Quiz on Sports

Quiz on Sports

Vijayalakshmi Iyer

GNOSIS

Publishers of Educational Books

Worldwide Circulation through Authorspress Global Network

First Published 2007
by
GNOSIS
E-35/103, Jawahar Park
Laxmi Nagar, Delhi-110 092
e-mail: authorspress@yahoo.com

An Imprint of Authorspress

Quiz on Sports
ISBN (PB) 81-89012-42-4

Printed in India at Virgo Press, Delhi.

Preface

Sport is an activity that is governed by a set of rules or customs and often engaged in competitively. Used by itself, sports commonly refer to activities where the physical capabilities of the competitor are the sole or primary determiner of the outcome (winning or losing), but the term is also used to include activities such as mind sports and motor sports where mental acuity or equipment quality are major factors. Sport has been a useful way for people to increase their mastery of nature and the environment, as well as a means of entertainment, both for the player as well as the viewer.

Various sports like football, basketball, rugby, etc., are popular the world over, and with increased are today highly regularised and organised. Industrialisation has brought increased leisure time to the citizens of developed and developing countries, leading to more time for citizens to attend and follow spectator sports, greater participation in athletic activities, and increased accessibility. These trends continue with the advent of mass media and global communication.

This book in the quiz series brings forth the reader an almost encyclopaedic amount of information on the various sports which have always been, continue to be, and are emerging, within human lives. The book strives towards equipping the readers with a large amount of information on the rules, history, cultural and national significance, the organisations and the sporting events of the various sports, as well as trivia and facts on the various personalities who have dominated the sporting arena. The focus is not just on increasing the readers' knowledge about sports, but also on fostering and encouraging readers to try out new sports, by providing them insightful and exciting knowledge on the subject. It is hoped that the compendious and informative nature of the book finds favour with the readers, and any suggestions to improve upon the book's content is most welcome.

Vijalakshmi Iyer

Contents

1

Olympics

1. In which year did Olympics commence and since then fully recorded until AD 381 when Theodosius banned it?

a) *920 BC* b) *776 BC*

c) *525 BC* d) *375 AD*

2. How many countries participated in the 1896 Olympics at Athens?

a) *10* b) *11* c) *14* d) *15*

3. Who was the first modern Olympia Winner in the 1896 Olympics?

a) *Robert Garrett* b) *Canl Samson*

c) *James Connolly* d) *Rowen Edison*

4. Who composed the Olympic anthem in 1896, which now has become the official hymn of the Olympic movement?

a) *Spyros Samaras* b) *Prince Constantine*

c) *Desertions Bekilas* d) *George Averoff*

5. This great Athenian soldier travelled two days and two nights to seek aid from the Epigrams more than 150 miles away. With his mission failed he returned to fight at the great battle of Marathon. Since then, the marathons is a regular feature of Olympics. Who was he?

a) *Robert Thycycide* b) *Pheidippides*

c) *Spartaus* d) *Herodotus*

6. **What is the motto of the Olympics in Latin, meaning "Faster, Higher, Stronger"?**

a) *Citius, Fortius, Altius* b) *Citius, Altius, Fortuis*
c) *Veni, Vidi, Viei* d) *Pro, Hae, Vici*

7. **In which Olympics the Olympia Flag and the Olympia Oath introduced?**

a) *1932, Los Angeles* b) *1928, Amsterdam*
c) *1920, Antwerp* d) *1912, Stockholm*

8. **In which Olympics was the Olympic Flame Introduced?**

a) *1920, Antwerp* b) *1924, Paris*
c) *1928, Amsterdam* d) *1932, Los Angeles*

9. **During which Olympics were the Games televised for the first time?**

a) *1936, Berlin* b) *1948, London*
c) *1952, Helsinki* d) *1956, Melbourne*

10. **At the victory ceremonies for the first time winners stood on a victor stand and the flag of the winner was raised. Which Olympics was it?**

a) *1932, Los Angeles* b) *1936, Berlin*
c) *1948, London* d) *1952 Helsinki*

11. **When was the official automatic timing and photo finish camera introduced?**

a) *1928, Amsterdam* b) *1932, Los Angeles*
c) *1936, Berlin* d) *1948, London*

12. **From which Olympics onward was the practice of Olympic torch relay begun?**

a) *1912, Stockholm* b) *1924, Paris*
c) *1936, Berlin* d) *1952, Helsinki*

13. **When was basketball introduced into the Olympics?**

a) *1936, Berlin* b) *1952, Helsinki*
c) *1960, Rome* d) *1968, Mexico*

14. When did Russia participate in the Olympics for the first time?

a) *1936, Berlin* b) *1948, London*
c) *1952, Helsinki* d) *1956, Melbourne*

15. In which Olympics did every single nation with an Olympic Committer show up including Cuba, North Korea and South Africa?

a) *1972, Munich* b) *1980, Moscow*
c) *1988, Seoul* d) *1992, Barcelona*

16. In which year did the Olympics Games return to their origins, Athens?

a) *1960* b) *1972* c) *1984* d) *2004*

17. For the first time games were held in a Communist Country. Which one?

a) *Moscow* b) *Romania*
c) *Poland* d) *Herzegovina*

18. In which Olympics did a black African win a gold medal for the first time?

a) *1956, Melbourne* b) *1960, Rome*
c) *1964, Tokyo* d) *1968, Mexico city*

19. Name the place and year where for the first time women competed in track and field events.

a) *1920, Antwy* b) *1924, Paris*
c) *1928, Amsterdam* d) *1932, Los Angeles*

20. During which Olympics did athletes march into the stadium behind their nations' flags for the first time?

a) *1912, Stockholm* b) *1908, London*
c) *1920, Antwerp* d) *1932, Los Angeles*

21. Name the place where the Games were held at the highest altitude ever.

a) *1964, Tokyo* b) *1968, Mexico City*
c) *1972, Munich* d) *1976, Montreal*

22. **Which two nations were not invited for the Olympics held at London in 1948?**

a) *Italy and Germany* b) *Germany and Japan*

c) *Japan and France* d) *Japan and Italy*

23. **Which three nations boycotted the Melbourne Olympics in 1956?**

a) *Spain, Switzerland and England*

b) *Netherlands, Germany and Spain*

c) *Netherlands, Spain and Switzerland*

d) *Switzerland, Netherlands and Germany*

24. **How many countries boycotted the Los Angeles Olympics due to security reasons?**

a) *Three* b) *Seven*

c) *Eleven* d) *Fourteen*

25. **Athletes form all nations entered the stadium in unity in the losing ceremonies for the first time. Where was this held?**

a) *1956, Melbourne* b) *1960, Rome*

c) *1964, Tokyo* d) *1968 Mexico City*

26. **Eleven Israeli athletes were killed when Palestinian militants stormed the Israeli team headquarters. When and where did this happen?**

a) *1960, Rome* b) *1972, Munich*

c) *1988, Seoul* d) *2000 Sydney*

27. **How much did Japan spend to rebuild Tokyo for the Olympics in 1964?**

a) *$ 1 billion* b) *$ 2 billion*

c) *$ 3 billion* d) *$ 4 billion*

28. **Which country refused to participate in the Games during the Olympic at Melbourne in 1956?**

a) *Russia* b) *China*

c) *New Zealand* d) *South Africa*

29. Which nation boycotted the Games at Montreal?

a) *Russia and China* b) *Taiwan and African nations*
c) *Japan and Netherlands* d) *USA and Britain*

30. Which Olympics did America boycott?

a) *1936, Berlin* b) *1964, Tokyo*
c) *1980, Moscow* d) *1988, Seoul*

31. In which Olympics did North Korea, Cuba and Ethiopia not participate?

a) *1964, Tokyo* b) *1980, Moscow*
c) *1988, Seoul* d) *1996, Atlanta*

32. Which Asian nation was the first to take part in Olympics and where?

a) *China in Athens* b) *Japan in London*
c) *India in Paris* d) *Russia in Rome*

33. Which Games remain the longest in the entire Olympic history and were called the Five Month Games?

a) *1896, Athens* b) *1900, Paris*
c) *1904, St. Louis* d) *1908, London*

34. Name the mascot which had a red belt with the emblem of the Games symbolising the ribbon to which the winners medal was attached.

a) *Waldi, the dachshund* b) *Amik, the beaver*
c) *Misha, the bear* d) *Cobi, the dog*

35. Name the animals which represented the earth, air and water at the Sydney Games in 2000?

a) *Kangaroo, panda, dingo* b) *Dingo, duck, kookaburra*
c) *Kookaburra, platypus, echidna*
d) *Duck, kangaroo, platypus*

36. Which games had an Olympics emblem portraying an olive wreath entwined in a crèche?

a) *1932, Los Angeles* b) *1952, Helsinki*
c) *1988, Seoul* d) *2004, Athens*

37. In 776 BC running naked Coroeous became the first recorded Olympic champion as he won foot race approximately 200 yards long? What was his prize?

a) *A red ribbon with a flower pinned to it*

b) *Fruits in a basket*

c) *A crown made of figs*

d) *A wreath of wild olive leaves*

38. Who officially opened the Games at Melbourne in 1956?

a) *The Duke of Edinburgh*

b) *Queen Elizabeth II*

c) *Sir William Deans*

d) *King Guan Carobs I*

39. For the first time releasing doves as a symbol of peace was seen at which Games?

a) *1900, Paris* b) *1920, Antwerp*

c) *1948, London* d) *1956 Melbourne*

40. For the first time the ritual of raising three flags at the closing ceremony was seen at the 1924 Paris Olympics. Whose flags were these?

a) *The country with maximum pacts, the host nation, International Olympic committee*

b) *International Olympic committee, host nation, next host nation*

c) *International Olympic committee, next host nation, UN*

d) *UN, host nation, next host nation*

41. When did the officials take the Olympic Oath for the first time?

a) *1972, Munich* b) *1976, Montreal*

c) *1980, Moscow* d) *1984, Los Angeles*

42. Cricket was held once in 1900 in Paris. Great Britain emerged victors. Whom did they beat in the final?

a) *France* b) *Australia*

c) *India* d) *South Africa*

43. Lacrosse was held in the Games of 1904 and 1908. Who won both times ?

a) *England* b) *Canada*
c) *Australia* d) *Spain*

44. The original Olympic Games began in 776 BC in ———.

a) *Elis* b) *Delphi*
c) *Phocis* d) *Olympia*

45. For what event did K. D. Jadhav India win a bronze in 1952?

a) *Boxing* b) *Wrestling*
c) *Shooting* d) *Archery*

46. When was Hockey played on an artificial pitch for the first time?

a) *1948, London* b) *1956, Melbourne*
c) *1968, Mexico* d) *1976, Montreal*

47. During which Games did East and West Germany participate as a combined team?

a) *1964, Tokyo* b) *1960, Rome*
c) *1956, Melbourne* d) *1952, Helsinki*

48. When was the first commemorative Olympic stamp released?

a) *1896* b) *1900* c) *1904* d) *1908*

49. Where was the first specially designed Olympic village constructed for the Games?

a) *Melbourne, 1956* b) *Los Angeles, 1932*
c) *Atlanta 1996* d) *Sydney, 2000*

50. Who qualified for seven races at Munich in 1972, and not only won them but set world records in all seven?

a) *Jesse Owens* b) *Alvin Kraenzlin*
c) *Mark Spitz* d) *Charlotte Cooper*

51. Who became the first athlete in Olympic history to die while participating in the Games at Stockholm in 1912?

a) *Francisco Lazaro* b) *Dorado Piers*
c) *Jim Thorpe* d) *Johnny Weissmyuller*

52. Who won the 100 m run at Antwerp in 1920 and became the first man to be labelled the "World's Fastest Human"?

a) *Charlie Paddock* b) *Harold Abraham*

c) *Durand Petra* d) *Jim Thorpe*

53. Who was the first Aborigine to win an individual medal in the Olympics at Sydney?

a) *Maurice Greene* b) *Jan Thorpe*

c) *Cathy Freeman* d) *Marion Jones*

54. Who was the first female black African Olympian champion of the 10,000m run at Barcelona in 1992?

a) *Marvin Jones* b) *Cathy Freeman*

c) *Charlotte Copper* d) *Derart Tulu*

55. Who was the first paraplegic athlete to take part in a medal event competing in a wheelchair at Los Angeles in 1984?

a) *Thomas Fahrner* b) *Sebastian Coe*

c) *Pertti Karpinnen* d) *Neroli Fairhall*

56. When women's marathon was introduced in the Olympics at Los Angeles in 1984, who won the women's inaugural marathon ?

a) *Newel El Moutawekes* b) *Joan Benoil*

c) *Connie Carpenter-Phinney* c) *Neroli Fairhall*

57. Nadia Comaneci became the first gymnast in Olympic history to score a perfect 10. Where did she achieve this feat?

a) *1972, Munich* b) *1976, Montreal*

c) *1980, Moscow* d) *1984, Los Angels*

58. Who became the first woman swimmer to win three gold medals at a single Games?

a) *Vera Cavallas* b) *Florence Griffith-Joyner*

c) *Debbie Mayer* d) *Yuliya Pecnonkina*

59. When was the last time that Olympic Summer Games and Winter Games were held in the same year ?

a) *1988* b) *1992* c) *1996* d) *2000*

60. The 1984 Summer Olympics in Los Angeles was notable for the absence of whom?

a) *African nations* b) *New Lealand*
c) *Almost all Eastern bloc countries*
d) *Swaziland*

61. Who was the first Indian woman to appear in the final of an Olympic event?

a) *Shiny Abraham* b) *Anjou Bobby George*
c) *P. T. Usha* d) *Bula Choudhury*

62. Suleymanoglu the first weight-lifter who won gold at three successive Olympics. To which country did he belong?

a) *Turkey* b) *Indonesia*
c) *Pakistan* d) *Egypt*

63. In which event did Burros Dumas of Greece break his own record at the Mexico Olympics in Atlanta?

a) *400 m race* b) *Shooting*
c) *Swimming* d) *Pole Vault*

64. Where was the 2006 Winter Olympics held ?

a) *Beijing* b) *Turin*
c) *Berlin* d) *Atlanta*

65. Who is said to be the father of Modern Olympics?

a) *Pierre de Coubertin* b) *Carl Pritchard*
c) *Norman Pritchard* d) *George Averaff*

66. Who was the first Olympic gold medallist in swimming?

a) *Alfred Hajos* b) *Cathy Bald*
c) *Candia Poll* d) *Corbos Maya*

67. Which country won every Olympic men's hockey gold medal from 1928 to 1964?

a) *Australia* b) *India*
c) *Holland* d) *Germany*

68. During the 1964 Tokyo Olympics a country joined with another haring. Name the country?

a) *Thailand* b) *Malaysia*
c) *Limbabwe* d) *Zambia*

69. When was tennis introduced in the Olympics as a medal event?

a) *1984* b) *1988* c) *1992* d) *1996*

70. The Danish cyclist Knud Enemark Jensen died during the road cycle race owing to the heat. During which Olympics did it happen?

a) *1960, Rome* b) *1964, Tokyo*
c) *1968, Mexico* d) *1972, Munich*

71. Emil, an army officer, won the 10,000m and 5,000m titles in his very first marathon decimating the world's greatest. To which country did he belong?

a) *Poland* b) *Czechoslovakia*
c) *Bulgaria* d) *Romania*

72. Bob Matthias, a 17-year-old, who had not tackled decathlon before that year, emerged to beat the world's greatest all-rounders at the London Olympics in 1948. From which country did he hail?

a) *England* b) *Canada*
c) *USA* d) *Australia*

73. When did China and Columbia make an entry into Olympic Games?

a) *1900, Paris* b) *1912, Stockholm*
c) *1924, Paris* d) *1932, Los Angeles*

74. Which Olympics was de Coubertin last appearance as an official of the Olympic?

a) *1900, Paris* b) *1912, Stockholm*
c) *1924, Paris* d) *1932, Los Angeles*

75. Which are the two official languages of the International Olympics Committee?

a) *English and French* b) *English and Chinese*
c) *English and German* d) *German and French*

76. Which first athlete failed an Olympic sex chromosome testing in 1964, and later stripped of the records?

a) *Games Connolly* b) *Kostis Palmas*
c) *Aladar Greenish* d) *Eva Klobukowska*

77. Dhyan Chand scored eight goals in an Olympics hockey that India won. Who was the opposition team?

a) *USA* b) *Germany*

c) *Australia* d) *Holland*

78. Spyros Samaras and Kostis Palmas composed the Olympic anthem that was played at the opening ceremonies. At which place did this commence?

a) *Athens, 1896* b) *Paris, 1900*

c) *St Roués, 1904* d) *London, 1908*

79. When were the golden, silver and bronze medals for the first second and third places introduced?

a) *1904, St Louis* b) *1912, Stockholm*

c) *1932, Los Angeles* d) *1952, Helsinki*

80. Which nations participated as a single delegation under the name of Australasia in 1908 at the London Games?

a) *Australia & Tasmania*

b) *Australia & The Pacific Islands*

c) *Australia & New Zealand*

d) *Australia & Papua New Guinea*

81. When was a public address system first used?

a) *1896, Athens* b) *1904, St Louis*

c) *1908, London* d) *1912, Stockholm*

82. This cycling road race was 320 kilometres the longest post race of any kind in Olympics history. Where was it held?

a) *Athens, 1896* b) *London, 1904*

c) *Stockholm, 1912* d) *Antwerp, 1920*

83. For the first time at which Olympics did the winners undergo a doping test?

a) *Mexico, 1968* b) *Munich, 1972*

c) *Montreal, 1976* d) *Moscow, 1980*

84. During which Games were blocks introduced to facilitate the start for the athletes in spring races?

a) *Berlin, 1936* b) *London, 1948*

c) *Munich, 1972* d) *Los Angeles, 1984*

85. When did the tradition of Greece leading the parade of nations and the hosts following last at the opening ceremony become a permanent Olympic tradition?

a) *1924, Paris* b) *1928, Amsterdam*

c) *1932, Los Angeles* d) *1936, Berlin*

86. During which Games was a twelve-foot clingy sealing race the only event in Olympic history held in two countries?

a) *1920, Antwerp* b) *1936, Berlin*

c) *1952, Helsinki* d) *1960, Rome*

87. When was fibre glass pole used for the first time in the pole vaulting competition?

a) *1956, Melbourne* b) *1960, Rome*

c) *1964, Tokyo* d) *1968, Mexico*

88. During which Olympics was the synthetic material tartan used for the first time?

a) *1968, Mexico* b) *1972, Mumucl*

c) *1976, Montreal* d) *1980, Moscow*

89. Who were the mascots at the Athens 2004 Games?

a) *Olly, Syd and millce* b) *Sam*

c) *Cobi* d) *Phevos and Athena*

90. What are the colours of the five rings on the Olympic flag?

a) *Red, green, blue, yellow, and black*

b) *Red, green, blue, yellow, and white*

c) *Red, blue, yellow, black, and white*

d) *Red, green, yellow, blue, and purple*

91. Heckki Savalainen took the oath at the start of the Games on behalf of the competitors at Helsinki in 1952. What game did he compete in?

a) *Gymnastics* b) *Track and field event*

c) *Weightlifting* d) *Basketball*

92. Who took the oath at the Sydney Olympics in 2000?

a) *Lanesa Edwards* b) *Edwin Mores*

c) *Rechelle Hawke* d) *John Landy*

93. In the Athens Games in which complex were beach volleyball, handball and volleyball competitions held?

a) *Athens Olympic Sports Complex*

b) *Faliro Coastal Zone Olympic Complex*

c) *Helliniko Olympic Complese*

d) *Goudi Olympic Complese*

94. How many nations participated at the Sydney Olympics?

a) *159* b) *169*

c) *197* d) *200*

95. Which aristocratic game was held in 1900 in which the French dominated winning all the medals in both singles and doubles and never held thereafter?

a) *Croquet* b) *Badminton*

c) *Tennis* d) *Rackets*

96. During which game was the Olympic flame sent by air in the form of an electronic signal by a telephone cable towards the transmitter in the direction of a satellite from the lintels at network? It was then forwarded to the receiver and the stored energy activated a laser beam giving it the original appearance?

a) *1976, Montreal* b) *1984, Los Angeles*

c) *1988, Seoul* d) *1996, Atlanta*

97. To whom did Leander Paes lose in the tennis semi-final at Atlanta in 1996?

a) *Pete Samaras* b) *Roger Federer*

c) *Bjorn Borg* d) *Andre Agassi*

98. Karoly Tukas's right hand was shattered by a grenade. Ten years later he won his first Olympic gold medal in shooting using his left hand. Where did he achieve this feat?

a) *London, 1948* b) *Tokyo, 1964*

c) *Seoul, 1988* d) *Sydney, 2000*

99. Lasse Verne of Finland stumbled and full in the middle of the 10,000m race. After a few seconds, he got up and stormed to victory. Name the place?

a) *Munich, 1972* b) *Montreal, 1976*

c) *Sydney, 2000* d) *Athens, 2004*

100. Who set the world record in the 400 m freestyle, and helped his country's squad in the 4 × 200 m free style?

a) *Ian Thorpe* b) *Maurice Greene*

c) *Steve redgrace* d) *Mark Spitz*

2

South Asian Federation Games

1. Known as SAF Games, where were the multi-sports first held?

a) *India* b) *Pakistan*

c) *Sri Lanka* d) *Nepal*

2. In which year were the SAF Games inaugurated?

a) *1984* b) *1988*

c) *1992* d) *1994*

3. From 2006, what are SAF Games be retitled as?

a) *SAARC Games*

b) *South Asian Games*

c) *South Asian Association Games*

d) *SAARC Sports and Events*

4. Which country topped medal tally in the 1999 SAF Games?

a) *India* b) *Sir Lanka*

c) *China* d) *Pakistan*

5. Where were the 2004 SAF Games held?

a) *Dhaka* b) *Chennai*

c) *Kalama bad* d) *Islamabad*

6. How many countries participated in the 8th SAF Games in 1999?

a) *9* b) *12*

c) *7* d) *10*

7. **Two commemorative coins were issued in December 1991 for the SAF Games. Where did this happen?**

   a) *Dhaka* b) *Colombo*
   c) *Islamabad* d) *Delhi*

8. **Who were the new entry to the Games in 2006 Games?**

   a) *Mauritius* b) *Afghanistan*
   c) *Myamnar* d) *Malaysia*

9. **Which country's government donated 25 million rupees to the Sri Lankan government for the 2006 Games ?**

   a) *USA* b) *China*
   c) *Japan* d) *Singapore*

10. **How many participants did India send for the 2006 Games at Colombo?**

    a) *150* b) *250* c) *325* d) *400*

11. **Who won the 2004 100 metres race?**

    a) *Piyush Kumar* b) *Anil Kumar*
    c) *Chintake De Zoysa* d) *Bimal Chandra Tarafdar*

12. **Who won the javelin event in the 2004 Games?**

    a) *Gurmeet Kaur* b) *Vijita P. Amarasekara*
    c) *Anne Maheshi De Silva* d) *Razia Sheikh*

13. **In 1991, who won the marathon?**

    a) *Baikuntha Manandhar* b) *V.K.L. Samarasinghe*
    c) *K.A. Karunaratne* d) *Sarath Prasanna Gamage*

14. **Name the 1984 Long Jump winner.**

    a) *Benildus Fernando* b) *Hemant Kumar Patel*
    c) *Shyam Kumar Sunder* d) *Maha Singh*

15. **Name the Pakistani winner of the Triple Jump event in 1991.**

    a) *Mujibar Rahman Malik* b) *Haider Ali Shah*
    c) *Benaras Khan* d) *Aqarab Abbas*

16. Which Indian won the 2004 discus event?

a) Surjeet Singh *d) Shakti Singh*

c) Hridayanand Singh *d) Manjeet Singh*

17. Which woman won the shot putt event at the 1993 Games?

a) Amandeep Kaur *b) Surinderjeet Kaur*

c) Rajwinder Kaur *d) Nicholas Latha*

18. In 1999 who won the 1500 metres race?

a) Suman Rawat *b) Sriyani Dhammika Menike*

c) Rosa Kutty *d) Sunita Rani*

19. Name the winner of the 3000 metres steeplechase event in the 1999 Games.

a) Shamsuddin *b) Abdul Razzaq*

c) Narinder Singh *d) Amrish Kumar*

20. In 1985, who won the 110 metres hurdles?

a) Manzoor Ahmed *b) Ashish Mondal*

c) Ghulam Abbas *d) Mahesh Perera*

3

Asian Games

1. In which year were the first Asian Games held?

a) *1950* b) *1951* c) *1952* d) *1953*

2. When did the Olympic Council of Asia take over the organization of the Asian Games?

a) *1955* b) *1965* c) *1972* d) *1982*

3. The Asian Games, aimed at promoting and propagating the importance of an Asian identity and fostering unity amongst Asians through sports and games, is held once in how many years?

a) *Two* b) *Three*

c) *Four* d) *Five*

4. In 1951 which nation was the first to host the Asian Games?

a) *China* b) *Japan*

c) *India* d) *Indonesia*

5. When were the five Olympic Rings added to the emblem of the Asian Games?

a) *1983* b) *1987* c) *1991* d) *1995*

6. Where are the XIII Asian Games to be held?

a) *Thailand* b) *North Korea*

c) *Singapore* d) *China*

7. Where were the 2006 Asian Games held?

A) *Malaysia* b) *Bahrain*

c) *Qatar* d) *Sandi Arabia*

8. How many stadiums will the country have for the various events?

a) *5* b) *9* c) *12* d) *14*

9. What is the motto of the Asian Games?

a) *Peace, Prosperity, Friendship*
b) *Unity, Friendship, Prosperity*
c) *Unity and Friendship*
d) *Friendship Beyond Frontiers*

10. In the 2002 Games which three nations topped the medal tally?

a) *China, Japan Iran*
b) *China, South Korea, Japan*
c) *China, South Korea, Philippines*
d) *Japan, South Korea, Indonesia*

11. Where will the 2010 Asian Games be held?

a) Guangzhou, China *b) Doha, Qatar*
c) Beijing, China *d) Seoul, S.Korea*

12. In Which year was rowing introduced?

a) 1990 *b) 1994* *c) 1998* *d) 2002*

13. Where were the first Winter Asian Games held?

a) Harbin, China *b) Kangwon, south Korea*
c) Aomori, Japan *d) Sapporo, Japan*

14. Which country the most gold medals in the Indoor Games of 2005?

a) India *b) China*
c) Thailand *d) Hong Kong*

15. Where will the first Asian Beach Games be held in 2008?

a) Oman *b) Haiyang, China*
c) Bali, Indonesia *d) Boracay, Philippines*

16. What is the total number of golds that India has won so far in the Asian Games?

a) 112 *b) 118* *c) 125* *d) 132*

17. In which country were the 2002 Games held?

a) Qatar *b) Thailand*

c) South Korea *d) Japan*

18. Since which year has judo been included in the Asian Games?

a) 1982 *b) 1986* *c) 1994* *d) 1998*

19. The Olympic Council of Asia agreed to exclude which country from participating the Asian Games?

a) Kazhakistan *b) Kyrgystan*

c) Uzbekistan *d) Israel*

20. Which was the second country to host the Asian Games?

a) New Delhi *b) Philippines*

c) Indonesia *d) Japan*

4

Commonwealth Games

1. How many countries participate in the Commonwealth Games?

a) *60* b) *65* c) *68* d) *71*

2. Who hosted the 2006 Commonwealth Games in March?

a) *London* b) *Melbourne*
c) *Kuala Lumpur* d) *Auckland*

3. Which Indian gold medallist of India was named as the winner of the Daird Dixon Award for the most outstanding athlete of the 2006 Commonwealth Games?

a) *Samaresh Jung* b) *Pixyish Kumar*
c) *Rohan Anil Kumar* d) *Gulab Chand*

4. When was the Commonwealth Games Federation formed?

a) *1930* b) *1935* c) *1948* d) *1050*

5. Who was instrumental in founding the Games?

a) *Herb Elliot* b) *Catherine Freeman*
c) *Bobby Robinson* d) *Ron Clarke*

6. What are the three foundation principles of the Commonwealth Games Federation?

a) *Success, Unity and Peace*
b) *Liberty, Equality, Unity*
c) *Humanity, Equality and Destiny*
d) *Prosperity, Peace and Unity*

7. **Where were the first Commonwealth Games held?**

a) *Hamilton* b) *London*
c) *Sydney* d) *Kuala Lumpur*

8. **Which country will be hosting the 2010 Commonwealth Games?**

a) *Britain* b) *Canada*
c) *Malaysia* d) *India*

9. **Which nation staged a stunning display of its culture at the closing ceremony making the handover from Melbourne 2006?**

a) *Britain* b) *Canada*
c) *India* d) *New Lealand*

10. **At an interval of how many years are the Commonwealth Games held?**

a) *Three* b) *Four*
c) *Five* d) *Two*

11. **Who win the netball gold at the 2006 Games?**

a) *South Africa* b) *New Zealand*
c) *Malaysia* d) *Canada*

12. **Who launched the Games website for the 2006 Games?**

a) *Malayan Mouthy*
b) *Bill Gates*
c) *Queen Elizabeth II*
d) *Prime Minister John Winston Howard*

13. **Who was the great dignitary to open the Games at Melbourne in March 2006?**

a) *Queen Elizabeth II*
b) *Prime Minister J. W. Howard*
c) *Gov Gen Michael Gaffer*
d) *Tony Blair*

14. Who was the flag bearer of the Opening Ceremony of the 2006 Games?

a) *Natalie Du Toit, S. African Swimming champion*

b) *Tracey Hallam, England's Badminton champion*

c) *Mathew Hayman, Austria's cyclists champion*

d) *Sharath Achanta, India's Table Lenis champion*

15. Which country topped the medal tally in the 1998 Games?

a) *England* b) *Australia*

c) *Canada* d) *South Africa*

16. What was the mascot of the 1998 Games?

a) *Mocha* b) *Appu*

c) *Wira* d) *Lobi*

17. Who won the Men's Cycling Rood Race at Melbourne in the 2006 Games?

a) *David George, South Africa*

b) *Allan David, Australia*

c) *Mathew Hayman, Australia*

d) *Pets Nicole, England*

18. Which country hosted the 16th Commonwealth Games in 1998?

a) *Malaysia* b) *Australia*

c) *South Africa* d) *England*

19. Where were the 17th Commonwealth Games held in 2002?

a) *Kuala Lumpur* b) *Bangkok*

c) *Manchester* d) *Toronto*

20. Which country snared all three medals in the women's Table Tennis Singles competition in 2006?

a) *Malaysia* b) *Singapore*

c) *India* d) *England*

5

Cricketing Moments

1. Which country won the 1999 World cup?

a) *Australia* b) *South Africa*

c) *West Indies* d) *Pakistan*

2. Against which country did Sachin Glandular make his debut?

a) *England* b) *Pakistan*

c) *West Indies* d) *England*

3. Who is the only Indian bowler to have taken 10 or more wickets in a test match against Australia?

a) *Kapil Dev* b) *Harbhajan Singh*

c) *Javagal Srinath* d) B) *S. Chandrashekhar*

4. Who is the only Indian Test cricketer to have played Sheffield Shield cricket in Australia?

a) *Rusi Surti* b) *Sunil Gavaskar*

c) *Kapil Dev* d) *Lala Amarnath*

5. Who was the first Indian to score a century in Tests against Australia?

a) *M. H. Mankad* b) *H. R. Adhekari*

c) *V. S. Hazare* d) *Lala Amarnath*

6. Which bowler claimed the last wicket of the 1992 World Cup Tournament?

a) *Wasim Akram* b) *Imran Khan*

c) *Mushtaq Ahmed* d) *Aaqib Javed*

7. Which New Zealand batsman struck six sixes against Sri Lanka in a pool-A match of the 2003 World Cup at Bloemfontein?

a) *Chris Cairns* b) *Scott Styris*
c) *Chris Harris* d) *Lou Vincent*

8. Who was the first batsman to be dismissed in the nineties in the World Cup 1999 Tournament?

a) *Rahul Dravid* b) *Mark Boucher*
c) *Roshan Mahanama* d) *Sourav Ganguly*

9. Where was World Cup 1992 held?

a) *South Africa* b) *India*
c) *Australia* d) *England*

10. Who scored highest runs from England side in the 2005 Ashes Series?

a) *Michael Vaughan* b) *Andrew Strauss*
c) *Levin Petersen* d) *Andrew Fflintoff*

11. Which famous Indian cricketer is named Jammy?

a) *Rahul Dravid* b) *Javagal Srinath*
c) *Kapil Dev* d) *Ravi Shastri*

12. Born in West Indies, who used to play for India?

a) *Robin Singh* b) *Connor Williains*
c) *Abey Kuruvilla* d) *Jacob Martin*

13. Which former Indian pacer was recently appointed as a Match referee by the ICC?

a) *Mohandas Amarnath* b) *Venkatesh Prasad*
c) *Javagal Srinath* d) *Kapil Dev*

14. By what margin did Australia beat India in the 4-Lest series in October-November 2004?

a) *3-1* b) *2-1* c) *3-0* d) *2-0*

15. In which year was the famous "blackwash" series when England were beaten 5-0 on home soil by the west Indies?

a) *1976* b) *1999* c) *1984* d) *2003*

16. Though Sachin has the highest number of ODI tons he took a pretty long time to crack his first. Which was the match in question?

a) *His 70th* b) *His 75th*
c) *His 78th* d) *His 80th*

17. Sir Don Bradman's Test average is 99.94. What is his average against India?

a) *69.26* b) *178.75* c) *98.50* d) *101.44*

18. Which player of India hit six sixes in the first Twenty-20 World Cup?.

a) *Mahendra Singh Dhoni* b) *Robin Uttappa*
c) *Yuvraj Singh* d) *Virender Sehwag*

19. While the Kiwis have returned winless on previous tours the Indians scored a major point when they recorded a rare series victory. Who was the skipper of the victorious team?

a) *Ajit Wadekar* b) *Tiger Pataudi*
c) *Chandu Borde* d) *Sunil Gavaskar*

20. Which player claimed the most catches in the outfields in the 1996 World Cup?

a) *Sanath Lamasery* b) *Chris Crains*
c) *Anil Kumble* d) *Alistair Campbell*

21. Who was the first batsman dismissed 'run out' in the 2003 World Cup?

a) *Brain Lara* b) *Nathan Astle*
c) *Arvinda de Silva* d) *Andy Flower*

22. Who was the only South African batsman to have scored a century in the 1999 World Cup?

a) *Jacques Kallis* b) *Heschelle Gibbs*
c) *Gary Kirsten* d) *Daryll Cullinan*

23. Who was the leading wicket taker for England in the 1992 World Cup?

a) *Philip DeFreitas* b) *Dermot Reeve*

c) *Chres Lewis* d) *Ian Botham*

24. Which English batsman was dismissed off the first ball he faced in the final of the 1987 World Cup?

a) *Graham Gooch* b) *Bill Athey*

c) *Tim Robinson* d) *Mike Getting*

25. Which Pakistani player was awarded the Man of the Match despite losing to England in their first Group-A league encounter at Lords in the 1983 World Cup?

a) *Zaheer Abbas* b) *Mudassar Nazar*

c) *Imran Khan* d) *Abdul Oadir*

26. How many England batsmen were dismissed without scoring a run in the final of the 1979 World Cup?

a) *Two* b) *Three*

c) *Four* d) *Five*

27. Who had the best match-bowling figures in the 1975 World Cup?

a) *Gary Gilmour* b) *Mohinder Amarnath*

c) *Richard Hadlee* d) *John Snow*

28. Which umpire standing at short leg was accidentally hit by a sweep shot played by Richie Richardson in the Australia-West Indies semi-final in the 1996 World Cup?

a) *S. Venkataraghavan* b) *David Shepherd*

c) B.C. *Cooray* d) *Steve Dunne*

29. In which year did India play its first test match?

a) *15th March 1877* b) *25th June 1932*

c) *16th October 1952* d) *23rd June 1928*

30. Which Indian opener blasted a double century against Australia at the MCG when legendary leg-spinner Shane Warne made his debut with unfaltering figures of 1 for 150 from 45 overs in 1992?

a) *Manoj Prabhakar* b) *Sachin Tendulkar*

c) *Ravi Shastri* d) *Navjot Siddhu*

31. Which opening batsman claimed to be deliberately got himself out on the same score as Bradman, after their massive partnership together?

a) *Syd F. Barnes* b) *Sid G. Barnes*

c) *Arthur Morris* d) *Bill Woodfull*

32. Alec Beaser was one of England's greatest medium pace bowlers. Which batsman did he dismiss 18 times in test matches, leading to him being dubbed "Bedser's Bunny"?

a) *Neil Harvey* b) *Everton Weekes*

c) *Don Bradman* d) *Arthur Morris*

33. Who was the first man to get 36 runs off a six-ball over?

a) *Sir Garfield Sobers* b) *Adam Gilchrist*

c) *Sir Donald Bradman* d) *Ravi Shastri*

34. Who became the first Sri Lankan wicket keeper to score a test double-hundred?

a) *Romesh Kaluwitharana* b) *Maravan Attappattu*

c) *Kumara Sangakara* d) *Brendon Kuruppu*

35. This first saw Sunil Gavaskar becoming the first player to make 100 consecutive appearances. It also saw Kiran More being substituted by Chandrakant Pandit behind the stumps after 50 minutes of play on Day 1. The match also saw Dean Jones being rushed to the hospital after a marathon inning which saved the match for his country. But this match is famous for another reason. What is that?

a) *All 11 Australians bowled in the match.*

b) *The test had five debutantes a world record.*

c) *It was history's second tied test.*

d) *The match saw a number of centuries.*

36. Who was the only Indian to score in double figure in India's disastrous 42 all out against England at Lords in 1974? .

a) *Syed Abid Ali* b) *M. L. Jaisimha*
c) *Eknath Solkar* d) *Dilip Sardesai*

37. What landmark did Chetan Sharma reach in the Healingly test against England in 1986?

a) *First Indian to take a test hat trick abroad.*
b) *First Indian to take 5 wickets and score 50 in an inning against England.*
c) *First Indian to take 10 wickets in a Lest overseas.*
d) *First Indian to score zero in test and go wicketless.*

38. Which Indian had this quixotic idea which he actually executed, of hitting four sixes in succession and thus saving the follow on in a test match against England?

a) *Kapil Dev* b) *M.A.K. Pataudi*
c) *Atul Bedade* d) *Ravi Shastri*

39. In 1974, when the touring Indian team played the Combined Universities, one non-British Oxford graduate player lift a deep impact on the match. This person went on to become a well known cricketer. Who was he?

a) *Martin Crowe* b) *Allan Border*
c) *Imran Khan* d) *Robin Singh*

40. Sunday Express had a unique headline after India riffled off England in the NatWest Trophy finals. What was it?

a) *Mountain comes to Mohammad*
b) *English Lion no match for Bengal Tiger*
c) *India Lords England*
d) *Browns Better than Whiters*

41. An amateur guitarist for 30 years, a science teacher and first class opening batsman for 16 years. Which Kiwi are we talking about?

a) *Fervor Franklin* b) *John Wright*
c) *Andrew goners* d) *Stephen Fleming*

42. Against which team did Sanath Jayasuriya register his first century in a World Cup?

a) *Pakistan* b) *Zimbabwe*

c) *India* d) *New Zealand*

43. Which bowler claimed the first wicket for Namibia during the 2003 World Cup?

a) *Lennie Louw* b) *Riaan Walters*

c) *Gerri Snyman* d) *Bryan Murgtatroyd*

44. Which all-rounder had a batting average of 117 without scoring a single century in the 1999 World Cup?

a) *Tom Moody* b) *Minhajul Abedin*

c) *Sanath Jayasuriya* d) *Wasim Akram*

45. Which bowler conceded the most wides in the 1992 World Cup Tournament?

a) *Wasim Akram* b) *Craig McDermott*

c) *Chris Lewis* d) *Allan Donald*

46. Which cricketer was part of the English team that lost both the 1979 and the 1987 World Cup finals?

a) *David Gower* b) *Alan Lamb*

c) *Ian Botham* d) *Graham Gooch*

47. In the Benson and Hedges Word Series Cup in 1986 the match between India and Australia saw this player wearing the wicketkeeper's gloves after W. B. Philips was injured. What was unusual was that he had also bowled four overs prior to sifting behind the stumps. Who is the player ?

a) *Steve Waugh* b) *Dave Gilbert*

c) *Allan Border* d) *Ken Hughes*

48. Which player holds the record for the most runs in a single Test inning?

a) *Mathew Hayden* b) *Graham Gooch*

c) *Clive Lloyd* d) *Brian Lara*

49. In which year was the first cricket Test played?

a) *1870* b) *1873* c) *1877* d) *1880*

50. At which ground did Anil kumble take his record 10 for 74 against Pakistan?

a) *Eden Garden* b) *Mohali*
c) *Ferozeshah Kotla* d) *Chinnaswami Stadium*

51. How many centuries did Sir Don Bradman score against India?

a) *None* b) *Two*
c) *Three* d) *Four*

52. Who scored 137 in his debut Test against Australia at Kanpur in the 1969-70 series?

a) *Sunil Gavaskar* b) *Gundappa Vishwanath*
c) *Ajit Wadekar* d) *M. L. Jaisimha*

53. What is Steve Waugh's highest Test score against India?

a) *99* b) *150* c) *175* d) *199*

54. Who was the captain of the India team for the tri-series of the Coco Cola Champions Cup in 1998 played at Sharjah?

a) *Sachin Tendulkar* b) *Saurav Ganguly*
c) *Rahul Dravid* d) *M. Azharuddin*

55. Who was the first batsman dismissed for 99 on his Test debut?

a) *Asim Kamal* b) *Arthur Chipperfield*
c) *Robert Chrestiani* d) *Rahul Dravid*

56. Who is the only Indian Test cricketer to also have played Davis Cup final?

a) *Pankaj Roy* b) *Nawab of Pataudi Sir*
c) *Cotah Ramaswami* d) *Viyay Hazare*

57. Who was the first player to score a hundred and claim 10 wickets in the same match?

a) *Imran Khan* b) *Ian Botham*
c) *Gary Sobers* d) *Kapil Dev*

58. Which player became the first batsman to be stumped in the 2003 World Cup?

a) *Brian Lara* b) *Carl Hooper*
c) *Jonty Rhodes* d) *Boeta Dippenaar*

59. Which batsman got the first duck in the 1999 World Cup Tournament?

a) *Sadagopan Ramesh* b) *Hashan Tillekaratne*
c) *Herschelle Gibbs* d) *Ricky Ponting*

60. Which nation won the World Cup 1996?

a) *Pakistan* b) *Australia*
c) *Sri Lanka* d) *West Indies*

61. Who has the most number of centuries in the ODI?

a) *Brian Lara* b) *Steve Waugh*
c) *Ricky Ponting* d) *Sachin Tendulkar*

62. Who amongst the following is the fastest 50 wicket taker in ODI Matches?

a) *Ajit Agarkar* b) *Abdul Razak*
c) *Anil Kumble* d) *Lance Klusener*

63. Where was the 2007 World Cup held?

a) *South Africa* b) *England*
c) *West Indies* d) *Australia*

64. Who did McGrath dismiss for his 500th test wicket?

a) *Andrew Strauss* b) *Michael Vaughan*
c) *Marcus Trescothick* d) *Paul Collinwood*

65. Whom did the West Indies beat to get to the 2004 ICC Champions final?

a) *England* b) *Australia*
c) *Pakistan* d) *Sir Lanka*

66. Which Indian has scored the slowest century (508 minutes) in Test match cricket?

a) *K. Srikaanth* b) *Sanjay Manjrekar*
c) *Ravi Shastri* d) *Mohinder Amarnath*

67. Which West Indies cricketer has named his daughter Sydney because of his famous knock of 277 in 1992-93?

a) *Jimmy Adams* b) *Brian Lara*
c) *Phil Simmons* d) *Keith Arthurton*

68. Which Indian cricketer was a national level skating champion at the age of 12?

a) *Mohammad Kaif* b) *Irfan Pathan*
c) *Suresh Raina* d) *Yuvraj Singh*

69. On which ball was Sanath Jayasuriya out during his knock of 189 against India?

a) *No Ball* b) *Bouncer*
c) *Yorker* d) *Wide Ball*

70. Which South African was nicknamed Mantzburg Mamba? Mamba is the fastest moving poisonous snake?

a) *Jonty Rhodes* b) *Mark Boucher*
c) *Hansie Cronje* d) *Shaun Pollock*

71. Who was the first batsman in the history of ODIs given out by the third umpire?

a) *Sachin Tendulkar* b) *Gary Kirsten*
c) *Mark Waugh* d) *Arjuna Ranatunga*

72. Which cricketer was struck by lightning during an ODI and was hospitalised?

a) *Darren Gough* b) *Chris Cairns*
c) *Gavial Srinath* d) *Mervyn Dillon*

73. What is the name of the famous green hat worn by Australian cricket player?

a) *Wattle Hat* b) *Austin Cap*
c) *Green and Gold* d) *Baggy Green*

74. Which Test venue boasts of the biggest official capacity in the world?

a) *MCG, Melbourne* b) *Lords, London*
c) *Eden Gardens, Kolkata* c) *Kandy, Sri Lanka*

75. The matches for Pura Cup (the premier cricket trophy) is held at————.

a) *New Zealand* b) *South Africa*
c) *Bangladesh* d) *Australia*

76. Which batsman holds the record for the fastest one-day century (34 balls)?

a) *Adam Glichrist* b) *Stephen Fleming*
c) *Shahid Afridi* d) *Sanath Jayasuriya*

77. Which bowler has the best ever Test bowling figures of 9 for 37 and 10 for 53?

a) *Jim Laker, England* b) *Anil Kumble, India*
c) *Sir Garfield Sobers, West Indies*
d) *Muthiah Muralitharan, Sri Lanka*

78. The lowest ever ODI score is 36 all out. They were soundly thrashed by Sri Lanka. Which country was it?

a) *Holland* b) *Kenya*
c) *Canada* d) *Bangladesh*

79. Who led the Indian team to Sharjah in 1988 to play for the Sharjah Cup?

a) *Sunil Gavaskar* b) *Kapil Dev*
c) *Ravi Shastri* d) *Dileep Vengsarkar*

80. Which country scored the lowest Test total of 26 in Test history in 1954-55?

a) *New Zealand* b) *South Africa*
c) *Australia* d) *India*

81. In 1974 India registered its lowest score of 42. Against Which nation was this dubious total scored?

a) *New Zealand* b) *England*
c) *Australia* d) *West Indies*

82. When did Australia play its first ever cricket Test?

a) *15 March, 1879* b) *10 November, 1902*

c) *10 January, 1920* d) *12 March, 1889*

83. To begin with the venue for the final—the first ODI played at Eden Gardens—saw a reversal of fortunes with a player tilting the scales in his and his team's favour after being almost dropped form the team. Who was he?

a) *Salim Malik* b) *Anwar Hussain*

c) *M. Azharuddin* d) *kaipl Dev*

84. Which batsman at the non-strikers end did Courtney Walsh warn in the last over of the Pakistan-West Indies Group B league match at Lahore in the 1987 World Cup?

a) *Wasim Akram* b) *Imran Khan*

c) *Shoaib Mohammad* d) *Salim Jaffer*

85. Which two unlucky batsmen were dismissed in the nineties in the second West Indies-England Group B match in the 1987 World Cup?

a) *Gooch and Richardson* b) *Gooch and Viv Richards*

c) *Gatting and Gooch* d) *Viv Richards and Lamb*

86. The Lal Bahadur Shastri Stadium witnessed to two of India's highest ODI performances. Which of these?

a) *Tendulkar 186, Ganguly 173*

b) *Tendulkar 186, Manjrekar 105*

c) *Tendulkar 186, Dravid 153*

d) *Tendulkar 186, Laxman 185*

87. Which stadium was promoted by a film named *The Dream Comes True* after its inaugural Test match between India and West Indies which the Windies won?

a) *Green Park, Kanpur*

b) *Barabatyi Stadium, Cuttack*

c) *Chinnaswamy Stadium, Bangalore*

d) *Chepauk Grounds, Chennai*

88. Matthew Hayden became the owner of a record highest runs in Test in a calendar year for Australia when he scored 1391 in 2001. Whose record did he break?

a) *Mark Waugh* b) *Neil Harvey*
c) *Bobby Simpson* d) *Allan Border*

89. Which of the umpires, who till recently officiated in ODI cup Test matches, has more than 10,000 runs in first class cricket?

a) *S. Venkatraghavan* b) *David Shepherd*
c) *Neil Mallender* d) *Dickie Bird*

90. Though he is not in the current New Zealand side he can lay claim to an unusual birthplace—a taxi ! He was in the limelight during the 1999 World Cup as he headed the averages for his country in that tournament. Who was he?

a) *Roger Twose* b) *Bryan Young*
c) *Andrew Jones* d) *Chris Cairns*

91. Which Kiwi cricketer is nicknamed Billy Ray?

a) *Roger Twose* b) *Stephen Flyris*
c) *Chris Cairns* d) *Scott Styris*

92. This Wisden player-of-the-year in 1965 had a good tour of India in 1964 claiming 10 wickets for 91 runs in Australia's win at Madras. He later gave way in the early seventies to the younger lot led by Bob Massie and company. Who was he?

a) *Graham McKenzie* b) *Neil Hawke*
c) *Alan Connolly* d) *Bobby Simpson*

93. The first ever Test between India and Australia saw the latter winning by an innings and 226 runs. However this match at Brisbane is famous for another reason. What is it?

a) *Only time C. S. Nayudu was out obstructing the field.*
b) *Only time Sir Don Bradman was out hit wicket.*
c) *Only time Vinoo Mankad was out first ball in both innings.*
d) *Only time the openers of both teams got out cheaply in both innings.*

94. The Benson & Hedges series was an all-out Ravi Shastri affair in 1986. However in the India wickets his being adjudged man-of-the-match raised quite a few eyebrows as the hallmark of the match as a hurricane innings by someone else. Who?

a) *K. Srikkanth* b) *Dileep Vengsarkar*

c) *Kapil Dev* d) *Sunil Gavaskar*

95. Who was the only West Indian batsman to be dismissed in West Indies' nine-wicket victory over India at Birmingham in the league phase of the 1979 World Cup?

a) *Desmond Haynes* b) *Gordon Greenidge*

c) *Vivian Richards* d) *Collin King*

96. Which Indian claimed one wicket at the cost of six runs in the 12 overs he bowled against East Africa in the 1975 World Cup?

a) *Madan Lal* b) *Abid Ali*

c) *S. Venkataraghavan* d) *Bishan Singh Bedi*

97. When did Sri Lanka played its first Test match?

a) *16 October, 1952* b) *18 October, 1992*

c) *17 February, 1982* d) *10 January, 1930*

98. Which South African captain opened the batting for another country in the 1980's before playing 16 Tests for his home nation in the 1990's?

a) *Shaun Pollock* b) *Kepler Wessels*

c) *Hansie Cronje* d) *Andrew Hudson*

99. Which player scored a double century for Zimbabwe in that country's historic first Test victory over Pakistan in 1995?

a) *Andy Flower* b) *Mark Dekker*

c) *Guy Whittall* d) *Grant Flower*

100. Which Indian was the first to play 300 ODIs ?

a) *Sachin Tendulkar* b) *Sunil Gavaskar*

c) *M. Azharuddin* d) *Kapil Dev*

6

Tennis

1. Which male tennis player has hit the fastest serve ever?

a) *Pete Sampras* b) *Mark Philipousses*
c) *Greg Ruseaski* d) *Andy Roddick*

2. Who was the only person in professional tennis to ever win a "Golden Set"?

a) *Rode Laver* b) *Pete Sampras*
c) *Fred Perry* d) *Bill Scanlon*

3. Which tennis player wrote the book *You Cannot Be Serious*?

a) *Patrick McEnroe* b) *Pete Sampras*
c) *John McEnroe* d) *Brad Gilbert*

4. Which nation had the most men ranked in the top ten of the ATP rankings at the end of 2005?

a) *Argentina* b) *Spain*
c) *Switzerland* d) *US*

5. If your opponent hits a winner and his/her foot touches the bottom of the net whose point is it?

a) *Nobody's point* b) *Replay the point*
c) *Your point* d) *Your opponent's point*

6. Which of the following players has won all four of the Grand Slams in singles?

a) *Pete Sampras* b) *John McEnroe*
c) *Layton Hewitt* d) *Andre Agassi*

7. Who won the 2005 Roland Garros Singles title?

a) *Amelie Mauresmo* b) *Justine Henin-Hardenne*

c) *Kim Clijsters* d) *Serena Williams*

8. How old was Boris Becker when he won his first Wimbledon title?

a) *16* b) *17* c) *18* d) *19*

9. Who is the only player to defeat Steffi Graf and Monica Seles at Wimbledon in the same year?

a) *Zina Garrison* b) *Martina Navratilova*

c) *Jana Novotna* d) *Grbriela Sabitini*

10. Who was the first non-British player to win the Men's Singles Championship at Wimbledon?

a) *Norman Brookes* b) *Anthony Wilding*

c) *Jeff Jarring* d) *Groan Ivanisefic*

11. In which year did Billie Jean King win her first and last Ladies Singles Championship at Wimbledon?

a) *1965 and 1976* b) *1966 and 1974*

c) *1965 and 1974* d) *1966 and 1975*

12. Who is the only member of the British royal family ever to have competed in a first day's tennis tournament when he entered the men's doubles event at Wimbledon in 1926?

a) *Edward VIII* b) *Edward VII*

c) *George V* d) *George VI*

13. Who shocked the tennis world and defeated defending champion Steffi Graf in the first round of Wimbledon in 1994?

a) *Lori McNeill* b) *Monica Seles*

c) *Pam Shiver* d) *Jennifer Capriati*

14. Who played against Pete Sampras in the quarterfinals of the Australian Open in 1995, when a member of the crowd yelled out "Do it for your coach"? This caused Pete to break down and weep for his cancer-stricken coach and friend ?

a) *Yevgemy Kafelnikov* b) *Andre Agassi*

c) *Jim Courier* d) *Patrick Rafter*

15. **Which player said this: "I don't care if the player is seeded or not. It's just a player I have to win. I have to play my game and win"?**

a) *Lina Krasnoroutskaya* b) *Pavlina Nola*
c) *Nicolas Eacude* d) *Arnaud Clement*

16. **Which two tennis players have the nickname Spice Girls when playing the doubles?**

a) *Lisa Raymond and Rennae Stubbs*
b) *Venus Williams and Serena Williams*
c) *Denials Hantuchova and Anna Kournikouva*
d) *Martina Hingis and Anna Kournikouva*

17. **In 1999, Leander Peas and Mahesh Bhupathi clinched the doubles title of:**

a) *Wimbledon, French Open*
b) *China Open, US Open*
c) *Australia Open, Wimbledon*
d) *US Open, Australia Open*

18. **Which player sent Roger Federer home in the first round of the Wimbledon 2002?**

a) *Mario Ancic* b) *Thomas Johanson*
c) *Marat Safin* d) *Lleyton Hewitt*

19. **Which of the following players has not won six singles slams?**

a) *Stefan Edberg* b) *Ken Rossewell*
c) *Boris Becker* d) *Mats Wilander*

20. **Who won the 2000 Wimbledon title?**

a) *Pete Sampras* b) *Richard Krajicek*
c) *Patrick Rafter* d) *Andre Agassi*

21. **In which year did Ivan Lendl win the Wimbledon?**

a) *1987* b) *1991* c) *1992* d) *Never*

22. **Tie-breakers are played at what score in a set?**

a) *5-5* b) *6-6* c) *6-5* d) *5-6*

23. Which player has won the most Grand Slam Men's Singles titles?

a) *Andre Agassi* b) *Ivan Lendl*
c) *Rod Landl* d) *Pete Sampras*

24. Which professional female tennis player held the first ranking the longest?

a) *Martina Navratilova* b) *Monica Seles*
c) *Steffi Graf* d) *Chris Evert*

25. Who wrote the book, *How To Play Tennis* ?

a) *Billy jean King* b) *Martina Hingis*
c) *Jennifer Capriati* d) *Venus and Serena Williams*

26. Who was the first player to win a Grand Slam?

a) *Donald Budge* b) *Nikolay Davydenkao*
c) *Rod Laver* d) *Lim Henman*

27. Players from which nation have captured the most French Open Men's singles titles in the last five years?

a) *Argentina* b) *Brazil*
c) *Spain* d) *United States*

28. Which of the following was the sponsor of the WTA Tour in 2005?

a) *David Nalbandian* b) *Albert Costa*
c) *Xavier Malisse* d) *Fabrics Santoro*

29. Who became the official sponsor of the WTA Tour in 2005.

a) *Sony Ericsson* b) *Volvo*
c) *Sanex* d) *Canon*

30. Who won the Women's Singles title at 2003's French Open?

a) *Kim Clijsters* b) *Justine Henin-Hardenne*
c) *Serena Williams* d) *Lindsay Davenport*

31. **Hana Mandlikova was a Czech tennis player during the 1980's she won four Grand slam titles but Wimbledon was not among them. Who did she lose to at the 1986 Wimbledon?**

a) *Chris Evert* b) *Martina Mavratilova*
c) *Wendy Iurnkull* d) *Silvia Hanika*

32. **Who was the first player to defeat Andre Agassi at Wimbledon?**

a) *John McEnroe* b) *Henri Leconte*
c) *Jimmy Connors* d) *Yannick Noah*

33. **In which of the following years did two Frenchmen oppose each other in the fight for the title of Men's Singles Champion?**

a) *1924* b) *1916* c) *1911* d) *1922*

34. **Which New Zealand player won four Singles Championships in a row in the early 1910's?**

a) *Laurie Doherty* b) *Anthony Wilding*
c) *Maurice McLaughlin* d) *Jack Crawford*

35. **At what age did Virginia Wade win the Ladies Singles Championship at Wimbledon?**

a) *33* b) *32* c) *31* d) *30*

36. **In the Australian Open (2006) how many tie-breakers were played throughout the course of the event?**

a) *53* b) *56* c) *59* d) *51*

37. **At the inaugural modern Olympic Games held at Athens in 1896, two lawn tennis titles were won by an Irish law student. Who was he?**

a) *John Donald Budge* b) *John Patrick McEnroe*
c) *John Mary Pius Boland* d) *Jean Borotra*

38. **Which is the only Grand Slam Tournament that allows fifth set tie-breakers?**

a) *French Open* b) *Wimbledon*
c) *Australian Open* d) *US Open*

39. **Who was quoted as saying: "The best doubles team in the world is McEnroe and whoever he's playing with"?**

a) *Peter Fleming* b) *John Newcombe*
c) *Arthur Ashe* d) *Bud Collins*

40. **For which country does M.Lucic play?**

a) *Yugoslavia* b) *Croatia*
c) *Romania* d) *Slovenia*

41. **Who won the women's 2000 Wimbledon crown?**

a) *Serena Williams* b) *Venus Williams*
c) *Lindsay Davenport* d) *Martina Hingis*

42. **In 2001, Juan Carlos Ferrero mainly played doubles with one partner. Who was this player?**

a) *Tommy Robredo* b) *Mark Philippoussis*
c) *Todd Martin* d) *Goran Ivanisevic*

43. **Which male player once opened Star Café with Monica Seles?**

a) *Pete Sampras* b) *Andre Agassi*
c) *Yevgeny Kafelnickov* d) *Chies Woodruff*

44. **Who won the Tennis Masters Cup in 2001?**

a) *Andre Agassi* b) *Yevgeny Kafelnickov*
c) *Gustavo Kuerten* d) *Lleyton Hewitt*

45. **Which two players participated in the final of the Australian Open 2002?**

a) *Thomas Johansson & Marat Safin*
b) *Pete Sampras & Lleyton Hewitt*
c) *Juan Carlos Ferrero & Albert Costa*
d) *Jiri Novak & Andre Agassi*

46. **Which woman has won the most Grand Slams?**

a) *Martina Navratilova* b) *Steffi Graf*
c) *Margaret Smith Court* d) *Helen Wills Moody*

47. How many racquets are you allowed to use in one match?

a) *3* b) *4*
c) *5* d) *As many as it takes*

48. Who amongst the following men has won the most tournaments ever?

a) *Jimmy Connors* b) *John Mcenroe*
c) *Bjorn Borg* d) *Ivan Lendl*

49. Who wrote the book, *I Know Absolutely Nothing About Tennis* ?

a) *Greg Rusedski* b) *Tracy Austin*
c) *Chirst Evert* d) *Bud Callins*

50. Who won the WTA 's season-ending Championship in 2005?

a) *Venus Williams* b) *Amelie Mauresmo*
c) *Kim Clijsters* d) *Justine Henin*

51. Who won the 2005 Wimbledon's single's title?

a) *Justin Henin-Hardenne* b) *Venus Williams*
c) *Lendsay Davenport* d) *Serena Williams*

52. How many Grand Slam titles has Pete Sampras won?

a) *10* b) *12* c) *14* d) *15*

53. Swiss standout Martina Hingis made a comeback in 2006 after three years out of professional tennis. Before her temporary retirement she won five Grand Slam titles but which tournament was not among them?

a) *US Open* b) *French Open*
c) *Wimbledon* d) *Australian Open*

54. Who defeated Boris Becker in his last singles match at Wimbledon?

a) *Andre Agassi* b) *Pat Rafter*
c) *Pete Sampras* d) *Goran Ivanisevic*

55. How old was the American Bill Tilden when he won his Men's Singles Championship?

a) *40* b) *38* c) *36* d) *34*

56. **Who was the first US woman to win the Tennis Grand Slam?**

a) *Shirley Fry* b) *Althea Gibson*
c) *Maureen Connolly* d) *Helen Wills*

57. **Which of these players did not compete in the US Open 2005 as a qualifier?**

a) *Bjorn Phau* b) *Daniel Bracciali*
c) *Jonas Bjorkman* d) *Arnaud Clement*

58. **Who was handed the 28th seed for the Australian Open 2006?**

a) *Filippo Volandri* b) *Taylor Dent*
c) *Max Mirnyi* d) *Fernando Verdasco*

59. **What was unusual about Virginia Wade's opponent in her opening match of the US Open in 1977?**

a) *She was one of identical twins who took turns to play.*
b) *She served underarm.*
c) *She had previously competed as a man.*
d) *She had an artificial legs.*

60. **Bill Telden and which other US player have finished the season ranked number one in the world six times?**

a) *John McEnroe* b) *Pete Sampras*
c) *Jimmy Connors* d) *Andre Agassi*

61. **What is upon the top of the trophy awarded to the men's singles championship at Wimbledon?**

a) *An eagle* b) *A terrier*
c) *A strawberry* d) *A pineapple*

62. **Melon-head is the nickname given to which player ?**

a) *Mark Phillippoussis* b) *Todd Martin*
c) *Thomas Enqvist* d) *Roger Federer*

63. **Which Australian player is the only one to win conductive US Open titles?**

a) *Mark Phillippoussis* b) *Lleyton Hewitt*
c) *Todd Woodbridge* d) *Patrick Rafter*

64. How many years had the car manufacturer Ford sponsored the first Grand Slam of the year in a row before it decided to stop and was replaced by another car manufacturer Ka Motors, in 2002?

a) *14* b) *16* c) *18* d) *22*

65. Where was the Tennis Masters Cup 2001 held?

a) *Sydney* b) *Mumbai*
c) *Paris* d) *New York*

66. Which four nations went on to the semi-final of the Davis Cup 2002?

a) *US, Australia, France, Brazil*
b) *US, Russia, France, Argentina*
c) *Australia, Russia, Spain, France*
d) *Spain, Russia, France, Argentina*

67. Who won the 1997 US Open women's singles?

a) *Lindsay Davenport* b) *Monica Seles*
c) *Martina Hingis* d) *Venus Williams*

68. Who amongst the women has won the most tournaments ever?

a) *Margaret Smith Court* b) *Martina Navratilova*
c) *Steffi Graf* d) *Christ Evert*

69. Who amongst the following hit virtually all of his backhands with one hand?

a) *Layton Hewitt* b) *Roger Federer*
c) *Andy Roddick* d) *Rafael Nadal*

70. Who played tennis for Harvard University before turning pro?

a) *Andy Roddick* b) *André Agassi*
c) *Robby Ginepri* d) *James Blake*

71. Who amongst the following attacked most often at the net?

a) *Chris Evert* b) *Jana Novotna*
c) *Arantxa Sanchez-Vicario* d) *Gabriella Sabatini*

72. **Who reached the quarter finals or better at all 15 WTA Tour events she played in 2005?**

a) *Kim Clijsters* b) *Elena Dementieva*
c) *Maria Sharapova* d) *Mary Pierce*

73. **From which country Roger Federer hail?**

a) *Spain* b) *Switzerland*
c) *Brazil* d) *US*

74. **Boris Becker won six Grand Slam title but a French Open was not among them. What was his best finish?**

a) *Finalist* b) *Fourth round*
c) *Quarterfinalist* d) *Semifinalist*

75. **The late 1970s made Argentinian Guillermo Vilas a household name in tennis. What tournament prevented him from winning the career Grand Slam?**

a) *US Open* b) *Wimbledon*
c) *Australian Open* d) *French Open*

76. **Except Marat Safin, who is the last winner of the US Open men's singles who did not win it more than once?**

a) *Andre Agassi* b) *Mats Wilander*
c) *Arthur Ashe* d) *Boris Becker*

77. **How many years in a row did Suzanne Lenglen of Fance win the women's singles Championship at Wimbledon in the 1910's and 1920's?**

a) *4* b) *5* c) *3* d) *6*

78. **Who was the first Australian among women to win the Championship at Wimbledon?**

a) *Margaret Smith* b) *Juliet Atkinson*
c) *Evonne Goolagong* d) *Ann Hayden Jones*

79. **In the US Open 2005, who was the only player to lose a match through a walkover?**

a) *Victor Hanescu* b) *Nicolas Massu*
c) *Marat Safin* d) *Jiri Novak*

80. **Which Australian player was nieknamed as Muscles?**

a) *Lew Hoad* b) *Patrick Rafter*
c) *Rod Laver* d) *Ken Rosewall*

81. **Which of the following players entered the 2006 Australian Open as a lucky loser?**

a) *Bjorn Rehnquist* b) *Amer Delic*
c) *Jacob Adaktusson* d) *Federico Luzzi*

82. **Which early royal tennis enthusiast was to find that lost tennis balls cost him his life?**

a) *Kin Henry VIII* b) *Ivan IV*
c) *Louis XVI* d) *King James I of Scotland*

83. **Can you name this former world number one who won Wimbledon thrice in his career?**

a) *Boris Becker* b) *Henri Lecanto*
c) *Lim Mayetta* d) *Joakim Nostrum*

84. **"I may have exaggerated a bit when I said that 80 per cent of the top 100 women are fat pigs. What I meant to say was 75 per cent of the top 100 women are fat pigs." Which ATP player said this?**

a) *Jim Courier* b) *John McEnroe*
c) *Richard Krajicek* d) *Goran Ivanisevic*

85. **Which US player made a guest appearance in an episode of *Sabrina, The Teenage Witch*?**

a) *Pete Sampras* b) *Andy Roddick*
c) *Andre Agassi* d) *Jan-Michael Gambill*

86. **Who amongst the following has won the most career prize money?**

a) *Martina Hingis* b) *Monica Seles*
c) *Steffi Graf* d) *Margaret Court*

87. **Where were the AATP Championships and ATP Tournament held?**

a) *San Jose* b) *Chennai*
c) *Adelaide* d) *Acapulco*

88. Who won the junior title of Roland Garros 2001?

a) *Amine Quahab* b) *Brian Dabul*
c) *Carlos Cuadrado* d) *Alejandro Falla*

89. How many times did Goran Ivanisevic participate in the Wimbledon final before winning it in 2001?

a) *Once* b) *Twice*
c) *Thrice* d) *Four times*

90 Which player was a sensation in Roland Garros 2002 after beating Kim Clijsters to Venus Williams in the semi-finals?

a) *Paola Suarez* b) *Clarissa Fernandez*
c) *Silvia Farina Elia* d) *Elena Bovina*

91. How many players enter a single's draw for a Grand Slam?

a) *64 Players* b) *128 players*
c) *256 players* d) *100 players*

92. Which of these players virtually uses a one-handed backhand?

a) *Serena Williams* b) *Amelia Mauresmo*
c) *Kim Clijsters* d) *Lindsay Davenport*

93. Who won the first Grand Slam singles title of her cancer in 2005?

a) *Mary Pierce* b) *Maria Sharapova*
c) *Media Pervade* d) *Kim Clijsters*

94. The four tournaments that make up the Grand Slam are French Open, US Open, Australian Open and—

a) *Brazil Open* b) *China Open*
c) *Wimbledon* d) *Davis Cup*

95. Who ended 2005 with the number one singles ranking?

a) *Lindsay Davenport* b) *Kim Clijsters*
c) *Serena Williams* d) *Amelia Mauresmo*

96. American Pete Sampras, who was top-ranked for much of his career, won 14 Grand Slam titles, but the French Open was not among them. When was his best finish?

a) *1996* b) *1995* c) *1997* d) *1994*

97. Stefan Edger was former number one rank who never won the French Open. The Swede did reach the finals in 1989. Who did he lose to?

a) *Mats Wilander* b) *Jim Couricer*

c) *Michael Chang* d) *Ivan Lendl*

98. Czech tennis legend Ivan Lendl won eight Grand Slam titles, but Wimbledon was not among them. At what stage was he knocked out of Wimbledon in 1986 and 1987?

a) *Fourth Round* b) *Quarter-Finals*

c) *Semi-Finals* d) *Finals*

99. Which US player dominated the women's singles at Wimbledon during the late 1920's?

a) *Helen Jacobs* b) *Helen Wills Moody*

c) *Mary K. Browne* d) *Dorothy Round*

100. In the 2006 Australian Open, which of these players did Roger Federer lose the most number of games to?

a) *Tommy Haas* b) *Marcos Baghdatis*

c) *Nikolay Davydenko* d) *Nicolas Keifer*

7

Golf

1. How many holes are there on a regulation golf course?

a) *27* b) *36* c) *110* d) *18*

2. Who is known as the Black Knight?

a) *Tiger Woods* b) *Vijay Singh*
c) *Gary Player* d) *Phil Mickelson*

3. Which was the first Irish course at which the British Open was held?

a) *Royal Porters* b) *Ballybunion*
c) *Royal County Down* d) *K-Chub*

4. Who did Ryder Cup captain, Lonnie Watkins overlook as a captain's pick for the 1995 US Ryder Cup team, despite the fact that this player had won twice earlier in the year?

a) *Payne Steward* b) *Lee Tanzen*
c) *Brad Faxon* d) *Steve Jones*

5. Who was the first golfer to shoot a competitive 59?

a) *Chip Beck* b) *Sam Snead*
c) *Jack Nicklaus* d) *Al Goberger*

6. If you hit a ball in a water hazard how many penalty strokes do you receive?

a) *Two* b) *One* c) *Three* d) *Four*

7. Three under par for hale is a(n)—

a) *Albatross* b) *Birdie*
c) *Eagle* d) *Turkey*

8. Which course has a floating island green that can be moved to play at different lengths?

a) *PGA West*
b) *TPC, Sawgrass*
c) *Coeur D'Alene*
d) *Kapalua*

9. Name the first Golf Club to be set up in India during the British Raj?

a) *Royal Calcutta Golf Club*
b) *Bombay Golf Club*
c) *Bangalore Golf Club*
d) *Madras Gymkhana Golf Club*

10. Who played with Tiger Woods in the final paring of the 1997 US Masters?

a) *Tom Kite*
b) *Phil Mickelson*
c) *David Duval*
d) *Costantino Rocca*

11. Which Glof Club hosted the US Open in the same year of Bobby Jones Grand Slam?

a) *Merion*
b) *Pebble Beach*
c) *Interlachen*
d) *Olympic Club*

12. Between 1991 and 2001, what is the only PGA Tour event that both Stuart Appleby and Robert Allenby have each won?

a) *Advil Western Open*
b) *Shell Houston Open*
c) *Kemper Open*
d) *Honda Classic*

13. Who was the first golfer to shoot a 58 in competitive play?

a) *Tiger Woods*
b) *Shigeki Maruyama*
c) *David Duval*
d) *Steve Lowery*

14. Which of these is the most dangerous to a golfer?

a) *Rain*
b) *Lightning*
c) *Thunder*
d) *Hot weather*

15. The allowance made, in putting, for a slope is a ________.

a) *Lend*
b) *Borrow*
c) *Give*
d) *Take*

16. This course was designed by Pete Dye and hosted the 1991 Ryder Cup Matches. Name it?

a) *Murefield Village* b) *Oak Hills*
c) *TPC, Sawgrass* d) *Kiawah Island*

17. In 1888 where in India was the Cosmopolitan Golf Club established?

a) *Bombay* b) *Calcutta*
c) *Bangalore* d) *Madras*

18. Which city in North India was the first to have a course?

a) *Shimla* b) *Ranikhet*
c) *Sringar* d) *Gulmarg*

19. What score did David Duval shoot in the final round of the 1999 Bob Chrysler Classic to win the tournament?

a) *61* b) *59* c) *66* d) *62*

20. What is the name of the 18th hole at Augusta National?

a) *Holly* b) *Camellia*
c) *Golden Bell* d) *Chinese Fu*

21. Who won the Money title on the 1990 Hogan Tourists first year of existence?

a) *Jeff Maggert* b) *Brandel Chamblee*
c) *John Daly* d) *Olin Browne*

22. What was the home golf course of Bobby Jones?

a) *East Lake GC* b) *Augusta National GC*
c) *Atlanta Athletic GC* d) *Peachtree GC*

23. If you hit a ball out of the range of play you are said to have gone—

a) *Out of Range* b) *Out of Bounds*
c) *Out Beyond* d) *Beyond Range*

24. Which court hosts the Byron Nelson Classic annually?

a) *TPC, Woodlands* b) *La Cantera*
c) *The Colonial* d) *TPC, Las Colinas*

25. In which year did world restoration finally come to India when it was invited to the Alfred Dunhill Cup, a premier 16-nation team event at the old Course of St. Andrews, Scotland?

a) *1993* b) *1994* c) *1995* d) *1996*

26. Who won the 2000 Women's British Open?

a) *Kerrie Webb* b) *Meg Mellon*
c) *Charlotte Sorenstam* d) *Sophie Gustafson*

27. On April 23, 2003, who resigned as a league representative on the PGA Tour Policy Board because he wanted more time to prepare for the next Ryder Cup where he would captain?

a) *David Toms* b) *David Duval*
c) *Hal Sutton* d) *Steve Ballesteros*

28. Who shot the first 58 in PGA Tour sanctioned event during the Canadian Laura Bayer Championship?

a) *Franklin Langham* b) *Jace Bugg*
c) *Jason Bohn* d) *Chip Beck*

29. Who was the first winner of a Hogan Tour event the 1990 Bakersfield Open?

a) *Jim McGovern* b) *Mike Springer*
c) *Dick Mast* d) *Barry Chessman*

30. Which golfer has the most official victories on any golf tour whatsoever in the USA?

a) *Sam Snead* b) *Jack Nicklaus*
c) *Mickey Wright* d) *Kathy Whitworth*

31. What is the term for the surface you hit that has the pin on it?

a) *Brown* b) *Rough*
c) *Smooth* d) *Green*

32. Which famous course has holes named Magnolia, Lea Olive and Golden Bell?

a) *Augusta National* b) *Oakmont*
c) *Pinehurst* d) *Pebble Beach*

33. In which city in India was the Wills Indian Open Golf Championship organised in March 2000?

a) *Mumbai* b) *New Delhi*

c) *Jaipur* d) *Kolkotta*

34. What position did Tiger Woods finish the 1998 season ranked in the putting category?

a) *147th* b) *1st* c) *17th* d) *95th*

35. On what course did Ken Ventura win the 1964 US Open?

a) *Congressional* b) *Riviera*

c) *Sahalee* d) *Winged Foot*

36. What is the name of the trophy presented to the player with the lowest scoring average on the European Tour?

a) *Volvo Trophy* b) *Seve Trophy*

c) *Brabazon Trophy* d) *Vardon Trophy*

37. On which course was the British Open held in 1975?

a) *Carnoustie* b) *Troon*

c) *Midfield* d) *Birkdale*

38. He won the 1998 and 1999 Hero Honda Masters to become only the second player in the history of Asean PGA Tour to successfully defend his title. Who was he?

a) *Jyoti Randhawa* b) *Gaurav Ghei*

c) *Jeev Milkha Singh* d) *Ali Sher*

39. When was the India Golf Union formed?

a) *1945* b) *1950* c) *1955* d) *1960*

40. Who was the first to win three Masters titles?

a) *Jack Nicklaus* b) *Gene Sarazen*

c) *Arnold Palmes* d) *Jimmy Demaret*

41. Hazards are defined by what colour stakes or lines?

a) *Yellow* b) *White*

c) *Red* d) *Green*

42. What is the warning shouted to anyone in danger of being hit by the ball?

a) *Four* b) *Five* c) *For* d) *Fore*

43. What famous course is known as the Home of Golf?

a) *Royal Troon* b) *St. Andrews*
c) *Augusta National* d) *Royal Lytham*

44. Who holds the record for the highest earning on the European Civility ?

a) D. B. *Close* b) *Hal Sutton*
c) *Nick Faldo* d) *Lim Duncan*

45. What is the maximum number of clubs with which player may start a game?

a) *13* b) *14* c) *15* d) *16*

46. How many minutes does a player get to search for his ball before it must be declared lost?

a) *Three* b) *Five* c) *Seven* d) *Ten*

47. Where was the first Indian Open played in the year 1962?

a) *Banglore* b) *New Delhi*
c) *Srinagar* d) *Ambala*

48. In the IX Asian Games held in Delhi which nation won the golf championship?

a) *Japan* b) *Korea* c) *India* d) *Singapore*

49. Which Australian golfer five-time winner of the British Open, became the winner of the first Indian Open at the Delhi Golf Club?

a) *J. F. Macnair* b) *David Daval*
c) *Peter Thompson* d) *David Toms*

50. Who was the 2002-2003 player of the year?

a) *Davis Love* b) *Tiger Woods*
c) *Mark Omeara* d) *Gohn Daly*

51. Who is the only player to have won five World Matchplay titles?

a) Gary Player *b) Seve Ballesteros*
c) Nick Faldo *d) Ernie Els*

52. Farmer William Lowe was fined £1000 for what?

a) Grazing cattle on Royal Birkdale
b) Digging up part of one of Carnoustie's greens that he believes is on his property
c) Killing 150 fish at The Belfry
d) Hitting lost balls back onto the course and endangering players at St Mellion

53. Which of these players never won an Open Championship at St Andrews?

a) Tom Watson *b) Seve Ballesteros*
c) Jack Nicklaus *d) Arnold Palmer*

54. What year was the European Tour qualifying school introduced?

a) 1973 *b) 1974* *c) 1975* *d) 1976*

55. What is the name of the championship course at Turnberry?

a) Ailsa *b) Alicia* *c) Elsa* *d) Allissa*

56. Which is the second oldest Open Championship on the European Tour after the British Open?

a) The French Open *b) The German Open*
c) The Spanish Open *d) The Swiss Open*

57. In which year did Tony Jacklin win the US Open Championship?

a) 1969 *b) 1970* *c) 1971* *d) 1972*

58. In what year was Ian Baker-Finch the Open Champion?

a) 1988 *b) 1989* *c) 1990* *d) 1991*

59. Which is the odd one out?

a) Royal Lytham & St Annes *b) Royal Troon*
c) Royal St Georges *d) Royal Birkdale*

60. **Which one of the following players was not involved in a play off for the '87 Masters?**

a) Seve Ballesteros *b) Larry Mize*
c) Curtis Strange *d) Greg Norman*

61. **What year did Greg Norman win his first Open Championship?**

a) 1984 *b) 1985* *c) 1986* *d) 1987*

62. **Who presented Bernhard Langer with his green jacket upon winning the 1993 Masters?**

a) Ian Woosnam *b) Nick Faldo*
c) Fred Couples *d) Sandy Lyle*

63. **All of the holes on which Major Championship course are named after flowers?**

a) Turnberry *b) Pebble Beach*
c) Augusta National *d) Ballybunion*

64. **Who was joint runner-up to Nick Faldo in the 1990 Open at St Andrews?**

a) Ian Baker-Finch *b) Greg Norman*
c) Payne Stewart *d) Paul Azinger*

65. **Which year did Harry Varon win his record breaking 6th Open Championship?**

a) 1899 *b) 1906* *c) 1912* *d) 1920*

66. **Who was the first player to win all four major championships?**

a) Gene Saracen *b) Sam Snead*
c) Jack Nicklaus *d) Arnold Palmer*

67. **The Open Championship was held on the same course for its first 12 years. Which was it?**

a) Troon *b) Prestwick*
c) St Andrews *d) Musselburgh*

68. **Who lost to Paul Azinger in a play-off for the 1993 USPGA Championship?**

a) Greg Norman *b) Nick Price*
c) Lee Janzen *d) Chip Beck*

69. During the 1981 "Cock of the North Open" in Zambia, Sandy Lyle was not given a free drop when his ball came to rest where?

a) In a rattle snakes nest
b) On the bones of a dead elephant
c) In a swarm of black ants
d) On the grave of a holy Zulu leader

70. Which make of ball did Henry Cotton play when he won the 1934 Open Championship?

a) Dunlop *b) Top Flite*
c) Wilson *d) Titleist*

71. Which Open Championship course has a hole called "Risk-an-Hope" (14th)?

a) Turnberry *b) Troon*
c) St Andrews *d) Wentworth*

72. Which players arguments caused referee Colonel Tony Duncan to quit on the spot during a recent World Matchplay Championship?

a) Gary Player *b) Seve Ballesteros*
c) Jack Nicklaus *d) Curtis Strange*

73. What year did Seve Ballesteros win his first Open Championship?

a) 1979 *b) 1983* *c) 1987* *d) 1989*

74. Who won the 1986 Masters Championship at Augusta?

a) Ben Crenshaw *b) Seve Ballesteros*
c) Larry Mize *d) Jack Nicklaus*

75. Where is Tuctu GC.? At 14,335 feet above sea level, it is the highest course in the world.

a) Chile *b) Nepal* *c) Peru* *d) India*

76. Which player was not involved in the play-off for the 1989 Open at Royal Troon?

a) Mark Calcavecchia *b) Greg Norman*
c) Wayne Grady *d) Payne Stewart*

77. What year was the first World Cup of Golf held?

a) 1893 *b) 1927* *c) 1944* *d) 1953*

78. Who won the 1967 Dutch Open?

a) K.Moon *b) R.Daltry*
c) J.Entwistle *d) P.Townsend*

79. On which Open Championship course is the famous "Postage Stamp" hole?

a) Carnoustie *b) Muirfield*
c) Sandwich *d) Troon*

80. Who was runner-up to Curtis Strange in the 1998 US Open after an 18 hole play-off?

a) Ian Woosnam *b) Nick Faldo*
c) Jose Maria Olazabel *d) Sandy Lyle*

81. When was golf last played in the Olympics?

a) 1928 *b) 1932* *c) 1936* *d) 1940*

82. In which city did Ian Woosnam win his first USPGA tour event?

a) Chicago *b) New Mexico*
c) New Orleans *d) New York*

83. On which course was the 1984 US Open held?

a) Webbed Foot *b) Golden Claw*
c) Red Eye Creek *d) Shotgun Valley*

84. Which of these players did not win a Major Championship in 1993?

a) Nick Faldo *b) Bernhard Langer*
c) Lee Jansen *d) Greg Norman*

85. What year did Sandy Lyle win the Open Championship at Sandwich?

a) 1983 *b) 1985* *c) 1987* *d) 1989*

86. Which player won the Open Championship four times between the wars?

a) Henry Cotton *b) Bobby Jones*
c) James Braid *d) Walter Hagen*

87. Who finished 2nd to Sandy Lyle in the 1988 Masters Championship?

a) Scott Hoch *b) Curtis Strange*

c) Mark Calcavecchia *d) Tom Kite*

88. What year did Nick Faldo first win on the USPGA Tour?

a) 1980 *b) 1984* *c) 1988* *d) 1990*

89. Who was the first European to win the US Masters?

a) Seve Ballesteros *b) Tony Jacklin*

c) Bernhard Langer *d) Peter Aliss*

90. Who lost the 1999 Open at Carnoustie in dramatic style?

a) Paul Lawrie *b) Justin Leonard*

c) Jean Van De Velde *d) Justin Leonard*

91. What year did Jose Maria Olazabel win his first US Masters title?

a) 1982 *b) 1984* *c) 1986* *d) 1988*

92. Which was the first all ticket golf tournament in the British Isles?

a) 1990 Benson & Hedges *b) 1990 Open*

c) 1989 Ryder Cup *d) 1989 Pga Championship*

93. Ramsey Golf Club is on which island off the British Isles?

a) Isle of White *b) Hayling Island*

c) Isle of Man *d) Orkney Isles*

94. Who was runner-up to Hal Suton in the 2000 Players Championship at Sawgrass?

a) Tiger Woods *b) Sergio Garcia*

c) Davis Love III *d) Lee Westwood*

95. Who did Fanny Sunesson carry for before she got Nick Faldo's bag?

a) Sam Torrence *b) Gordon Brand Jnr*

c) Howard Clark *d) Mark James*

96. Which is the highest course above sea level in England?

a) Kingston *b) Kingslynn*

c) Kington *d) Kingstanton*

97. Which legendary player designed the multi-million pound Kildare Club in Ireland?

a) Arnold Palmer *b) Jack Nicklaus*

c) Lee Trevino *d) Tom Watson*

98. George Walker, donator of the Walker Cup has a famous grandson. Who is he?

a) Ronald Reagan *b) George Bush*

c) Bill Clinton *d) Richard Nixon*

99. Englishman Bernie Hunt was leading money winner on the 1961 European Tour. What were his total earnings for the season?

a) £4,492 *b) £11,657*

c) £29,501 *d) £86,012*

100. How many holes at St Andrews are named after former champions?

a) None *b) One* *c) Two* *d) Three*

8

Football

1. In which year was the Federation of International Football Associations (FIFA) formed?

a) *May 1900* b) *August 1902*
c) *May 1904* d) *August 1906*

2. Where is the headquarters of the FIFA?

a) *Zurich* b) *Paris*
c) *Rome* d) *Barcelona*

3. How many teams qualify into the final stage form each of the regional federations?

a) *16* b) *20* c) *24* d) *28*

4. Who was chosen as the FIFA Footballer of the year in 1993?

a) *Rosario, Holland* b) *Leonidas da Silva, Brazil*
c) *Antonio Carvazal, Mexico* d) *Roberto Baggio of Italy*

5. Who is credited with scoring the first ever hat-trick?

a) *Leonidas da Silva of Brazil* b) *Szengeller, Hungary*
c) *Gunnison, Sweden* d) *Colossi, Italy*

6. Where was the first World Cup in 1930 held?

a) *Italy* b) *Uruguay*
c) *France* d) *Brazil*

7. In the 18th World Cup 2006, which country won the FIFA World Cup?

a) *France* b) *Germany*
c) *Argentina* d) *Italy*

8. The participation of Romania was largely due to the efforts of their King. He not only picked the team for the 1930 World Cup in Uruguay, but also secured the release of some of the players from their employers. Who was this King?

a) *King Wilhelm* b) *King Carol*
c) *King George V* d) *Emperor Gutenberg*

9. South America was poorly represented in the 1934 World Cup held in Italy. Only Brazil and Argentina took part in the Cup. Even then Argentina didn't send its full strength squad, due to fears of poaching by top Italian clubs. Which Argentinean player switched sides (to Italy) before the 1930 World Cup finals?

a) *Orsi* b) *Tattering*
c) *Michelle* d) *Sela*

10. Cuba made its lone entry in the twentieth century into the World Cup during the 1938 World Cup. How far did they progress in the tournament?

a) *Second Round* b) *First Round*
c) *Final* d) *Semi Final*

11. Who scored Uruguay's winning goal against Brazil in the 1950 World Cup?

a) *Sehiaffino* b) *Ghiggia*
c) *Miguez* d) *Vidal*

12. In the 1954 Swaziland World Cup, which team scored the most goals during the tournament?

a) *West Germany* b) *Masco*
c) *Switzerland* d) *Hungary*

13. Who beat Brazil in the 1958 World Cup in Sweden to win their first ever World Cup?

a) *Sweden* b) *West Germany*
c) *Italy* d) *Hungary*

14. Who won the 1962 World Cup held in Chile after a 3-victory over European opposition?

a) *Brazil* b) *Argentina*
c) *Uruguay* d) *Chile*

15. Who scored both goals for England in their semi-final match against Portugal in 1966 in England?

a) *Bobby Charlton* b) *Martin Peters*
c) *Geoff Hurst* d) *Roger Hurt*

16. What injury caused Franz Beckenbauer to play the last part of the semi-final against Italy with his arm in a sling strapped to his side?

a) *Broken arm* b) *Dislocated shoulder*
c) *Dislocated collar bone* d) *Broken fingers*

17. Which Argentinean player scored tinier in the final against the Netherlands in the 1978 World Cup in Argentina?

a) *Loquat* b) *Kempes*
c) *Ardilles* d) *Maradona*

18. Which country won the 1982 World Cup in Spain?

a) *Brazil* b) *Italy*
c) *Argentina* d) *West Germany*

19. Why did Colombia, the original host country for the 1986 World Cup, step down in which Mexico took their place to host?

a) *Due to bad whether* b) *Due to lack of playgrounds*
c) *Due to financial deficiency* d) *Due to fear of terrorism*

20. Which Country won the 1999 FIFA World Youth Football Championship in Laogs, Nigeria in April 1999?

a) *Japan* b) *Spain*
c) *Croatia* d) *Brazil*

21. Which was the only team not to score a goal at the 1944 World Cup in USA?

a) *Greece* b) *Morocco*
c) *Cameroon* d) *Bolinas*

22. Who sang the World Cup theme song at the 1998 World Cup in Africa?

a) *Ricky Martin* b) *Enrique Iglesias*
c) *Gennefer Lopez* d) *Guho Iglesias*

23. Who hit the post in the World Cup final in 2002 in an amazing free kick between Germany and Brazil?

a) *Michael Ballack* b) *Mehmet Scholl*
c) *Miroslav Klose* d) *Oliver Neville*

24. Which team finished the 2006 tournament in Germany with the fewest yellow cards?

a) *Saudi Arabia* b) *Japan*
c) *Spain* d) *Paraguay*

25. FIFA'S Technical Study Group selects a Man of the Match after each game. Which player finished the tournament in the 2006 World Cup with the most Man of the Match awards?

a) *Te Roberto* b) *Muroslav Klose*
c) *Andrea Pirlo* d) *Zinedine Zidane*

26. To which player was the 2006 Golden Ball awarded at the closing ceremony of the 2006 World Cup?

a) *Miroslav Klose* b) *Zinedine Zidane*
c) *Crespo Herman* d) *Ronaldo*

27. Which player won the Golden Shoe Award in the 2006 FIFA World Cup?

a) Miroslav Klose *b) Zinedine Zidane*
c) Crespo Hernan *d) Ronaldo*

28. In the 2006 Cup, who was shown the yellow card the maximum number of time?

a) Gyan Asamoah
b) Andre of Angola
c) Costtinha of Portugal
d) Boulahrouz Khalid of Netherlands

29. Who won the Golden Ball Award, for the best player in the 1994 World Cup—

a) Romario, Brazil *b) Roberto Baggio, Italy*

c) Sandor Puhl, Hungary *d) Oleg Salenko, Russia*

30. Who won the Silver Shoe Award at the 2006 World Cup?

a) Minoslav Klose, Germany *b) Hernan Crespo, Argentina*

c) Ronaldo, Brazil *d) Zinedine, Zidane, France*

31. Which team conceded the most goals during the 1930 World Cup?

a) USA *b) Mexico*

c) Argentina *d) Uruguay*

32. Who won the 1934 FIFA World Cup?

a) Czechoslovakia *b) Italy*

c) Germany *d) Hungary*

33. After their World campaign in the 1938 World Cup was over, the American team went to New York. There the entire team went to watch another sporting event. What was it?

a) Ice hockey *b) Cricket*

c) Croquet *d) Boxing*

34. Which country was the only one who failed to score a goal in the 1950 tournament?

a) Bolivia *b) Mexico*

c) Chile *d) Paraguay*

35. Who was the team captain for West Germany in the finals of the 1954 World Cup?

a) Bernhard Klodt *b) Max Morlock*

c) Fritz Walter *d) Toni Turek*

36. Which major European power was absent from the 1958 finals after failing to qualify?

a) USSR *b) West Germany*

c) Italy *d) France*

37. Which player appeared in the final match of this 1962 World Cup for the winning team, and later managed this team as winners in two World Cup finals?

a) Zagalo, Brazil *b) Garrincha, Brazil*

c) Backbencher, West Germany *d) Zito, Brazil*

38. Which player scored the most goals in the 1966 tournament?

a) Helmut Haller *b) Eusebio*

c) Geoff Hurst *d) Franz Beckenbauer*

39. Eight members of England's 1966 winning side were in the squad for Mexico. Who was the only one not to take part in any game?

a) Jack Charlton *b) Nobby Stiles*

c) Alan Ball *d) Martin Peters*

40. There was an upset in Group D of the 1974 West Germany World Cup when Haiti scored first to lead 1-0 against Italy. What is the name of the Haitian player who scored that goal?

a) Sanon *b) Manon*

c) Hanon *c) Canon*

41. In the first game of the 1974 World Cup that Holland played against Uruguay, there was a Dutch player who scored both goals. Who was he?

a) Rob Rensenbrink *b) Willy van de Kerkhof*

c) Theode Tong *d) Johnny Rep*

42. During the 1978 World Cup in Argentina two players scored five goals. Who were they?

a) Mario Kempes and Hans Krankle

b) Leopoldo Luque and Teofilio Cedillas

c) Teofilio and Rob Rensenbrink

d) Rob Rensenbrink and Mario Kempes

43. How many teams participated in World Cup in Spain in 1982?

a) 16 *b) 24* *c) 32* *d) 20*

44. Which team did Brazil kick out of the quarter finals on penalties in the 1986 World Cup final in Mexico?

a) France *b) Italy*

c) West Germany *d) Sweden*

45. What was the name of the younger brother of Diego Maradona, who was named in the Argentina squad but did not travel to Italy as he did not make in the final squad?

a) Pedro *b) Javier*

c) Carlos *d) Hugo*

46. How far is the penalty spot from the goal line?

a) 14 yards *b) 8 yards*

c) 12 yards *d) 10 yards*

47. What is the most basic technique used to pass the ball over distances of 15 or fewer yards?

a) Side-volley pass *b) Inside-of-the-foot pass*

c) Instep pass *d) Outside-of-the-foot pass*

48. Who scored the last goal in Germany's thrashing 8-0 against Saudi Arabia in the 2002 World Cup?

a) Miroslav Klose *b) Bernd Schneider*

c) Thomas Linke *d) Carsten Janker*

49. Frank Lampard finished the tournament with more shots than any other player, 24 in total but of those that were recorded as shots on goal, none made it to the back of the net. Which striker had the most number of shots on goal in the 2006 World Cup?

a) Lukas Podolski *b) Crestoano Ronaldo*

c) Miroslav Klose *d) Thierry Henry*

50. This stadium in Germany was originally built in 1936 for the Olympics, and is appropriately named the Olympic Stadium. Which city is it?

a) Berlin *b) Hamburg*

c) Frankfurt *d) Stuttgart*

51. Which two teams earned the World Cup 2006 FIFA Fair Play Award for sportsmanship?

a) England And Spain *b) England and Ecuador*
c) Brazil and Spain *d) Brazil and England*

52. Germany won in the highest scoring opening matching 2006 World Cup history. Who did they play and what was the score?

a) England 3-1 *b) Argentina 6-0*
c) Costa Rica 4-2 *d) Spain 4-0*

53. Who became the first Argentinean official to referee at the FIFA World Cup final in Germany in 2006?

a) Horacio Elizondo *b) Arnaldo Coelho*
c) Romualdo Arppi Filho *d) Codesal*

54. Before the start of the 1930 World Cup, Uruguay started practising with full earnest. They had to follow a strict regime and discipline. Which inspirational player was sacked from the team after he got sneaking into his room after the curfew time?

a) Castro *b) Nazassi*
c) Mazzali *d) Cea*

55. Who emerged as the leading goal scorer of the 1930 World Cup?

a) CEA *b) Dorado*
c) Subiabre *d) Stabile*

56. The final between Argentina and Uruguay was marked by a certain controversy in the 1930 World Cup. It was regarding which ball to use. Both teams wanted to play the match with their balls. Which ball was finally used?

a) Neither country's was used
b) Argentina's
c) Both balls were used
d) Uruguay's

57. **The Italian desire to win started with the ambition to host the 1934 World Cup. How many FIFA Congresses were held to decide the venue before Italy became the host?**

a) *One* b) *Four*

c) *Eight* d) *Fifteen*

58. **Austria was expected to post a formidable challenge to the Italians at the 1934 World Cup. Called popularly 'Wonderteam' they were coached by a highly respected figure in the soccer world. Who was he?**

a) *Matthias Sindelar* b) *Saris*

c) *Semitic* d) *Hugo Meisl*

59. **How many South American teams took part in the 1938 World Cup held in France?**

a) *One* b) *Two*

c) *None* d) *Five*

60. **The manager of the Italian side considered his side to be much better than the side which won the 1934 World Cup. How many players played in both the 1934 and 1938 World Cup?**

a) *Nine* b) *Six*

c) *Four* d) *Eight*

61. **In the 1950 World Cup the participating teams were placed in four groups from which the winner qualified for the second and final round. Which of the following is not true regarding Group D?**

a) *The group consisted of only South American nations.*

b) *The group winner was European.*

c) *There were only two European.*

d) *The group winner scored an average of eight goals per match.*

62. **In the 1950 World Cup, where was the first game of the tournament played?**

a) *Curitiba*

b) *Belo Horizontal*

c) *Rio de Janeiro*

d) *Sao Paulo*

63. Group A was won by Brazil as anticipated in the 1950 World Cup. The Brazilians won two of their three games. What the outcome of their other match?

a) A draw (1-1) against Yugoslavia

b) A draw (2-2) against Switzerland

c) A draw (1-2) against Argentina

d) A draw (3-3) against Mexico

64. How many teams participated in the 1954 World Cup, Which was held in Switzerland?

a) 20 *b) 16* *c) 24* *d) 30*

65. Which player scored the most goals during the tournament in 1954?

a) Josef Hugi, Switzerland *b) Nat Lofthouse, England*

c) Sandor Kocsis, Hungary *d) Carlos Borges, Uruguay*

66. In the 1958 World Cup in Sweden, which Brazilian players scored two goals each in the final?

a) Vava and Zagalo *b) Pele and Garrincha*

c) Pele and Zagalo *d) Vava and pele*

67. Which player finished the 1958 World Cup tournament as the top goal scorer and with a World Cup scoring record of 13 goals in one tournament?

a) Just Fontaine, France

b) Gird Muller, West Germany

c) Pele, Brazil

d) Roymond Kopa, France

68. In the 1962 World Cup held in Chile, who were the only British representatives at the finals?

a) England *b) Wales*

c) Northern Ireland *d) Scotland*

69. How many representatives from South America were present in Chile for the World Cup in 1962?

a) Four *b) Six*

c) Three *d) Five*

70. In the World Cup held in England, who were in England's first round group?

a) North Korea, Italy and China

b) Argentina, Spain and Switzerland

c) Uruguay, Mexico and France

d) Hungary, Brazil and Bulgaria

71. Who was the manager of the England team in 1966?

a) Walter Winterbottom

b) Ron Greenwood

c) Don Rare

d) Alf Ramsey

72. Which Brazilian star of the 1970 World Cup held in Mexico City became a player agent, and was credited with discovering superstar Ronaldo?

a) Carlos Alberto *b) Tostao*

c) Jairzinho *d) Gerson*

73. Which stadium in Mexico saw the highest number of goals being scored per match in the 1970 World Cup?

a) Guanajuato Stadium *b) Luis Dorsal Stadium*

c) Jelisco Stadium *d) Azteca Stadium*

74. In the 1974 World Cup held in West Germany, which African nation in Group B played against Brazil Scotland and Yugoslavia?

a) Zaire *b) Tunisia*

c) South Africa *d) Nigeria*

75. What was the name of the referee in the final match of the 1974 World Cup?

a) Van Gamert *b) Taylor*

c) Holzenbein *d) Di Pinto*

76. In the 1978 World Cup held in Argentina how many games were played during the tournament?

a) 38 *b) 36* *c) 34* *d) 40*

77. **Which Dutch player almost scored in the 90th minute of final against Argentina in the 1978 World Cup, when it was still 1-1?**

a) Willy Van der Kerkhof *b) Jan Poortuliet*
c) Dick Nanninga *d) Rob Rensenbrink*

78. **Which player finished the 1982 World Cup Tournament with six goals and won the Golden Boot as top scorning player?**

a) Zbigniew Boniek *b) Zico*
c) Paolo Rossi *d) Karl-Heinz Rummaging*

79. **Which player scored after just 27 seconds against France in the 1982 World Cup?**

a) Trevor Brooking *b) Paul Mariner*
c) Bryan Robson *d) Glenn Hoddle*

80. **Which African nation got through to the second round in the World Cup in 1986?**

a) Nigeria *b) South Africa*
c) Egypt *d) Morocco*

81. **What was thrown onto the pitch on June 1, 1986, during the match between France and Canada?**

a) Beaver *b) Toilet paper*
c) Beer Bottle *d) Rooster*

82. **In the 1990 World Cup held in Italy which England player had a goal from a free kick disallowed against Holland in the group stages?**

a) Stuart Pearce *b) Chris Waddle*
c) John Barnes *d) Paul Gascoigne*

83. **Who scored for Sire in the opening match against England in the 1990 World Cup?**

a) Kevin Sheedy *b) Ray Houghton*
c) Tony Cascarino *d) David O'Leary*

84. **How many European teams made its to the last 16 in the 1994 World Cup held in USA?**

a) 8 *b) 10* *c) 9* *d) 11*

85. **How many games in USA 1994 were settled by a penalty shoot out?**

a) *One* b) *Three*

c) *Two* d) *Four*

86. **For the 1998 World Cup, who qualified by winning Group 2?**

a) *Tunisia* b) *Liberia*

c) *Egypt* d) *Namibia*

87. **Who scored the first goal of the 1998 World Cup?**

a) *Cesar Simpatico* b) *Own Goal*

c) *Bebeto* d) *John Collins*

88. **Which famous footballer is nicknamed as "The Phenomenon."**

a) *Ronaldo* b) *Maradona*

c) *Pele* d) *Zidane*

89. **Against what team was Thierry Henry sent off in the first round in the 2006 tournament?**

a) *Denmark* b) *Uruguay*

c) *Senegal* d) *Argentina*

90. **In the 2006 World Cup Serbia and Montenegro hit the headlines for all the wrong reasons when they lost 0-6 to Argentina. They subsequently ended up by conceding more goals than any other team at the tournament. One team acceded 9 goals in total. Which team was it?**

a) *Saudi Arabia* b) *Japan*

c) *Ukraine* d) *Costa Rica*

91. **Which city stadium in Germany caries the name of German football legend, Fritz Walter?**

a) *Munich* b) *Berlin*

c) *Kaiserslautern* d) *Leverkusen*

92. **Which team earned the Most Entertaining Team Award at the 2006 World Cup Tournament?**

a) *France* b) *Germany*

c) *Portugal* d) *Italy*

93. Who was given the title of Athlete of the Century by the International Olympic Committee ?

a) Pele *b) Maradona* *c) Batistuta* *d) Matthäus*

94. Which player at the 2006 World Cup declined an award and was one of three players to have already been honoured twice with a top FIFA World Cup award?

a) Ronaldo *b) Zinedine Zadine*
c) Oliver Kahn *d) Miroslav Klose*

95. Which goalkeeper earned the Yashin Award for his outstanding performance in goal throughout the final competition of the 2006 World Cup?

a) Jens Lehman *b) Pascal Zuberbuehler*
c) Oliver Kahn *d) Gianluigi Buffon*

96. Ronaldo of Brazil became the leading scorer in World Cup history in the match against Ghana in the 2006 World Cup. How many goals did he have?

a) 15 *b) 13* *c) 14* *d) 16*

97. Which World Cup great was sent off in the 1982 finals?

a) Karl Heinz-Rummaging *b) Diego Maradona*
c) Kevin Keegan *d) Horst Hrubesch*

98. Which English player retired after the 1990 World Cup tournament, after becoming the most capped player for his nation?

a) Peter Beardsley *b) Terry Butcher*
c) Peter Shilton *d) Gary Linekarss*

99. During the 1998 World Cup tournament who scored the first golden goal in World Cup history?

a) Laurent Blanc *b) Thierry Henry*
c) Dennis Bergkamp *d) Michael Owen*

100. Which three countries made their debuts in 1994 World Cup?

a) Saudi Arabia, Greece and Nigeria
b) Belgium, Hungary and Switzerland
c) Uruguay, Sweden and Yugoslavia
d) South Korea, China and Japan

9

Hockey

1. Which of the following countries won the 1999 Champions Trophy Hockey Tournament?

a) South Korea *b) The Netherlands*
c) Australia *d) Germany*

2. What is the name of the cup awarded to Netherlands, the winning team of the Champion Hockey Trophy held at China in December 1996?

a) Huber Cup *b) Rangaswamy Cup*
c) Santosh Trophy *d) C. K. Nayudu Trophy*

3. Who amongst the following teams won the Asia Cup Hockey tournament held in November 1999?

a) Holland *b) Pakistan*
c) South Korea *d) India*

4. Which Olympic hockey tournament was played a couple of months before the rest of the Olympics?

a) 1936 Berlin *b) 1980 Moscow*
c) 1928 Amsterdam *d) 1976 Montreal*

5. Who was the captain of the Indian team in the 1975 World Cup?

a) Lakshman Singh *b) Ajit Pal Singh*
c) Michael Kindo *d) Peter Ekka*

6. Where was the first Asia Cup in hockey held?

a) 1980 Mumbai *b) 1982 Karachi*
c) 1984 Bangkok *d) 1986 Kuala Lumpur*

7. **Who was the first Indian to be conferred the Helm's Award?**

   a) Dhyan Chand *b) Bagicha Singh*
   c) K. D. Singh Babu *d) R. Rawat*

8. **When was the bully for starting and restarting the game abolished?**

   a) 1985 *b) 1987* *c) 1981* *d) 1983*

9. **Who was India's first hockey captain?**

   a) Pankaj Gupta *b) Sanjay Tulsiani*
   c) Rahul Bara *d) Deepak Ahuja*

10. **Between which two nations was the first recorded international match held?**

    a) New Zealand and West Germany
    b) India and Pakistan
    c) Ireland and New Zealand
    d) England and Ireland

11. **In which year was hockey introduced in the Olympics?**

    a) 1928 *b) 1916*
    c) 1908 *d) 1930*

12. **India had two captains for a team. What was the event?**

    a) 1980 Moscow Olympics
    b) 1976 Montreal Olympics
    c) 1988 Mexico Olympics
    d) 1972 Munich Olympics

13. **From how many yards is a penalty stroke taken?**

    a) 5 Yards *b) 7 Yards*
    c) 9 Yards *d) 10 Yards*

14. **Who was the only Indian player to figure in the World Eleven side during the 1994 World Cup at Sydney?**

    a) Dhyan Chand *b) Dhanraj Pillai*
    c) Roop Singh *d) Sandeep Singh*

15. In which year was Dhanraj Pillai awarded the prestigious Rajiv Gandhi Khel Ratna Award?

a) 1989　*b) 1995*　*c) 1999*　*d) 2002*

16. Which Indian hockey player was termed Hockey Wizard due to his quicksilver ability on the field as a centre-forward and captain of the Indian hockey team?

a) Dhyan Chand　*b) Amarjeet Singh Rana*
c) Prithipal Singh　*d) Surinder Singh Sodhi*

17. Who offered to buy Dhyan Chand's hockey stick which was once taken apart. Olympic officials in Holland to see if there was a magnet inside?

a) The Olympic Referee　*b) Vienna Sports Club*
c) Adolf Hitler　*d) London Museum*

18. Which sports club has a statue of Dhyan Chand depicting him with four arms holding four hockey sticks?

a) London Sports Club　*b) Punjab Sports Club*
c) Vienna Sports Club　*d) India Sports Club*

19. In the 1936 Berlin Games Dhyan Chand was the captain and led India to victory in the final. Which country did India beat to win the award?

a) Germany　*b) Holland*
c) Australia　*d) England*

20. Out of the 338 goals scored by the Indians in 37 matches in 1932 how many did Dhyan Chand contribute?

a) 105　*b) 92*　*c) 133*　*d) 121*

21. In which year did India issue a stamp in honour of Dhyan Chand?

a) 1968　*b) 1972*　*c) 1976*　*d) 1980*

22. In the 1928 Olympic Games, who did India beat in the final match to win the gold?

a) Germany　*b) England*
c) Holland　*d) Spain*

23. **Who was the Indian goalkeeper, who did not concede a single goal in the 1928 Olympics?**

a) Roop Singh *b) Balbir Singh*
c) Richard James Allen *d) Kedar Singh*

24. **India holds the world record for the biggest victory margin in a hockey match, In 1932 at Los Angeles, Whom did they beat 24-1?**

a) Holland *b) Canada*
c) USA *d) Germany*

25. **At the Berlin Olympics in 1936 he could not play the final against Germany as he was hurt in the foot. At half point India led by only 1-0. This worried player removed his shoes, entered the field and took India to a stunning victory scoring six goal. Who was he?**

a) Gurmeet Singh *b) Gurcharan Singh*
c) Dhyan Chand *d) Balbir Singh*

26. **In which year were the first women's World Cup held?**

a) 1974 *b) 1978* *c) 1980* *d) 1982*

27. **When was the astroturf first used in the Olympics?**

a) 1972 Munich *b) 1976 Montreal*
c) 1980 Moscow *d) 1984 Los Angeles*

28. **Who is Australia's most capped player?**

a) Rechelle Hawkers *b) Juliet Haslam*
c) Sharon Buchan *d) Renita Garard*

29. **Where was the first Indian hockey club in India formed?**

a) Calcutta *b) Bombay*
c) Madras *d) Delhi*

30. **Adolf Hitler was so impressed by Dhyan Chand's performance that he offered to elevate him to Lance Naik Dhyan to which rank if he migrated to Germany?**

a) Second Lieutenant *b) Lieutenant*
c) Major *d) Colonel*

31. Whom did Australia play in the gold medal match at the Sydney 2000 Olympics?

a) England *b) Argentina*
c) India *d) Canada*

32. Women's Hockey World Cup since ——

a) 1974 b) 1972
c) 1984 d) 1971

33. In the 27th Sahara Champions Trophy in 2000 held in Chennai, what was India's position in ranking?

a) Second *b) Third*
c) Fourth *d) Last*

34. What product is painted by Dhanraj Pillai on his hockey stick?

a) Tyre *b) Liquor*
c) Mineral Water *d) Cell phone*

35. Whom did India beat in the finals of the nine nation prime Minister's Gold Cup international in Dhaka?

a) Pakistan *b) Egypt*
c) Japan *d) Bangladesh*

36. In the Asia Champions for juniors in 2001, whom did India beat to win the cup at Ipoh?

a) Japan *b) Uzbekistan*
c) China *d) Pakistan*

37. By how many goals did the Indian Juniors beat Argentina at Hobart, Australia in October 2001 to win the World Cup?

a) 6-1 *b) 5-3* *c) 3-2* *d) 2-1*

38. In the Champion Challenge Cup held in Kuala Lumpur in 2001, whom did India beat to lift the trophy?

a) Argentina *b) Australia*
c) South Africa *d) Singapore*

39. In a thrilling league match of the Champions Trophy hockey tournament in Cologne in 2002, whom did India beat 3-2?

a) Germany *b) Spain*
c) Pakistan *d) Japan*

40. In the Singapore International Hockey Challenge tournament in 2006, which junior team defeated Malaysia 6-0 in its opening match?

a) Japan *b) China*
c) India *d) Pakistan*

41. Who scored a hat-trick to help India notch a convincing win over Singapore in the four-nation International Hockey Challenge at Singapore on August 3, 2006?

a) Ajit Singh *b) Prabhjot Singh*
c) Vikramjit Singh *d) Dilip J.*

42. S. P. Dass Bable, joint secretary of Indian Hockey federation, has been appointed manager of the Indian hockey team for the World Cup in September 2006. Where was the tournament held?

a) England *b) Germany*
c) Spain *d) Lance*

43. Who orchestrated a blitzkrieg that annihilated Olympic champions and holders 6-2 in the final of the 15th Sultan Azlam Shah Hockey tournament in Kuala Lumpur in June 2006?

a) India *b) New Zealand*
c) Netherlands *d) Germany*

44. In the Challenge Open men's U-21 tourney, by how many goals did India beat Poland in the final in June 2006?

a) 3-0 *b) 3-2* *c) 2-1* *d) 3-1*

45. In their opening match of the under-21 Invitation Hockey Tournament at Griezno Poland in May 2006, by how many goals did India drub Pakistan?

a) 3-1 *b) 3-2* *c) 4-2* *d) 4-0*

46. When was Dhanraj Pillai conferred with the coveted Padma Shri?

a) 1998 *b)* 1999 *c)* 2000 *d)* 2001

47. Where is Shivaji Hockey Stadium located?

a) Amritsar *b)* Kolkata
c) Varanasi *d)* New Delhi

48. Name the object used in ice-hockey instead of a ball.

a) Block *b)* Disc
c) Puck *d)* Chip

49. Who now sponsors the Indian hockey team?

a) MRF Tyres *b)* Pepsi
c) Sahara India *d)* Videocon

50. In which country was modern hockey created?

a) Ireland *b)* England
c) Finland *d)* Netherlands

51. Who has won the most World Cup titles?

a) Germany *b)* Brazil
c) Italy *d)* India

52. In which year was the Hockey Association formed?

a) 1864 *b)* 1875 *c)* 1899 *d)* 1902

53. Who introduced Hockey to the U.S.A. in 1901?

a) Senator Bill Wainwright
b) Constance Applebee
c) James Naylor Junior
d) Florence Gummage

54. Hockey World Cup was first conceived by Pakistan's Air Marshal Nur Khan and India's ————.

a) Dhyan Chand
b) Lakshman Singh
c) Jimmy Nagarwalla
d) Abdul Hafeez Kardar

55. Who won the first men's hockey world cup, which was held in 1971?

a) India *b) Pakistan*

c) Germany *d) Australia*

56. Which country was the first to win two world titles?

a) Italy *b) England*

c) Uruguay *d) Germany*

57. In which decade did players start to tape their sticks for extra grip?

a) 1900's *b) 1910's* *c) 1920's* *d) 1930's*

58. What is Hockey's most coveted international prize called?

a) The Golden Sticks *b) The Wedgwood Bowl*

c) The World Cup *d) The Stainington Trophy*

59. Who is the only player to score a golden goal in World Cup play?

a) France's Laurent Blanc *b) Germany's Karl*

c) Austria's Reeve Dermot *d) Italy's Giovani*

60. Who was the first black man to play hockey?

a) Booker T. *b) Willy O Ree*

c) Smart *d) Jim Abit*

61. Which of the following is a Manipuri version of Hockey?

a) Khong Kangjei *b) Hiyang Tanaba*

c) Yubi Lakpi *d) Yubi-Lakpi*

62. In which country was the first World Cup played?

a) Brazil *b) Italy*

c) Uruguay *d) France*

63. Who is generally accredited with inventing the 'bent stick'?

a) Robby Dull *b) Bobby Hull*

c) Nobby Gull *d) Dobby Full*

64. When was the first U.S. national team selected at the National Tournament in Philadelphia?

a) 1922 *b) 1936* *c) 1948* *d) 1962*

65. Which team scored three unanswered second-half goals to stun Argentina in the first World Cup final, in 1930?

a) Uruguay *b) Germany*
c) Brazil *d) India*

66. Which material are most hockey sticks made of nowadays?

a) Wood *b) Plastic*
c) Latex Composite *d) Aluminium*

67. In 1927 who met Westchester Biltmore in the first recorded game of men's field hockey in the United States?

a) The Bostonian Gentlemen
b) New York Sticks
c) Centennial Allbackers
d) Germantown Cricket Club

68. Which nation has played the most World Cup games without earning a win or a draw?

a) El Salvador *b) South Korea*
c) Haiti *d) New Zealand*

69. When was hockey first played as an Olympic Sport?

a) 1908 *b) 1912* *c) 1920* *d) 1924*

70. Which medal did the USA Women's hockey team win at the 1994 World Cup in Dublin, Ireland?

a) Gold *b) Silver*
c) Bronze *d) They didn't*

71. In which city was hockey included in the Olympics as a female sport for the first time?

a) Los Angeles *b) Seoul*
c) Melbourne *d) Moscow*

72. **In which South American country were the 1962 World Cup finals held:**

a) Brazil *b) Chile*

c) Argentina *d) Uruguay*

73. **What do the initials U.S.F.H.A. stand for?**

a) United States Foremost Health Association

b) United States Field Hockey Accreditation

c) United States Field Hockey Association

d) United States Female Hockey Association

74. **In each of the past six World Cups, the winner of the tournament's Golden Boot has scored what number of goals?**

a) Six *b) Two*

c) Seven *d) Five*

75. **Which nation has been eliminated from the World Cup on penalty kicks on three different occasions?**

a) Mexico *b) Italy*

c) England *d) Romania*

10

Miscellaneous

1. **From where does the gymnast Mary Lou Retton hail?**

   a) Russia *b) Britain*
   c) USA *d) France*

2. **With which sport is Michael Dohan associated?**

   a) Golf *b) Football*
   c) Rugby *d) Motorbike racing*

3. **How many innings are there in a game of baseball?**

   a) 10 *b) 9* *c) 8* *d) 7*

4. **In what year was the first three point made in NBA?**

   a) 1982 *b) 1980* *c) 1979* *d) 1981*

5. **In which country was lacrosse invented?**

   a) USA *b) Greece*
   c) England *d) Ireland*

6. **The game of softball had a different name when it was invented by George Hancock. What was it called at first?**

   a) Girlball *b) Streetball*
   c) Slickball *d) Indoor*

7. **There are four infielders in the game of baseball. First baseman, Second baseman, Third baseman and—**

   a) Pitcher *b) Catcher*
   c) Shortstop *d) Umpire*

8. **Peter Maple and Ahmad Barada played which of the following tournaments held in 1999 in which Ahmad was defeated?**

   a) World Open Jennies *b) World Open Badminton*
   c) World Open Squash *d) World Open Table Tennis*

9. **In 1987 who was the first goalie in the NHL to have scored a goal?**

   a) Mark Jamison *b) Bobby Franklin*
   c) Ron Hextall *d) Tyler Francis*

10. **What did DR. George F. Grant invent?**

    a) Golf Tee *b) Football Helmet*
    c) Batting Glove *d) Jock strap*

11. **Who was the first person to run a mile in under four minutes?**

    a) Roger Bannister *b) Howard Lee*
    c) Ray Lentz *d) Jermain Stevenson*

12. **Which athlete was portrayed by Ian Charleston in the film *Chariots of Fire*?**

    a) Roger Bannister *b) Eric Liddell*
    c) Allan Wells *d) Ben Johnson*

13. **Who was the first West Indies cricketer to play 100 test matches?**

    a) Michael Holding *b) Clive Lloyd*
    c) Gary Sobers *d) Viv Richards*

14. **Which swimmer was the first to swim 100 yards in less then a minute?**

    a) Johnny Weismuller *b) Mark Spitz*
    c) Buster Crab *d) Michael Gorse*

15. **What is the place where pitchers warm up before a game of baseball starts?**

    a) Ring *b) Diamond*
    c) Bullpen *d) Pitch*

16. In 1970 who became the first African nation to play in the finals of the Football World Cup?

a) Egypt *b) Morocco*
c) Tunisia *d) Nigeria*

17. By what nickname is the American rugby team commonly known?

a) The Bears *b) The Cougars*
c) The Eagles *d) The Buffaloes*

18. Over which bridge do competitors run in the London Marathon?

a) Tower *b) Putney*
c) London *d) Victoria*

19. The Salgaocar Club Football team won the Durand Cup final match in December 1999. Whom did they beat?

a) Mohammedan Sporting *b) Mohan Bagan*
c) Air India *d) Services*

20. Who succeeded Alex Ferguson as manager of the Scotland Football team in 1986?

a) Andy Rexburg *b) Craig Brown*
c) Kenny Dalglsh *d) John Stein*

21. In which year did Boris Becker win Wimbledon for the first time?

a) 1984 *b) 1983* *c) 1986* *d) 1985*

22. Who was the runner up in the Formula 1 World Championship in 1997?

a) Heinz Herald Frentzen *b) Michael Schumaker*
c) Damon Hill *d) Eddie Irvine*

23. What sports did James Gibbs introduce in 1890?

a) Badminton *b) Table Tennis*
c) Snooker *d) Field Hockey*

24. Who was Cliff Thorburn plaiting when in 1983 he became the first man to score a 147 break at the Embassy World Snooker Championship?

a) Steve Davis *b) Dennis Taylor*

c) Kirk Stevens *d) Terry Griffiths*

25. With what sports is Bhagyashree Thipstay associated?

a) Archery *b) Chess*

c) Table Tennis *d) Weight-lifting*

26. What is the exact distance of a marathon?

a) 26 miles 585 yards *b) 26 miles 285 yards*

c) 26 miles 485 yards *d) 26 miles 385 yards*

27. How many gold medals did Mark Spitz win at the 1972 Olympics in Munich?

a) 6 *b) 7* *c) 8* *d) 5*

28. Which of the following professional golfers was the first to beat Tiger Wood on the final detour of tournament competition on the PGA tour?

a) Duffy Waldorf *b) Ed Fiji*

c) Brace Lietzke *d) Bob May*

29. Which of the following was once a top sport until abolished in 1922?

a) Marbles *b) Tug of war*

c) Checkers *d) Lacrosse*

30. Who finished second to be affirmed in every triple crown race of horse racing in 1978?

a) Alydar *b) Count Fleet*

c) Elroy *d) Darbee Creek Road*

31. Who was the Olympic gold medallist in the 1996 Atlanta Games in the sport of wrestling?

a) Rubin Gardner *b) Olindo Mare*

c) Olin Green *d) Kurt Angle*

32. **In which year did Jack Nicklaus win his fourth Masters championship?**

a) 1972 *b) 1974* *c) 1976* *d) 1978 s*

33. **What was the name of at the mascot for the 1996 Summer Olympics in Atlanta?**

a) Izzy *b) Cobi*

c) Hodori *d) Misha*

34. **One of hockey's greatest, Wayne Gretzky began his NHL career with which team?**

a) Chicago Blackhawks *b) New York Rangers*

c) Los Angeles Kings *d) Edmonton Oilers*

35. **Where in India was the National Triathlon Championship held?**

a) Mumbai *b) Chennai*

c) Visakhapatnam *d) Vadodara*

36. **What was heavyweight boxing champion Sonny Liston's real first name?**

a) Jackson *b) Charles*

c) Mordecai *d) Robert*

37. **One of the greatest football players in history was David Beckham. What is his born name?**

a) Davidio Antonio Beckham *b) David James Dinner*

c) Robert James Cornelius

d) David Robert Joseph Beckham

38. **Which of the following states led the medal tally in the fifth National Games held in 1999 at Imphal?**

a) Punjab *b) Maharashtra*

c) Kerala *d) Karnataka*

39. **Who won the Under 19 World Cup Cricket tournament in 2000?**

a) West Indies *b) Sri Lanka*

c) India *d) South Africa*

40. Which player won the 26th Junior National Chess Championship held in Thresher?

a) J. V. Ramana *b) K. Sasikiran*
c) Abhijit Kunte *d) Mansher Singh*

41. "Little Sam" is a term associated with which game?

a) Bridge *b) Billiards*
c) Badminton *d) Squash*

42. Of which country is bullfighting a popular sport?

a) Spain *b) UK*
c) Germany *d) Romania*

43. Who among the following has played a test cricket for India?

a) Vijay Mallya *b) Vijay Tendulkar*
c) Vijay Merchant *d) Vijay Amritraj*

44. Name the oldest football club in India.

a) Mohammad Sporting *b) Mohan Bagan*
c) East Bengal *d) Calcutta Football Club*

45. Which individual game was developed in Jabalpur by Col. Neville Chamberlain in 1875?

a) Snooker *b) Billiards*
c) Badminton *d) Scrabble*

46. P. K. Banerjee, Chunni Goswami and Jarnail Singh are associated with which sport?

a) Hockey *b) Football*
c) Cricket *d) Tennis*

47. Which Indian batsman hit six fours in a single over of Bob Willis in the 1982 Manchester Cricket?

a) Kapil Dev *b) Sandeep Patil*
c) Ravi Shastri *d) Sunil Gavaskar*

48. Which of these Grand Slams is played in the beginning of the year?

a) French Open *b) Wimbledon*
c) Australian Open *d) US Open*

49. Which tennis player was stabbed in count at Hamburg in 1993?

a) *Steffi Graf* b) *Martina Navratilova*
c) *Martina Hinges* d) *Monica Seles*

50. In one-day cricket, how many fielders can stay outside the 15 yard circle for the first 15 over?

a) *Three* b) *Four*
c) *Five* d) *Two*

51. Which of these Indian batsmen scored 2000 runs in Test cricket without scoring a century?

a) *Kapil Dev* b) *Chetan Chauhan*
c) *Ravi Shastri* d) *Mohinder Amarnath*

52. Who was the first Indian to reach the All England Badminton Championship's final?

a) *Prakash Padukone* b) *Vijay Madgavkar*
c) *Prakash Nath* d) *Gopichand*

53. Which West Indies cricketer was nicknamed the Super Cat?

a) *Vivian Richards* b) *Clive Lloyd*
c) *Malcolm Marshall* d) *Michael Holding*

54. Which of these is a convention in the game of cataract Bridge?

a) *Pisala* b) *Gerber*
c) *Angor* d) *Auction*

55. In the game of chess normally how many squares can the king move at a time?

a) *One* b) *Two and a half*
c) *Two* d) *Three*

56. Who is the first woman chess Grandmaster of India?

a) *Anupama Abeyance* b) *Subhaswami Vijayalakshmi*
c) *Rohini Kardeker* d) *Vishwanath Anand*

57. Which Austrian cricketer is associated with Udayan, a children's home in India?

a) *Steve Waugh* b) *Shane Warne*
c) *Allan Border* d) *Adam Gilchrist*

58. If you were a beginner in judo, what colour belt would you wear?

a) White *b) Red*

c) Green *d) Black*

59. Where were the first Winter Olympics held in 1924?

a) USA *b) Russia*

c) France *d) Australia*

60. Of which country is Water Buffalo Race a popular sport?

a) Korea *b) Thailand*

c) Malaysia *d) Indonesia*

61. Where did the game of bridge originate?

a) England *b) Russia*

c) America *d) Germany*

62. Who was the heavy-weight boxing champion in 1996-97?

a) Mike Tyson *b) Bruce Sheldon*

c) Games Douglas *d) Mohammedan Ali*

63. A checked flag of which two colours is waved to indicate the end of a motorcar race?

a) Black and white *b) Black and red*

c) Black and blue *d) Black and white*

64. Who was the youngest Indian to captain the test cricket team?

a) Tendulkar *b) Pataudi*

c) Azharuddin *d) Kapil Dev*

65. Who is the youngest Indian to score a century in test cricket?

a) Mansur Ali Khan Pataudi *b) Sachin Tendulkar*

c) Mohammad Azharuddin *d) Abbas Ali Baig*

66. Which cricketer was nicknamed 'Guy the Gorilla'?

a) Vivian Richards *b) Ian Botham*

c) Wasim Akram *d) Mohammad Azharuddin*

67. For which event did Carl Lewis win four successive medals in Olympics?

a) 4x100m relay *b) Long jump*
c) 100m sprint *d) 800m*

68. Which 1932 Olympic great won two gold medals, one silver, and later became a historic professional golfer?

a) Wilma Rudolph *b) Babe Didricksen*
c) Jim Thorpe *d) Jesse Owens*

69. Who became the World Snooker Champion for 2005?

a) Mark Williams *b) Ronnie O'Sullivan*
c) Shaun Murphy *d) Stepher Hendry*

70. Which country won the Six Nations Rugby title in 2006?

a) Ireland *b) Scotland*
c) England *d) France*

71. Where were the 1994 Winter Olympic games held?

a) Calgary, Canada *b) Lillehammer, Norway*
c) Nagano Japan *d) Salt Lake City, USA*

72. Who set a 100 metres world record time of 9.77 seconds?

a) Marlon Devonish *b) Asafa Powell*
c) Patrick Johnson *d) Uchenna Emedolu*

73. With which sport would you associate Willie Shoemakers?

a) Motor racing *b) Athletics*
c) Bob-Alighting *d) Horse racing*

74. Which cyclist won the tour de France for five consecutive years in the 1990?

a) Greg Lemond *b) Laurent Fignon*
c) Jan Ulrich *d) Miguel Indurain*

75. Who won the 2005 US Open in Golf?

a) Tiger Woods *b) Darren Clarke*
c) Ernie Els *d) Michael Campbell*

76. Which of these tennis greats never won the Men's Singles title at Wimbledon?

a) Andre Agassi *b) Stefan Edbery*

c) Ivan Lendl *d) Goran Ivanesevic*

77. Which little known unseeded player defeated Kern Current to win the Wimbledon Tennis Championship in 1985 and went on to become of the greatest players in recent history?

a) Mats Wilander *b) Stefan Edberg*

c) Boris Becker *d) Pat Cash*

78. Anton Geesink defeated Akio Kaminaga to win the 1964 Olympic Judo gold Medal. Which country did he represent?

a) Denmark *b) USA*

c) Germany *d) The Netherlands*

79. Australia was defeated in the 1996 Cricket world Cup final by which little fancied nation?

a) Zimbabwe *b) Sir Lanka*

c) Bangladesh *d) New Zealand*

80. West Germany was defeated in the preliminary rounds of the 1974 Football World Cup in one of the most famous matches in World Cup history. Who was their opponent?

a) Australia *b) Cameroon*

c) Portugal *d) East Germany*

81. In the 1980 Moscow Olympic Games, the heavily by favoured Soviet Union did not win the Gold Medal in Basketball. Which team won?

a) Germany *b) France*

c) Japan *d) Yugoslavia*

82. In the Grand Prix the 1966 World Drivers Championship was won by a man who designed and built his own Car. Who was he?

a) Juan Manuel Fangio *b) Jack Brabham*

c) Nike Landa *d) Bruce McLaren*

83. Luisito Monte played for Argentina in the 1930 World Cup Football. In 1934, he played for another country. Which one?

a) Mexico *b) France*
c) Columbia *d) Italy*

84. Which of these British royals was playing squash with his private secretary when his first child was born?

a) Prince Andrew, The Duke of York
b) Prince Charles, The Prince of Wales
c) Prince Philip, The Duke of Edinburgh
d) King Edward VIII

85. By what altogether different name was Long Jump known in the first modern Olympics and for some time later?

a) Parallel Jump *b) Last Jump*
c) Double Jump *d) Running Broad Jump*

86. Juctu Golf Club Course, the highest golf course in the world, is located in which country?

a) Mexico *b) Scotland*
c) Peru *d) Japan*

87. Whom did the English cricketers refer to as 'Rent a Wagon'?

a) Imran Khan *b) Ian Healy*
c) Andy Roberts *d) S. Venkatraghavan*

88. Who was the only British boxer to go the distance with Muhammad Ali in a World Title Bout?

a) Joe Bugner *b) Richard Dunn*
c) Henry Cooper *d) Frank Bruno*

89. During which years were English football teams banned from European Competition?

a) 1986-1991 *b) 1983-1991*
c) 1984-1991 *d) 1985-1991*

90. What is the first event in the Heptathlon?

a) Javelin *b) 100m hurdles*
c) 800m *d) Long Jump*

91. In which sport would you encounter a bedpost, a six pack, a blow and a deuce?

a) American Football *b) Ten pin bowling*
c) Lacrosse *d) Ice hockey*

92. Which British city hosted both the 1970 and the 1986 Commonwealth Games?

a) Manchester *b) Birmingham*
c) Glasgow *d) Edinburgh*

93. Which Tennis Grand Slam is played on clay courts?

a) French Open *b) US Open*
c) Australian Open *d) Wimbledon*

94. Who won the Formula 1 Motor Racing World Championship in 2005?

a) Fernando Alonso *b) Juan Pablo Montoya*
c) Michael Schumacher *d) Kiwis Reckoned*

95. What sport did Konrad Koch introduce in Germany in the late 1890's?

a) Curling *b) Squash*
c) Handball *d) Basketball*

96. Who was the first man to win two golds in the marathon in consecutive Olympics?

a) Frank Shorter *b) Wami Biratu*
c) Abebe Bikala *d) Kip Keno*

97. From which 2000 Olympics event did Gene Senile get disqualified?

a) Race Walking *b) Judo*
c) Swimming *d) Gymnastics*

98. Which skater was known as the Swan of Odessa?

a) Tenley Allbright *b) Katrina Witt*
c) Oskana Baiul *d) Sonja Henie*

99. How many grams of gold are there in an Olympic gold medal?

a) Three *b) Six*

c) Twenty-One *d) Nine*

100. Who invented volleyball?

a) William G. Morgan *b) K. C. Elamma*

c) Jimmy George *d) Cyril C. Valoor*

101. Where was the first shooting range of club founded?

a) St Petersburg *b) Kentucky*

c) Berne *d) Frankfurt*

102. Who was the first modern marathon winner?

a) Emil Zatopek *b) Spyridon Louis*

c) Ron Clanked *d) Henry Rono*

103. Who among the following became the oldest world heavyweight boxing champion?

a) Sonny Liston *b) Casius Clay*

c) George Foreman *d) Joe Frazier*

104. Which game is the Indian equivalent of the game Ludo?

a) Chattering *b) Pachisi*

c) Moksha-Patamu *d) Spartan*

105. Australia set a new world record winning streak in March 2001. With 16 consecutive cricket victories, who ended this amazing sequence?

a) India *b) West Indies*

c) England *d) Sri Lanka*

106. In ice hockey, which player infamously broke the neck of his Colorado Avalanche opponent Steve Moore, in March of 2004?

a) Marty McSorley *b) Brad May*

c) Todd Bertuzzi *d) Markus Naslund*

107. Who became the first 17-year-old ever to score at a World Cup Football finals?

a) Pele *b) Maradona*

c) Baggio *d) Ronaldo*

108. Which two teams were eliminated in the first round of the 1990 World Cup Football?

a) USA and France *b) USA and Sweden*
c) France and Spain *d) Spain and Russia*

109. Which athlete reached the Men's 110m hurdles Olympic Final in four consecutive games between 1988 and 2000, and his only medal being a silver in 1988?

a) Tony Jarred *b) Roger Kingdom*
c) Colin Jackson *d) Allen Jackson*

110. Which country won the Olympic Football Gold Medal at the 2004 Athens Olympics?

a) Nigeria *b) Brazil*
c) Argentina *d) Cameroon*

111. Which boxing World Champion from the 1980's was nicknamed 'The Hitman'?

a) Robert Duran *b) Thomas Hearns*
c) Ray Leonard *d) Marvin Haggler*

112. Which player lost in the 1992, 1994 and 1998 Men's Finals, before finally winning the tennis title in 2001 with victory over Austria's Pat Rafter?

a) Goran Ivanisevic *b) Andre Agassi*
c) Roger Federer *d) Mark Phillippousses*

113. For which athletics event was Cuban Javier Solo Mayor Olympic champion in 1992 and silver medallist in 2000?

a) Long Jump *b) High Jump*
c) Triple Jump *d) Pole Vault*

114. Which event in the Olympic Games determined the best of all round athlete?

a) Marathon *b) Supertathlon*
c) Olympiathon *d) Pentathlon*

115. Who amongst the following set a record for most test match catches?

a) Mark Waugh *b) Vivian Richards*
c) Mark Taylor *d) Don Bradman*

116. Which Indian is known as the Flying Sikh?

a) Bishen Singh *b) Balvinder Singh*
c) Milkha Singh *d) Robin Singh*

117. With which game is Thomas Cup associated?

a) Rugby *b) Badminton*
c) Polo *d) Golf*

118. From which country did Diego Maradona hail?

a) Bolivia *b) Uruguay*
c) Venezuela *d) Argentina*

119. Which cricketer is known as the Sultan of Swing?

a) Richard Hadlee *b) Kapil Dev*
c) Dennis Lillee *d) Imran Khan*

120. Which cricketer scored a zero in his last test innings?

a) Donald Bradman *b) Sunil Gavaskar*
c) Allan Border *d) Vivian Richards*

121. Which country's basketball team was called the Dream Team?

a) Russia *b) Spain*
c) USA *d) Romania*

122. Whose athletic records did Carl Lewis emulate in 1984?

a) Jesse Owens *b) Daley Thompson*
c) Edwin Moses *d) S. Bubka*

123. From which nation does Ben Johnson, the athlete, banned for using steroids?

a) Jamaica *b) Canada*
c) USA *d) New Zealand*

124. Who is called the Golden Bear in the field of sports?

a) Mike Tampon *b) Jack Nicklaus*
c) Carl Lewis *d) Richard Barry*

125. Santosh Trophy is awarded for which sport?

a) Football *b) Cricket*
c) Chess *d) Hockey*

126. Who is the officially recommended lady umpire in India?

a) Anjali Sharma *b) Anne Rajagopal*

c) Mita Basu *d) Anjali Rajagopal*

127. What game did the British army in India invent on a rainy afternoon?

a) Rummy *b) Snooker*

c) Table Tennis *d) Caroms*

128. Who first jumped 8.9 metres in the Olympics?

a) Carl Lewis *b) Daley Thompson*

c) Bob Beamon *d) Sergi Bukka*

129. For which sport did Randhir Singh receive the Arjuna Award?

a) Hockey *b) Kabaddi*

c) Golf *d) Shooting*

130. Which Indian tennis player won a medal for India in Olympics?

a) Mahesh Bhupati *b) Vijay Amritraj*

c) Leander Paes *d) Ramesh Krishnan*

131. Which of the following countries won the final of the triangular cricket series held in durban in februarry 1997 ?

a) India *b) New zealand*

c) South Africa *d) Zimbabwe*

132. With which sport is the 'Choudhury Trophy' associated?

a) Golf

b) Circumnavigation of the earth by car

c) Formula One racing

d) Buggy-Jumping

133. Who was the first Indian to reach the semi final in Wimbledon Tennis Championship?

a) Ramanathan Krishnan *b) Ramesh Krishnan*

c) Laender Paes *d) Mahesh Bhupati*

134. Who was the first Indian to win an individual medal in Olympics?

a) Milkha Singh *b) P.T.Usha*

c) Karnam Malleshwari *d) K.D.Yadav*

135. Where did India play its 1st one day international match?

a) Lords *b) Headingley*

c) Taunton *d) The Oval*

136. What Major League Baseball player holds the record for all-time career high batting average?

a) Ty Cobb *b) Larry Walker*

c) Jeff Bagwell *d) Frank Thomas*

137. What is the name of the person that controls a football match?

a) A referee *b) An umpire*

c) A spectator *d) A goalkeeper*

138. Which player has scored the most runs in a single Test innings?

a) Graham Gooch *b) Matthew Hayden*

c) Brian Lara *d) Agarkar*

139. Undertaker wrestled Yokozuna at the 1994 "Royal Rumble". This was a Casket Match. Undertaker wrestled in another Casket Match at the 1998 "Royal Rumble". Who did he wrestle?

a) Yokozuna *b) Shawn Michaels*

c) Mabel *d) Triple H*

140. Who did The Rock wrestle in the main event at the 1999 edition of "Wrestlemania"?

a) Stone Cold Steve Austin *b) Triple H*

c) Mankind *d) Undertaker*

141. The nickname of Glenn McGrath is what?

a) Ooh Ahh *b) Penguin*

c) Big Bird *d) Pigeon*

142. Which county did Mohammad Azharuddin play for?

a) Yorkshire *b) Hampshire*
c) Lancashire *d) Derbyshire*

143. Which two counties did Anil Kumble play for?

a) Nottinghamshire & Lancashire
b) Nottinghamshire & Leicestershire
c) Northamptonshire & Leicestershire
d) Northamptonshire & Lancashire

144. What is the middle name of Bhajji (Harbhajan Singh)?

a) Plaba *b) Plaha*
c) Kholi *d) Asrani*

145. How many wickets did Zaheer Khan pick up in his ODI debut?

a) Zero *b) Three*
c) Five *d) Two*

146. Since the turn of the new millennium, five of the six Le Mans 24 hour endurance races were won by the same make of car. Name the manufacturer.

a) Porsche 930 SC *b) McLaren F1 GTR*
c) Audi R8 *d) Mazda 787B*

147. Which nation hosted and won the first ever Soccer World Cup?

a) Uruguay *b) West Germany*
c) Argentina *d) Brazil*

148. How many teams in the NFL have names of birds?

a) Six *b) Five*
c) Three *d) Two*

149. Which athlete was portrayed by Ian Charleston in the film Chariots of Fire?

a) Roger Bannister *b) Ben Johnson*
c) Allan Wells *d) Eric Liddell*

150. How many individual bets make up a Yankee?

a) 9 *b) 11* *c) 10* *d) 12*

151. Who won the Badminton Gold Medal at 1996 Atlant[a] Olympics?

a) Jiang Dang *b) Hendrawan*
c) Rashid Sidek *d) Paul-Erik Hoyer-Larsen*

152. How old was Roger Bannister (subsequently Dr Bannister) when he became the first man to run a mile in under 4 minutes?

a) 25 *b) 21* *c) 19* *d) 23*

153. He is the uncle of a famous sportsman. He was also a good footballer when he used to play. He used to play under Johan Cruyff at Barcelona. Name him.

a) Cervantes Gonzalez *b) Felipe Gonzalez Alonso*
c) Miguel Angel Nadal *d) Luis Meija Ferrero*

154. What sport was the first to be filmed?

a) Boxing *b) Tennis* *c) Baseball* *d) Football*

155. In what year's Olympics were electric timing devices and a public address system used for the first time?

a) 1956 *b) 1928* *c) 1912* *d) 1936*

156. Which one of these sports is estimated to be over 4,000 years old and requires the characteristics of both wrestling and rugby?

a) Yubi Lakpi *b) Kang Shanaba*
c) Kabaddi *d) Tchoukball*

157. Which sport that has Gaelic origins is also played on ice with granite stones?

a) Hacky-Sack *b) Curling*
c) Tchoukball *d) Hurling*

158. For which sport is the Eisenhower trophy awarded?

a) Rugby Union *b) Tennis*
c) Golf *d) Cricket*

159. Who defeated Jack Dempsey to win the World Heavyweight Boxing title in 1926?

a) Max Schmeling *b) Gene Tunney*
c) Jack Johnson *d) Jack Sharkey*

160. Which country won the Euro 1996 Soccer competition?

a) England *b) France*
c) Czech Republic *d) Germany*

161. In which year did Milkha Singh win the first National title in the 400 m race?

a) 1955 *b) 1956* *c) 1957* *d) 1970*

162. When was Amateur Athletics Federation of India established?

a) 1936 *b) 1946* *c) 1956* *d) 1966*

163. In which Indian state did the game of Polo originate?

a) Meghalaya *b) Rajasthan*
c) Manipur *d) West Bengal*

164. How many gold medals did P.T.Usha win in the 1986 Seoul Asian Games?

a) One *b) Two* *c) Three* *d) Four*

165. Where did the 1st ODI match was played in India?

a) New Delhi *b) Ahmedabad*
c) Kolkata *d) Mumbai*

166. The first hang gliders to be flown were flown in. _____.

a) 1600s *b) 1700s* *c) 1800s* *d) 1900s*

167. Which track and field star overcame childhood polio to become one of the greatest athletes of her time?

a) Wilma Rudolph *b) Gail Devers*
c) Florence Griffith Joyner *d) Jackie Robinson*

168. Stripped of his heavyweight title in 1967 for refusing induction into the U.S. military, Muhammad Ali regained the heavyweight championship on October 30, 1974, in Kinshasa, Zaire with an eighth-round knockout of which prizefighter?

a) George Foreman *b) Joe Frazier*
c) Leon Spinks *d) Sputnik*

169. In what year was the first international cricket match held?

a) 1892 between England and India

b) 1869 between England and Australia

c) 1883 between Australia and Wales

d) 1844 between Canada and the USA

170. How long are professional Golf Tour players allotted per shot?

a) 45 seconds *b) 25 seconds*

c) 1 minute *d) 2 minutes*

171. Which football hero was nicknamed "The Sundance Kid"?

a) Jim Kiick *b) Troy Aikman*

c) Brett Favre *d) Joe Montana*

172. 'Dizzy' is the nickname of what Australian player?

a) Adam Gilchrist *b) Jason Gillespie*

c) Glenn McGrath *d) Brett Lee*

173. Which county did Ravi Shastri play for?

a) Glamorgan *b) Leicestershire*

c) Gloucestershire *d) Lancashire*

174. What is the middle name of Sourav Ganguly?

a) Chandidas *b) Mohandas*

c) Chandradas *d) Tarwadi*

175. Ajit Agarkar's first match was against Australia on April 1, 1998 at Kochi. Which Australian batsman was dismissed by Agarkar in that match?

a) Ponting *b) Warne*

c) Martyn *d) Gilchrist*

176. All of these footballers played in the Premiership in 2005. Which of these are English?

a) Ugo Ehiogu *b) Brett Emerton*

c) Michael Essien *d) Robbie Keane*

177. Which is the most recent addition in the field of adventure sports?

a) *Orienteering* b) *Barefooting*
c) *Canopying* d) *Bungee Jumping*

178. Modern day Polo, a game with origins traced to the mythological age when the game was believed to have been played by gods, is derived from the Indian game of

a) *Kabaddi* b) *Sagol Kangjei*
c) *Yubi Lakpi* d) *Kang Shanaba*

179. Which one of the following games is also played as a competitive underwater sport?

a) *Soccer* b) *Rugby*
c) *Tchoukball* d) *Hockey*

180. Which horse won the 2005 Derby, which took place at Epsom in June?

a) *Walk in the Park* b) *Oratorio*
c) *Motivator* d) *The Geezer*

181. Rugby Union: Which nation won gold at the Olympic Games in 1924?

a) *New Zealand* b) *England*
c) *USA* d) *Australia*

182. Which sprinter set a new 100m world record at the 1996 Olympic Games?

a) *Maurice Greene* b) *Linford Christie*
c) *Donovan Bailey* d) *Michael Johnson*

183. Which is considered by many to be the fastest sport in the world?

a) *Canopying* b) *Korfball*
b) *Hurling* c) *Curling*

184. Which game combines the court strategy of tennis with the spiking strategy of volleyball?

a) *Hacky-Sack* b) *Netball*
b) *Hurling* d) *Kabaddi*

185. Lacrosse was invented in which country?

a) Ireland *b) England* *c) USA* *d) Greece*

186. Who was the first President of the International Olympic Committee?

a) Dimitrias Vikelas *b) Avery Brundage*
c) Sigfrid Egstrom *d) Lord Killanin*

187. Who won the tennis gold medal at the 1996 Atlanta Olympics?

a) Pete Sampras *b) Boris Becker*
c) Goran Ivanisevic *d) Andre Agassi*

188. Which venue hosted the Asian Games in 1954?

a) New Delhi *b) Manila*
c) Jakarta *d) Tokyo*

189. Which team won the Hero Cricket Cup in 1993?

a) Australia *b) West Indies*
c) Pakistan *d) India*

190. At which venue did Martina Navratilova, become the oldest player to win a title on the WTA circuit on May 26, 2002?

a) Paris *b) Madrid*
c) Hamburg *d) Rome*

191. How old was Boris Becker when he became the youngest ever winner of a singles title at Wimbledon?

a) 20 *b) 18* *c) 17* *d) 19*

192. Which of the following bowlers has conceded the most runs in a single ODI match?

a) Mick Lewis *b) Martin Snedden*
c) Muttiah Muralitharan *d) Roger Telemachus*

193. At the Barcelona Olympics in 1992, why were coconut shells imported from India?

a) To make key chains *b) To use for selling juice*
c) To use as caps *d) To serve ice cream in*

194. "With Time to Spare", was the autobiography of which elegant left-handed cricket batsman?

a) *Alan Border* b) *Clive Lloyd*
c) *Salim Durani* d) *David Gower*

195. Nadia Comenaci was the first person to score a perfect 10 in Olympic gymnastics competition. What was her nationality?

a) *Romanian* b) *Ukrainian*
c) *Hungarian* d) *Latvian*

196. Which English football club was called "Dial Square" when they were founded?

a) *Manchester United F.C.* b) *Chelsea F.C.*
c) *Arsenal F.C* d) *Leeds United F.C.*

197. What is the distance between bases on a little league baseball field?

a) *70 feet* b) *40 feet*
c) *60 feet* d) *50 feet*

198. What was the first sport in which women were invited to compete at the Olympics?

a) *Golf* b) *Track and field*
c) *Tennis* d) *Swimming*

199. What card game gave us the term bilk?

a) *Gin* b) *Bridge*
c) *Poker* d) *Cribbage*

200. How wide is the netted goal in ice hockey?

a) *4 feet* b) *6 feet*
c) *5 feet* d) *7 feet*

201. Under what name did Dr. Joshua Pim of Great Britain enter and win the Wimbledon tennis tournament in 1893?

a) *Dr. X* b) *Mr. X*
c) *John Doe* d) *Renee Richards*

202. **Which popular sport did Joe Sobek invent at the Greenwich, Connecticut YMCA in 1950?**

a) Badminton *b) Handball*
c) Racquetball *d) Squash*

203. **In blackjack, players try to get cards that add up to 21, and no higher. What is the count sought in baccarat?**

a) 9 *b) 11* *c) 7* *d) 13*

204. **Who was the first Olympic gold medalist to win a professional world boxing title?**

a) Cassius Clay *b) Floyd Patterson*
c) George Foreman *d) Joe Frazier*

205. **How many world records did swimmer Mark Spitz set when he won seven gold medals at the 1972 Olympics?**

a) Three *b) Seven*
c) Five *d) Six*

206. **What is the maximum weight permitted for calves in rodeo calf roping competition?**

a) 350 lbs *b) 250 lbs*
c) 200 lbs *d) 300 lbs*

207. **How long is the average pool cue?**

a) 60 inches *b) 57 inches*
c) 48 inches *d) 53 inches*

208. **How many of the four Grand Slam trophies in tennis are gold?**

a) One *b) Three* *c) Two* *d) Four*

209. **Which famous boxer received critical praise as an actor in, "The Adventures of Huckleberry Finn?**

a) Oscar de la Hoya *b) Archie Moore*
c) Rocky Marciano *d) Floyd Patterson*

210. **Which sport features acro, aerials, and moguls?**

a) Freestyle Skiing *b) Synchronised Swimming*
c) Freestyle Skating *d) Kabbadi*

211. In which country did Tae Kwon Do originate?

a) *China* b) *Cambodia*
c) *Thailand* d) *Korea*

212. With which sport was Francis Rogallo associated?

a) *Hang Gliding* b) *Parachuting*
c) *Archery* d) *Deep sea diving*

213. With which sport was the term 'criterium' associated?

a) *Cycling* b) *Wrestling*
c) *Swimming* d) *Weightlifting*

214. Who was the first amateur to have won the Grand Slam of tennis?

a) *Alice Marble* b) *Don Budge*
c) *Fred Perry* d) *Helen Jacobs*

215. Which boxer was also called 'The Brockton Blockbuster'?

a) *Jersey Joe Walcott* b) *Rocky Marciano*
c) *Barney Ross* d) *Joe Louis*

216. Where was the first English cycling race held?

a) *Middlesex* b) *Cumbria*
c) *Yorkshire* d) *Somerset*

217. What material was the golf ball originally made of?

a) *Feather* b) *Steel*
c) *Wood* d) *Rubber*

218. What term in Baseball, refers to what a pitcher can commit with a runner or runners on base?

a) *Caught* b) *Pitched*
c) *Putout* d) *Bowled*

219. In which year did Sandy Lyle win the U.S. Masters in golf?

a) *1987* b) *1988*
c) *1982* d) *1985*

220. In which country did badminton originate?

a) *Pakistan* b) *England*
c) *India* d) *USA*

221. Where were the 1968 Summer Olympic Games held?

a) Rome *b) Munich*
c) Mexico City *d) Tokyo*

222. Which of the following is a Manipuri version of Hockey?

a) Khong Kangjei *b) Hiyang Tanaba*
c) Yubi Lakpi *d) Yubi-Lakpi*

223. Who is the first Indian woman to win an Asian Games gold in 400m run?

a) M.L.Valsamma *b) P.T.Usha*
c) Kamaljit Sandhu *d) K.Malleshwari*

224. The Indian football team made its first appearance at Olympics in _____.

a) 1936 *b) 1948* *d) 1952* *d) 1956*

225. The first hand glider was designed by _____.

a) Leonardo DaVinci *b) The Wright brothers*
c) Francis Rogallo *d) Galileo*

226. Track and field star Carl Lewis won how many gold medals at the 1984 Olympic Games?

a) Two *b) Three* *c) Four* *d) Eight*

227. When was the first cricket Test match played?

a) 1873 *b) 1877* *c) 1870* *d) 1788*

228. Who is the leading wicket taker in the history of Test cricket?

a) Shane Warne *b) Brian Lara*
c) Courtney Walsh *d) Muttiah Muralitharan*

229. Wrestling; Whom did The Rock beat to win his first WWE Title?

a) Triple H *b) Stone Cold Steve Austin*
c) Mankind *d) Bret Hart*

230. Mark Waugh is commonly called what?

a) Afganistan *b) Junior*
c) Tugga *d) Julio*

231. **Pravin Amre and Vinod Kambli played for which province in South Africa?**

a) *Border* b) *Boland*
c) *Griqualand West* d) *Gauteng*

232. **Which cricketer died on the field in Bangladesh while playing for Abahani Club?**

a) *Subhash Gupte* b) *M.L.Jaisimha*
c) *Lala Amarnath* d) *Raman Lamba*

233. **What is the middle name of Rahul Dravid?**

a) *Naren* b) *Sharad*
c) *Srivatsav* d) *Shyam*

234. **Where did Yuvraj Singh make his ODI debut?**

a) *Nairobi, Kenya* b) *Mumbai, India*
c) *London, England* d) *Lahore, Pakistan*

235. **Rugby Union: The All Blacks of New Zealand offer their opponents a Haka before kick off. But what exactly is a "Haka"?**

a) *A tasty cake made by the All Blacks the night before a big game*
b) *A Maori chant involving stamping and gestures*
c) *A promise by the All Blacks to ease up if they get 40 points ahead*
d) *Each All Black player gives an opponent a Haka flower and shakes his hand*

236. **Who played soccer for the USA national team over 80 occasions and later played in the Premiership?**

a) *Brian McBride* b) *Russell Blaze*
c) *Tony Womack* d) *Anthony Mundine*

237. **Which batsman scored the most runs in Test cricket in the 1990's?**

a) *Sachin Tendulkar* b) *Alec Stewart*
c) *Brian Lara* d) *Steve Waugh*

238. **Which Jockey rode West Tip (1986) and Minnehoma (1994) to victory in the Grand National?**

a) Richard Dunwoody *b) Peter Scudamore*
c) Tony Dobbin *d) John Francombe*

239. **What was the score at the end of the final of the first-ever Football World Cup in Uruguay?**

a) Uruguay 2- Argentina-1
b) Uruguay 4- Argentina-2
c) Uruguay 1- Argentina-0
d) Uruguay 3- Argentina-2

240. **Which 2 players had the second-highest individual score in One Day International Cricket with 189?**

a) Vivian Richards and Sanath Jayasuriya
b) Gary Kirsten and Sachin Tendulkar
c) Sanath Jayasuriya and Gary Kirsten
d) Only Jayasuriya holds the record

241. **When Nigel Mansell won his first motor-racing World Drivers Championship, how old was he?**

a) 31 *b) 27* *c) 39* *d) 35*

242. **Which Indian emulated Bob Massie's feat of 16 wickets on test debut?**

a) Sunil Gavaskar *b) Roger Binny*
c) Madan Lal *d) Narendra Hirwani*

243. **Everyone remembers the 1994 San Marino Grand Prix for Ayrton Senna's death. However, there was another rider who also died during the qualifying rounds for the event. Who was he?**

a) Nicola Larini *b) Roland Ratzenberger*
c) Olivier Beretta *d) Pedro Lamy*

244. **Which famous Hungarian footballer of the 20th century was nicknamed, "The Galloping Major"?**

a) Marco van Basten *b) Franz Beckenbaur*
c) Johan Cruyff *d) Ferenc Puskas*

245. In the very first Boston Marathon, 15 runners competed. How many finished?

a) *10* b) *1* c) *0* d) *15*

246. Which footballer was credited with inventing 'total football'?

a) *Rinus Michels* b) *Pele*
c) *Franz Beckenbaur* d) *Johan Cruyff*

247. What does "Whist" refer to?

a) *A card game* b) *A badminton play*
c) *A chess move* d) *A quick movement*

248. Which is the oldest of the classic American horse races?

a) *Kentucky Derby* b) *Belmont Stakes*
c) *Preakness Stakes* d) *Hambletonian Stakes*

249. With which sport would you associate Willie Shoemaker?

a) *Motor Racing* b) *Athletics*
c) *Bobsleighing* d) *Horse Racing*

250. The 'Dronacharya Award' is given to _____.

a) *Sportsmen* b) *Coaches*
c) *Umpires* d) *Sports Editors*

251. India reached the final of the Davis Cup for the first time in _____.

a) *1964* b) *1966* c) *1970* d) *1974*

252. How many gold medals have been won by India in the Olympics so far?

a) *Four* b) *Six* c) *Eight* d) *Ten*

253. Who was the 1st president of BCCI (Board of Control for Cricket in India)?

a) *R.E. Grant Govan*
b) *Dr. Maharajkumar Sir Vijaya Ananda*
c) *Sikandar Hyat Khan*
d) *Anthony S. D'Mello*

254. Which NBA player scored 8 points in the final 7 seconds of a game to lead his team to victory?

a) Baron Davis | *b) Kevin Garnett*
c) Stephon Maurbury | *d) Reggie Miller*

255. Who has scored the most runs in a single First-class innings?

a) Hanif Mohammad | *b) Brian Lara*
c) Sir Donald Bradman | *d) Sachin Tendulkar*

256. Who did Stone Cold Steve Austin wrestle at the 1998 edition of "Over the Edge"?

a) Cactus Jack | *b) Mankind*
c) Dude Love | *d) Mick Foley*

257. What Australian player was known as 'Fruitfly' amongst the rest of the team?

a) Geoff Lawson | *b) Merv Hughes*
c) Mike Veletta | *d) Mike Whitney*

258. Which county did the outspoken spin great Bishen Singh Bedi play for?

a) Essex | *b) Surrey*
c) Northamptonshire | *d) Sussex*

259. Who had a torrid time with Lancashire in 2000?

a) Sachin Tendulkar | *b) Nayan Mongia*
c) Javagal Srinath | *d) Saurav Ganguly*

260. What is the middle name of the Ajit Agarkar, a top class all rounder?

a) Karan | *b) Bhalchandra*
c) Dalmiya | *d) Rohan*

261. Against which team did Virender Sehwag make his one day international debut?

a) New Zealand | *b) Sri Lanka*
c) Pakistan | *d) South Africa*

262. Who set a record for the biggest winning margin in Super Bowls with their victory in Super Bowl XXIV in 1990?

a) San Francisco 49ers *b) Washington Redskins*
c) Dallas Cowboys *d) Denver Broncos*

263. By what nickname is the American rugby team commonly known?

a) The Eagles *b) The Buffaloes*
c) The Cougars *d) The Bears*

264. Olga Korbut won three gold medals at the same Olympiad, but how old was she?

a) 11 *b) 13*
c) 17 *d) 15*

265. Which was the oldest continuing harness horseracing series in the United States?

a) World Driving Championship
b) Grand Circuit
c) International Pace Series
d) Roosevelt International Trot

266. The name Kunjarani Devi is associated with?

a) Weight Lifting *b) Target shooting*
c) Athletics *d) Swimming*

267. Who was the 1st ODI captain for India?

a) Ajit Wadekar *c) Bishen Singh Bedi*
c) Nawab Pataudi *d) Vinoo Mankad*

268. Who beat Duke in the Great Alaskan Shootout Finals in 1998?

a) Syracuse *b) University of Cincinnati*
c) Notre Dame *d) UCLA*

269. Who has scored the most Test hundreds ever?

a) Steve Waugh *b) Sachin Tendulkar*
c) Shane Warne *d) Sunil Gavaskar*

270. **What NHL goaltender has the most career wins?**

a) *Grant Fuhr* b) *Patrick Roy*
c) *Chris Osgood* d) *Mike Vernon*

271. **Former Australian captain Allan Border was sometimes known as "Captain Grumpy". What was his other nickname?**

a) *Abe* b) *Captain Junior*
c) *AB* d) *Groucho*

272. **Which county did Javagal Srinath sign for in 2003?**

a) *Surrey* b) *Durham*
c) *Sussex* d) *Essex*

273. **What is the middle name of the world class batsman Sachin Tendulkar?**

a) *Rohan* b) *Ramesh*
c) *Rahul* d) *Ravi*

274. **When did Sourav Ganguly made his ODI debut?**

a) *20 March 1993* b) *11 January 1992*
c) *1 December 1987* d) *1 June 1998*

275. **Rugby League: Who set a world record by getting himself sent off 12 seconds into Great Britain's 2003 Ashes series against Australia?**

a) *Andy Farrell* b) *Paul Sculthorpe*
c) *Adrian Morley* d) *Sean Long*

276. **At what age did Steffi Graf win her first Grand Slam?**

a) *21* b) *17* c) *19* d) *23*

277. **In which sport/game, was the Sicilian Defence used?**

a) *Chess* b) *Italian Football*
c) *Karate* d) *Chequers*

278. **How many times did Geet Sethi win the IBSF World Billiards title?**

a) *2* b) *3* c) *4* d) *5*

279. **India won the World Championship of Cricket defeating Pakistan in the final by 8 wickets. Who was the man of tournament?**

a) *Kris Srikaant* b) *Sunil Gavaskar*
c) *Ravi Shastri* d) *Kapil Dev*

280. **What do African-American football players Ernie Davis, Archie Griffin, and Tony Dorsett have in common?**

a) *They all played for Pittsburgh*
b) *They all won the Heisman Trophy*
c) *They all led to Super Bowl titles*
d) *They dont have any similarity*

281. **Who holds second and third place for most yards rushing in a single season in the NFL?**

a) *Barry Sanders* b) *Jim Brown*
c) *O.J. Simpson* d) *Dick Lane*

282. **The nickname of wicketkeeping great Rod Marsh was what?**

a) *Billabong* b) *Swampy*
c) *Bacchus* d) *Lagoon*

283. **Which two counties did Kapil Dev play?**

a) *Northamptonshire & Worcestershire*
b) *Northamptonshire & Warwickshire*
c) *Nottinghamshire & Worcestershire*
d) *Nottinghamshire & Warwickshire*

284. **How many runs did VVS Laxman score in his ODI debut?**

a) *100* b) *1* c) *99* d) *0*

285. **At what age did Zola Budd break the official 5,000 metres World Record?**

a) *16* b) *18* c) *14* d) *20*

286. **Who was called 'The Boston Strong Boy'?**

a) *Floyd Patterson* b) *James J Corbett*
c) *John Lawrence Sullivan* d) *Joe Louis*

287. Who was the first Indian to win the World Amateur Billiards title?

a) Geet Sethi *b) Wilson Jones*
c) Michael Ferreira *d) Manoj Kothari*

288. In the match between India and Pakistan at Jaipur on 02-10-1983, which new rule was introduced?

a) Limit of overs was reduced to 50 overs
b) The rule of field restriction was taken.
c) Over throw runs were batsman's score
d) No-balls & wides were debited to bowlers analysis

289. Which was the 1st non Test playing country to beat India in an international match?

a) Canada *b) Sri Lanka*
c) Zimbabwe *d) East Africa*

290. Who was the first captain of Indian Test team?

a) Vijay Hazare *b) C K Nayudu*
c) Lala Amarnath *d) Vijay Merchant*

291. Which country won the World Cup Cricket in 1999?

a) Australia *b) South Africa*
c) Pakistan *d) England*

292. Former Australian captain Mark Taylor has had several nicknames over his playing career. Which of the following was NOT one of them??

a) Tubby *b) Stodge*
c) Helium Bat *d) Stumpy*

293. Which county did Sachin Tendulkar play for?

a) Nottinghamshire *b) Yorkshire*
c) Lancashire *d) Leicestershire*

294. Which country, which made its debut in the Norwich Union League in 2003, signed Rahul Dravid as their overseas player?

a) Holland *b) Ireland*
c) Wales *d) Scotland*

295. What was the bowling figures (O-M-R-W) of Anil Kumble in his ODI debut against Sri Lanka?

a) 1.1-0-27-0 *b) 10-7-10-5*
c) 10-0-42-1 *d) 8.2-2-33-2*

296. Against which team did Rahul Dravid made his ODI debut?

a) Kenya *b) Pakistan*
c) Sri Lanka *d) Australia*

297. Soccer - who succeeded Alex Ferguson as manager of Scotland in 1986?

a) Andy Roxburgh *b) Craig Brown*
c) Kenny Dalglish *d) Jock Stein*

298. How old was Graham Gooch when he made his First Class cricket debut?

a) 18 *b) 24* *c) 22* *d) 20*

299. India won its first Olympic hockey gold in _____.

a) 1928 *b) 1932* *c) 1936* *d) 1948*

300. Hampden Park staged the Soccer European Cup final in 1960 and 2002. What did these two games have in common?

a) The final score was the same
b) Both games were abandoned due to waterlogged pitch
c) Fans in kilts and Jimmy wigs invaded the pitch
d) Real Madrid were the winners

301. In what sport did Graeme Obree make his name?

a) Cycling *b) Swimming*
c) Archery *d) Polo*

302. Who won the women's soccer World Cup in 2003?

a) Australia *b) USA*
c) England *d) Germany*

303. In which sport is the Thomas Cup a prize?

a) Downhill Skiing *b) Badminton*
c) Table Tennis *d) Canoeing*

304. How many Formula 1 Championships did Jackie Stewart win?

a) Three *b) Five*
c) Two *d) Four*

305. In which Olympic event did Abebe Bikila gain a medal?

a) The 10,000 metres *b) The 400 metres*
c) The Marathon *d) The 5000 metres*

306. Which athlete was referred to as "The Flying Finn"?

a) Erik Vilen *b) Ville Ritola*
c) Paavo Nurmi *d) Albin Stenroos*

307. Who won the 1988 World Snooker Championship?

a) Joe Johnson *b) Terry Griffiths*
c) Dennis Taylor *d) Steve Davis*

308. In which sporting event would a competitor wear the Maillot Jaune?

a) The Open Golf Championship
b) The Boat Race
c) The Tour de France
d) The Grand National

309. Which game is divided in to Chukkas?

a) Ice Hockey *b) Rugby Sevens*
c) Bowls *d) Polo*

310. With which sport do you associate the Calcutta Cup?

a) Soccer *b) Snooker* *c) Baseball* *d) Rugby*

311. Who was the first man to break the 10-second barrier for the 100m sprint in professional competition?

a) Carl Lewis *b) Charles Greene*
c) Ben Johnston *d) Jim Hines*

312. Who was the first non Brit to win the Snooker World Championship?

a) Ken Doherty *b) Cliff Thorburn*
c) Eddie Charlton *d) Marco Fu*

313. **Who was the first batsman to reach 10,000 Test match runs?**

a) *Sachin Tendulkar* b) *Allan Border*

c) *Sunil Gavaskar* d) *Brian Lara*

314. **Mark Spitz won an unprecedented SEVEN swimming gold medals for the USA. At which Olympic Games did he achieve this feat?**

a) *Munich 1972* b) *Montreal 1976*

c) *Los Angeles 1984* d) *Moscow 1980*

315. **In August 2006, sprinter Asafa Powell equaled the men's 100 metres world record. What nationality is he?**

a) *Jamaica* b) *South Africa*

c) *West Indies* d) *USA*

316. **How many points would a snooker player get for potting the brown ball?**

a) *Six* b) *Three* c) *Four* d) *Five*

317. **Who won the 1996 Wimbledon men's single tennis championship?**

a) *Pete Sampras* b) *Richard Krajicek*

c) *Malivai Washington* d) *Boris Becker*

318. **Which county did Sunil Gavaskar play for?**

a) *Somerset* b) *Worcestershire*

c) *Warwickshire* 4d) *Glamorgan*

Answers

Olympics

1. 776 BC
2. 14
3. James Connolly
4. Spyros Samaras
5. Pheidippides
6. Citius, Altius, Fortuis
7. 1920 Antwerp
8. 1928 Amsterdam
9. 1936 Berlin
10. 1932 Los Angeles
11. 1932 Los Angeles
12. 1936 Berlin
13. 1936 Berlin
14. 1952 Helsinki
15. 1992 Barcelona
16. 2004
17. Moscow
18. 1960 Rome
19. 1928 Amsterdam
20. 1908 London
21. 1968 Mexico city
22. Germany and Japan
23. Netherlands, Spain and Switzerland
24. Fourteen
25. 1956 Melbourne
26. 1972 Munich
27. $3 billion
28. China
29. Taiwan and African nations
30. 1980 Moscow
31. 1988 Seoul
32. India in Paris (1900)
33. 1900, Paris
34. Amik, the beaver (Montreal, 1976)
35. Kookaburra, Platypus, Echidna
36. 2004, Athens
37. A Weath of wild olive leaves

38. The Duke of Edinburgh
39. 1920, Antwerp
40. International Olympic committee host nation next host nation
41. 1972, Munich
42. France
43. Canada
44. Olympia
45. Wrestling
46. 1976, Montreal
47. 1956, Melbourne
48. 1896
49. Los Angeles, 1932
50. Mark Spitz
51. Francisco Lazaro
52. Charlie Paddock
53. Cathy Freeman
54. Derart Tulu
55. Neroli Fairhall
56. Joan Benoil
57. 1976, Montreal
58. Debbie Meyer
59. 1992
60. Almost all Eastern bloc countries
61. P. T. Usha
62. Turkey
63. 400m race
64. Turin (Italy)
65. Pierre de Coubertin
66. Alfred Hajos
67. India
68. Ethiopia
69. 1988
70. 1960, Rome
71. Czechoslovakia
72. USA
73. 1924, Paris
74. 1932, Los Angeles
75. English and French
76. Eva Klobukowska
77. USA
78. Athens, 1896
79. 1904, St Louis
80. Australia & New Zealand
81. 1912, Stockholm
82. Stockholm, 1912
83. Mexico, 1968
84. London, 1948
85. 1928, Amsterdam
86. 1920, Antwerp
87. 1964, Tokyo
88. 1968, Mexico
89. Phevos and Athena
90. Red, green, blue, yellow and black
91. Gymnastics
92. Rechelle Hawkes
93. Faliro Coastal Zone Olympic Complex

94. 200
95. Croquet
96. 1976, Montreal
97. Andre Agassi
98. London, 1948
99. Munich, 1972
100. Ian Thorpe

South Asian Federation Games

1. Nepal
2. 1984
3. South Asian Games
4. India
5. Islamabad
6. 7
7. Colombo
8. Afghanistan
9. China
10. 400
11. Piyush Kumar
12. Anne Maheshi De Silva
13. K.A. Karunaratne
14. Hemant Kumar Patel
15. Haider Ali Shah
16. Hridayanand Singh
17. Amandeep Kaur
18. Sunita Rani
19. Amrish Kumar
20. Manzoor Ahmed

Asian Games

1. 1951
2. 1982
3. Four
4. India
5. 1983
6. Thailand
7. Qatar
8. 14
9. Friendship Beyond Frontiers
10. China, South Korea, Japan
11. Guangzhou, China
12. 1990
13. Sapporo, Japan
14. China
15. Bali, Indonesia
16. 112
17. South Korea
18. 1986
19. Israel
20. Philippines

Commonwealth Games

1. 71
2. Melbourne
3. Samaresh Jung
4. 1930

5. Bobby Robinson
6. Humanity, Equality and Destiny
7. Hamilton in Ontario, Canada
8. India
9. India
10. Four
11. New Zealand
12. Bill Gates
13. Queen Elizabeth II
14. Natalie Du Toit, S. African Swimming champion
15. Australia
16. Wira
17. Mathew Hayman, Australia
18. Malaysia
19. Manchester
20. Singapore

Cricketing Moments

1. Australia
2. Pakistan
3. Harbhajan Singh
4. Rusi Surti
5. M. H. Mankad
6. Imran Khan
7. Scott Styris
8. Sourav Ganguly
9. Australia
10. Michael Vaughan
11. Rahul Dravid
12. Robin Singh
13. Javagal Srinath
14. 2-1
15. 1984
16. His 78th
17. 178.75
18. Yuvraj Singh
19. Tiger Pataudi
20. Anil Kumble
21. Nathan Astle
22. Herschelle Gibbs
23. Ian Bothom
24. Tim Robinson
25. Zaheer Abbas
26. Five
27. Gary Gilmour
28. B. C. Cooray
29. 25th June 1932
30. Ravi Shastri
31. Syd F. Barnes
32. Arthur Morris
33. Sir Garfield Sobers
34. Brendon Kuruppu

35. It was history's second tied Test
36. Eknath Solkar
37. First Indian to take a Test hat trick abroad
38. Kapil Dev
39. Imran Khan
40. Mountain Comes to Mohammad
41. John Wright
42. New Zealand
43. Lennie Louw
44. Tom Moody
45. Wasim Akram
46. Graham Gooch
47. Allan Border
48. Brian Lara
49. 1877
50. Ferozeshah Kotla
51. Four
52. Gundappa Vishwanath
53. 150
54. Azharuddin
55. Arthur Chipperfield
56. Cotah Ramaswami
57. Ian Botham
58. Boeta Dippenaar
59. Hashan Tillekaratne
60. Sri Lanka
61. Sachin Tendulkar
62. Ajit Agarkar
63. West Indies
64. Marcus Trescothick
65. Pakistan
66. Sanjay Manjrekar
67. Brian Lara
68. Yuvraj Singh
69. Wide ball
70. Jonty Rhodes
71. Sachin Tendulkar
72. Mervyn Dillon
73. Baggy Green
74. Eden Gardens, Kolkata
75. Australia
76. Shahid Afridi
77. Jim Laker, England
78. Canada
79. Ravi Shastri
80. New Zealand
81. England
82. 15 March, 1879
83. Salim Malik
84. Salim Jaffar
85. Gooch and Richardson
86. Tendulkar 186, Dravid 153
87. Chinnaswamy Stadium, Bangalore
88. Bobby Simpson
89. David Shepherd
90. Roger Twose
91. Scott Styris

92. Graham McKenzie
93. Only time Sri Don Brahman was out hit wicket
94. K. Srikkanth
95. Desmond Haynes
96. Bishen Singh Bedi
97. 17 February, 1982
98. Kepler Wessels
99. Grant Flower
100. M. Azharuddin

TENNIS

1. Andy Roddick
2. Bill Scanlon
3. John McEnroe
4. Argentina
5. Your Point
6. Andre Agassi
7. Justine Henin Hardenne
8. 17
9. Zina Garrison
10. Norman Brookes
11. 1966 and 1975
12. George VI
13. Lori McNeill
14. Jim Courier
15. Arnaud Clement
16. Martina Hingis and Anna Kournikouva
17. Wimbledon, French Open
18. Mario Ancic
19. Ken Rosewell
20. Pete Sampras
21. Never
22. 6-6
23. Pete Sampras
24. Steffi Graf
25. Venus and Serena Williams
26. Donald Budge
27. Spain
28. David Nalbandian
29. Sony Ericsson
30. Justin Henin-Hardenne
31. Martina Navratilova
32. Henri Leconte
33. 1924
34. Anthony Wilding
35. 31
36. 56
37. John Mary Pius Boland
38. US Open
39. Peter Fleming
40. Croatia
41. Venus Williams
42. Tommy Robredo
43. Andre Agassi

44. Lleyton Hewitt
45. Thomas Jonansson & Marat Safin
46. Margaret Smith Court
47. As many as it takes
48. ·Jimmy Connors
49. Tracy Austin
50. Amelie Mauresmo
51. Venus Williams
52. 14
53. French Open
54. Pat Rafter
55. 38
56. Maureen Connolly
57. Bjorn Phau
58. Fernando Verdasco
59. She had previously competed as a man
60. Pete Sampras
61. A pineapple
62. Thomas Enqvist
63. Patrick Rafter
64. 16
65. Sydney
66. US, Russia, France, Argentina
67. Martina Hingis
68. Martina Navratilova
69. Roger Fededer
70. James Blake
71. jana Novotna
72. Maria Sharapova
73. Switzerland
74. Semi-finalist
75. Wimbledon
76. Boris Becker
77. 5
78. Margaret Smith
79. Jiri Novak
80. Ken Rosewall
81. Frederico Luzzi
82. King James I of Scotland
83. Boris Becker
84. Richard Krajicek
85. Andy Roddick
86. Steffi Graf
87. Adelaide
88. Carlos Cuadrado
89. Thrice
90. Clarissa Fernandez
91. 128 players
92. Amelia Mauresmo
93. Kim Clijsters
94. Wimbledon
95. Lindsay Davenport
96. 1996
97. Michael Chang
98. Finals
99. Helen Wills Moody
100. Nikolay Davydenko

Golf

1. 18
2. Gary Player
3. Royal Porters
4. Lee Tanzen
5. Al Goberger
6. One
7. Albatross
8. Coeur D'Alene
9. Royal Calcutta Golf Club
10. Costantino Rocca
11. Interlachen
12. Shell Houston Open
13. Shigeki Maruyama
14. Lightning
15. Borrow
16. Kiawah Island
17. Madras
18. Srinagar
19. 59
20. Holly
21. Jeff Maggert
22. East Lake GC
23. Out of Bounds
24. TPC, Las Colinas
25. 1996
26. Sophie Gustafson
27. Hal Sutton
28. Jason Bohn
29. Mike Springer
30. Kathy Whitworth
31. Green
32. Augusta National
33. New Delhi
34. 147th
35. Congressional
36. Vardon Trophy
37. Carnoustie
38. Jyoti Randhawa
39. 1955
40. Jimmy Demaret
41. Yellow
42. Fore
43. St Andrews
44. Nick Faldo
45. 14
46. Five
47. New Delhi
48. India
49. Peter Thompson
50. Tiger Woods
51. Gary Player
52. Killing 150 fish at The Belfry
53. Tom Watson
54. 1975
55. Ailsa
56. The French Open
57. 1969
58. 1991
59. Royal Troon
60. Curtis Strange

61. 1986
62. Fred Couples
63. Augusta National
64. Payne Stewart
65. 1920
66. Gene Saracen
67. Prestwick
68. Greg Norman
69. In a swarm of black ants
70. Dunlop
71. Turnberry
72. Jack Nicklaus
73. 1979
74. Jack Nicklaus
75. Peru
76. Payne Stewart
77. 1953
78. P.Townsend
79. Troon
80. Nick Faldo
81. 1936
82. New Orleans
83. Webbed Foot
84. Nick Faldo
85. 1985
86. Walter Hagen
87. Mark Calcavecchia
88. 1984
89. Seve Ballesteros
90. Jean Van De Velde
91. 1984
92. 1989 Ryder Cup
93. Isle of Man
94. Tiger Woods
95. Howard Clark
96. Kingston
97. Jack Nicklaus
98. George Bush
99. £4,492
100. Two

Football

1. May 1904 (in Paris)
2. Zurich
3. 24
4. Roberto Baggio of Italy
5. Leonidas da Silva
6. Uruguay
7. Italy
8. King Carol
9. Orsi
10. Second round
11. Ghiggia
12. Hungary
13. Sweden
14. Brazil
15. Bobby Charlton
16. Dislocated shoulder
17. Kempes
18. Italy
19. Due to financial deficiency
20. Spain

21. Greece
22. Ricky Martin
23. Oliver Neville
24. Saudi Arabia
25. Andrea Pirlo
26. Zinedine Zidane
27. Miroslav Klose
28. Costtinha of Portugal
29. Romario, Brazil
30. Herman Crespo
31. Mexico
32. Italy
33. Boxing
34. Bolivia
35. Fritz Walter
36. Italy
37. Zagalo (Brazil)
38. Eusebio
39. Nobby Stiles
40. Canon
41. Johnny Rep
42. Teofilio and Rob Rensenbrink
43. 24
44. France
45. Hugo
46. 12 yards
47. Inside-of-the-foot pass
48. Bernd Schneider
49. Thierry Henry
50. Berlin
51. England and Spain
52. Costa Rica 4-2
53. Horacio Elizondo
54. Mazzali
55. Stabile
56. Both balls were used
57. Eight
58. Hugo Meisl
59. One
60. Four
61. The group winner was European
62. Rio de Janeiro
63. A draw (2-2) against Switzerland
64. 16
65. Sandor Kocsis, Hungary
66. Vava and Pele
67. Just Fontaine
68. England
69. Five
70. Uruguay, Mexico and France
71. Alf Ramsey
72. Jairzinho
73. Guanajuato Stadium
74. Zaire
75. Taylor
76. 38

77. Rob Rensenbrink
78. Puolo Rossi
79. Bryan Robson
80. Morocco
81. Rooster
82. Stuart Pearce
83. Kevin Sheedy
84. 10
85. Four
86. Tunisia
87. Cesar Simpatico
88. Ronaldo
89. Uruguay
90. Costa Rica
91. Kaiserslautern
92. Portugal
93. Pele
94. Ronaldo
95. Gianluigi Buffon
96. 15
97. Diego Maradona
98. Peter Shilton
99. Laurent Blanc
100. Saudi Arabia, Greece and Nigeria

Hockey

1. The Netherlands
2. Huber Cup
3. South Korea
4. 1928 Amsterdam
5. Ajit Pal Singh
6. 1982 Karachi
7. K. D. Singh Babu
8. 1983
9. Pankaj Gupta
10. England and Ireland
11. 1908
12. 1988 Mexico Olympics
13. 7 yards
14. Dhanraj Pillai
15. 1999
16. Dhyan Chand
17. Adolf Hitler
18. Vienna Sports Club
19. Germany
20. 133
21. 1980
22. Holland
23. Richard James Allen
24. USA
25. Dhyan Chand
26. 1974
27. 1976 Montreal
28. Rechelle Hawkers
29. Calcutta
30. Colonel
31. Argentina
32. 1974
33. Last
34. Mineral water
35. Pakistan
36. Uzbekistan

37. 6-1
38. South Africa
39. Pakistan
40. Pakistan
41. Vikramjit Singh
42. Germany
43. Netherlands
44. 3-0
45. 4-0
46. 2000
47. New Delhi
48. Puck
49. Sahara India
50. England
51. Brazil
52. 1875
53. Constance Applebee
54. Jimmy Nagarwalla
55. Pakistan
56. Italy
57. 1920's
58. The World Cup
59. France's Laurent Blanc
60. Willy O Ree
61. Khong Kangjei
62. Uruguay
63. Bobby Hull
64. 1922
65. Uruguay
66. Aluminum
67. Germantown Cricket Club
68. El Salvador
69. 1908
70. Bronze
71. Moscow
72. Chile
73. United States FieldHockey Association
74. Six
75. Italy

Miscellaneous

1. USA
2. Motorbike racing
3. 9
4. 1979
5. USA
6. Indoor
7. Shortstop
8. World Open Squash
9. Ron Hextall
10. Golf Tee
11. Roger Bannister
12. Eric Liddell
13. Clive Lloyd
14. Johnny Weismuller
15. Bullpen
16. Morocco
17. The Eagles
18. Tower
19. Mohan Bagan
20. Andy Rexburg

21. 1985
22. Heinz Herald Frentzen
23. Table Tennis
24. Terry Griffiths
25. Chess
26. 26 miles 585 yards
27. 7
28. Ed Fiji
29. Tug of war
30. Alydar
31. Kurt Angle
32. 1972
33. Izzy
34. Edmonton Oilers
35. Visakhapatnam
36. Charles
37. Davidio Antonio Beckham
38. Kerala
39. India
40. Abhijit Kunte
41. Bridge
42. Spain
43. Vijay Merchant
44. Mohan Bagan
45. Snooker
46. Football
47. Sandeep Patil
48. Australian Open
49. Monica Seles
50. Two
51. Chetan Chauhan
52. Prakash Nath
53. Clive Lloyd
54. Auction
55. One
56. Subhaswami Vijayalakshmi
57. Steve Waugh
58. White
59. France
60. Thailand
61. Russia
62. Mike Tyson
63. Black and white
64. Pataudi
65. Sachin Tendulkar
66. Ian Botham
67. Long jump
68. Babe Didricksen
69. Shaun Murphy
70. France
71. Lillehammer, Norway
72. Asafa Powell
73. Motor racing
74. Miguel Indurain
75. Michael Campbell
76. Ivan Lendl
77. Boris Becker
78. The Netherlands
79. Sri Lanka
80. East Germany
81. Yugoslavia
82. Jack Brabham

83. Italy
84. Prince Philip, the Duke of Edinburgh
85. Running Broad Jump
86. Peru
87. S. Venkataraghavan
88. Joe Bugner
89. 1985-1991
90. 100m hurdles
91. Ten pin bowling
92. Edinburgh
93. French Open
94. Fernando Alonso
95. Handball
96. Abebe Bikala
97. Race Walking
98. Oskana Baiul
99. Six
100. William G. Morgan
101. St Petersburg
102. Spyridon Louis
103. George Foreman
104. Pachisi
105. India
106. Todd Bertuzzi
107. Pele
108. USA and Sweden
109. Colin Jackson
110. Argentina
111. Thomas Hearns
112. Goran Ivanisevic
113. High Jump
114. Pentathlon
115. Mark Taylor
116. Milkha Singh
117. Badminton
118. Argentina
119. Richard Hadlee
120. Donald Bradman
121. USA
122. Jesse Owens
123. Canada
124. Jack Nicklaus
125. Football
126. Anjali Rajagopal
127. Snooker
128. Bob Beamon
129. Kabaddi
130. Leander Paes
131. South Africa
132. Circumnavigation of the earth by car
133. Ramanathan Krishnan
134. K.D.Yadav
135. Headingley
136. Ty Cobb
137. A referee
138. Brian Lara
139. Shawn Michaels
140. Stone Cold Steve Austin
141. Pigeon
142. Derbyshire

143. Northamptonshire & Leicestershire
144. Plaha
145. Three
146. Audi R8
147. Uruguay
148. Five
149. Eric Liddell
150. 11
151. Paul-Erik Hoyer-Larsen
152. 25
153. Miguel Angel Nadal
154. Boxing
155. 1912
156. Kabaddi
157. Curling
158. Golf
159. Gene Tunney
160. Germany
161. 1957
162. 1956
163. Meghalaya
164. Four
165. Ahmedabad
166. 1800s
167. Wilma Rudolph
168. George Foreman
169. 1844 between Canada and the USA
170. 45 seconds
171. Jim Kiick
172. Jason Gillespie
173. Glamorgan
174. Chandidas
175. Gilchrist
176. Ugo Ehiogu
177. Canopying
178. Sagol Kangjei
179. Underwater Rugby
180. Motivator
181. USA
182. Donovan Bailey
183. Hurling
184. Hacky-Sack
185. USA
186. Dimitrias Vikelas
187. Andre Agassi
188. Manila
189. India
190. Madrid
191. 17
192. Mick Lewis
193. To serve ice cream in
194. David Gower
195. Romanian
196. Arsenal F.C.
197. 60 feet
198. Tennis
199. Cribbage
200. 6 feet
201. Mr.X
202. Racquetball
203. 9

204. Floyd Patterson
205. Seven
206. 350 lbs
207. 57 inches
208. One
209. Archie Moore
210. Freestyle Skiing
211. Korea
212. Hang Gliding
213. Cycling
214. Don Budge
215. Rocky Marciano
216. Middlesex
217. Wood
218. Putout
219. 1988
220. India
221. Mexico City
222. Khong Kangjei
223. Kamaljit Sandhu
224. 1948
225. Leonardo DaVinci
226. Four
227. 1877
228. Shane Warne
229. Mankind
230. Junior
231. Boland
232. Raman Lamba
233. Sharad
234. Nairobi, Kenya
235. A Maori chant involving stamping and gestures
236. Brian McBride
237. Alec Stewart
238. Richard Dunwoody
239. Uruguay 4- Argentina-2
240. Vivian Richards and Sanath Jayasuriya
241. 39
242. Narendra Hirwani
243. Roland Ratzenberger
244. Ferenc Puskas
245. Ten
246. Franz Beckenbaur
247. A card game
248. Belmont Stakes
249. Horse Racing
250. Coaches
251. 1966
252. Ten
253. R.E. Grant Govan
254. Reggie Miller
255. Brian Lara
256. Dude Love
257. Merv Hughes
258. Northamptonshire
259. Saurav Ganguly
260. Bhalchandra
261. Pakistan
262. San Francisco 49ers
263. The Eagles
264. 17
265. Grand Circuit
266. Weight Lifting

267. Ajit Wadekar
268. University of Cincinnati
269. Sachin Tendulkar
270. Patrick Roy
271. AB
272. Durham
273. Ramesh
274. 11 January 1992
275. Adrian Morley
276. 17
277. Chess
278. Three
279. Ravi Shastri
280. They all won the Heisman Trophy
281. O.J. Simpson
282. Bacchus
283. Northamptonshire & Worcestershire
284. Zero
285. 18
286. John Lawrence Sullivan
287. Wilson Jones
288. No-balls & wides were debited to bowlers analysis
289. Sri Lanka
290. C K Nayudu
291. Australia
292. Stumpy
293. Yorkshire
294. Scotland
295. 10-0-42-1
296. Sri Lanka
297. Andy Roxburgh
299. 20
299. 1928
300. Real Madrid were the winners
301. Cycling
302. Germany
303. Badminton
304. Three
305. The Marathon
306. Paavo Nurmi
307. Steve Davis
308. The Tour de France
309. Polo
310. Rugby
311. Jim Hines
312. Cliff Thorburn
313. Sunil Gavaskar
314. Munich 1972
315. Jamaican
316. Four
317. Richard Krajicek
318. Somerset

DESTROYER

In naval terminology, a destroyer is a fast and maneuverable yet long-endurance warship intended to escort larger vessels in a fleet, convoy or battle group and defend them against smaller, short-range but powerful attackers (originally torpedo boats, later submarines and aircraft).

Before World War II, destroyers were light vessels without the endurance for unattended ocean operations; typically a number of destroyers and a single destroyer tender operated together. During and after the war, larger and more powerful destroyers capable of independent operation were built, particularly as cruisers ceased to be used in the 1950s and 60s.

At the dawn of the 21st Century, destroyers are the heaviest surface combatant ships in general use, with only four nations (the United States, Russia, France and Peru) operating the heavier class cruisers and none operating battleships or true battlecruisers. Modern destroyers, also known as guided missile destroyers, are equivalent in tonnage but vastly superior in firepower to cruisers of the World War II era, capable of carrying nuclear missiles.

Emergence and development of the destroyer, up until World War II, was related to the invention of the self-propelled torpedo in the 1860s. A navy now had the potential to destroy a superior enemy battle fleet using steam launches to drop torpedoes. Fast boats armed with torpedoes were built and called torpedo boats. By the 1880s, these had evolved into small ships of 50-100 tons, fast enough to evade enemy picket boats.

At first, the danger to a battle fleet was considered only to exist when at anchor, but as faster and longer range torpedoes were developed, the threat extended to cruising at sea. In response to this new threat more heavily-gunned picket boats called "catchers" were built which were used to escort the battle fleet at sea. They needed the same seaworthiness and endurance, and as they necessarily became larger, they became officially designated "torpedo boat destroyers", soon contracted to destroyer in English. The anti-torpedo boat origin of this type of ship is retained in its name in other languages, including French (*contre-torpilleur*), Italian (*cacciatorpediniere*), Portuguese (*contratorpedeiro*), Polish (*kontrtorpedowiec*), Czech (*torpédoborec*), Greek (*antitorpiliko*) and so on. Once destroyers became more than just catchers guarding an anchorage, it was realized that they were also ideal to take over the role of torpedo boats themselves, so they were fitted with torpedo tubes as well as guns. At that time, and even into World War I, the only function of destroyers was to protect their own battle fleet from enemy torpedo attacks and to make such attacks on the battleships of the enemy. The task of escorting merchant convoys was still in the future.

An important development came in 1884 with HMS *Swift*, a large torpedo boat with six 47 mm quick-firing guns and three torpedo tubes. While still not fast enough to engage torpedo boats reliably, she at least had the armament to deal with them.

The Japanese *Kotaka* (*Falcon*) of 1885 was "the forerunner of torpedo boat destroyers that appeared a decade later" Designed to Japanese specifications and ordered from the London Yarrow shipyards in 1885, she was transported in parts to Japan, where she was assembled and launched in 1887. She was armed with four 1-pounder (37 mm) quick-firing guns and six torpedo tubes, reached 19 knots (35 km/h), and at 203 tons, was the largest torpedo boat yet. In her trials in 1889, *Kotaka* demonstrated that she could go beyond a role of coastal defence, and was capable of following larger ships on the high seas. The Yarrow shipyards, builder of the parts for the *Kotaka*, "considered Japan to have effectively invented the destroyer".

Almost immediately after the order of *Kotaka* was placed, Fernando Villaamil, second officer of the Ministry of the Navy of Spain where he was put in charge of developing the concept of a new ship designed to combat torpedo boats placed an order for a large torpedo gunboat in November 1885, with the British builder James and George Thompson, of Clydebank, not far from where the Yarrow shipyards would move from London twenty years later. The ship, named *Destructor* (literally *Destroyer*), was laid down at the end of the year, launched in 1886, and commissioned in 1887. Her displacement was 380 tons, and she was armed with one 90 mm Hontoria guns, four 57 mm Nordenfelt guns, two 37 mm Hotchkiss cannons and 3 Schwarzkopf torpedo tubes. Her complement was 60 men. In terms of gunnery, speed (22.5 knots in trials) and dimensions, the specific design to chase torpedo boats and her high seas capabilities, *Destructor* is widely considered the first torpedo-boat destroyer ever built.

The Spanish *Destructor* is thought to have influenced the designation and concept of later destroyers developed by the British Navy.

Shortly afterwards, Britain began experiments with the *Rattlesnake* class 'torpedo boat catcher', a class of 17 large torpedo boats-the first precursors of destroyers to be built as a class, rather than as single ships. On tests, *Rattlesnake* proved to be marginally faster than torpedo boats, but not fast enough to be decisive.

The first ships to bear the formal designation "Torpedo boat destroyer" (TBD) were the *Daring* class of two ships and *Havock* class of two ships of the Royal Navy, developed in 1892 under the newly appointed Third Sea Lord Rear Admiral "Jackie" Fisher. The *Daring* and *Decoy* were ordered on 27 June 1892 from Thornycroft at Chiswick, while the *Havock* and *Hornet* were ordered five days later from Yarrow at Poplar. All were launched in 1893-94. Each was armed with a single 12-pounder (76 mm) gun, three 6-pounders (57 mm), and three 46 cm torpedo tubes. They also had the range and speed to travel effectively with a battle fleet.

The French navy, an extensive user of torpedo boats, built its first destroyer in 1899, with the *Durandal*-class 'torpilleur d'escadre'. The United States commissioned its first destroyer, USS *Bainbridge*, Destroyer No. 1, in 1902 and by 1906 there were 16 destroyers in service with the US Navy.

Destroyer design evolved around the turn of the 20th century in several key ways. The first was the introduction of the steam turbine. The spectacular unauthorized demonstration of the turbine powered *Turbinia* at the 1897 Spithead Navy Review, which, significantly, was of torpedo boat size, prompted the Royal Navy to order a prototype turbine powered destroyer, HMS *Viper* of 1899. This was the first turbine warship of any kind and achieved a remarkable 36 knots (67 km/h) on sea trials. By 1910 the turbine had been widely adopted by all navies for their faster ships.

The second development was the replacement of the boat-style turtleback foredeck by a raised forecastle, which provided better sea-keeping as well as more space below deck.

The British experimented with oil propulsion for the Tribal class of 1905 but switched temporarily back to coal for the later *Beagle* class in 1909. Other navies also adopted oil, for instance the USN with the *Paulding* class of 1909. In spite of all this variety, destroyers adopted a largely similar pattern. The hull was long and narrow, with a relatively shallow draft. The bow was either raised in a forecastle or covered under a turtleback; underneath this were the crew spaces, extending 1/4 to 1/3 the way along the hull.

Aft of the crew spaces was as much engine space as the technology of the time would allow: several boilers and engines or turbines. Above deck, one or more quick-firing guns were mounted in the bows, in front of the bridge; several more were mounted amidships and astern. Two torpedo tube mountings (later on, multiple mountings) were generally found amidships.

Between 1890 and 1914 destroyers became markedly larger: initially 300 tons was a good size, but by the start of the First World War 1000 tons was not unusual. However, construction remained focused on putting the biggest possible engines into a small hull, resulting in a somewhat flimsy construction. Often hulls were built of steel only 1/8in thick.

By 1910 the steam-driven displacement (i.e. not hydroplaning) torpedo boat had become redundant as a separate type. Germany nevertheless continued to build such torpedo boats until the end of WWI, although these were effectively small coastal destroyers. In fact Germany never distinguished between the two types, giving them pennant numbers in the same series and never giving names to destroyers. Ultimately the term *torpedo boat* came to be attached to a quite different vessel-the very fast hydroplaning motor driven MTB.

LIFE ON EARLY DESTROYERS

Early destroyers were extremely cramped places to live. In the *Havock*-class no crew member could ever get undisturbed rest, with officers sleeping on cushioned chairs around the wardroom instead of beds. Spray and condensation made life miserable. The first British class to have separate cabins for officers, or a heating stove for the captain, was the River class of 1902.

Early Destroyer Tactics and Engagements

The destroyer's initial purpose was to protect against torpedo boats, but navies soon appreciated the flexibility of the fast, multi-purpose vessel that resulted. Vice-Admiral Sir Baldwin Walker laid down destroyer duties for the Royal Navy

- Screening the advance of a fleet when hostile torpedo craft are about
- Searching a hostile coast along which a fleet might pass
- Watching an enemy's port for the purpose of harassing his torpedo craft and preventing their return
- Attacking an enemy fleet

The destroyer's first major use came in the devastating Japanese attack on the Russian fleet in Port Arthur at the opening of the Russo-Japanese War in 1904. Three destroyer divisions attacked the Russian fleet in port, firing a total of 18 torpedoes, and severely damaging two Russian battleships.

World War I

While capital ship engagements were scarce in World War I, destroyer units were almost continually engaged in raiding and patrol actions. The first shot of the war at sea was fired on 5 August 1914 by a destroyer of the 2nd Flotilla, *Lance*, in an engagement with the German auxiliary minelayer *Königin Luise*. The first British naval casualty was *Amphion*, the light cruiser leading the 3rd Flotilla, which ran into a mine laid by *Königin Luise*. Destroyers were involved in the skirmishes that prompted the Battle of Heligoland Bight, and filled a range of roles in the Battle of Gallipoli, acting as troop's transports and fire support vessels, as well as their fleet-screening role. Over 80 British destroyers and 60 German torpedo-boats took part in the Battle of Jutland, which involved pitched small-boat actions between the main fleets, and several foolhardy attacks by unsupported destroyers on capital ships. Jutland also concluded with a messy night action between the German High Seas Fleet and part of the British destroyer screen.

The threat evolved by World War I with the development of the submarine, or U-boat. The submarine had the potential to hide from gunfire and close underwater to fire torpedoes. Early-war destroyers had the speed and armament to intercept submarines before they submerged, either by gunfire or by ramming. Destroyers also had a shallow enough draft that torpedoes would find it difficult to hit them.

The desire to attack submarines underwater led to rapid destroyer evolution during the war, which were quickly equipped with strengthened bows for ramming, depth charges and hydrophones for identifying submarine targets. The first submarine casualty to a destroyer was the German *U-19*, rammed by *Badger* on 29 October 1914. While *U-19* was only damaged, the next month *Garry* successfully sank *U-18*. The first depth-charge sinking was on 4 December 1916, when *UC-19* was sunk by *Llewellyn*.

The submarine threat meant that many destroyers spent their time on anti-submarine patrol; once Germany adopted unrestricted submarine warfare in January 1917, destroyers were called on to escort merchant convoys. US Navy destroyers were among the first American units to be dispatched upon the American entry to the war, and a squadron of Japanese destroyers even joined Allied patrols in the Mediterranean. Patrol duty was far from safe; of the 67 British destroyers lost in the war, collisions accounted for 18, while 12 were wrecked. At the end of the war the state-of-the-art was represented by the British W class.

Inter-war

The trend during World War I had been towards larger destroyers with heavier armaments. A number of opportunities to fire at capital ships had been missed during the War, because destroyers had expended all their torpedoes in an initial salvo. The British 'V' & 'W' classes of the late war had sought to address this by mounting six torpedo tubes in two triple mounts, instead of the four or two on earlier models. The 'V' and 'W's set the standard of destroyer building well into the 1920s.

The next major innovation came with the Japanese *Fubuki* class or 'special type', designed in 1923 and delivered in 1928. The design was initially noted for its powerful armament of six five-inch (127 mm) guns and three triple torpedo mounts. The second batch of the class gave the guns high-angle turrets for anti-aircraft warfare, and the 24-inch (61 cm) oxygen-fueled 'Long Lance' Type 93 torpedo. The later *Hatsuharu* class of 1931 further improved the torpedo armament by storing its reload torpedoes close at hand in the superstructure, allowing reloading within 15 minutes.

Most other nations replied with similar larger ships. The US *Porter* class adopted twin five-inch (127 mm) guns, and the subsequent *Mahan* class and *Gridley* class (the latter of 1934) increased the number of torpedo tubes to 12 and 16 respectively.

In the Mediterranean, the Italian Navy's building of very fast light cruisers of the *Condottieri* class prompted the French to produce exceptional destroyer designs. The French had long been keen on large destroyers, with their *Chacal* class of 1922 displacing over 2,000 tons and carrying 130 mm guns; a further three similar classes were produced around 1930. The *Le Fantasque* class of 1935 carried five 5.5-inch (140 mm) guns and nine torpedo tubes, but could achieve speeds of 45 knots (83 km/h), which remains the record speed for a steamship and for any destroyer.The Italians' own destroyers were almost as swift, most Italian designs of the 1930s being rated at over 38 knots (70 km/h), while carrying torpedoes and either four or six 120 mm guns.

Germany started to build destroyers again during the 1930s as part of Hitler's rearmament program. The Germans were also fond of large destroyers, but while the initial Type 1934 displaced over 3,000 tons, their armament was equal to smaller vessels. This changed from the Type 1936 onwards, which mounted heavy 150 mm guns. German destroyers also used innovative high-pressure steam machinery: while this should have helped their efficiency, it more often resulted in mechanical problems.

Once German and Japanese rearmament became clear, the British and American navies consciously focused on building destroyers that were smaller but more numerous than those used by other nations. The British built a series of destroyers (the A Class to I Class) which were about 1,400 tons standard displacement, had four 4.7-inch (119 mm) guns and eight torpedo tubes; the American *Benson* class of 1938 similar in size, but carried five 5-inch (127 mm) guns and ten torpedo tubes. Realizing the need for heavier gun armament, the British built the Tribal class of 1936 (sometimes called "Afridi" after one of two lead ships).

These ships displaced 1,850 tons and were armed with eight 4.7-inch (119 mm) guns in four twin turrets and four torpedo tubes. These were followed by the J Class and L class destroyers, with six 4.7-inch (119 mm) guns in twin turrets and eight torpedo tubes

Anti-submarine sensors included sonar (or ASDIC), although training in their use was indifferent. Anti-submarine weapons changed little, and ahead-throwing weapons, a need recognized in World War I, had made no progress.

Operations in the Inter-war Period

During the 1920s and 1930s destroyers were often deployed to areas of diplomatic tension or humanitarian disaster. British and American destroyers were common on the Chinese coast and rivers, even supplying landing parties to protect colonial interests.

World War II the threat had evolved once again. Submarines were more effective, and aircraft had become important weapons of naval warfare; once again the fleet destroyers were ill-equipped for combating these new targets. They were fitted with new anti-aircraft guns, radar, and forward-launched ASW weapons, in addition to their existing light guns, depth charges, and torpedoes. By this time the destroyers had become large, multi-purpose vessels, expensive targets in their own right. As result casualties on destroyers were one of the highest. This led to the introduction of smaller and cheaper specialized anti-submarine warships called corvettes and frigates by the Royal Navy and destroyer escorts by the USN. A similar programme was belatedly started by the Japanese. These ships had the size and displacement of the original torpedo boat destroyers that the contemporary destroyer had evolved from.

Post-war

Some conventional destroyers were completed in the late 1940s and 1950s which built on wartime experience. These vessels were significantly larger than wartime ships and had fully automatic main guns, unit Machinery, radar, sonar, and antisubmarine weapons such as the Squid mortar. Examples include the British *Daring* class, US *Forrest Sherman*-class, and the Soviet Kotlin-class destroyers.

Some World War II–vintage ships were modernized for anti-submarine warfare, and to extend their service lives, to avoid having to build (expensive) brand-new ships. Examples include the US FRAM I programme and the British Type 15 frigates converted from fleet destroyers.

The advent of surface-to-air missiles and surface-to-surface missiles, such as the Exocet, in the early 1960s changed naval warfare. Guided missile destroyers (DDG in the US Navy) were developed to carry these weapons and protect the fleet from air, submarine and surface threats. Examples include the Soviet Kashin-class, the British County class, and the American *Charles F. Adams*-class.

Modern Destroyers

The Royal Navy currently operates 7 ships of the Type 42 class with HMS *Southampton* reducing to extended readiness in 2008. The destroyers (as well as frigates) are, as always, the workhorses of the fleet, the former optimized for air defence and the latter for surface and subsurface warfare. They are equally at home in large task groups or on independent operations which may include sanctions enforcement, humanitarian relief or anti-drug patrols. British destroyers (of recent times) have an average displacement of around 5000 tonnes, and are armed with a mixture of guns and missiles including 114 mm (4.5 inch) Mk 8 guns, Sea Dart Missiles, 20 mm Close range guns, Vulcan Phalanx close in weapons system (CIWS), and anti submarine torpedo tubes. These ships are due to be replaced by the new Type 45 or *Daring*-class destroyers which will displace roughly 7,200 tonnes. A class of 6 ships is envisaged. They will be equipped with the UK variant of the Principal Anti-Air Missile System (PAAMS) and BAE Systems SAMPSON radar. The ships are assembled at Scotstoun, by BAE Systems Surface Ships. HMS Daring, the first of her class, was launched on 1 February 2006.

The Italian navy (Marina Militare) currently operates 2 each of the *Luigi Durand de la Penne* and *Orizzonte*-class of destroyers.

The Canadian Navy currently operates the *Iroquois*-class destroyers, a class of four helicopter-carrying, anti-aircraft, guided missile destroyers. Launched in the 1970s, the *Iroquois* were the first Canadian all gas turbine powered military ships, using two turbines for cruise power, and another two fast-starting "boost" turbines for speeds of up to 29 knots (54 km/h) (such an arrangement is known as COGOG). Previously the Soviet Navy had used all-gas turbine propulsion on their Kashin class destroyers of the 1960s but the Iroquois were the first to be built to this scheme either in Canada or in the US. The design of the Iroquois was a major inspiration for the US's later *Spruance* class ships. They were originally fitted out for anti-submarine warfare, but the entire class underwent major retrofits as a part of the Tribal Class Update and Modernization Program, or TRUMP, in the 1990s. These refits had the effect of re-purposing the ships for air-defence, and the ships are now referred to as area air-defence destroyers.

The Indian Navy operates three *Delhi*-class destroyers. These ships are armed with Kh-35 missiles, which have a range of 130 km, in the anti-ship role. They will be replaced by the Brahmos cruise missiles. Shtil (AKA SA-N-7 Gadfly) system is installed to counter airborne threats. The Barak point-defence missile system has been installed in *Delhi* and will soon be installed in the other two ships of its class. These destroyers also carry the RBU-6000 rockets in the anti-submarine role and are provided with five 533 mm torpedo launch tubes that can launch the SET-65E, Type 53-65 torpedoes. The destroyers have the capability to carry two Sea King helicopters. The *Delhi*-class will be augmented by the new *Kolkata*-class destroyers, the first of which was launched in March 2006.

The Chinese People's Liberation Army Navy has recently commissioned a number of new modern destroyers in addition to the four *Sovremenny*-class. Three new classes were launched since 2003, known as the Luyang, Luyang II and *Luzhou*-class. The latter two are armed with long range air defence missiles, the indigenous HQ-9 and the Russian S-300 respectively. It has been speculated that once the PLAN has been satisfied with one of the two designs (either the 052C or 051C), it would be selected for series production as the next generation of advanced air defence destroyers for China. In the US Navy, destroyers operate in support of carrier battle groups, surface action groups, amphibious groups and replenishment groups. The destroyers currently in use by the US Navy are the *Arleigh Burke*-class. Destroyers (with a DD hull classification symbol) primarily perform anti-submarine warfare duty while guided missile destroyers (DDGs) are multi-mission (anti-submarine, anti-aircraft, and anti-surface warfare) surface combatants.

The relatively-recent addition of cruise missile launchers has greatly expanded the role of the destroyer in strike and land-attack warfare. As the expense of heavier surface combatants has generally removed them from the fleet, destroyer tonnage has grown (a modern *Arleigh Burke*-class destroyer has the same tonnage as a World War II light cruiser). *Arleigh Burke* is billed by her builders as ton-for-ton the most powerful warship in history.

The Russian Navy and the People's Liberation Army Navy of the People's Republic of China operate the *Sovremenny* class, a class of large multi-purpose missile destroyers. They are powered by pressure-fired boilers, making them capable of speeds in excess of 30 knots (56 km/h). Their armament consists of 8 SS-N-22 Sunburn anti-ship missiles, launchers for SA-N-7 Gadfly anti-air missiles and two AK-130 twin-barreled 130 mm automatic naval guns which can fire laser-guided shells. While they also carry 533 mm torpedo tubes and RBU-6000 rocket launchers for use against submarines, their primary mission is to attack surface ships. Their anti-aircraft missiles have a surface attack mode, and both the 130 mm guns and the torpedoes are useful against ships at close range.

Future Destroyers

The last US Navy *Spruance*-class destroyer in service, USS *Cushing*, was decommissioned on September 21, 2005. The *Zumwalt* class are planned to replace them; on November 1, 2001, the US Navy announced the issuance of a revised Request for Proposal (RFP) for the Future Surface Combatant Program. Formerly known as DD 21, the program will now be called DD(X) to more accurately reflect the program purpose, which is to produce a family of advanced technology surface combatants, not a single ship class. DD(X), also called *Zumwalt* class, is much larger than traditional destroyers, being nearly three thousand tons heavier than a

Ticonderoga-class cruiser (c.12,500 tonnes, larger than most heavy cruisers from the World War II era). It will potentially employ advanced weaponry and an all-electric Integrated Power System; however, the construction programme was subsequently reduced to just two vessels, and there is currently only funding for three in total. With the retirement of the *Spruance* class, the Navy began commissioning an advanced variant of the *Arleigh Burke* class with expanded ASW capabilities, the *Arleigh Burke* Flight IIA, beginning with USS *Oscar Austin*. As of 2006, 22 of these vessels are in service, with at least seven more under construction.

The $5.2 billion Command & Control and Air-Defence Capability Replacement project is meant to replace Canada's *Iroquois* class destroyers whose primary role shifted to area air-defence after TRUMP refits in the 1990s. Although the area air-defence capability had not previously existed, the Canadian Navy now regards "wide area air defence" as part of Canada's core naval capabilities. When the project began, Canadian Navy destroyers were expected to need replacing by 2005, they are now expected to serve until 2010. There was some work on a replacement design, known to Navy-watchers as the *Province* class destroyers, but this was confined largely to studies of a much-improved multi-function three dimensional phased array radar system being developed in conjunction with the Dutch and German navies, known as Active Phased Array Radar. Current speculation is that the ships themselves would be similar to a "stretched" *Halifax*-class frigate.

UNRESTRICTED SUBMARINE WARFARE

Unrestricted submarine warfare is a type of naval warfare in which submarines sink merchant ships without warning, as opposed to attacks per prize rules. While providing the submarine with strongly increased lethality and greater chances of survival against its hunters, it is also considered by many as a substantial breach of the rules of war, especially when employed against neutral country vessels in a war zone. There have been four major campaigns of unrestricted submarine warfare:

1. The U-boat campaign of World War I, waged intermittently by Germany between 1915 and 1918 against Britain and

her allies. This warfare was also ostensibly the *casus belli* for the United States and Brazil's entry into the war in 1917.

2. The Battle of the Atlantic during World War II between 1939 and 1945, waged by Germany and, from 1940 to 1943, by Italy, against Britain and her allies.
3. The Naval War on the Eastern Front, also during World War II between 1941 and 1945, waged by Germany and the USSR against each other, primarily on the Baltic Sea, especially from 1942.
4. The Pacific War during World War II, also between 1941 and 1945, waged by the United States against Japan.

All the four cases centred around attempts to navally blockade countries, especially those heavily dependent on merchant shipping to supply their war industries and feed their populations (like Britain and Japan), even though the countries waging the unrestricted submarine warfare were unable to institute a typical naval blockade.

HISTORY

Before WWI

In 1912, British Admiral Sir John "Jackie" Fisher, by then a retired First Sea Lord, presented a paper to the Cabinet. He developed the argument that submarines would find adherence to Prize Rules impossible, for practical reasons: a submarine could not capture a merchant ship, for it would have no spare manpower to deliver the prize to a neutral port, neither could it take survivors or prisoners, for lack of space. "*...there is nothing a submarine can do except sink her capture.*" If a merchant ship were armed, as was permitted by a conference in London in 1912, then a submarine would be under even more pressure to destroy it. He asked: "*What if the Germans were to use submarines against commerce without restriction?*" This last comment was thought to be unsupportable. Winston Churchill, then First Lord of The Admiralty and political head of the Navy, supported by senior naval opinion, said it was inconceivable that "*...this would ever be done by a civilised power.*" It was Fisher who was proved correct, though—as will be shown in the following section—the Germans themselves did not plan for this kind of warfare and went in practice through the stages which Fisher had predicted.

World War I

The evidence suggests that Imperial Germany had not started World War I with an appreciation of the impact on commerce and supply that submarines could have. They had fewer than 30 operational boats, all with small torpedo capacities. At first, merchant ships would be stopped, occupants safely evacuated and then the vessel sunk, usually by gunfire, all following Cruiser Rules. This relatively dangerous, time-consuming process placed the German submarine—U-boat—at risk from Q-ships, defensive patrols and other anti-submarine measures adopted by the British admiralty.

Germany had practical strategic problems. War-weariness affected the German home situation. The best chance of achieving an early advantageous peace with Britain was considered to be the stifling of its trade and imports. The gamble that was taken was that unrestricted submarine warfare would critically damage Britain before an incensed United States could make a practical impact. Even before the entry of the United States into the war, the US had already effectively been on the side of Britain, trading heavily with the United Kingdom, while the UK in turn prevented all attempts at US-German trade via a classical surface ship naval blockade, only ineffectually circumvented by German merchant submarines like the *Deutschland*. Thus, commercial interests were already in favour of a US that was increasingly assertive in its own strength and its right to trade with whatever nation it desired to, technically neutral or not.le the success of the submarines was no small blow to British supply lines, the gamble ultimately failed when it drew the United States into the war, and when the introduction of the convoy system cut shipping losses heavily again.

World War II

London Rules on naval warfare

The submarine sinking of merchant ships without warning is in violation of the 1930 First London Naval Treaty, which specifies that "...except in the case of persistent refusal to stop on being duly summoned, or of active resistance to visit or search, a warship, whether surface vessel or submarine, may not sink or render incapable of navigation a merchant vessel without having first placed passengers, crew and ship's papers in a place of safety. For this purpose the ship's boats are not regarded as a place of safety..."

However, the London Rules were obsolete before they were signed (though the *Kriegsmarine* based its Prize Rules on them). The use of disguised guns on auxiliary cruisers increased the risk inherent in stop-and-search rules, but the primary danger came from the wide-spread adoption of radio, which meant that a merchant could call for help as soon as a submarine appeared, even before it could issue its demands. Coupled with the rapidly-growing speed, range, and destructive power of combat aircraft, this technology ensured that complying with these rules would be suicide for any submarine.

Germany in the Atlantic

Battle of the Atlantic (1939–1945)

For the first few weeks of World War II, the German Navy attempted to honour Nazi Germany's treaty obligations, but that attempt was in trouble almost immediately following the sinking of SS *Athenia* by *U 30*, and it was abandoned at the end of November or the beginning of December 1939 with the issuing of War Order No. 154.

United States in the Pacific: Allied submarines in the Pacific War

The United States, from the first day it entered the Pacific War against the Japanese Empire, decided that unrestricted submarine warfare was to be carried out in the Pacific Ocean.

Post-WWII Concept

Since the introduction of long-range anti-ship missiles after World War II, which are able to destroy a ship from beyond the horizon, the London Rules are universally regarded as entirely void. It is indicative that despite the rules being used in the indictment of Admiral Karl Dönitz, and although he was found guilty of breaching the 1936 Naval Protocol, his sentence was not assessed (no penalty was issued) on the ground of his breaches of the international law of submarine warfare at the Nuremberg Trials because evidence was presented to the court that both the Royal Navy and the United States Navy had issued similar orders.atalino Ronzitti pointed out that due to the advent of supersonic aircraft and missiles, that at times of war fleets of warships can justifiably have a moving *cordon sanitaire* under which shipping or aircraft within the cordon can be attacked without warning.

He also states that The Royal Navy had such a zone around their fleet during the 1982 Falkland War and that as this action was in the relatively empty South Atlantic it did not raise the diplomatic problems that such an action might cause in a busy sea such as the Mediterranean. Ronzitti states that D. P. O'Connell considers such a cordon sanitaire in restricted shipping lanes, in the context of anti-submarine warfare, and found it to be lawful providing it is properly advertised.

Ronzitti was also of the opinion that during the 1982 Falkland War although the static "Maritime Exclusion Zone" the British issued around the Falkland Islands that excluded Argentinian shipping from within 200 miles of the islands was legal, but the issuing of the static "Total Exclusion Zone" (TEZ), if based on the Dönitz's Nuremberg Trial was not, because it excluded neutral as well as Argentinian shipping.

The 1982 TEZ did not raise much of a diplomatic protest, but Ronzitti points out that when Saddam Hussein declared a similar 50 mile zone around Kharg Island it was condemned in three United Nations Security Council Resolutions (552, 582, and 598).

However Ronzitti also pointed out though that some authors have suggested that if one borrows from the laws and customs of land, then attacks on neutral shipping carrying supplies which could aid an enemy's war effort (even if only economically) could be attacked, and that this is an area of the laws of war which are still in need of clarification.Naval warfare is divided into three operational areas: surface warfare, air warfare and underwater warfare. The latter may be subdivided into submarine warfare and anti-submarine warfare as well as mine warfare and mine countermeasures. Each area comprises specialized platforms and strategies used to exploit tactical advantages unique and inherent to that area.

Modern submarine warfare consists primarily of diesel and nuclear submarines using weapons (like torpedoes, missiles or nuclear weapons), as well as advanced sensing equipment, to attack other submarines, ships, or land targets. Submarines may also be used for reconnaissance and landing of special forces as well as deterrence. In some navies they may be used for task force screening. The effectiveness of submarine warfare partly depends on the anti-submarine warfare carried out in response.

4

Nuclear Weapon

A nuclear weapon is an explosive device that derives its destructive force from nuclear reactions, either fission or a combination of fission and fusion. Both reactions release vast quantities of energy from relatively small amounts of matter; a modern thermonuclear weapon weighing little more than a thousand kilograms can produce an explosion comparable to the detonation of more than a billion kilograms of conventional high explosive. Thus, even single small nuclear devices no larger than traditional bombs can devastate an entire city by blast, fire and radiation. Nuclear weapons are considered weapons of mass destruction, and their use and control has been a major focus of international relations policy since their debut.

In the history of warfare, only two nuclear weapons have been detonated offensively, both near the end of World War II. The first was detonated on the morning of 6 August 1945, when the United States dropped a uranium gun-type device code-named "Little Boy" on the Japanese city of Hiroshima. The second was detonated three days later when the United States dropped a plutonium implosion-type device code-named "Fat Man" on the city of Nagasaki, Japan. These bombings resulted in the immediate deaths of around 120,000 people (mostly civilians) from injuries sustained from the explosion and acute radiation sickness, and even more deaths from long-term effects of ionizing radiation. The use of these weapons was and remains controversial.

Since the Hiroshima and Nagasaki bombings, nuclear weapons have been detonated on over two thousand occasions for testing purposes and demonstration purposes. A few states have possessed such weapons or are suspected of seeking them. The only countries known to have detonated nuclear weapons—and that acknowledge possessing such weapons—are (chronologically) the United States, the Soviet Union (succeeded as a nuclear power by Russia), the United Kingdom, France, the People's Republic of China, India, Pakistan, and North Korea.

Israel is also widely believed to possess nuclear weapons, though it does not acknowledge having them.

HISTORY OF NUCLEAR WEAPONS

The history of nuclear weapons chronicles the development of nuclear weapons. Nuclear weapons are devices that possess enormous destructive potential derived from nuclear fission or nuclear fusion reactions. Starting with the scientific breakthroughs of the 1930s which made their development possible, and continuing through the nuclear arms race and nuclear testing of the Cold War, the issues of proliferation and possible use for terrorism still remain in the early 21st century.

The first fission weapons, also known as "atomic bombs," were developed jointly by the United States, Britain and Canada during World War II in what was called the Manhattan Project. In August 1945 two were dropped on Japan ending the Pacific War. An international team was dispatched to help work on the project. The Soviet Union started development shortly thereafter with their own atomic bomb project, and not long after that both countries developed even more powerful fusion weapons called "hydrogen bombs."

During the Cold War, the Soviet Union and United States each acquired nuclear weapons arsenals numbering in the thousands, placing many of them onto rockets which could hit targets anywhere in the world.

Currently there are at least nine countries with functional nuclear weapons. A considerable amount of international negotiating has focused on the threat of nuclear warfare and the proliferation of nuclear weapons to new nations or groups. There have been (at least) four major false alarms, the most recent in 1995, that resulted in the activation of either the US's or Russia's nuclear attack early warning protocols.

Physics and Politics in the 1930

In nuclear fission, the nucleus of a fissile atom (in this case, enriched uranium) absorbs a thermal neutron, becomes unstable, and splits into two new atoms, releasing some energy and between one and three new neutrons, which can perpetuate the process.

In the first decades of the twentieth century, physics was revolutionized with developments in the understanding of the nature of atoms. In 1898, French physicist Pierre Curie and his Polish wife Maria Sklodowska-Curie had discovered that present in pitchblende, an ore of uranium, was a substance which emitted large amounts of radioactivity, which they named radium. This raised the hopes of both scientists and lay people that the elements around us could contain tremendous amounts of unseen energy, waiting to be tapped.

Experiments by Ernest Rutherford in 1911 indicated that the vast majority of an atom's mass was contained in a very small nucleus at its core, made up of protons, surrounded by a web of whirring electrons. In 1932, James Chadwick discovered that the nucleus contained another fundamental particle, the neutron, and in the same year John Cockcroft and Ernest Walton "split the atom" for the first time, the first occasion on which an atomic nucleus of one element had been successfully changed to a different nucleus by artificial means.

In 1934 the idea of chain reaction via neutron was proposed by Leó Szilárd, who patented the idea of the atomic bomb. The patent was transferred in secret to Britain's Royal Navy in 1936. In a very real sense, Szilárd was the father of the atomic bomb academically. In 1934, French physicists Irène and Frédéric Joliot-Curie discovered that artificial radioactivity could be induced in stable elements by bombarding them with alpha particles, and in the same year Italian physicist Enrico Fermi reported similar results when bombarding uranium with neutrons.

In December 1938, the German chemists Otto Hahn and Fritz Strassmann sent a manuscript to *Naturwissenschaften* reporting they had detected the element barium after bombarding uranium with neutrons; simultaneously, they communicated these results to Lise Meitner. Meitner, and her nephew Otto Robert Frisch, correctly interpreted these results as being nuclear fission. Frisch confirmed this experimentally on 13 January 1939.

Even before it was published, Meitner's and Frisch's interpretation of the work of Hahn and Strassmann crossed the Atlantic Ocean with Niels Bohr, who was to lecture at Princeton University. Isidor Isaac Rabi and Willis Lamb, two Columbia University physicists working at Princeton, heard the news and carried it back to Columbia. Rabi said he told Fermi; Fermi gave credit to Lamb. Bohr soon thereafter went from Princeton to Columbia to see Fermi. Not finding Fermi in his office, Bohr went down to the cyclotron area and found Herbert Anderson. Bohr grabbed him by the shoulder and said: "Young man, let me explain to you about something new and exciting in physics."

It was clear to a number of scientists at Columbia that they should try to detect the energy released in the nuclear fission of uranium from neutron bombardment. On 25 January 1939, an experimental team at Columbia University conducted the first nuclear fission experiment in the United States, which was done in the basement of Pupin Hall; the members of the team were Herbert L. Anderson, Eugene T. Booth, John R. Dunning, Enrico Fermi, G. Norris Glasoe, and Francis G. Slack.

As the Nazi army marched into first Czechoslovakia in 1938, and then Poland in 1939, beginning World War II, many of Europe's top physicists had already begun to flee from the imminent conflict. Scientists on both sides of the conflict were well aware of the possibility of utilizing nuclear fission as a weapon, but at the time no one was quite sure how it could be done. In the early years of the Second World War, physicists abruptly stopped publishing on the topic of fission, an act of self-censorship to keep the opposing side from gaining any advantages.

FROM LOS ALAMOS TO HIROSHIM

Proportions of uranium-238 (blue) and uranium-235 (red) found naturally versus grades that are enriched by separating the two isotopes atom-by-atom using various methods that all require a massive investment in time and money.

By the beginning of World War II, there was concern among scientists in the Allied nations that Nazi Germany might have its own project to develop fission-based weapons. Organized research first began in Britain as part of the "Tube Alloys" project, and in the United States a small amount of funding was given for research into uranium weapons starting in 1939 with the Uranium Committee under Lyman James Briggs.

At the urging of British scientists, though, who had made crucial calculations indicating that a fission weapon could be completed within only a few years, by 1941 the project had been wrested into better bureaucratic hands, and in 1942 came under the auspices of a Military Policy Committee led by General Leslie Groves as the Manhattan Project.

Scientifically led by the American physicist Robert Oppenheimer, the project brought together the top scientific minds of the day (many exiles from Europe) with the production power of American industry for the goal of producing fission-based explosive devices before Germany could. Britain and the U.S. agreed to pool their resources and information for the project, but the other Allied power—the Soviet Union under Joseph Stalin—was not informed.

A massive industrial and scientific undertaking, the Manhattan Project involved many of the world's great physicists in the scientific and development aspects. The United States made an unprecedented investment into wartime research for the project, which was spread across more than 30 sites in the U.S. and Canada. Scientific knowledge was centralized at a secret laboratory known as Los Alamos, previously a small ranch school near Santa Fe, New Mexico.

Uranium appears in nature primarily in two isotopes: uranium-238 and uranium-235. When the nucleus of uranium-235 absorbs a neutron, it undergoes nuclear fission, splitting into two "fission products" and releasing energy and 2.5 neutrons on average. Uranium-238, on the other hand, absorbs neutrons but does not split, effectively putting a stop to any ongoing fission reaction.

It was discovered that an atomic bomb based on uranium would need to be made of almost completely pure uranium-235 (at least 80% pure), or else the presence of uranium-238 would quickly curtail the nuclear chain reaction. The team of scientists working on the Manhattan Project immediately realized that one of the largest problems they would have to solve was how to remove uranium-235 from natural uranium, which was composed of 99.3% uranium-238.

Two methods were developed during the wartime project, both of which took advantage of the fact that uranium-238 has a slightly greater atomic mass than uranium-235: electromagnetic separation and gaseous diffusion—methods which separated isotopes based on their differing weights. Another secret site was erected at rural Oak Ridge, Tennessee, for the large-scale production and purification of the rare isotope.

It was a massive investment: at the time, one of the Oak Ridge facilities (K-25) was the largest factory under one roof. The Oak Ridge site employed tens of thousands of employees at its peak, most of whom had no idea what they were working on.

Massive new physics machines were assembled at secret installations around the United States for the production of enriched uranium and plutonium. Though uranium-238 cannot be used for the initial stage of an atomic bomb, when U-238 absorbs a neutron, it transforms first into an unstable element, uranium-239, and then decays into neptunium-239, and finally the relatively stable plutonium-239, an element which does not exist in nature. Plutonium is also fissile and can be used to create a fission reaction, and after Enrico Fermi achieved the world's first sustained and controlled nuclear chain reaction in the creation of the first "atomic pile"—a primitive nuclear reactor—in a basement at the University of Chicago, massive reactors were secretly created at what is now known as Hanford Site in the state of Washington, using the Columbia River as cooling water, to transform uranium-238 into plutonium for a bomb.

For a fission weapon to operate, there must be a critical mass—the amount needed for a self-sustaining nuclear chain reaction—of fissile material bombarded with neutrons at any one time. The simplest form of nuclear weapon is a gun-type fission weapon, where a sub-critical mass of fissile material (such as uranium-235) would be shot at another sub-critical mass of fissile material. The result would be a super-critical mass which, when bombarded with neutrons, would undergo fission at a rapid rate and create the desired explosion. The weapons envisaged in 1942 were the two gun-type weapons, Little Boy (uranium) and Thin Man (plutonium), and the Fat Man plutonium implosion bomb.

In early 1943 Oppenheimer determined that two projects should proceed forwards: the "Thin Man" project (plutonium gun) and the "Fat Man" project (plutonium implosion). The plutonium gun was to receive the bulk of the research effort, as it was the project with the most uncertainty involved. It was assumed that the uranium gun-type bomb could then be adapted from it.

But in April 1944 it was found by Emilio Segrè that plutonium produced by the Hanford reactors had too high a level of background neutron radiation, and underwent spontaneous fission to a very small extent, due to the presence of impurities of the Pu-240 isotope. If such plutonium were used in a "gun assembly," the chain reaction would start in the split seconds before the critical mass was assembled, blowing the weapon apart before it would have any great effect (this is known as a fizzle).

So development of Fat Man, the implosion bomb, was given high priority. Chemical explosives were used to implode a sub-critical sphere of plutonium, thus increasing its density and making it into a critical mass. The difficulties with implosion were in the problem of making the chemical explosives deliver a perfectly uniform shock wave upon the plutonium sphere— if it were even slightly asymmetric, the weapon would fizzle (which would be expensive, messy, and not a very effective military device). This problem was circumvented by the use of hydrodynamic "lenses"—explosive materials of differing densities—which would focus the blast waves inside the imploding sphere, akin to the way in which an optical lens focuses light rays. After D-Day, General Groves had ordered a team of scientists—Project Alsos—to follow eastward-moving victorious Allied troops into Europe in order to assess the status of the German nuclear program (and to prevent the westward-moving Russians from gaining any materials or scientific manpower). It was concluded that while Nazi Germany had also had an atomic bomb program, headed by Werner Heisenberg, the government had not made a significant investment in the project, and had been nowhere near success.

Historians claim to have found a rough schematic showing a Nazi nuclear bomb. Research was conducted in the German nuclear energy project. In March 1945, a Nazi scientific team was directed by the physicist Kurt Diebner to develop a primitive nuclear device in Ohrdruf, Thuringia.

By the unconditional surrender of Germany on May 8, 1945, the Manhattan Project was still months away from a working weapon. That April, after the death of American President Franklin D. Roosevelt, former Vice-President Harry S. Truman was told about the secret wartime project for the first time. Because of the difficulties in making a working plutonium bomb, it was decided that there should be a test of the weapon, and Truman wanted to know for sure if it would work before his meeting with Joseph Stalin at an upcoming conference on the future of postwar Europe. On July 16, 1945, in the desert north of Alamogordo, New Mexico, the first nuclear test took place, code-named "Trinity," using a device nicknamed "the Gadget." The test, a plutonium implosion type device, released the equivalent of 19 kilotons of TNT, far mightier than any weapon ever used before. The news of the test's success was rushed to Truman, who used it as leverage at the upcoming Potsdam Conference, held near Berlin.

After hearing arguments from scientists and military officers over the possible uses of the weapons against Japan (though some recommended using them as "demonstrations" in unpopulated areas, most recommended using them against "built up" targets, a euphemistic term for populated cities), Truman ordered the use of the weapons on Japanese cities, hoping it would send a strong message which would end in the capitulation of the Japanese leadership and avoid a lengthy invasion of the island.

There were suggestions to drop the atomic bomb on Tokyo, the capital of Japan, but concerns about Tokyo's cultural heritage changed the plan. On May 10–11, 1945 The Target Committee at Los Alamos, led by J. Robert Oppenheimer, recommended Kyoto, Hiroshima, Yokohama, and the arsenal at Kokura as possible targets. On August 6, 1945, a uranium-based weapon, "Little Boy", was let loose on the Japanese city of Hiroshima. Three days later, a plutonium-based weapon, "Fat Man", was dropped onto the city of Nagasaki. The atomic bombs killed at least one hundred thousand Japanese outright, most of them civilians, with the heat, radiation, and blast effects.

Many tens of thousands would die later of radiation sickness and related cancers. Truman promised a "rain of ruin" if Japan did not surrender immediately, threatening to eliminate Japanese cities, one by one; Japan surrendered on August 15. Truman's threat was in fact a bluff, since the US had but one remaining uranium-gun type bomb completed.

Soviet Atomic Bomb Project

The Soviet Union was not invited to share in the new weapons developed by the United States and the other Allies. During the war, information had been pouring in from a number of volunteer spies involved with the Manhattan Project (known in Soviet cables under the code-name of *Enormoz*), and the Soviet nuclear physicist Igor Kurchatov was carefully watching the Allied weapons development. It came as no surprise to Stalin when Truman had informed him at the Potsdam conference that he had a "powerful new weapon." Truman was shocked at Stalin's lack of interest.

The Soviet spies in the U.S. project were all volunteers and none were Russians. One of the most valuable, Klaus Fuchs, was a German émigré theoretical physicist who had been a part in the early British nuclear efforts and had been part of the UK mission to Los Alamos during the war. Fuchs had been intimately involved in the development of the implosion weapon, and passed on detailed cross-sections of the "Trinity" device to his Soviet contacts. Other Los Alamos spies—none of whom knew each other—included Theodore Hall and David Greenglass. The information was kept but not acted upon, as Russia was still too busy fighting the war in Europe to devote resources to this new project.

In the years immediately after World War II, the issue of who should control atomic weapons became a major international point of contention. Many of the Los Alamos scientists who had built the bomb began to call for "international control of atomic energy," often calling for either control by transnational organizations or the purposeful distribution of weapons information to all superpowers, but due to a deep distrust of the intentions of the Soviet Union, both in postwar Europe and in general, the policy-makers of the United States worked to attempt to secure an American nuclear monopoly. A half-hearted plan for international control was proposed at the newly formed United Nations by Bernard Baruch ("The Baruch Plan"), but it was clear both to American commentators—and to the Soviets—that it was an attempt primarily to stymie Russian nuclear efforts. The Soviets vetoed the plan, effectively ending any immediate postwar negotiations on atomic energy, and made overtures towards banning the use of atomic weapons in general.

All the while, the Soviets had put their full industrial and manpower might into the development of their own atomic weapons. The initial problem for the Soviets was primarily one of resources—they had not scouted out uranium resources in the Soviet Union and the U.S. had made deals to monopolise the largest known (and high purity) reserves in the Belgian Congo. The USSR used penal labour to mine the old deposits in Czechoslovakia—now an area under their control—and searched for other domestic deposits (which were eventually found).

Two days after the bombing of Nagasaki, the U.S. government released an official technical history of the Manhattan Project, authored by Princeton physicist Henry DeWolf Smyth, known colloquially as the Smyth Report. The sanitized summary of the wartime effort focused primarily on the production facilities and scale of investment, written in part to justify the wartime expenditure to the American public.

The Soviet program, under the suspicious watch of former NKVD chief Lavrenty Beria (a participant and victor in Stalin's Great Purge of the 1930s), would use the Report as a blueprint, seeking to duplicate as much as possible the American effort. The "secret cities" used for the Soviet equivalents of Hanford and Oak Ridge literally vanished from the maps for decades to come.

At the Soviet equivalent of Los Alamos, Arzamas-16, physicist Yuli Khariton led the scientific effort to develop the weapon. Beria distrusted his scientists, however, and he distrusted the carefully collected espionage information. As such, Beria assigned multiple teams of scientists to the same task without informing each team of the other's existence. If they arrived at different conclusions, Beria would bring them together for the first time and have them debate with their newfound counterparts. Beria used the espionage information as a way to double-check the progress of his scientists, and in his effort for duplication of the American project even rejected more efficient bomb designs in favour of ones which more closely mimicked the tried-and-true "Fat Man" bomb used by the U.S. against Nagasaki.

Working under a stubborn and scientifically ignorant administrator, the Soviet scientists struggled on. On August 29, 1949, the effort brought its results, when the USSR tested its first fission bomb, dubbed "Joe-1" by the U.S., years ahead of American predictions. The news of the first Soviet bomb was announced to the world first by the United States, which had detected the nuclear fallout it generated from its test site in Kazakhstan.

The loss of the American monopoly on nuclear weapons marked the first tit-for-tat of the nuclear arms race. The response in the U.S. was one of apprehension, fear, and scapegoating, which would lead eventually into the Red-baiting tactics of McCarthyism. Yet recent information from unclassified Venona intercepts and the opening of the KGB archives after the fall of the Soviet Union show that the USSR had useful spies that helped their program, although none were identified by the McCarthy. Before this, though, President Truman would announce his decision to begin a crash program to develop a far more powerful weapon than those which were used against Japan: the hydrogen bomb.

THE FIRST THERMONUCLEAR WEAPONS

Hungarian physicist Edward Teller toiled for years trying to discover a way to make a fusion bomb. The notion of using a fission weapon to ignite a process of nuclear fusion can be dated back to 1942. At the first major theoretical conference on the development of an atomic bomb hosted by J. Robert Oppenheimer at the University of California, Berkeley, participant Edward Teller directed the majority of the discussion towards Enrico Fermi's idea of a "Super" bomb which would utilize the same reactions which powered the Sun itself.

It was thought at the time that a fission weapon would be quite simple to develop and that perhaps work on a hydrogen bomb would be possible to complete before the end of the Second World War. However, in reality the problem of a "regular" atomic bomb was large enough to preoccupy the scientists for the next few years, much less the more speculative "Super." Only Teller continued working on the project—against the will of project leaders Oppenheimer and Hans Bethe.

After the atomic bombings of Japan, many scientists at Los Alamos rebelled against the notion of creating a weapon thousands of times more powerful than the first atomic bombs. For the scientists the question was in part technical—the weapon design was still quite uncertain and unworkable—and in part moral: such a weapon, they argued, could only be used against large civilian populations, and could thus only be used as a weapon of genocide.

Many scientists, such as Bethe, urged that the United States should not develop such weapons and set an example towards the Soviet Union. Promoters of the weapon, including Teller, Ernest Lawrence, and Luis Alvarez, argued that such a development was inevitable, and to deny such protection to the people of the United States—especially when the Soviet Union was likely to create such a weapon themselves—was itself an immoral and unwise act.

Oppenheimer, who was now head of the General Advisory Committee of the successor to the Manhattan Project, the Atomic Energy Commission, presided over a recommendation against the development of the weapon. The reasons were in part because the success of the technology seemed limited at the time (and not worth the investment of resources to confirm whether this was so), and because Oppenheimer believed that the atomic forces of the United States would be more effective if they consisted of many large fission weapons (of which multiple bombs could be dropped on the same targets) rather than the large and unwieldy predictions of massive super bombs, for which there were a relatively limited amounts of targets of the size to warrant such a development. Furthermore, were such weapons developed by both the U.S. and the USSR, they would be more effectively used against the U.S. than by it, as the U.S. had far more regions of dense industrial and civilian activity which would serve as ideal targets for the large weapons than the Soviet Union did. In the end, President Truman made the final decision, looking for a proper response to the first Soviet atomic bomb test in 1949. On January 31, 1950, Truman announced a crash program to develop the hydrogen (fusion) bomb. At this point, however, the exact mechanism was still not known: the "classical" hydrogen bomb, whereby the *heat* of the fission bomb would be used to ignite the fusion material, seemed highly unworkable. However, an insight by Los Alamos mathematician Stanislaw Ulam showed that the fission bomb and the fusion fuel could be in separate parts of the bomb, and that *radiation* of the fission bomb could first work in a way to *compress* the fusion material before igniting it.

Teller pushed the notion further, and used the results of the boosted-fission "George" test (a boosted-fission device using a small amount of fusion fuel to boost the yield of a fission bomb) to confirm the fusion of heavy hydrogen elements before preparing for their first true multi-stage, Teller-Ulam hydrogen bomb test. Many scientists initially against the weapon, such as Oppenheimer and Bethe, changed their previous opinions, seeing the development as being unstoppable.

The first fusion bomb was tested by the United States in *Operation Ivy* on November 1, 1952, on Elugelab Island in the Enewetak (or Eniwetok) Atoll of the Marshall Islands, code-named "Mike". "Mike" used liquid deuterium as its fusion fuel and a large fission weapon as its trigger. The device was a prototype design and not a deliverable weapon: standing over 20 ft (6 m) high and weighing at least 140,000 lb (64 t) (its refrigeration equipment added an additional 24,000 lb as well), it could not have been dropped from even the largest planes.

Its explosion yielded 10.4 megatons of energy—over 450 times the power of the bomb dropped onto Nagasaki— and obliterated Elugelab, leaving an underwater crater 6240 ft (1.9 km) wide and 164 ft (50 m) deep where the island had once been. Truman had initially tried to create a media blackout about the test—hoping it would not become an issue in the upcoming presidential election—but on January 7, 1953, Truman announced the development of the hydrogen bomb to the world as hints and speculations of it were already beginning to emerge in the press.

The basics of the Teller-Ulam design for a hydrogen bomb: a fission bomb uses radiation to compress and heat a separate section of fusion fuel.

Not to be outdone, the Soviet Union exploded its first thermonuclear device, designed by the physicist Andrei Sakharov, on August 12, 1953, labeled "Joe-4" by the West. This created concern within the U.S. government and military, because, unlike "Mike," the Soviet device was a deliverable weapon, which the U.S. did not yet have. This first device though was arguably not a "true" hydrogen bomb, and could only reach explosive yields in the hundreds of kilotons (never reaching the megaton range of a "staged" weapon). Still, it was a powerful propaganda tool for the Soviet Union, and the technical differences were fairly oblique to the American public and politicians.

Following the "Mike" blast by less than a year, "Joe-4" seemed to validate claims that the bombs were inevitable and vindicate those who had supported the development of the fusion program. Coming during the height of McCarthyism, the effect was most pronounced by the security hearings in early 1954 which revoked former Los Alamos director Robert Oppenheimer of his security clearance, on the grounds that he was unreliable, had not supported the American hydrogen bomb program, and had made long-standing, left-wing ties in the 1930s. Edward Teller participated in the hearing as the only major scientist to testify against Oppenheimer, a role which resulted in his virtual expulsion from the physics community.

On February 28, 1954, the U.S. detonated its first deliverable thermonuclear weapon (which used isotopes of lithium as its fusion fuel), known as the "Shrimp" device of the "Castle Bravo" test, at Bikini Atoll, Marshall Islands. The device yielded 15 megatons of energy, over twice its expected yield, and became the worst radiological disaster in U.S. history. The combination of the unexpectedly large blast and poor weather conditions caused a cloud of radioactive nuclear fallout to contaminate over 7,000 square miles, including Marshall Island natives and the crew of a Japanese fishing boat, as a snow-like mist. The contaminated islands were evacuated (and are still uninhabitable), but the natives received enough of a radioactive dose that they suffered far elevated levels of cancer and birth defects in the years to come. The crew of the Japanese fishing boat, *Lucky Dragon 5,* returned to port suffering from radiation sickness and skin burns. Their cargo, many tons of contaminated fish, managed to enter into the market before the cause of their illness was determined. When a crew member died from the sickness and the full results of the contamination were made public by the U.S., Japanese concerns were reignited about the hazards of radiation and resulted in a boycott on eating fish (a main staple of the island country) for some weeks.

Fallout from a large nuclear exchange would potentially blanket a country—perhaps even the whole world—with radioactive fission products. Note: This image depicts the aftermath of a retaliatory strike, predicated on attacks on US missile bases, using ICBM trajectories only

The hydrogen bomb age had a profound effect on the thoughts of nuclear war in the popular and military mind. With only fission bombs, nuclear war could be considered something which could easily be "limited." Dropped by planes and only able to destroy the most built up areas of major cities, it was possible to consider fission bombs simply a technological extension of previous wartime bombing (such as the extensive firebombing which took place against Japan and Germany during World War II), and claims that such weapons could lead to worldwide death or harm were easily brushed aside as grave exaggeration.

Even the decades before the development of fission weapons there had been speculation about the possibility for human beings to end all life on the planet by either accident or purposeful maliciousness, but technology had never allowed for such a capacity. The far greater power of hydrogen bombs made this seem ever closer. The "Castle Bravo" incident itself raised a number of questions about the survivability of a nuclear war. Government scientists in both the U.S. and the USSR had insisted that fusion weapons, unlike fission weapons, were "cleaner" as fusion reactions did not result in the dangerously radioactive by-products as did fission reactions. While technically true, this hid a more gruesome point: the last stage of a multi-staged hydrogen bomb often used the neutrons produced by the fusion reactions to induce fissioning in a jacket of natural uranium, and provided around half of the yield of the device itself.

This fission stage made fusion weapons considerably more "dirty" than they were made out to be, a fact made evident by the towering cloud of deadly fallout which followed the "Bravo" test. When the Soviet Union tested its first megaton device in 1955, the possibility of a limited nuclear war seemed even more remote in the public and political mind: even if a city or country was not the direct target of a nuclear attack, the clouds of fallout and harmful fission products would disperse along with normal weather patterns and embed themselves in the soil and water of non-targeted areas of the planet as well.

Speculation began to look towards what would happen as the fallout and dust created by a full-scale nuclear exchange would affect the world as a whole, rather than just the cities and countries which had been directly involved. In this way, the fate of the world was now tied to the fate of the bomb-wielding superpowers.

Deterrence and Brinkmanship

Throughout the 1950s and the early 1960s a number of trends were enacted between the U.S. and the USSR as they both endeavored in a tit-for-tat approach to disallow the other power from acquiring nuclear supremacy. This took form in a number of ways, both technologically and politically, and had massive political and cultural effects during the Cold War.

The first atomic bombs dropped on Hiroshima and Nagasaki were large, custom-made devices, requiring highly trained personnel for their arming and deployment. They could be dropped only from the largest bomber planes—at the time the B-29 Superfortress—and each plane could only hold a single bomb in its hold. The first hydrogen bombs were similarly massive and complicated. This ratio of one plane to one bomb was still fairly impressive in comparison with conventional, non-nuclear weapons, but against other nuclear-armed countries it was considered to be a grave danger. In the immediate postwar years, the U.S. expended much effort on making the bombs "G.I.-proof"—capable of being used and deployed by members of the U.S. Army, rather than Nobel Prize–winning scientists, and in the

1950s a program of nuclear testing was undertaken in order to improve the nuclear arsenal.

Starting in 1951, the Nevada Test Site (in the Nevada desert) became the primary location for all U.S. nuclear testing (in the USSR, Semipalatinsk Test Site in Kazakhstan served a similar role). Tests were divided into two primary categories: "weapons related" (verifying that a new weapon worked or looking at exactly how it worked) and "weapons effects" (looking at how weapons behaved under various conditions or how structures behaved when subjected to weapons).

In the beginning, almost all nuclear tests were either "atmospheric" (conducted above ground, in the atmosphere) or "underwater" (such as some of the tests done in the Marshall Islands). Testing was used as a sign of both national and technological strength, but also raised questions about the safety of the tests, which released nuclear fallout into the atmosphere (most dramatically with the Castle Bravo test in 1954, but in more limited amounts with almost all atmospheric nuclear testing).

Because testing was seen as a sign of technological development (the ability to design usable weapons without some form of testing was considered dubious), halts on testing were often called for as stand-ins for halts in the nuclear arms race itself, and many prominent scientists and statesmen lobbied for a ban on nuclear testing. In 1958, the U.S., USSR, and the United Kingdom (a new nuclear power) declared a temporary testing moratorium for both political and health reasons, but by 1961 the Soviet Union had broken the moratorium and both the USSR and the U.S. began testing with great frequency.

As a show of political strength, the Soviet Union tested the largest-ever nuclear weapon in October 1961, the massive Tsar Bomba, which was tested in a reduced state with a yield of around 50 megatons—in its full state it was estimated to have been around 100 Mt. The weapon was largely impractical for actual military use, but was hot enough to induce third-degree burns at a distance of 62 mi (100 km) away. In its full, "dirty" design, it would have increased the amount of worldwide fallout since 1945 by 25%.

In 1963, all nuclear and many non-nuclear states signed the Limited Test Ban Treaty, pledging to refrain from testing nuclear weapons in the atmosphere, underwater, or in outer space. The treaty permitted underground tests. Most tests were considerably more modest, and worked for direct technical purposes as well as their potential political overtones. Weapons improvements took on two primary forms. One was an increase in efficiency and power, and within only a few years fission bombs were being developed which were many times more powerful than the ones created during World War II. The other was a program of miniaturization, reducing the size of the nuclear weapons themselves.

Smaller bombs meant that bombers could carry more of them, and thus become even more of a threat against even the most rigorous air defenses, and they could also be used in conjunction with the development in rocketry during the 1950s and 1960s. U.S. rocket efforts had received a large boost in the postwar years, largely from the acquiring of engineers who had worked on the Nazi rocketry program during the war, such as Wernher von Braun, who had been involved in the design and manufacture of the V-2 rockets which were launched across the English Channel. An American program, Project Paperclip, had endeavored to move scientists of this sort into American hands (and kept out of Soviet hands) and put them to work on projects for the U.S.

Weapons Improvement

The first nuclear-tipped rockets, such as the MGR-1 Honest John, first deployed by the U.S. in 1953, were surface-to-surface missiles with relatively short ranges (around 15 mi/25 km maximum) with yields around twice the size of the first fission weapons. The limited range of these weapons meant that they could only be used in certain types of potential military situations—the U.S. rocket weapons could not, for example, threaten the city of Moscow with the threat of an immediate strike, and could only be used as "tactical" weapons (that is, for small-scale military situations).

For "strategic" weapons—weapons which would serve to threaten an entire country—for the time being, only long-range bombers capable of penetrating deep into enemy territory would work. In the U.S. this resulted in the creation of the Strategic Air

Command in 1946, a system of bombers headed by General Curtis LeMay (who had previously presided over the firebombing of Japan during WWII), which kept a number of nuclear-armed planes in the sky at all times, ready to receive orders to attack Moscow whenever commanded.

These technological possibilities enabled nuclear strategy to develop a logic considerably different than previous military thinking had allowed. Because the threat of nuclear warfare was so awful, it was first thought that it might make any war of the future impossible. President Dwight D. Eisenhower's doctrine of "massive retaliation" in the early years of the Cold War was a message to the USSR, saying that if the Red Army attempted to invade the parts of Europe not given to the Eastern bloc during the Potsdam Conference (such as West Germany), nuclear weapons would be used against the Soviet troops and potentially the Soviet leaders.

With the development of more rapid-response technologies (such as rockets and long-range bombers), this policy began to shift. If the Soviet Union also had nuclear weapons and a policy of "massive retaliation" was carried out, it was reasoned, then any Soviet forces not killed in the initial attack, or launched while the attack was ongoing, would be able to serve their own form of nuclear "retaliation" against the U.S. Recognizing this to be an undesirable outcome, military officers and game theorists at the RAND think tank developed a nuclear warfare strategy that would eventually become known as Mutually Assured Destruction (MAD).

MAD divided potential nuclear war into two stages: first strike and second strike. A first strike would be the first use of nuclear weapons by one nuclear-equipped nation against another nuclear-equipped nation. If the attacking nation did not prevent the attacked nation from a nuclear response, then a second strike could be deployed against the attacking nation. In this situation, whether the U.S. first attacked the USSR or the USSR first attacked the U.S., the end result would be that both nations would be damaged perhaps to the point of utter social collapse.

According to game theory, because starting a nuclear war would be suicidal, no logical country would willfully enter into a nuclear war. However, if a country were capable of launching a first strike which would utterly destroy the ability of the attacked country to respond in kind, then the balance of power would be disturbed and nuclear war could then be safely undertaken.

MAD played on two seemingly opposed modes of thought: cold logic and emotional fear. The phrase by which MAD was often known, "nuclear deterrence", was translated as "dissuasion" by the French and "terrorization" by the Russians. This apparent paradox of nuclear war was summed up by British Prime Minister Winston Churchill as "the worse things get, the better they are"—the greater the threat of mutual destruction, the safer the world would be.

This philosophy made a number of technological and political demands on participating nations. For one thing, it said that it should always be assumed that an enemy nation may be trying to acquire "first strike capability," something which must always be avoided. In American politics this translated into demands to avoid "missile gaps" and "bomber gaps" where the Soviet Union could potentially "out shoot" American efforts (most of these supposed "gaps" proved to be political figments, but this hardly mattered at the time). It also encouraged the production of thousands of nuclear weapons by both the U.S. and the USSR, far more than would be needed to simply destroy the major civilian and military infrastructures of the opposing country.

These policies and strategies were satirized in the 1964 Stanley Kubrick film Dr. Strangelove, in which the Soviets, unable to keep up with the US's first strike capability, instead plan for MAD by building a Doomsday Machine, and thus, after a (literally) mad US General orders a nuclear attack on the USSR, the end of the world is brought about.

With early warning systems, it was thought that the strikes of nuclear war would come from dark rooms filled with computers, not the battlefield of the wars of old. The policy also encouraged the development of the first early warning systems. Conventional war, even at its fastest, was fought over time scales of days and weeks. With long-range bombers, the time from the start of an attack to its conclusion was reduced to mere hours. With rockets, it could be reduced to minutes. It was reasoned that conventional command and control systems could not be expected to adequately respond to a nuclear attack, and so great lengths were taken to develop the first computers which could look for enemy attacks and direct rapid responses.

In the U.S., massive funding was poured into the development of SAGE, a system which would track and intercept enemy bomber aircraft using information from remote radar stations, and was the first computer system to feature real-time processing, multiplexing, and display devices—the first "general" computing machine, and a direct predecessor of modern computers.

Anti-nuclear

Bombers and short-range rockets were not reliable: planes could be shot down, and earlier nuclear missiles could cover only a limited range— for example, the first Soviet rockets' range limited them to targets in Europe. However, by the 1960s, both the United States and the Soviet Union had developed intercontinental ballistic missiles, which could be launched from extremely remote areas far away from their target; and submarine-launched ballistic missiles, which had less range but could be launched from submarines very close to the target without any radar warning. This made any national protection from nuclear missiles increasingly impractical.

The military realities made for a precarious diplomatic situation. The international politics of brinkmanship led leaders to exclaim their willingness to participate in a nuclear war rather than concede any advantage to their opponents, feeding public fears that their generation may be the last. Civil defence programs undertaken by both superpowers, exemplified by the construction of fallout shelters and urging civilians about the "survivability" of nuclear war, did little to ease public concerns.

The climax of brinksmanship came in early 1962, when an American U-2 spy plane photographed a series of launch sites for medium-range ballistic missiles being constructed on the island of Cuba, just off the coast of the southern United States, beginning what became known as the Cuban Missile Crisis. The U.S. administration of John F. Kennedy concluded that the Soviet Union, then led by Nikita Khrushchev, was planning to station

Russian nuclear missiles on the island, which was under the control of Communist Fidel Castro. On October 22, Kennedy announced the discoveries in a televised address, and declared that a naval quarantine would be put around Cuba to turn back any Soviet nuclear shipments, and warned that the military was prepared "for any eventualities." The missiles would have a range of 2,400 miles (4,000 km), and allow the Soviet Union to easily destroy many major American cities on the Eastern Seaboard if a nuclear war were started.

The leaders of the two superpowers stood nose to nose, seemingly poised over the beginnings of a third world war. Khrushchev's ambitions for putting the weapons on the island were motivated in part by the fact that the U.S. had stationed similar weapons in Britain, Italy, and nearby Turkey, and had previously attempted to sponsor an invasion of Cuba the year before in the failed Bay of Pigs Invasion. On October 26, an offer was sent from Khrushchev to Kennedy offering to withdraw all missiles if Kennedy would commit to a policy of no future invasions of Cuba. Khrushchev worded the threat of assured destruction eloquently:

"You and I should not now pull on the ends of the rope in which you have tied a knot of war, because the harder you and I pull, the tighter the knot will become. And a time may come when this knot is tied so tight that the person who tied it is no longer capable of untying it, and then the knot will have to be cut. What that would mean I need not explain to you, because you yourself understand perfectly what dreaded forces our two countries possess."

A day later, however, the Russians put forward another offer, this time demanding that the U.S. remove its missiles from Turkey before any missiles would be withdrawn from Cuba. On the same day, a U-2 plane was shot down over Cuba and another was almost intercepted over Russia, and Soviet merchant ships were nearing the quarantine zone. Kennedy responded by accepting the first deal publicly, and sending his brother Robert to the Soviet embassy to accept the second deal in private. On October 28, the Soviet ships stopped at the quarantine line and, after some hesitation, turned back towards the Soviet Union. Khrushchev announced that he had ordered the removal of all missiles in Cuba, and U.S. Secretary of State Dean Rusk was moved to comment, "We went eyeball to eyeball, and the other fellow just blinked."

The Crisis was later seen as the closest the U.S. and the USSR ever came to nuclear war and had been narrowly averted by last-minute compromise by both superpowers. Fears of communication difficulties led to the installment of the first hotline, a direct link between the superpowers which would allow them to more easily discuss future military activities and political maneuverings. It had been made clear that with their missiles, bombers, submarines, and computerized firing systems, the escalation of any situation to Armageddon could be done far more easily than anybody desired.

After stepping so close to the brink, both the U.S. and the USSR worked to reduce their nuclear tensions in the years immediately following. The most immediate culmination of this work was the signing of the Partial Test Ban Treaty in 1963, in which the U.S. and USSR agreed to no longer test nuclear weapons in the atmosphere, underwater, or in outer space. Testing underground continued, allowing for further weapons development, but the worldwide fallout risks were purposefully reduced, and the era of using massive nuclear tests as a form of saber-rattling ended.

In December 1979, NATO decided to deploy cruise and Pershing II missiles in Western Europe in response to Soviet deployment of intermediate range mobile missiles, and in the early 1980s, a "dangerous Soviet-US nuclear confrontation" arose. In New York on June 12, 1982, one million people gathered to protest nuclear weapons, and to support the second UN Special Session on Disarmament. As the nuclear abolitionist movement grew, there were many protests at the Nevada Test Site. For example, on February 6, 1987, nearly 2,000 demonstrators, including six members of Congress, protested against nuclear weapons testing and more than 400 people were arrested. Four of the significant groups organizing this renewal of anti-nuclear activism were Greenpeace, The American Peace Test, The Western Shoshone, and Nevada Desert Experience.

Initial Proliferation

The United Kingdom had been an integral part of the Manhattan Project following the Quebec Agreement in 1943. The passing of the McMahon Act by the United States in 1946 unilaterally broke this partnership and prevented the passage of any further information to the United Kingdom. The British Government under Clement Attlee determined that it would be essential for there to be a British Bomb. Because of the involvement in the Manhattan Project Britain had extensive knowledge in some areas, but not in others.

An improved version of 'Fat Man' was developed, and on 26th February 1952, Prime Minister Winston Churchill announced that the United Kingdom also had an atomic bomb and a successful test took place on the 3rd October 1952. At first these were free-fall bombs and then there was a missile, Blue Steel, and a later-canceled MRBM, Blue Streak. Anglo-American cooperation on Nuclear weapons was restored by the 1958 US-UK Mutual Defence Agreement. As a result of this and the Polaris Sales Agreement, the United Kingdom has bought United States designs for submarine missiles and fitted its own warheads. It retains full independent control over the use of the missiles. It no longer possesses any free-fall bombs.

France had been heavily involved in nuclear research before World War II through the work of the Joliot-Curies. This was discontinued after the war because of the instability of the Fourth Republic and the lack of finance available. However, in the 1950s a civil nuclear research program was started, a byproduct of which would be plutonium.

In 1956 a secret Committee for the Military Applications of Atomic Energy was formed and a development program for delivery vehicles started. With the return of Charles de Gaulle to the presidency of France in 1958 the final decisions to build a bomb were taken, and a successful test took place in 1960. Since then France has developed and maintained its own nuclear deterrent.

In 1951 China and the Soviet Union signed an agreement whereby China would supply uranium ore in exchange for technical assistance in producing nuclear weapons. In 1953 China had established a research program under the guise of civilian nuclear energy.

Throughout the 1950s the Soviet Union provided large amounts of equipment, but as the relations between the two countries worsened, the amount of assistance was reduced, and in 1959 the donation of a bomb for copying purposes was refused. Despite this, rapid progress was made with the test of an atomic bomb on the 16th October 1964 at Lop Nur, a nuclear missile on 25th October 1966, and of a hydrogen bomb on the 14th June 1967.

Nuclear warheads were produced from 1968 and thermonuclear warheads from 1974. It is also thought that Chinese warheads have been successfully miniaturised from 2200 kg to 700 kg through the use of designs obtained by espionage from the United States. The current number of weapons is unknown owing to strict secrecy, but it is thought that up to 2000 warheads may have been produced, though far fewer may be available for use. China is the only nuclear weapons state to have guaranteed the non-first use of nuclear weapons.

COLD WAR

After World War II, the balance of power between the Eastern and Western blocs, resulting in the fear of global destruction, prevented the further military use of atomic bombs. This fear was even a central part of Cold War strategy, referred to as the doctrine of Mutually Assured Destruction ("MAD" for short). So important was this balance to international political stability that a treaty, the Anti-Ballistic Missile Treaty (or ABM treaty), was signed by the U.S. and the USSR in 1972 to curtail the development of defenses against nuclear weapons and the ballistic missiles which carry them. This doctrine resulted in a large increase in the number of nuclear weapons, as each side sought to ensure it possessed the firepower to destroy the opposition in all possible scenarios and against all perceived threats.

Early delivery systems for nuclear devices were primarily bombers like the United States B-29 Superfortress and Convair B-36, and later the B-52 Stratofortress. Ballistic missile systems, based on Wernher von Braun's World War II designs (specifically the

V2 rocket), were developed by both United States and Soviet Union teams (in the case of the U.S., effort was directed by the German scientists and engineers although the Soviet Union also made extensive use of captured German scientists, engineers, and technical data).

These systems, after testing, were used to launch satellites, such as Sputnik, and to propel the Space Race, but they were primarily developed to create the capability of Intercontinental Ballistic Missiles (ICBMs) with which nuclear powers could deliver that destructive force anywhere on the globe. These systems continued to be developed throughout the Cold War, although plans and treaties, beginning with the Strategic Arms Limitation Treaty (SALT I), restricted deployment of these systems until, after the fall of the Soviet Union, system development essentially halted, and many weapons were disabled and destroyed.

There have been a number of potential nuclear disasters. Following air accidents U.S. nuclear weapons have been lost near Atlantic City, New Jersey (1957); Savannah, Georgia (1958); Goldsboro, North Carolina (1961); off the coast of Okinawa (1965); in the sea near Palomares, Spain (1966); and near Thule, Greenland (1968). Most of the lost weapons were recovered, the Spanish device after three months' effort by the DSV Alvin and DSV Aluminaut.

The Soviet Union was less forthcoming about such incidents, but the environmental group Greenpeace believes that there are around forty non-U.S. nuclear devices that have been lost and not recovered, compared to eleven lost by America, mostly in submarine disasters. The U.S. has tried to recover Soviet devices, notably in the 1974 Operation Jennifer using the specialist salvage vessel *Hughes Glomar Explorer*.

On January 27, 1967, more than 60 nations signed the Outer Space Treaty, banning nuclear weapons in space. The end of the Cold War failed to end the threat of nuclear weapon use, although global fears of nuclear war reduced substantially. In a major move of symbolic de-escalation, Boris Yeltsin, on January 26, 1992, announced that Russia planned to stop targeting United States cities with nuclear weapons.

Second Nuclear Age

Although it had started before the end of the Cold War, the *second nuclear age*-proliferation of nuclear weapons among lesser powers and for reasons other than the American-Soviet rivalry-really began with the end of the Cold War.

India's first atomic-test explosion was in 1974 with Smiling Buddha, which it described as a "peaceful nuclear explosion". India tested fission and perhaps fusion devices in 1998, and Pakistan successfully tested fission devices that same year, raising concerns that they would use nuclear weapons on each other. All of the former Soviet bloc countries with nuclear weapons (Belarus, Ukraine, and Kazakhstan) returned their warheads to Russia by 1996. In January 2004, Pakistani metallurgist and weapons scientist Abdul Qadeer Khan confessed to having been a part of an international proliferation network of materials, knowledge, and machines from Pakistan to Libya, Iran, and North Korea.

South Africa also had an active program to develop uranium-based nuclear weapons, but dismantled its nuclear weapon program in the 1990s. It is not believed that it actually tested such a weapon though it later claimed to have constructed several crude devices which it eventually dismantled. In the late 1970s American spy satellites detected a "brief, intense, double flash of light near the southern tip of Africa." Known as the Vela Incident, it was speculated to have been a South African or possibly Israeli nuclear weapons test, though some feel that it may have been caused by natural events. Israel is widely believed to possess an arsenal of potentially up to several hundred nuclear warheads, but this has never been officially confirmed or denied (though the existence of their Dimona nuclear facility were confirmed by Mordechai Vanunu in 1986).

North Korea announced in 2003 that it also had several nuclear explosives though it has not been confirmed and the validity of this has been a subject of scrutiny amongst weapons experts. The first detonation of a nuclear weapon by the Democratic People's Republic of Korea was the 2006 North Korean nuclear test, conducted on October 9, 2006. On the 25th of May 2009 North Korea continued nuclear testing, violating United Nations Security Council Resolution 1718.

In Iran, Ayatollah Ali Khamenei issued a fatwa forbidding the production, stockpiling and use of nuclear weapons on August 9, 2005. The full text of the fatwa was released in an official statement at the meeting of the International Atomic Energy Agency (IAEA) in Vienna. Despite this, however, there is mounting concern in many nations about Iran's refusal to halt its nuclear power program, which many (including some members of the US Government) fear is a cover for weapons development.

TYPES OF NUCLEAR WEAPONS

There are two basic types of nuclear weapon. The first type produces its explosive energy through nuclear fission reactions alone. Such fission weapons are commonly referred to as atomic bombs or atom bombs (abbreviated as A-bombs), though their energy comes specifically from the nucleus of the atom. In fission weapons, a mass of fissile material (enriched uranium or plutonium) is assembled into a supercritical mass—the amount of material needed to start an exponentially growing nuclear chain reaction—either by shooting one piece of sub-critical material into another (the "gun" method), or by compressing a sub-critical sphere of material using chemical explosives to many times its original density (the "implosion" method). The latter approach is considered more sophisticated than the former, and only the latter approach can be used if plutonium is the fissile material.

A major challenge in all nuclear weapon designs is to ensure that a significant fraction of the fuel is consumed before the weapon destroys itself. The amount of energy released by fission bombs can range between the equivalent of less than a ton of TNT upwards to around 500,000 tons (500 kilotons) of TNT.

The second basic type of nuclear weapon produces a large amount of its energy through nuclear fusion reactions. Such fusion weapons are generally referred to as thermonuclear weapons or more colloquially as hydrogen bombs (abbreviated as H-bombs), as they rely on fusion reactions between isotopes of hydrogen (deuterium and tritium). However, all such weapons derive a significant portion – and sometimes a majority – of their energy from fission (including fission induced by neutrons from fusion reactions). Unlike fission weapons, there are no inherent limits on the energy released by thermonuclear weapons. Only six countries—United States, Russia, United Kingdom, People's Republic of China, France and India—have conducted thermonuclear weapon tests. (Whether India has detonated a "true," multi-staged thermonuclear weapon is controversial.)

Thermonuclear bombs work by using the energy of a fission bomb in order to compress and heat fusion fuel. In the Teller-Ulam design, which accounts for all multi-megaton yield hydrogen bombs, this is accomplished by placing a fission bomb and fusion fuel (tritium, deuterium, or lithium deuteride) in proximity within a special, radiation-reflecting container. When the fission bomb is detonated, gamma and X-rays emitted first compress the fusion fuel, then heat it to thermonuclear temperatures. The ensuing fusion reaction creates enormous numbers of high-speed neutrons, which then can induce fission in materials which normally are not prone to it, such as depleted uranium. Each of these components is known as a "stage," with the fission bomb as the "primary" and the fusion capsule as the "secondary." In large hydrogen bombs, about half of the yield, and much of the resulting nuclear fallout, comes from the final fissioning of depleted uranium.

By chaining together numerous stages with increasing amounts of fusion fuel, thermonuclear weapons can be made to an almost arbitrary yield; the largest ever detonated (the Tsar Bomba of the USSR) released an energy equivalent to over 50 million tons (50 megatons) of TNT. Most thermonuclear weapons are considerably smaller than this, due for instance to practical constraints in fitting them into the space and weight requirements of missile warheads. There are other types of nuclear weapons as well. For example, a boosted fission weapon is a fission bomb which increases its explosive yield through a small amount of fusion reactions, but it is not a fusion bomb. In the boosted bomb, the neutrons produced by the fusion reactions serve primarily to increase the efficiency of the fission bomb. Some weapons are designed for special purposes; a neutron bomb is a thermonuclear weapon that yields a relatively small explosion but a relatively large amount of neutron radiation; such a device could theoretically be used to cause massive casualties while leaving infrastructure mostly intact and creating a minimal amount of fallout.

The detonation of a nuclear weapon is accompanied by a blast of neutron radiation. Surrounding a nuclear weapon with suitable materials (such as cobalt or gold) creates a weapon known as a salted bomb. This device can produce exceptionally large quantities of radioactive contamination. Most variety in nuclear weapon design is in different yields of nuclear weapons for different types of purposes, and in manipulating design elements to attempt to make weapons extremely small.

NUCLEAR STRATEGY

The United States' Peacekeeper missile was a MIRVed delivery system. Each missile could contain up to ten nuclear warheads (shown in red), each of which could be aimed at a different target. These were developed to make missile defence very difficult for an enemy country.

Nuclear warfare strategy is a way for either fighting or avoiding a nuclear war. The policy of trying to ward off a potential attack by a nuclear weapon from another country by threatening nuclear retaliation is known as the strategy of nuclear deterrence. The goal in deterrence is to always maintain a second strike status (the ability of a country to respond to a nuclear attack with one of its own) and potentially to strive for first strike status (the ability to completely destroy an enemy's nuclear forces before they could retaliate). During the Cold War, policy and military theorists in nuclear-enabled countries worked out models of what sorts of policies could prevent one from ever being attacked by a nuclear weapon.

Different forms of nuclear weapons delivery allow for different types of nuclear strategy, primarily by making it difficult to defend against them and difficult to launch a pre-emptive strike against them. Sometimes this has meant keeping the weapon locations hidden, such as putting it on submarines or train cars whose locations are very hard for an enemy to track, and other times this means burying them in hardened bunkers.

Other responses have included attempts to make it seem likely that the country could survive a nuclear attack, by using missile defence (to destroy the missiles before they land) or by means of civil defence (using early warning systems to evacuate citizens to a safe area before an attack). Note that weapons which are designed to threaten large populations or to generally deter attacks are known as strategic weapons. Weapons which are designed to actually be used on a battlefield in military situations are known as tactical weapons.

There are critics of the very idea of nuclear strategy for waging nuclear war who have suggested that a nuclear war between two nuclear powers would result in mutual annihilation. From this point of view, the significance of nuclear weapons is purely to deter war because any nuclear war would immediately escalate out of mutual distrust and fear, resulting in mutually assured destruction. This threat of national, if not global, destruction has been a strong motivation for anti-nuclear weapons activism.

Critics from the peace movement and within the military establishment have questioned the usefulness of such weapons in the current military climate. The use of (or threat of use of) such weapons would generally be contrary to the rules of international law applicable in armed conflict, according to an advisory opinion issued by the International Court of Justice in 1996.

Perhaps the most controversial idea in nuclear strategy is that nuclear proliferation would be desirable. This view argues that, unlike conventional weapons, nuclear weapons successfully deter all-out war between states, and they are said to have done this during the Cold War between the U.S. and the Soviet Union. Political scientist Kenneth Waltz is the most prominent advocate of this argument.

It has been claimed that the threat of potentially suicidal terrorists possessing nuclear weapons (a form of nuclear terrorism) complicates the decision process. Mutually assured destruction may not be effective against an enemy who expects to die in a confrontation, as they may feel they will be rewarded in a religious afterlife as martyrs and would not therefore be deterred by a sense of self-preservation. Further, if the initial act is from rogue groups of individuals instead of a nation, there is no fixed nation or fixed military targets to retaliate against. It has been argued, especially after the September 11, 2001 attacks, that this complication is the sign of the next age of nuclear strategy, distinct from the relative stability of the Cold War.

Weapons Delivery

The first nuclear weapons were gravity bombs, such as this "Fat Man" weapon dropped on Nagasaki, Japan. They were very large and could only be delivered by heavy bomber aircraft Nuclear weapons delivery—the technology and systems used to bring a nuclear weapon to its target—is an important aspect of nuclear weapons relating both to nuclear weapon design and nuclear strategy. Additionally, developing and maintaining delivery options is among the most resource-intensive aspects of nuclear weapons: according to one estimate, deployment of nuclear weapons accounted for 57% of the total financial resources spent by the United States in relation to nuclear weapons since 1940.

Historically the first method of delivery, and the method used in the two nuclear weapons actually used in warfare, is as a gravity bomb, dropped from bomber aircraft. This method is usually the first developed by countries as it does not place many restrictions on the size of the weapon, and *weapon miniaturization* is something which requires considerable weapons design knowledge. It does, however, limit the range of attack, the response time to an impending attack, and the number of weapons which can be fielded at any given time.

Additionally, specialized delivery systems are usually not necessary; especially with the advent of miniaturization, nuclear bombs can be delivered by both strategic bombers and tactical fighter-bombers, allowing an air force to use its current fleet with little or no modification. This method may still be considered the primary means of nuclear weapons delivery; the majority of U.S. nuclear warheads, for example, are represented in free-fall gravity bombs, namely the B61. More preferable from a strategic point of view are nuclear weapons mounted onto a missile, which can use a ballistic trajectory to deliver a warhead over the horizon. While even short range missiles allow for a faster and less vulnerable attack, the development of intercontinental ballistic missiles (ICBMs) and submarine-launched ballistic missiles (SLBMs) has allowed some nations to plausibly deliver missiles anywhere on the globe with a high likelihood of success.

More advanced systems, such as multiple independently targetable reentry vehicles (MIRVs) allow multiple warheads to be launched at several targets from any one missile, reducing the chance of any successful missile defence. Today, missiles are most common among systems designed for delivery of nuclear weapons. Making a warhead small enough to fit onto a missile, though, can be a difficult task.

Tactical weapons have involved the most variety of delivery types, including not only gravity bombs and missiles but also artillery shells, land mines, and nuclear depth charges and torpedoes for anti-submarine warfare. An atomic mortar was also tested at one time by the United States. Small, two-man portable tactical weapons (somewhat misleadingly referred to as suitcase bombs), such as the Special Atomic Demolition Munition, have been developed, although the difficulty to combine sufficient yield with portability limits their military utility.

GOVERNANCE, CONTROL, AND LAW

The International Atomic Energy Agency was created in 1957 in order to encourage the peaceful development of nuclear technology while providing international safeguards against nuclear proliferation Because of the immense military power they can confer, the political control of nuclear weapons has been a key issue for as long as they have existed; in most countries the use of nuclear force can only be authorized by the head of government or head of state.

In the late 1940s, lack of mutual trust was preventing the United States and the Soviet Union from making ground towards international arms control agreements, but by the 1960s steps were being taken to limit both the proliferation of nuclear weapons to other countries and the environmental effects of nuclear testing. The Partial Test Ban Treaty (1963) restricted all nuclear testing to underground nuclear testing, to prevent contamination from nuclear fallout, while the Nuclear Non-Proliferation Treaty (1968) attempted to place restrictions on the types of activities which signatories could participate in, with the goal of allowing the transference of non-military nuclear technology to member countries without fear of proliferation.

In 1957, the International Atomic Energy Agency (IAEA) was established under the mandate of the United Nations in order to encourage the development of the peaceful applications of nuclear technology, provide international safeguards against its misuse, and facilitate the application of safety measures in its use. In 1996, many nations signed and ratified the Comprehensive Test Ban Treaty which prohibits all testing of nuclear weapons, which would impose a significant hindrance to their development by any complying country.

Additional treaties have governed nuclear weapons stockpiles between individual countries, such as the SALT I and START I treaties, which limited the numbers and types of nuclear weapons between the United States and the Soviet Union.

Nuclear weapons have also been opposed by agreements between countries. Many nations have been declared Nuclear-Weapon-Free Zones, areas where nuclear weapons production and deployment are prohibited, through the use of treaties. The Treaty of Tlatelolco (1967) prohibited any production or deployment of nuclear weapons in Latin America and the Caribbean, and the Treaty of Pelindaba (1964) prohibits nuclear weapons in many African countries. As recently as 2006 a Central Asian Nuclear Weapon Free Zone was established amongst the former Soviet republics of Central Asia prohibiting nuclear weapons.

In the middle of 1996, the International Court of Justice, the highest court of the United Nations, issued an Advisory Opinion concerned with the "Legality of the Threat or Use of Nuclear Weapons". The court ruled that the use or threat of use of nuclear weapons would violate various articles of international law, including the Geneva Conventions, the Hague Conventions, the UN Charter, and the Universal Declaration of Human Rights.

Additionally, there have been other, specific actions meant to discourage countries from developing nuclear arms. In the wake of the tests by India and Pakistan in 1998, economic sanctions were (temporarily) levied against both countries, though neither were signatories with the Nuclear Non-Proliferation Treaty.

One of the stated *casus belli* for the initiation of the 2003 Iraq War was an accusation by the United States that Iraq was actively pursuing nuclear arms (though this was soon discovered not to be the case as the program had been discontinued). In 1981, Israel had bombed a nuclear reactor in Osirak, Iraq, in what it called an attempt to halt Iraq's previous nuclear arms ambitions.

Disarmament

Beginning with the 1963 Partial Test Ban Treaty and continuing through the 1996 Comprehensive Test Ban Treaty, there have been many treaties to limit or reduce nuclear weapons testing and stockpiles. The 1968 Nuclear Non-Proliferation Treaty has as one of its explicit conditions that all signatories must "pursue negotiations in good faith" towards the long-term goal of "complete disarmament". However, no nuclear state has treated that aspect of the agreement as having binding force.

Only one country—South Africa—has ever fully renounced nuclear weapons they had independently developed. A number of former Soviet republics—Belarus, Kazakhstan, and Ukraine—returned Soviet nuclear arms stationed in their countries to Russia after the collapse of the USSR.

Uses

The Sedan test from 1962 formed a crater 100 m (330 ft) deep with a diameter of about 390 m (1,300 ft), as a means of investigating the possibilities of using peaceful nuclear explosions for large-scale earth moving. Apart from their use as weapons, nuclear explosives have been tested and used for various non-military uses, and proposed, but not used for large-scale earth moving. When long term health and clean-up costs were included, there was no economic advantage over conventional explosives.

Synthetic elements, such as einsteinium and fermium, created by neutron bombardment of uranium and plutonium during thermonuclear explosions, were discovered in the aftermath of the first thermonuclear bomb test. In 2008 the worldwide presence of new isotopes from atmospheric testing beginning in the 1950s was developed into a reliable way of detecting art forgeries, as all paintings created after that period contain traces of cesium-137 and strontium-90, isotopes that did not exist in nature before 1945. Nuclear explosives have also been seriously studied as potential propulsion mechanisms for space travel..

NUCLEAR SUBMARINE

A nuclear submarine is a submarine powered by a nuclear reactor. The performance advantages of nuclear submarines over "conventional" (typically diesel-electric) submarines are considerable: nuclear propulsion, being completely independent of air, frees the submarine from the need to surface frequently, as is necessary for conventional submarines; the large amount of power generated by a nuclear reactor allows nuclear submarines to operate at high speed for long durations; and the long interval between refuellings grants a range limited only by consumables such as food. Current generations of nuclear submarines never need to be refueled throughout their 25-year lifespans Conversely, the limited power stored in electric batteries means that even the most advanced conventional submarine can only remain submerged for a few days at slow speed, and only a few hours at top speed; recent advances in air-independent propulsion have eroded this disadvantage somewhat. The high cost of nuclear technology means that relatively few states have fielded nuclear submarines.

History

The United States launched the USS *Nautilus*, the first nuclear submarine, in 1954. *Nautilus* could circle the world underwater for up to four months without resurfacing. Construction of the *Nautilus* was made possible by the successful development of a nuclear propulsion plant by a group of scientists and engineers at the Naval Reactors Branch of the Atomic Energy Commission. In July 1951, the U.S. Congress authorized construction of the world's first nuclear-powered submarine, under the leadership of Captain Hyman G. Rickover, USN.s Admiral Rickover came up with the idea of nuclear submarines.

The Westinghouse Corporation was assigned to build its reactor. After the submarine was completed, President Harry S. Truman broke the traditional bottle of champagne on *Nautilus'* bow. On January 17, 1955, it began its sea trials after leaving its dock inz. The submarine was 320 feet long, and cost about $55 million. The Soviet Union soon followed the United States in developing nuclear-powered submarines in the 1950s. Stimulated by the U.S. development of the *Nautilus*, Soviet work on nuclear propulsion reactors began in the early 1950s at the Institute of Physics and Power Engineering, in Obninsk, under Anatoliy P. Alexandrov, later to become head of the Kurchatov Institute. In 1956, the first Soviet propulsion reactor designed by his team began operational testing. Meanwhile, a design team under Vladimir N. Peregudov worked on the vessel that would house the reactor.

After overcoming many obstacles, including steam generation problems, radiation leaks, and other difficulties, the first nuclear submarine based on these combined efforts entered service in the Soviet Navy in 1958. At the height of the Cold War, approximately five to ten nuclear submarines were being commissioned from each of the four Soviet submarine yards (Sevmash in Severodvinsk, Admiralteyskiye Verfi in St. Petersburg, Krasnoye Sormovo in Nizhny Novgorod, and Amurskiy Zavod in Komsomolsk-on-Amur).

From the late 1950s through the end of 1997, the Soviet Union, and later Russia, built a total of 245 nuclear submarines, more than all other nations combined Today, six countries deploy some form of nuclear-powered strategic submarines: the United States, Russia, France, the United Kingdom, People's Republic of China, and India. Several other countries, including Argentina and Brazil, have ongoing projects in different phases to build nuclear-powered submarines. In the United Kingdom, all former and current nuclear submarines for the Royal Navy have been constructed in Barrow-in-Furness (at BAE Systems Submarine Solutions or its predecessor VSEL).

Technology

The main difference between conventional submarines and nuclear submarines is the power generation system. Nuclear submarines employ nuclear reactors for this task. They either generate electricity that powers electric motors connected to the propeller shaft or rely on the reactor heat to produce steam that drives steam turbines (cf. nuclear marine propulsion). Reactors used in submarines typically use highly enriched fuel (often greater than 20%) to enable them to deliver a large amount of power from a smaller reactor. The nuclear reactor also supplies power to the submarine's other subsystems, such as for maintenance of air quality, fresh water production by distilling salt water from the ocean, temperature regulation, etc. All naval nuclear reactors currently in use are operated with diesel generators as a backup power system. These engines are able to provide emergency electrical power for reactor decay heat removal as well as enough electric power to supply an emergency propulsion mechanism. Submarines may carry nuclear fuel for up to 30 years of operation. The only resource that limits the time underwater is the food supply for the crew and maintenance of the vessel.

The weakness of nuclear submarines is the need to cool the reactor even when the submarine is not moving; about 70% of the reactor output heat is coupled into the sea water. This leaves a "thermal wake", a plume of warm water of lower density which ascends to the sea surface and creates a "thermal scar" observable by thermal imaging systems, e.g. FLIR

LINEAGE

United States Navy

First Generation

- SCB-64: USS *Nautilus* (SSN-571)
- SCB-64A: USS *Seawolf* (SSN-575)
- SCB-121: *Skate* class attack submarines
- SCB-132: USS *Triton* (SSRN-586)
- SCB-137A: USS *Halibut* (SSGN-587)

Second Generation

- SCB-154: *Skipjack* class attack submarines
- SCB-178: USS *Tullibee* (SSN-597)
- SCB-180A: *George Washington* class ballistic missile submarines
- SCB-180: *Ethan Allen* class ballistic missile submarines
- SCB-188: *Permit* class attack submarines
- SCB-188A: *Sturgeon* class attack submarines
- SCB-216: *Lafayette* class ballistic missile submarines

- SCB-216: *James Madison* class ballistic missile submarines
- SCB-216: *Benjamin Franklin* class ballistic missile submarines

Third Generation

- *NR-1*
- SCB-245: USS *Narwhal* (SSN-671)
- SCB-302: USS *Glenard P. Lipscomb* (SSN-685)
- SCB-303: *Los Angeles* class attack submarines
- SCB-304: *Ohio* class ballistic missile submarines

Fourth Generation

- *Seawolf* class attack submarines
- *Virginia* class attack submarines

Soviet Navy/Russian Navy

First Generation

- Project 627 (November) attack submarines
- Project 645 test attack submarine *K-27*
- Project 658 (Hotel) ballistic missile submarines
- Project 659/675 (Echo) cruise missile submarines

Second Generation

- Project 661 (Papa) attack submarines
- Project 667 (Yankee) ballistic missile submarines
- Project 667B (Delta) ballistic missile submarines
- Project 670 (Charlie) cruise missile submarines
- Project 671 (Victor) attack submarines

Third Generation

- Project 678 (X-Ray) research submersible
- Project 685 (Mike) attack submarine K-278 *Komsomolets*
- Project 705 (Alfa) attack submarines
- Project 941 (Typhoon) ballistic missile submarines
- Project 945 (Sierra) attack submarines
- Project 949 (Oscar) cruise missile submarines
- Project 1910 (Uniform) special purpose submarines
- Project 971 (Akula) attack submarines

Fourth Generation

- Project 885 (Graney) attack submarines
- Project 935 (Borei) ballistic missile submarines

Royal Navy

First Generation

- HMS *Dreadnought* (S101)
- *Valiant* class attack submarines
- *Swiftsure* class attack submarines
- *Resolution* class ballistic missile submarines

Second Generation

- *Swiftsure* class attack submarines
- *Trafalgar* class attack submarines

Third Generation

- *Vanguard* class ballistic missile submarines

Fourth Generation

- *Astute* class attack submarines

French Navy

First Generation

- *Rubis* class attack submarines
- *Redoutable* class ballistic missile submarines

Second Generation

- *Triomphant* class ballistic missile submarines
- *Barracuda* class attack submarines

People's Liberation Army Navy (PLAN) of the People's Republic of China

First Generation

- Type 091 (Han) attack submarines (retired)
- Type 092 (Xia) ballistic missile submarines

Second Generation

- Type 093 (Shang) attack submarines
- Type 094 (Jin) ballistic missile submarines
- Type 095 attack submarines (planned)

Indian Navy

- *Arihant* class ballistic missile submarines

ANTI-SUBMARINE WARFARE

Anti-submarine warfare (ASW, or in older form A/S) is a branch of naval warfare that uses surface warships, aircraft, or other submarines to find, track and deter, damage or destroy enemy submarines.

Like many forms of warfare, successful anti-submarine warfare depends on a mix of sensor and weapon technology, training, experience and luck. Sophisticated sonar equipment for first detecting, then classifying, locating and tracking the target submarine is a key element of ASW. To destroy submarines both the torpedo and mine are used, launched from air, surface and underwater platforms. Other means of destruction have been used in the past but are now obsolete. ASW also involves protecting friendly ships.

History

The first attacks on a ship by an underwater vehicle are generally believed to have been during the American Revolutionary War of 1776 using what would now be called a naval mine but what then was called a torpedo, though various attempts to build submarines had been made before this. The first propelled torpedo was invented in 1863 and launched from surface craft. The first submarine with a torpedo was the Nordenfeld II built in 1886, though it had been proposed earlier. In the Russo-Japanese War of 1904-5 the submarine was a significant threat. By the start of the First World War nearly 300 submarines were in service. Ships were built with an armour band as protection against torpedoes.

World War I

During the First World War submarines were a major menace.

They operated in the Baltic, North Sea, Black Sea and Mediterranean as well as the North Atlantic. Previously they had been limited to relatively calm and protected waters. The vessels used to combat them were a range of small, fast surface ships using guns and good luck.

They mainly relied on the fact a submarine of the day was often on the surface for a range of reasons, such as charging batteries or crossing long distances. The first approach to protect warships was chainlink nets strung from the sides of battleships, as defence against torpedoes. Nets were also deployed across the mouth of a harbour or naval base to stop submarines entering or to stop torpedoes fired against ships. British warships were fitted with a ram with which to sink submarines, and *U15* was sunk in August 1914.

In July 1915 the British set up the civilian "Board of Invention and Research" to evaluate suggestions from the public as well as carrying out their own investigations. Some 14000 suggestions were received about combating submarines and wireless. In December 1916 the RN set up its own Anti-Submarine Division (from which came the term "Asdics") but relations with the BIR were poor. After 1917 most ASW work was carried out by ASD. In the US a Naval Consulting Board was set up in 1915 to evaluate ideas. After American entry into the war in 1917 they encouraged work on submarine detection. The US National Research Council, a civilian organization, brought in British and French experts on underwater sound to a meeting with their American counterparts in June 1917. In October 1918 there was a meeting in Paris on "supersonics" a term used for echo-ranging, but the technique was still in research by the end of the war.

By early 1917 the Royal Navy had also developed indicator loops which consisted of long lengths of cables lain on the seabed to detect the magnetic field of submarines as they passed overhead. At this stage they were used in conjunction with controlled mines which could be detonated from a shore station once a 'swing' had been detected on the indicator loop galvanometer. Indicator loops used with controlled mining were known as 'guard loops'. While dipping hydrophones appeared before war's end, the trials were abandoned.

Seaplanes and airships were also used to patrol for submarines. A number of successful attacks were made but the main value of air patrols was in driving the U-boat to submerge, rendering it virtually blind and immobile.

However, the most effective anti-submarine measure was the introduction of escorted convoys, which reduced the loss of ships entering the German's War Zone around the British Isles from 25% to less than 1%.

To attack submerged boats a number of anti-submarine weapons were derived, including the sweep with a contact-fused explosive. Bombs were dropped by aircraft and depth charge attacks were made by ships. Initially these were simply dropped off the back of a ship but then depth charge throwers were introduced. The Q-ship, a warship disguised as a merchantman, was used to attack surfaced U-boats while the *R1* was the first ASW submarine. A major contribution was the interception of German submarine radio signals and breaking of their code by "Room 40" of the Admiralty.

178 of the 360 U-boats were sunk during the war, from a variety of ASW methods:

- Mines 58
- Depth charges 30
- Submarine torpedoes 20
- Gunfire 20
- Ramming 19
- Unknown 19
- Accidents 7
- Sweeps 3
- Other (including bombs) 2

Inter-war Period

This period saw the development of active sonar (ASDIC) and its integration into a complete weapons system by the British, as well as the introduction of radar. During the period there was a great advance due to the introduction of electronics for amplifying, processing and display of signals. In particular the "range recorder" was a major step that provided a memory of target position. New materials for sound projectors were developed. Both the Royal Navy and the US Navy fitted their destroyers with ASDIC. In 1928 a small escort ship was designed and plans made to arm trawlers and to mass produce ASDIC sets. Depth sounders were developed that allowed measurement by moving ships and an appreciation obtained of the properties of the ocean affecting sound propagation. The bathythermograph was invented in 1937, which was soon fitted to ASW ships.

There were few major advances in weapons. However, the performance of torpedoes continued to improve.

Battle of the Atlantic

A depth charge thrower being loaded, aboard corvette HMS *Dianthus*, 14 August 1942.

A Leigh Light fitted to a Liberator of Royal Air Force Coastal Command, 26 February 1944.

Hedgehog, a 24-barreled anti-submarine mortar, mounted on the fo'c's'l of the destroyer HMS *Westcott*.

A Vought SB2U Vindicator from the USS *Ranger* (CV-4) flies anti-submarine patrol over Convoy WS12 en route to Cape Town, 27 November 1941.

The USS *Mission Bay* (CVE-59) operated primarily as an ASW carrier in the Atlantic. She is shown in August, 1944 off the East Coast, wearing Measure 32 Design 4A camouflage. Note the Grumman F6F Hellcats on deck and the large SK air search radar antenna on the mast.

During the Second World War, the submarine menace revived, threatening the survival of island nations like Britain and Japan which were particularly vulnerable because of their dependence on imports of food, oil, and other vital war materials. Despite this vulnerability, little had been done to prepare sufficient anti-submarine forces or develop suitable new weapons. Other navies were similarly unprepared, despite the fact every major navy had a large, modern submarine fleet, because all had fallen in the grip of Mahanian doctrine which held *guerre de course* could not win a war.

At the beginning of the war, most navies had few ideas how to combat submarines beyond locating them with sonar and then dropping depth charges on them. Sonar proved much less effective than expected, and was no use at all against submarines operating on the surface, as U-boats routinely did at night.

The Royal Navy had continued to develop indicator loops between the wars but this was a passive form of harbour defence that depended on detecting the magnetic field of submarines by the use of long lengths of cable lain on the floor of the harbour.

Indicator loop technology was quickly developed further and deployed by the US Navy in 1942. By then there were dozens of loop stations around the world. Sonar was far more effective and loop technology died straight after the war.

Allied anti-submarine tactics developed to defend convoys (the Royal Navy's preferred method), aggressively hunt down U-boats (the U.S. Navy approach), and to divert vulnerable or valuable ships away from known U-boat concentrations.

During the Second World War, the Allies developed a huge range of new technologies, weapons and tactics to counter the submarine danger. These included:

Vessels

- Allocating ships to convoys according to speed, so faster ships were less exposed.
- Larger convoys, which allowed escorts to better defend each convoy (the same number of total escorts for the same number of ships could actually cover smaller sectors in large convoys while it was mathematically determined by operations research that the enemy would not be able to inflict significantly more losses with the increase of targets provided the number of attacking U-Boats was unchanged).
- Huge construction programmes to mass-produce the small warships needed for convoy defence, such as corvettes, frigates, and destroyer escorts. These were more economical than using destroyers, which were better suited to fleet duties.

- Ships that could carry aircraft, such as the CAM ships, the merchant aircraft carrier, and eventually the purpose-built escort carriers.
- Support groups of escort ships that could be sent to reinforce the defence of convoys under attack. Free from the obligation to remain with the convoys, support groups could continue hunting a submerged submarine until its batteries and air supplies were exhausted and it was forced to surface.
- Hunter-killer groups, whose job was to actively seek out enemy submarines, as opposed to waiting for the convoy to come under attack. Later hunter-killer groups were centred around escort carriers.
- Huge construction programmes to mass-produce the transports and replace their losses. Once shipbuilding had ramped up to full efficiency, transports could be built faster than U-boats could sink them, playing a crucial role in the Allies winning the "Tonnage war".

AIRCRAFT

- Air raids on the German U-boat pens at Brest and La Rochelle.
- Long-range aircraft patrols to close the Mid-Atlantic gap.
- Escort carriers to provide the convoy with air cover, as well as close the mid-Atlantic gap.
- High frequency direction finding (HF/DF), including shipborne sets, to pinpoint the location of an enemy submarine from its radio transmissions.
- The introduction of seaborne radar which could enable the detection of surfaced U-boats.
- Airborne radar.
- The Leigh light airborne searchlight, in conjunction with airborne radar to surprise and attack enemy submarines on the surface at night.
- Magnetic anomaly detection
- Diesel exhaust sniffers
- Sonobuoys

Weaponry

- Torpedo countermeasures such as the Foxer acoustic decoy.
- The development of forward-throwing anti-submarine weapons such as Hedgehog and the Squid.
- The FIDO (Mk 24 'mine') homing torpedo.
- Pattern running torpedoes

Intelligence

- One of the best kept Allied secrets was the breaking of enemy codes including some of the German Naval Enigma codes (information gathered this way was dubbed Ultra) at Bletchley Park in England. This enabled the tracking of U-boat packs to allow convoy re-routings; whenever the Germans changed their codes (and when they added a fourth rotor to the Enigma machines in 1943), convoy losses rose significantly. By the end of the war, the Allies were regularly breaking and reading German naval codes.
- To prevent the Germans from guessing that Enigma had been cracked, the British planted a false story about a special infrared camera being used to locate U-boats. The British were subsequently delighted to learn that the Germans responded by developing a special paint for submarines that exactly duplicated the optical properties of seawater.

Many different aircraft from airships to four-engined sea-and land-planes were used. Some of the more successful were the Lockheed Ventura, PBY (Catalina or Canso, in British service), Consolidated B-24 Liberator (VLR Liberator, in British service), Short Sunderland, and Vickers Wellington. U-boats were not defenseless, since their deck guns were a very good anti-aircraft weapon. They claimed 212 Allied aircraft shot down for the loss of 168 U-boats to air attack. At one point in the war, there was even a 'shoot back order' requiring U-boats to stay on the surface and fight back, in the absence of any other option.

The provision of air cover was essential. The Germans at the time had been using their Focke-Wulf Fw 200 "Condor" long range aircraft to attack shipping and provide reconnaissance for U-boats, and most of their sorties occurred outside the reach of existing land-based aircraft that the Allies had; this was dubbed the *Mid-Atlantic gap*. At first, the British developed temporary solutions such as CAM ships and merchant aircraft carriers. These were superseded by mass-produced, relatively cheap escort carriers built by the United States and operated by the US Navy and Royal Navy. There was also the introduction of long-ranged patrol aircraft. Many U-boats feared aircraft, as the mere presence would often force them to dive, disrupting their patrols and attack runs.

There was a significant difference in the tactics of the two navies. The Americans favored aggressive hunter-killer tactics using escort carriers on search and destroy patrols, whereas the British preferred to use their escort carriers to defend the convoys directly. The American view was that defending convoys did little to reduce or contain U-boat numbers, while the British were constrained by having to fight the battle of the Atlantic alone for the early part of the war with very limited resources. There were no spare escorts for extensive hunts, and it was only important to neutralize the U-boats which were found in the vicinity of convoys. The survival of convoys was critical, and if a hunt missed its target a convoy of strategic importance could be lost. The British also reasoned that since submarines sought convoys, convoys would be a good place to find submarines.

Once America joined the war, the different tactics were complementary, both suppressing the effectiveness of and destroying U-boats. The increase in Allied naval strength allowed both convoy defence and hunter-killer groups to be deployed, and this was reflected in the massive increase in U-Boat sinking in the latter part of the war. The British developments of ASDIC, Centimetric Radar and the Leigh Light also reached the point of being able to support U-Boat hunting towards the end of the war, while at the beginning technology was definitely on the side of the submarine. Commanders such as F. J. "Johnnie" Walker of the Royal Navy were able to develop integrated tactics which made the deployment of hunter-killer groups a practical proposition.

Mediterranean

Italian and German submarines operated in the Mediterranean on the Axis side while French and British submarines operated on the side of the Allies. Similar ASW methods were used as in the Atlantic but an additional menace was the use by Italians of midget submarines.

Pacific Theatre

Japanese submarines pioneered many innovations, being some of the largest and longest range vessels of their type. However, they ended up playing little impact, especially in the latter half of the war. Instead of commerce raiding like their U-boat counterparts, they followed the Mahanian doctrine, serving in offensive roles against warships, which were fast, maneuverable and well-defended compared to merchant ships. In the early part of the Pacific War, Japanese subs scored several tactical victories, including two successful torpedo strikes on the US fleet carriers *Saratoga* and *Wasp*, the latter of which was sunk abandoned and scuttled as a result of the attack However, these are mostly considered incidental successes, due to limited resources in the US Navy at the time.

Once the US was able to ramp up construction of destroyers and destroyer escorts, as well as bringing over highly effective anti-submarine techniques learned from the British from experiences in the Battle of the Atlantic, they would take a significant toll on Japanese submarines, which tended to be slower and could not dive as deep as their German counterparts. Japanese submarines, in particular, never menaced the Allied merchant convoys and strategic shipping lanes to any degree that German U-boats did. One major advantages the Allies had was the breaking of the Japanese "Purple" code by the US, so allowing friendly ships to be diverted from Japanese submarines and allowing Allied submarines to intercept Japanese forces.

In 1942 and early 1943, US submarines posed little threat to Japanese ships, whether warships or merchant ships. They were initially hampered by poor torpedoes, which often failed to detonate on impact, ran too deep, or even ran wild. As the US submarine menace was slight in the beginning, Japanese commanders became complacent and as a result did not invest heavily into ASW measures or upgrade their convoy protection to any degree to what the Allies in the Atlantic did. Often encouraged by the Japanese not placing a high priority on the Allied submarine threat, US skippers were relatively complacent and docile compared to their German counterparts, who understood the "life and death" urgency in the Atlantic.

However, US Vice Admiral Charles A. Lockwood pressured the ordnance department to replace the faulty torpedoes; famously when they initially ignored his complaints, he ran his own tests to prove the torpedoes' unreliability. He also cleaned out the "deadwood", replacing many cautious or unproductive submarine skippers with younger (somewhat) and more aggressive commanders. As a result, in the latter half of 1943, US subs were suddenly sinking Japanese ships at a dramatically higher rate, scoring their share of key warship kills and accounting for almost half of the Japanese merchant fleet. Japanese naval command was caught off guard, as they had not the anti-submarine technology or doctrine, nor did the production capability to withstand a tonnage war of attrition, nor did they develop the organizations needed (unlike the Allies in the Atlantic).

Japanese antisubmarine forces consisted mainly of their destroyers, with sonar and depth charges. However, Japanese destroyer design, tactics, training, and doctrine emphasized surface nightfighting and torpedo delivery (necessary for fleet operations) over anti-submarine duties. By the time Japan finally developed a destroyer escort which was more economical and better suited to convoy protection, it was too late; coupled to incompetent doctrine and organization, it could have had little effect in any case. Late in the war, the Japanese Army and Navy used Magnetic Anomaly Detector MAD) gear in aircraft to locate shallow submerged submarines. The Japanese Army also developed two small aircraft carriers and Ka-1 autogyro aircraft for use in an antisubmarine warfare role.

The Japanese depth charge attacks by its surface forces initially proved fairly unsuccessful against U.S. fleet submarines. Unless caught in shallow water, a U.S. submarine commander could normally escape destruction, sometimes using temperature gradients (thermoclines). Additionally, IJN doctrine emphasized fleet action, not convoy protection, so the best ships and crews went elsewhere. Moreover, during the first part of the war, the

Japanese tended to set their depth charges too shallow, unaware U.S. submarines could dive below 150 feet (45m). Unfortunately, this deficiency was revealed in a June 1943 press conference held by U.S. Congressman Andrew J. May, and soon enemy depth charges were set to explode as deep as 250 feet (76m). Vice Admiral Charles A. Lockwood, COMSUBPAC, later estimated May's revelation cost the navy as many as ten submarines and 800 crewmen.

Much later in the war, active and passive sonobuoys were developed for aircraft use, together with MAD devices. Toward the end of the war, the Allies developed much better ATWs, such as Squid, Limbo and Mousetrap, in the face of new, much better German submarines, such as the Type XVII and Type XXI.

British and Dutch submarines also operated in the Pacific, mainly against coastal shipping.

Post-war

In the immediate postwar period, faced with the prospect of large numbers of Soviet submarines as capable as the Type XVIIs and XXIs, or better, new ASW weapons were essential. This led to the introduction of longer-ranged ATWs, such as Ikara, Weapon Alpha and ASROC. Nuclear submarines, even faster still, posed an even greater threat; in particular, shipborne helicopters (recalling the blimps of World War I) have emerged as essential anti-submarine platforms. A number of torpedo carrying missiles were developed, combining ahead-throwing capability (or longer-range delivery) with torpedo homing.

Since the introduction of submarines capable of carrying ballistic missiles, great efforts have been made to counter the threat they pose; here, maritime patrol aircraft (as in World War II) and helicopters have had a large role. The use of nuclear propulsion and streamlined hulls has resulted in submarines with high speed capability and increased maneuverability, as well as low "indiscretion rates" when a submarine is exposed on the surface. This has required changes both to the sensors and weapons used for ASW. Because nuclear submarines were noisy, there was an emphasis on passive sonar detection. The torpedo became the main weapon (though nuclear depth charges were developed).

The mine continued to be an important ASW weapon. In some areas of the ocean, where land forms natural barriers, long strings of sonobuoys, deployed from surface ships or dropped from aircraft, can monitor maritime passages for extended periods. Bottom mounted hydrophones can also be used, with land based processing. A system like this SOSUS was deployed by the USA in the GIUK gap and other strategically important places.

Airborne ASW forces developed better bombs and depth charges, while for ships and submarines a range of towed sonar devices were developed to overcome the problem of ship-mounting. Helicopters can fly courses offset from the ships and transmit sonar information to their combat information centres. They can also drop sonobuoys and launch homing torpedoes to positions many miles away from the ships actually monitoring the enemy submarine. Submerged submarines are generally blind to the actions of a patrolling aircraft until it uses active sonar or fires a weapon, and the aircraft's speed allows it to maintain a fast search pattern around the suspected contact.

Increasingly anti-submarine submarines, called attack submarines or hunter-killers, became capable of destroying, particularly, ballistic missile submarines. Initially these were very quiet diesel-electric propelled vessels but they are more likely to be nuclear-powered these days. The development of these was strongly influenced by the duel between *Venturer* and *U-864*.

A significant detection aid that has continued in service is the Magnetic Anomaly Detector (MAD), a passive device. First used in World War II, MAD uses the Earth's magnetosphere as a standard, detecting anomalies caused by large metallic vessels, such as submarines. Modern MAD arrays are usually contained in a long tail boom (fixed-wing aircraft) or an aerodynamic housing carried on a deployable tow line (helicopters). Keeping the sensor away from the plane's engines and avionics helps eliminate interference from the carrying platform.

At one time, reliance was placed on electronic warfare detection devices exploiting the submarine's need to perform radar sweeps and transmit responses to radio messages from home port. As frequency surveillance and direction finding became more sophisticated, these devices enjoyed some success. However, submariners soon learned not to rely on such transmitters in dangerous waters. Home bases can then use extremely low frequency radio signals, able to penetrate the ocean's surface, to reach submarines wherever they might be.

Modern Warfare

The military submarine is still a threat, so ASW remains a key to obtaining sea control. Neutralizing the SSBN has been a key driver and this still remains. However, non-nuclear powered submarines have become increasingly important. Though the diesel-electric submarine continues to dominate in numbers, several alternative technologies now exist to enhance the endurance of small submarines. Previously the emphasis had been largely on deep water operation but this has now switched to littoral operation where ASW is generally more difficult.

Current Technologies

There are a large number of technologies used in modern anti-submarine warfare:

Sensors

- Acoustics particularly in active and passive sonar, sonobuoys and fixed hydrophones and in the reduction of radiated noise.
- Pyrotechnics in the use of markers, flares and explosive devices
- Searchlights
- Radar
- Low frequency spread-spectrum electromagnetic surface wave devices
- Active spread-spectrum magnetic techniques
- Hydrodynamic pressure wave detection
- Blue-green laser airborne and satellite LIDAR
- Electronic countermeasures and Acoustic Countermeasures such as noisemakers
- Passive acoustic countermeasures such as concealment and design of sound-absorbing materials to coat reflecting underwater surfaces

- Magnetic anomaly detection
- Active and (more commonly) passive infra-red detection

In modern times infra-red (FLIR) detectors have been used to track the large plumes of heat that fast nuclear-powered submarines leave while rising to the surface. FLIR devices are also used to see periscopes or snorkels at night whenever a submariner might be incautious enough to probe the surface. The active sonar used in such operations is often of "mid-frequency", approximately 3.5 kHz. Because of the quietening of submarines, resulting in shorter passive detection ranges, there has been interest in low frequency active for ocean surveillance. However, there have been protests about the use of medium and low frequency high-powered active sonar because of its effects on whales. Others argue the high power level of some LFA (Low Frequency Active) sonars is actually detrimental to sonar performance in that such sonars are reverberation limited.

Weapons

- Mines,
- Torpedoes, acoustic, wire-guided, and wake homing.

Platforms

Satellites have been used to image the sea surface using optical and radar techniques, and it is claimedthese might be used for indirect detection of submarines, as could thermal imaging. Fixed wing aircraft provide both a sensor and weapons platform as do some helicopters, with sonobuoys and/or dipping sonars as well as aerial torpedoes. In other cases the helicopter has been used solely for sensing and rocket delivered torpedoes used as the weapon. Surface ships continue to be a main ASW platform because of their endurance, now having towed array sonars. Submarines are the main ASW platform because of their ability to change depth and their quietness, which aids detection.

Today some nations have seabed listening devices capable of tracking submarines. It is known to be possible to detect man-made marine noises across the southern Indian Ocean from South Africa to New Zealand. Some of the SOSUS arrayshave been turned over to civilian useand are now used for marine research.

Attack Submarines

During World War II submarines were typically hunted on the surface and only engaged underwater if contact was maintained when the submarine dived. There was no expectation of submarines tracking other submarines underwater and engaging in 'torpedo dogfights'. This type of anti-submarine action became a possibility after the duel between HMS *Venturer* and *U-864* in the North Sea, west of Bergen, Norway.

U-864 was carrying secret German weapons technology intended to assist Japan against US bombing raids. An ULTRA intercept alerted the Royal Navy, who dispatched a submarine to intercept the cargo. She was separated from her escort and, recognizing she was being trailed by an enemy submarine, submerged and began to zig-zag. This was a course of action which would normally render her invulnerable, but Jimmy Launders, the captain of *Venturer* submerged as well and tracked on hydrophones.

For several hours the cat-and-mouse hunt progressed, until Launders decided to perform the complex calculations necessary to obtain a firing solution in three dimensions. These were done manually, predicting the likely maneuvers of the target, and a spread of four torpedoes at 17 second intervals and varying depths was fired. *U-864* dived into the path of one of these, and was blown in half.

This possibly was the first attempt by one submarine to sink another while both were submerged, and the only successful one ever recorded up to the present day. It was a hugely influential action in the history of anti-submarine warfare, and modern attack submarine's tactics of attempting to track ballistic missile submarines from their bases underwater are directly derived from it. Modern computers provide the calculations which were originally done manually, and modern torpedoes are guided, but in all other respects the essentials of submerged anti-submarine warfare have remained the same.

GERMAN SUBMARINE U-864

German submarine *U-864* was a German Type IX U-boat sunk on 9 February 1945 by the British submarine HMS *Venturer*, killing all 73 onboard. It is the only instance in the history of naval warfare where one submarine has intentionally sunk another while both were submerged. The shipwreck was located in March 2003 by the Royal Norwegian Navy 2.2 miles west of the island of Fedje in the North Sea, at 150 metres.

Career

Early career: Commanded throughout its entire career by Korvettenkapitän Ralf-Reimar Wolfram she served with the 4th Submarine Flotilla (*4 Unterseebootflottille*) undergoing crew training from her commissioning until 31 October 1944. She was then reassigned to the 33rd Submarine Flotilla (*33. Unterseebootflottille*).

Final Voyage

Location of U-864.

According to decrypted intercepts of German naval communications with Japan, *U-864*'s mission was to transport military equipment to Japan destined for the Japanese military industry, including approximately 67 tons of metallic mercury in 1,857 32 kg steel flasks stored in her keel. That the mercury was contained in steel canisters was confirmed when one of the canisters containing mercury was located and brought to the surface during surveys on her wreck in 2005. Approximately 1,500 tons of mercury was purchased by the Japanese from Italy between 1942 and Italy's surrender in September 1943. This had the highest priority for submarine shipment to Japan and was used in the manufacture of explosives, especially primers.

There was some speculation as to whether *U-864* was carrying uranium oxide, as was *U-234*, which was captured by the US Navy in the Atlantic on 15 May 1945, but Det Norske Veritas (DNV) concluded that there was no evidence that uranium oxide was on board *U-864* when she departed Bergen. During the Norwegian Coastal Administration's investigation of the wreck of *U-864* in 2005, radiation measurements were made but no traces of uranium oxide were found.

According to her cargo list, *U-864* also carried parts and engineering drawings for German fighter aircraft and other military supplies for Japan, while among her passengers were

Messerschmitt engineers Rolf von Chlingensperg and Riclef Schomerus, Japanese torpedo expert Tadao Yamoto, and Japanese fuel expert Toshio Nakai.

U-864, commanded by Wolfram, left Kiel on 5 December 1944, arriving at Horten, Norway four days later. Before leaving Germany, *U-864* had been refitted with a snorkel mast. Several messages found in the ULTRA archives show that there were problems with the snorkel, which needed repairs before the *U-864* put to sea for her voyage to Japan. All Schnorkel trials and training were conducted at Horten near Oslo. *U-864* would have needed to be certified ready to sail at Horten before proceeding to Bergen. While en route to Bergen, *U-864* ran aground and had to stop in Farsund for repairs, not arriving in Bergen until 5 January 1945. While docked in the *Bruno* U-boat pens, *U-864* received minor damage on 12 January when the pens and shipping in the harbour were attacked by 32 Royal Air Force Lancaster bombers and one Mosquito bomber of Numbers 9 and 617 Squadrons. At least one Tallboy bomb penetrated the roof of the bunker causing severe damage inside, and left one of the seven pens unusable for the remainder of the war.

Sinking

Meanwhile, repairs and adjustments to her snorkel had been completed, and *U-864* had commenced submerged trials. British submarine HMS *Venturer*, commanded by Lieutenant James "Jimmy" S. Launders, was sent on her eleventh patrol from the British submarine base at Lerwick in the Shetland Islands to Fedje, north of Bergen. After German radio transmissions regarding *U-864* were decrypted, she was rerouted to intercept the U-boat. On 6 February *U-864* passed the Fedje area without being detected, but one of her engines began to misfire and she was ordered to return to Bergen. A signal stated that a new escort would be provided her at Hellisøy on 10 February. She made for there, but on 9 February *Venturer* heard *U-864*'s engine noise (Launders had decided not to use ASDIC since it would betray his position) and spotted the U-boat's periscope.

In an unusually long engagement for a submarine and in a situation for which neither crew had been trained, Launders waited

45 minutes after first contact before going to action stations, waiting in vain for *U-864* to surface and thus present an easier target. Upon realizing they were being followed by the British submarine and that their escort had still not arrived, *U-864* zig-zagged in attempted evasive manoeuvres and each submarine risked raising her periscope. *Venturer* had only eight torpedoes (four tubes and four reloads) as opposed to *U-864*'s total of 22, and so after three hours Launders decided to make a prediction of his opponent's zig-zag, and release a spread of his torpedoes into its predicted course. The first torpedo was released at 12:12 and then at 17 second intervals after that (taking four minutes to reach their target), and Launders then dived suddenly to evade any retaliation from his opponent. *U-864* heard the torpedoes coming and also dived deeper and turned away to avoid them, managing to avoid the first three but unknowingly steering into the path of the fourth. Imploding, she split in two, sinking with all hands and coming to rest more than 150 m (500 ft) below the surface on the seafloor, 2 nmi (3.7 km; 2.3 mi) west of the island of Fedje.

Rediscovery

In early 2003, the Royal Norwegian Navy, alerted by local fishermen, found the wreck. The mercury, contained in 1,857 rusting steel bottles located down in the vessel's keel, has started to leak and currently poses a severe environmental threat.

So far 4 kilograms per year of mercury is leaking out into the surrounding environment, resulting in high levels of contamination in cod, torsk and edible crab around the wreck. Boating and fishing near the wreck has been prohibited. Although attempts using robotic vehicles to dig into the half-buried keel were abandoned after the unstable wreck shifted, one of the steel bottles was recovered. Its original 5 mm thick wall was found to have corroded badly, leaving in places only a 1 mm thickness of steel.

The delicate condition of the 2,400-ton wreck, the rusting mercury bottles, and the live torpedoes on board would make a lifting operation extremely dangerous, with significant potential for an environmental catastrophe A three year study by the Norwegian Coastal Administration has recommended entombing the wreck in a 12 metre thickness of sand, with a reinforcing layer of gravel or concrete to prevent erosion. This is being proposed as a permanent solution to the problem, and the proposal notes that similar techniques have been successfully used around 30 times to contain mercury-contaminated sites over the past 20 years.

The proposal of entombing the wreck rather than removing it has been criticised by locals concerned about possible future leakage

On 11 November 2008 the Norwegian Coastal Administration awarded the contract for the possible salvage of the U-864 submarine and its cargo of mercury to salvage company Mammoet Salvage BV. Mammoet, which was awarded the contract for the salvage of Russian nuclear submarine *Kursk* in 2001 had proposed a method of raising the *U-864*'s wreck which would satisfy the environmental requirements, described as "a safe and innovative salvage solution". This was reported to be a safe, fully remotely-controlled operation which would raise the submarine and remove the source of pollution without the need for anyone working under water. On 29 January 2009, the Norwegian government approved the proposed method of raising the wreck, and the operation is scheduled to begin in 2010. The operation is estimated to cost 1 billion kroner ($USD 153 million).

5

Fire and Capital Ship

A fire ship, used in the days of wooden rowed or sailing ships, was a ship filled with combustibles, deliberately set on fire and steered (or, where possible, allowed to drift) into an enemy fleet, in order to destroy ships, or to create panic and make the enemy break formation. Ships used as fire ships were usually old and worn out or purpose-built inexpensive vessels. An explosion ship or *hellburner* was a variation on the fire ship, intended to cause damage by blowing up in proximity to enemy ships.

HISTORY

ANCIENT ERA, FIRST USES

Possibly the oldest account of the military use of a fire ship is recorded by the Greek historian Thucydides on the occasion of the failed Athenian Sicilian Expedition (415–413 BC). In the episode, the Athenian expeditionary force successfully repels an attack by the Syracusans: The rest of the Athenian force] the enemy tried to burn by means of an old merchantman which they filled with faggots and pine-wood, set on fire and let drift down the wind which blew full on the Athenians. The Athenians, however, alarmed for their ships, contrived means for stopping it and putting it out, and checking the flames and the nearer approach of the merchantman, thus escaped the danger.

A fire ship was used in the 208 Battle of Red Cliffs, when Huang Gai assaulted the enemy naval force with a fire ship filled with bundles of kindling, dry reeds, and fatty oil. The invention of Greek fire in 673 increased the use of fire ships, at first by the Greeks and afterward by other nations as they came into possession of the secret of manufacturing this compound. In 951 and again in 953 Russian fleets narrowly escaped destruction by fire ships.

Age of Sail, Refinement

Warships of the age of sail were highly vulnerable to fire. Made of wood, with seams caulked with tar, ropes greased with fat, and stores of gunpowder, there was little that would not burn. Accidental fires destroyed many ships, so fire ships presented a terrifying threat.

With the wind in exactly the right direction a fire ship could be cast loose and allowed to drift onto its target, but in most battles fire ships were equipped with skeleton crews to steer the ship to the target (the crew were expected to abandon ship at the last moment and escape in the ship's boat). Fire ships were most devastating against fleets which were at anchor or otherwise restricted in movement.

At sea, a well-handled ship could evade a fire ship and disable it with cannon fire. Other tactics were to fire at the ship's boats and other vessels in the vicinity, so that the crew could not escape and therefore might decide not to ignite the ship, or to wait until the fire ship had been abandoned and then tow it aside with small maneuverable vessels, such as galleys. During the period of the Crusades their use was frequent. Their use peaked during the 18th and 19th centuries, with fireships a permanent part of any naval fleet, ready to be deployed whenever necessary, such as the Battle of Tripoli Harbor.

Use in the Greek war of Independence

The attack on the Turkish flagship in the Gulf of Eressos at the Greek island of Lesvos by a fire ship commanded by Papanikolis during the Greek War of Independence-Painting by Volanakis

In the Greek War of Independence, 1821-1832, Greek fire ships were manned and sailed alongside a small and medium Turkish ship attached to her with hooks, ropes and grips, and then set on fire by the captain alone when the crew was in the escape boat. As the small fire ships were much more manoeuvrable than enemy ships of the line, especially in the coasts of the Aegean Sea where the islands, islets, reefs, gulfs and straits restrained big ships from being easily moved, they were a serious danger for the ships of the Turkish fleet. Many naval battles of the Greek war of independence were won by the use of fire ships.

Modern Age, Obsolescence

From the beginning of the nineteenth century steam propulsion and the use of iron, rather than wood, in shipbuilding gradually came into use, making fire ships useless, although ships or boats packed with explosives could still be effective. Such a case was Operation Chariot of World War II, in which the old destroyer HMS *Campbeltown* was packed with explosives and rammed into the dry dock at Saint-Nazaire, France, to deny its use to the battleship *Tirpitz*, which could not drydock anywhere else on the French west coast.

In the Mediterranean, the Italian Navy made good use of high-speed boats filled with explosives, mostly against moored targets. Each boat, called by the Italians MTM (*Motoscafo da Turismo Modificato*), carried a 300 kilograms (660 lb) explosive charge inside their bow. Their most known action was the 1941 assault on Souda Bay, which resulted in the destruction of cruiser HMS *York* and the Norwegian tanker *Pericles*, of 8,300 tn.

In 1946, as part of Operation Crossroads, the American landing ship *LSM-60* demonstrated the potential of explosives ships containing nuclear weapons. A total of eight vessels were sunk in the test in addition to *LSM-60*, including the aircraft carrier *Saratoga* The successful attack by terrorists in a speedboat packed with explosives on the USS Cole in 2000 is another extension of the idea.

NOTABLE USES

Notable fire ship attacks include:

- Alexander the Great's Siege of Tyre in 332 BC. The Tyrians used the fire ship in attempt to destroy Alexander's mole
- Syracuse in their battle with the Athenian fleet
- Huang Gai's attack on Cao Cao at the Battle of Chibi, 208.
- Siege of Antwerp in 1585. Both fire ships and exploding vessels were employed together for the first time.

- Francis Drake's attack on the Spanish Armada moored at Gravelines in 1588. The fire ships did no damage, but the Spanish scattered in panic and were easy prey for English ships.
- Maarten Tromp's attack on the Spanish fleet moored off the Kent coast in the Battle of the Downs in 1639. The Spanish fleet was destroyed.
- Michiel de Ruyter's attack on the anchored English fleet at the battle of Solebay in 1672 in which HMS *Royal James* was burned, killing Vice-Admiral Edward Montagu, and wounding *Royal James*'s captain, Richard Haddock.
- The destruction of 15 French ships of the line, including *Soleil Royal, Admirable* and *Triomphant* in 1692, after the Battle of La Hougue.
- US Attack on Tripoli during the First Barbary War in 1804 by USS Intrepid.
- The Russian attack on the Turkish fleet at the Battle of Chesma, 1770.
- Thomas Cochrane's attack on the French in the Battle of the Basque Roads, 1809.
- Many Greek attacks on large Turkish ships during the Greek War of Independence, 1821-1832.
- Chinese attacks on British ships during the Opium Wars, 1839-1842.

NAVAL DRIFTER

A naval drifter is a boat built along the lines of a commercial fishing drifter but fitted out for naval purposes. The use of naval drifters is paralleled by the use of naval trawlers.

Fishing trawlers were designed to tow heavy trawls, so they were easily adapted to tow minesweepers, with the crew and layout already suited to the task. Drifters were robust boats built, like trawlers, to work in most weather conditions, but designed to deploy and retrieve drift nets. They were generally smaller and slower than trawlers. If requisitioned by navies, they were typically armed with an anti-submarine gun and depth charges and used to maintain and patrol anti-submarine nets.

WORLD WAR I

Like fishing trawlers, the Royal Navy requisitioned many fishing drifters for conversion to naval use during World War I.

In addition, 362 naval drifters were ordered to Admiralty specifications (and thus are often referred to as "Admiralty drifters" Shipyards used to building fishing trawlers or drifters could easily switch to constructing naval versions. As a bonus these drifters could be sold to commercial fishing interests when the war ended.

There were two basic types of Admiralty built drifter, wooden hull and steel hull.

- The wooden hull vessels displaced 175 tons, were 86ft (26.2 m) long, with a beam of 19ft (5.8 m). They had a speed of 9 knots and carried one 6pdr gun. 91 wooden hull vessels were launched 1918–20, and 100 similar Canadian-built craft were ordered in January 1917.
- The steel hull vessels displaced 199 tons, were 86ft (26.2 m) long, with a beam of 18ft 6in (5.6 m). They also had a speed of 9 knots and carried one 6pdr gun. 123 steel-hulled vessels were launched 1917–1920, and 48 others were cancelled

Royal Navy drifters were named like the trawlers were, except for the Canadian-built vessels which were numbered CD 1 to CD 100.

During 1917, a fleet of British drifters, escorted by destroyers and light cruisers, maintained a blockade of the 100 km (62 miles) wide Otranto Straits, denying the Austro-Hungarian Navy access to the Mediterranean. On 15 May 1917, the Austro-Hungarian Navy raided the barrage.The Austro-Hungarians gave most drifter crews warning to abandon ship before opening fire Some drifter crews chose to fight, and the *Gowan Lee* returned fire on the Austro-Hungarian ships.

The drifter was heavily damaged, but remained afloat. Skipper Joseph Watt was later awarded the Victoria Cross for his actions during the battle. Of the 47 drifters in the barrage at the time, 14 were sunk and 4 were damaged The lack of sufficient Allied escorts forced the withdrawal of the remaining blockading ships, although only for a short time.

PRE-DREADNOUGHT BATTLESHIP

Pre-dreadnought battleship is the general term for all of the types of sea going battleships built between the mid-1890s and 1905. Pre-dreadnoughts replaced the ironclad warships of the 1870s and 1880s. Built from steel, and protected by hardened steel armour, pre-dreadnought battleships carried a main battery of very heavy guns in turrets supported by one or more secondary batteries of lighter weapons. They were powered by coal-fuelled triple-expansion steam engines.

In contrast to the chaotic development of ironclad warships in preceding decades, the 1890s saw navies worldwide start to build battleships to a common design as dozens of ships worldwide essentially followed the design of the British *Majestic* class. The similarity in appearance of battleships in the 1890s was underlined by the increasing number of ships being built. New naval powers like Germany, Japan and the United States began to establish themselves with fleets of pre-dreadnoughts, while the navies of Britain, France and Russia expanded to meet these new threats. The main clash of pre-dreadnought fleets would be fought between the Russians and Japanese during the Battle of Tsushima on 27 May 1905.

These dozens of battleships were abruptly made obsolete by the arrival of HMS *Dreadnought* in 1906. *Dreadnought* followed the trend in battleship design to heavier, longer-ranged guns by adopting an 'all-big-gun' armament scheme of ten 12-inch (305 mm) guns; her innovative steam turbine engines also made her faster. The existing pre-dreadnoughts were decisively outclassed; new battleships were from then on known as dreadnoughts while the ships laid down previously were designated pre-dreadnoughts. In spite of their obsolescence, the pre-dreadnought battleships played an important role in World War I and could even be found serving in World War II

Evolution

The pre-dreadnought developed from the ironclad battleship. The first ironclads—*La Gloire* and *Warrior*—looked much like a sailing frigate, with three tall masts and broadside battery, when they were commissioned at the start of the 1860s. Only eight years later HMVS Cerberus, the first breastwork monitor was launched followed three years later by HMS *Devastation*, a ship which looked much more like a pre-dreadnought battleship and was the first ocean going breastwork monitor. Mastless, both ships carried four heavy guns in two turrets fore and aft. *Devastation* was a breastwork monitor, built to attack enemy coasts and harbours; because of her very low freeboard, she lacked the seaworthiness needed to fight on the high seas; her decks would be swept by water and spray, interfering with the working of her gunsNavies worldwide continued to build masted, turretless battleships which had sufficient freeboard and were good enough sea-boats to fight on the high seas.

The distinction between coast-assault battleship and cruising battleship became blurred with the Admiral class, ordered in 1880. These ships reflected developments in ironclad design, being protected by iron-and-steel compound armour rather than wrought iron. Equipped with breech-loading guns of between 12 inch and 16¼ inch (305 mm and 413 mm) calibre, the Admirals continued the trend of ironclad warships towards gigantic weapons. The guns were mounted in open barbettes to save weight. Some historians see these ships as a vital step towards pre-dreadnoughts; others view them as a confused and unsuccessful design.

The subsequent *Royal Sovereign* class of 1889 retained barbettes but were uniformly armed with 13.5-inch (343 mm) guns; they were also significantly larger (at 14,000 tons displacement) and faster (due to triple-expansion steam engines) than the Admirals. Just as importantly, the *Royal Sovereigns* had a higher freeboard, making them unequivocally capable of the high-seas battleship role.

The pre-dreadnought design reached maturity with the *Majestic* class,of which the lead ship was launched in 1895. These ships were built and armoured entirely of steel, and their guns were mounted in fully-enclosed barbettes, inevitably referred to as turrets. They also adopted a 12-inch (305 mm) main gun, which, due to advances in casting and propellant, was lighter and more powerful than the previous guns of larger calibre. The *Majestics* provided the model for battleship-building in the Royal Navy and many other navies for years to come.

ARMAMENT

Pre-dreadnoughts carried several different calibres of guns for different roles in ship-to-ship combat. The main armament was four heavy guns, mounted in two centreline turrets fore and aft. Very few pre-dreadnoughts deviated from this arrangement. These guns were slow-firing and, initially, of limited accuracy; however they were the only guns heavy enough to penetrate the thick armour which protected the engines, magazines, and main guns of enemy battleships.

The most common calibre for the main armament was 12 inches; British battleships from the *Majestic* class onwards carried this calibre, as did French ships from the *Charlemagne* class (laid down 1894). Japan, importing most of its guns from Britain, used 12-inch guns. The United States used both 12-and 13-inch (330 mm) guns for most of the 1890s until the *Maine* class, laid down 1899, after which the 12-inch (305 mm) gun was universal. The Russians used both 12-and 10-inch (254 mm) as their main armament; the *Petropavlovsk class, Retvizan, Tsesarevich, Borodino class* had 12-inch (305 mm) main batteries while *Peresviet class* mounted 10-inch (254 mm) inch guns. The first German pre-dreadnought class used a 11-inch (279 mm) gun but decreased to a 9.4-inch (239 mm) gun for the two following classes, and returned to 11 in guns with the *Braunschweig* class.

While the calibre of the main battery remained quite constant, the performance of the guns improved as longer barrels were introduced. The introduction of slow-burning nitrocellulose and cordite propellant meant a longer barrel offered a higher muzzle velocity and hence range and penetrating power for the same calibre of shell. Between the *Majestic* class and *Dreadnought,* the length of the British 12-inch gun increased from 35 calibres to 45 and muzzle velocity increased from 2417 feet per second (737 m/s) to 2725 (830 m/s).

Pre-dreadnoughts also carried a secondary battery. This consisted of smaller guns, typically 6-inch (152 mm), though any calibre from 4 to 9.2 inches (100 to 230 mm) could be used. Virtually all secondary guns were 'quick firing', employing a number of innovations to increase the rate of fire. The propellant was provided in a brass cartridge, and both the breech mechanism and the mounting were suitable for rapid aiming and reloading. The role of the secondary battery was to damage the less well-armoured parts of an enemy battleship; while unable to penetrate the main armour belt, it might score hits on lightly armoured areas like the bridge, or start fires.

Equally important, the secondary armament was to be used against enemy cruisers, destroyers, and even torpedo boats. A medium-calibre gun could expect to penetrate the light armour of smaller ships, while the rate of fire of the secondary battery was important in scoring a hit against a small, maneuverable target. Secondary guns were mounted in a variety of ways; sometimes carried in turrets, they were just as often positioned in fixed armoured casemates in the side of the hull, or in unarmoured positions on upper decks.

During the ironclad age, the range of engagements increased; in the Sino-Japanese War of 1894–5 battles were fought at around 1 mile (2,000 m), while in the Battle of the Yellow Sea in 1904, the fleets were engaged at 3.5 miles (6,500 m). In part, the increase in engagement range was due to the longer range of torpedoes, and in part due to improved gunnery and fire control. In consequence, shipbuilders tended towards heavier secondary armament, of the same calibre that the 'intermediate' battery had been previously; the Royal Navy's last pre-dreadnought class, the *Lord Nelson* class, carried ten 9.2 in guns as her secondary armament. Ships with a uniform, heavy secondary battery are often referred to as 'semi-dreadnoughts'.

The pre-dreadnought's armament was completed by a tertiary battery of light, rapid-fire guns. These could be of any calibre from 3-inch (76 mm) down to machine guns. Their role was to give short-range protection against torpedo boats, or to rake the deck and superstructure of a battleship

In addition to their gun armament, many pre-dreadnought battleships were armed with torpedoes, fired from fixed tubes located either above or below the waterline. By the pre-dreadnought era the torpedo was typically 18 inches (46 cm) in diameter and had an effective range of several thousand yards. However, it was virtually unknown for a battleship to score a hit with a torpedo.

Protection

Pre-dreadnought battleships carried a considerable weight of steel armour. Experience showed that rather than giving the ship uniform armour protection, it was best to concentrate armour over critical areas. The central section of the hull, which housed the boilers and engines, was protected by the main belt, which ran from just below the waterline to some distance above it. This 'central citadel' was intended to protect the engines from even the most powerful shells. The main armament and the magazines were protected by projections of thick armour from the main belt. The beginning of the pre-dreadnought era was marked by a move from mounting the main armament in open barbettes to an all-enclosed, turret mounting.

The main belt armour would normally taper to a lesser thickness along the side of the hull towards bow and stern; it might also taper up from the central citadel towards the superstructure. The deck was typically lightly armoured with 2 in to 4 in of steel This lighter armour was to prevent high-explosive shells from wrecking the superstructure of the ship

The battleships of the late 1880s, for instance the *Royal Sovereign* class, were armoured with iron and steel compound armour. This was soon replaced with more effective case hardened steel armour made using the Harvey process developed in the United States. First tested in 1891, Harvey armour was commonplace in ships laid down in 1893–5. However, its reign was brief; in 1895, the German *Kaiser Friedrich III* pioneered the even better Krupp armour; Europe adopted Krupp plate within five years, only the United States persisted in using Harvey steel into the 20th Century. The improving quality of armour plate meant that new ships could have better protection from a thinner and lighter armour belt. Twelve inches of compound armour provided the same protection as just 7.5 inches of Harvey or 5.75 inches of Krupp.

Propulsion

All pre-dreadnoughts were powered by reciprocating steam engines. Most were capable of top speeds between 16 and 18 knots (21 mph; 33 km/h) The ironclads of the 1880s used Compound engine, but by the end of the 1880s the more efficient triple expansion engine was in use. Some fleets, though not the British, adopted the quadruple-expansion steam engine.

The main improvement in engine performance during the pre-dreadnought period came from the adoption of increasingly higher pressure steam from the boiler. The early cylindrical fire-tube boilers were superseded by more efficient water-tube boilers, allowing higher-pressure steam to be produced with less fuel consumption. Water-tube boilers were also safer, with less risk of explosion, and more flexible than fire-tube types. The Belleville-type water-tube boiler had been introduced in the French fleet as early as 1879, but it took until 1894 for the Royal Navy to adopt it for armoured cruisers and pre-dreadnoughts; other water-tube boilers followed in navies worldwide

The engines drove either two or three screw propellers. France and Germany preferred the three-screw approach, which allowed the engines to be shorter and hence more easily protected; they were also more maneuverable and had better resistance to accidental damage. Triple screws were, however, generally larger and heavier than the twin-screw arrangements preferred by most other navies.

Coal was the almost exclusive fuel for the pre-dreadnought period, though navies made the first experiments with oil propulsion in the late 1890s. An extra knot or two of speed could be gained by applying a 'forced draught' to the furnaces, where air was pumped into the furnaces, but this risked damage to the boilers.

PRE-DREADNOUGHT FLEETS AND BATTLES

The pre-dreadnought battleship in its heyday was the core of a very diverse navy. Many older ironclads were still in service. Battleships served alongside cruisers of many descriptions: modern armoured cruisers which were essentially cut-down battleships, lighter protected cruisers, and even older unarmoured cruisers, sloops and frigates whether built out of steel, iron or wood. The battleships were threatened by torpedo boats; it was during the pre-dreadnought era that the first destroyers were constructed to deal with the torpedo-boat threat, though at the same time the first effective submarines were being constructed..

The pre-dreadnought age saw the beginning of the end of the 19th century naval balance of power in which France and Russia vied for competition against the massive British Royal Navy, and saw the start of the rise of the 'new naval powers' of Germany, Japan and the USA. The new ships of the Imperial Japanese Navy and to a lesser extent the U.S. Navy supported those powers' colonial expansion.

While pre-dreadnoughts were adopted worldwide, there were no clashes between pre-dreadnought battleships until the very end of their period of dominance. The First Sino-Japanese War in 1894–95 influenced pre-dreadnought development, but the largest modern ships involved were cruisers The Spanish-American War of 1898 was a mismatch: with the American pre-dreadnought fleet engaging Spanish cruisers. Not until the Russo-Japanese War of 1904-05 did pre-dreadnoughts engage on an equal footing. This happened in three battles: the indecisive Battle of Port Arthur on 8 February 1904, the indecisive Battle of the Yellow Sea on 10 August 1904, and the decisive Japanese victory at the Battle of Tsushima on 27 May 1905.

Gunboat diplomacy was typically conducted by cruisers or smaller warships. A British squadron of three protected cruisers and two gunboats brought about the capitulation of Zanzibar in 1896; and while battleships participated in the combined fleet Western powers deployed during the Boxer rebellion, the naval part of the action was performed by gunboats, destroyers and sloops.

Europe

European navies remained dominant in the pre-dreadnought era. The British Royal Navy remained the world's largest fleet, though both Britain's traditional naval rivals and the new European powers increasingly asserted themselves against her supremacy.

In 1889, Britain formally adopted a 'Two Power Standard' committing her to building enough battleships to exceed the two largest other navies combined; at the time, this meant France and Russia, who became formally allied in the early 1890s. The *Royal Sovereign* class and *Majestic* class were followed by a regular programme of construction at a much quicker pace than in previous years. The *Canopus, Formidable, Duncan* and *King Edward VII* classes appeared in rapid succession from 1897 to 1905. Counting two ships ordered by Chile but taken over by the British, the Royal Navy had 39 pre-dreadnought battleships ready or building by 1904, starting the count from the *Majestics*. Over two dozen older battleships remained in service. The last British pre-dreadnoughts, the *Lord Nelson* class, appeared after *Dreadnought* herself.

France, Britain's traditional naval rival, had paused her battleship building during the 1880s because of the influence of the Jeune Ecole doctrine, which favoured torpedo boats to battleships. After the Jeune Ecole's influence faded, the first French battleship laid down was *Brennus*, in 1889. *Brennus* and the ships which followed her were individual, as opposed to the large classes of British ships; they also carried an idiosyncratic arrangement of heavy guns, with *Brennus* carrying three 13.4-inch (340 mm) guns and the ships which followed carrying two 12-inch and two 10.8-inch in single turrets. The *Charlemagne* class, laid down 1894–96, were the first to adopt the standard four 12-inch (305 mm) gun heavy armament. The Jeune Ecole retained a strong influence on French naval strategy, and by the end of the 19th century France had abandoned competition with Britain in battleships numbers. The French suffered the most from the Dreadnought revolution, with four ships of the *Liberté* class still building when *Dreadnought* launched, and a further six of the *Danton* class begun afterwards.

Germany was just beginning to build a navy at the start of the 1890s but by 1905 was wholeheartedly engaged in an arms race with Britain that would ultimately help cause World War I. Germany's first pre-dreadnoughts, the *Brandenburg* class, were laid down in 1890. By 1905, a further 19 battleships were built or under construction, thanks to the sharp increase in naval expenditure justified by the 1898 and 1900 Navy Laws. This increase was due to the determination of the navy chief Alfred von Tirpitz and the growing sense of national rivalry with the UK. Besides the *Brandenburg* class, German pre-dreadnoughts include the ships of the *Kaiser Friedrich III, Wittelsbach,* and *Braunschweig* classes-culminating in the *Deutschland* class, which served in both World Wars. On the whole, the German ships were less powerful than their British equivalents but equally robust. Russia equally entered into a programme of naval expansion in the 1890s; one of Russia's main objectives was to maintain her interests against Japanese expansion in the Far East. The *Petropavlovsk* class begun in 1892 took after the British *Royal Sovereigns*; later ships showed more French influence on their design, such as the *Borodino*-class. The weakness of Russian shipbuilding meant that many ships were built overseas for Russia; the best ship, the *Retvizan*, being largely constructed in America. The Russo-Japanese War of 1904–05 had been a disaster for the Russian pre-dreadnoughts; of the 15 battleships completed since *Petropavlovsk*, eleven were sunk or captured during the war. One of which, the famous *Potemkin* mutinied and was scuttled, however it was raised and recommissioned. After the war, Russia completed four more pre-dreadnoughts after 1905.

Between 1893 and 1904, Italy laid down eight battleships; the later two classes of ship were remarkably fast, though the *Regina Margherita* class was poorly protected and the *Regina Elena class* lightly armed. In some ways, these ships presaged the concept of the battlecruiser. The Austro-Hungarian Empire also saw a naval renaissance during the 1890s, though of the nine pre-dreadnought battleships ordered only the three of the *Habsburg* class arrived before *Dreadnought* herself made them obsolete.

America and the Pacific

The United States started building its first ever battleships in 1891. These ships were short-range coast-defence battleships that were similar to the British *Hood* except for an innovative intermediate battery of 8-inch guns. The US Navy continued to build ships that were relatively short-range and poor in heavy seas, until the *Virginia* class laid down in 1901–02 Nevertheless, it was these earlier ships that ensured American naval dominance against the antiquated Spanish fleet — which included no pre-dreadnoughts — in the Spanish-American War, most notably at Battle of Santiago de Cuba. *Virginia* and the two pre-dreadnought classes that followed her were completed after the completion of the *Dreadnought* and after the start of design work on the USN's own initial class of dreadnoughts. The US Great White Fleet of

16 pre-dreadnought battleships circumnavigated the world from 16 December 1907, to 22 February 1909.

Japan was involved in both of the major naval wars of the pre-dreadnought era. The first Japanese pre-dreadnought battleships, the *Fuji* class, were still being built at the outbreak of the First Sino-Japanese War of 1894–95, which saw Japanese armoured cruisers and protected cruisers defeat the Chinese Beiyang Fleet, composed of a mixture of old ironclad battleships and cruisers, at the Battle of the Yalu River. Following their victory, and facing Russian pressure in the region, the Japanese placed orders for four more pre-dreadnoughts; along with the two *Fuji*s these battleships formed the core of the fleet which twice engaged the numerically superior Russian fleets at the Battle of the Yellow Sea and the Battle of Tsushima. After capturing eight Russian battleships of various ages, Japan built several more classes of pre-dreadnought after the Russo-Japanese War.

Obsolescence

In 1906, the commissioning of HMS *Dreadnought* brought about the obsolescence of all existing battleships. *Dreadnought,* by scrapping the secondary battery, was able to carry ten 12-inch (305 mm) guns rather than four. She could fire eight heavy guns broadside, as opposed to four from a pre-dreadnought; and six guns ahead, as opposed to two. The move to an 'all-big-gun' design was a logical conclusion of the increasingly long engagement ranges and heavier secondary batteries of the last pre-dreadnoughts; Japan and the USA had designed ships with a similar armament before *Dreadnought,* but were unable to complete them before the British ship. It was felt that only the largest guns were effective in battle, and by mounting more 12-inch guns *Dreadnought* was two to three times more effective in combat than an existing battleship.

The armament of the new breed of ships was not their only crucial advantage. *Dreadnought* used steam turbines for propulsion, giving her a top speed of 21 knots, against the 18 knots typical of the pre-dreadnought battleships. Able both to outgun and outmaneuver their opponents, the dreadnought battleships decisively outclassed earlier battleship designs.

Nevertheless, pre-dreadnoughts continued in active service and saw significant combat use even when obsolete. Dreadnoughts and battlecruisers were believed vital for the decisive naval battles which at the time all nations expected, hence were jealously guarded against the risk of damage by mines or submarine attack, and kept close to home as much as possible. The obsolescence and consequent expendability of the pre-dreadnoughts meant that they could be deployed into more dangerous situations and more far-flung areas.

The only pre-dreadnought preserved today is the Japanese Navy's flagship at the Battle of Tsushima, the *Mikasa*, which is now located in Yokosuka, where it has been a museum ship since 1925.

World War I

During World War I, a large number of pre-dreadnoughts remained in service. The advances in machinery and armament meant that a pre-dreadnought was not necessarily the equal of even a modern armoured cruiser, and totally outclassed by a modern dreadnought battleship or battlecruiser. Nevertheless, the pre-dreadnought played a major role in the War.

This was first illustrated in the skirmishes between British and German navies around South America in late autumn 1914. As two German cruisers menaced British shipping, the Admiralty insisted that no battlecruisers could be spared from the main fleet and sent to the other side of the world to deal with them. Instead the British dispatched a pre-dreadnought of 1896 vintage, HMS *Canopus*. Intended to stiffen the British cruisers in the area, in fact her slow speed meant that she was left behind at the disastrous Battle of Coronel. *Canopus* redeemed herself at the Battle of the Falkland Islands, but only when grounded to act as a harbour-defence vessel; she fired at extreme range (13,500 yards) on the German cruiser SMS *Gneisenau*, and while the only hit was from an inert practice shell which had been left loaded from the previous night (the 'live' shells of the salvo broke up on contact with water; one inert shell ricocheted into one of *Gneisenau*'s funnels), this certainly deterred *Gneisenau* from a potentially damaging raid on a British squadron which was still taking on coal. The subsequent battle was decided by the two *Invincible*-class battlecruisers which had been dispatched after Coronel. This appears to have been the only meaningful engagement of an enemy ship by a British pre-dreadnought.

In the Black Sea five Russian pre-dreadnoughts saw brief action against the Ottoman battlecruiser Yavuz during the Battle of Cape Sarych in November 1914.

The principle that disposable pre-dreadnoughts could be used where no modern ship could be risked was affirmed by British, French and German navies in subsidiary theatres of war. The German navy used its pre-dreadnoughts frequently in the Baltic campaign. However, the largest number of pre-dreadnoughts was engaged at the Gallipoli campaign. Twelve British and French pre-dreadnoughts formed the bulk of the force which attempted to 'force the Dardanelles' in March 1915. The role of the pre-dreadnoughts was to support the brand-new dreadnought *Queen Elizabeth* engaging the Turkish shore defences. Three of the pre-dreadnoughts were sunk by mines, and several more badly damaged. However, it was not the damage to the pre-dreadnougl 3 which led to the operation being called off. The two battlecruisers were also damaged; since *Queen Elizabeth* could not be risked in the minefield, and the pre-dreadnoughts would be unable to deal with the Turkish battlecruiser lurking on the other side of the straits, the operation had failed. Pre-dreadnoughts were also used to support the Gallipoli landings, with the loss of three more: *Goliath*, *Triumph* and *Majestic*.

A squadron of German pre-dreadnoughts was present at the Battle of Jutland in 1916; German sailors called them the "five minute ships", which was the amount of time they were expected to survive in a pitched battle In spite of their limitations, the pre-dreadnought squadron played a useful role. As the German fleet disengaged from the battle, the pre-dreadnoughts risked themselves by turning on the British battlefleet as dark set Nevertheless, only one of the pre-dreadnoughts was sunk: SMS *Pommern* went down in the confused night action as the battlefleets disengaged.

Following the November 1918 Armistice, the U.S. Navy converted fifteen older battleships, eight armoured cruisers and two larger protected cruisers for temporary service as transports. These ships made one to six trans-Atlantic round-trips each, bringing home a total of more than 145,000 passengers.

World War II

After World War I, most battleships, dreadnought and pre-dreadnought alike, were disarmed under the terms of the Washington Naval Treaty. Largely this meant the ships being broken up for scrap; others were destroyed in target practice or relegated to training and supply duties. One, *Mikasa,* was given a special exemption to the Washington Treaty and was maintained as a museum and memorial ship.

Germany, losing most of her fleet under the terms of the Versailles treaty, was allowed to keep eight pre-dreadnoughts (of which only six could be in active service at any one time) which were counted as armoured coast-defence ships; two of which soldiered on into World War II. One of these, *Schleswig-Holstein,* shelled the Polish Westerplatte peninsula during the opening of the German invasion of Poland. *Schleswig-Holstein* served for most of the War as a training ship; she was sunk while under refit in December 1944, and broken up in situ in January 1945. The other, *Schlesien,* was mined and then scuttled in March 1945.

A number of the inactive or disarmed pre-dreadnoughts were nevertheless sunk in action during World War II, such as the Greek pre-dreadnoughts *Kilkis* and *Limnos,* bought from the U.S. Navy in 1914. While neither of the ships was in active service, they were both sunk by German divebombers after the German invasion in 1941. In the Pacific, the U.S. Navy submarine USS *Salmon* sank the disarmed Japanese pre-dreadnought *Asahi* in May 1942. A veteran of Tsushima, she was serving as a repair-ship.

CAPITAL SHIP

The capital ships of a navy are its most important warships; the ones with the heaviest firepower and armour. A capital ship is generally a leading or a primary ship in a fleet. There is usually no formal criterion for the classification, but it is a useful concept when thinking about strategy, for instance to compare relative naval strengths in a theatre of operations without having to get bogged down in the details of tonnage and gun diameters. A good example of this is the Mahanian doctrine, which was applied in the planning of the defence of Singapore in WWII, where the Royal Navy had to decide the allocation of their battleships and battlecruisers between the Atlantic and Pacific theatres. The Mahanian doctrine was also applied by the Imperial Japanese Navy which led to their pre-emptive move to attack Pearl Harbor and the US Pacific battleships. Another instance is the US Navy's chief warships being deployed in the Pacific, such as aircraft carriers and battleships. Although the United States and the United Kingdom agreed upon a Germany first grand strategy, Germany's surface fleet was small and the escort ships used in the Second Battle of the Atlantic were mostly destroyers and destroyer escorts to counter the U-boat threat.

Era of Sail

Before the advent of the all-steel navy in the late 19th century, a capital ship was a warship of the First, Second or Third rates:

- 1st Rate: 100 or more guns, typically carried on three or four decks. Four-deckers tended to have problems with the waterline and the lowest deck could seldom fire except on the calmest of seas.
- 2nd Rate: 90–98 guns
- 3rd Rate: 64 to 80 guns (although 64-gun third-raters were very small and not very numerous in any era).

Frigates were ships of the fourth or fifth rate; a corvette was a ship of the sixth rate.

Battleship / Battlecruiser

The definition of "capital ship" was formalized in the limitation treaties of the 1920s and 30s esulting from the dreadnought reWashington Naval Treaty, London Naval Treaty, and Second London Naval Treaty. This applied mainly to ships revolution; dreadnought battleships (also known first as dreadnoughts and later as battleships) and battlecruisers.

In the 20th century, especially in World Wars I and II, typical capital ships would be battleships and battlecruisers. All of the above ships were close to 20,000 tons displacement or heavier, with large caliber guns and heavy armour protection. Heavy cruisers, despite being important ships, were not considered capital ships. An exception to the above in World War II was the *Deutschland*-class cruiser. Though this class was technically similar to a heavy cruiser, albeit with considerably heavier guns, they were generally regarded as capital ships (hence the British label "Pocket battleship"). The *Alaska*-class cruisers, despite being oversized heavy cruisers and *not* true battleships/battlecruisers, were also considered by some to be capital ships.

During the Cold War, a Soviet *Kirov*-class large missile cruiser had a displacement great enough to rival WWII-era capital ships, perhaps defining a new battlecruiser for that era. However, others consider the *Kirov* is just a supersized guided-missile cruiser.

Aircraft Carrier

It took until late 1942 before aircraft carriers were universally considered capital ships. The US Navy was forced to rely primarily on their aircraft carriers after the attack on Pearl Harbor sank or damaged eight of their Pacific Fleet battleships.

In the 21st century, the aircraft carrier is the last remaining capital ship, with capability defined in decks available and aircraft per deck, rather than in guns and calibers. The United States is generally considered to possess supremacy, in both categories of aircraft carriers, possessing not only 11 active duty supercarriers each capable of carrying and launching nearly 100 tactical aircraft, but an additional 12 amphibious assault ships every bit as capable (in the "Sea Control Ship" configuration) as the light VSTOL carriers of other nations.

Ballistic missile submarines (or "boomers"), while important ships and in tonnage are similar to early battleships, are usually counted as part of a nation's nuclear deterrent force and do not share the sea control mission of traditional capital ships. Many navies, including the Royal Navy and the United States Navy consider these ships to be capital ships.

Naming

Some navies reserve specific names for their capital ships. Names reserved for capital ships include chiefs of state (eg

Bismarck), important places (eg HMAS *Australia*), historical events (eg USS *Constitution*), traditional names (eg HMS *Ark Royal*). However there are some exceptions to the rule, a British destroyer later adopted the name used by the dreadnought HMS *Agincourt*.

In fiction

The term has also been adopted into science fiction literature and culture to describe large spaceships used in military contexts, particularly where other naval terms have also been adopted in similar fashion; for example, sci-fi capital spaceships are often "carriers", that carry small fighters analogous to the way the real-world naval equivalent carries fighter aircraft, as well as functioning as "battleships".

6

Ballistic and Anti-ship Missile

A ballistic missile is a missile that follows a sub-orbital ballistic flightpath with the objective of delivering one or more warheads (often nuclear) to a predetermined target. The missile is only guided during the relatively brief initial powered phase of flight and its course is subsequently governed by the laws of orbital mechanics and ballistics. To date, ballistic missiles have been propelled during powered flight by chemical rocket engines of various types.

History

The first ballistic missile was the A-4, commonly known as the V-2 rocket, developed by Nazi Germany in the 1930s and 1940s under direction of Walter Dornberger. The first successful launch of a V-2 was on October 3, 1942 and began operation on September 6, 1944 against Paris, followed by an attack on London two days later. By the end of World War II May 1945 over 3,000 V-2s had been launched. A total of 30 nations have deployed operational ballistic missiles. Development continues, with around 100 ballistic missile flight tests (not including those of the US) in 2007, mostly by China, Iran and the Russian Federation.

Flight

A ballistic missile trajectory consists of three parts: the powered flight portion, the free-flight portion which constitutes most of the flight time, and the re-entry phase where the missile re-enters the Earth's atmosphere. Ballistic missiles can be launched from fixed sites or mobile launchers, including vehicles (transporter erector launchers, TELs), aircraft, ships and submarines. The powered flight portion can last from a few tens of seconds to several minutes and can consist of multiple rocket stages.

When in space and no more thrust is provided, the missile enters free-flight. In order to cover large distances, ballistic missiles are usually launched into a high sub-orbital spaceflight; for intercontinental missiles the highest altitude (apogee) reached during free-flight is about 1200 km. The re-entry stage begins at an altitude where atmospheric drag plays a significant part in missile trajectory, and lasts until missile impact.

MISSILE TYPES

Ballistic missiles can vary widely in range and use, and are often divided into categories based on range. Various schemes are used by different countries to categorize the ranges of ballistic missiles:

- Tactical ballistic missile: Range between about 150 km and 300 km
    - Battlefield range ballistic missile (BRBM): Range less than 200 km
- Theatre ballistic missile (TBM): Range between 300 km and 3500 km
    - Short-range ballistic missile (SRBM): Range 1000 km or less
    - Medium-range ballistic missile (MRBM): Range between 1000 km and 3500 km
- Intermediate-range ballistic missile (IRBM) or long-range ballistic missile (LRBM): Range between 3500 km and 5500 km
- Intercontinental ballistic missile (ICBM): Range greater than 5500 km
- Submarine-launched ballistic missile (SLBM): Launched from ballistic missile submarines (SSBNs), all current designs have intercontinental range.

Short-and medium-range missiles are often collectively referred to as theatre or tactical ballistic missiles (TBMs). Long and medium-range ballistic missiles are generally designed to deliver nuclear weapons because their payload is too limited for conventional explosives to be efficient (though the U.S. may be evaluating the idea of a conventionally-armed ICBM for near-instant global air strike capability despite the high costs) The flight phases are like those for ICBMs, except with no exoatmospheric phase for missiles with ranges less than about 350 km.

Quasi Ballistic Missiles

A quasi ballistic missile (also called a semi ballistic missile) is a category of missile that has a low trajectory and/or is largely ballistic but can perform maneuvers in flight or make unexpected changes in direction and range. At a lower trajectory than a ballistic missile, a quasi ballistic missile can maintain higher speed, thus allowing its target less time to react to the attack, at the cost of reduced range. Missiles that combine a maneuverable reentry vehicle (MaRV) with a terminal guidance system, allowing them to adjust the flight path as they near their target, are thought to be under development in China for use as anti-ship ballistic missiles.

Specific Missiles

China

- *DF-1*: MRBM
- *DF-2*: MRBM
- *DF-3A*: IRBM
- *DF-4*: ICBM
- *DF-5*: ICBM
- *DF-11*: SRBM
- *DF-15*: SRBM
- *DF-21*: IRBM
- *DF-21*: ASBM (anti-ship ballistic missile)
- *DF-25*: IRBM
- *DF-31*: ICBM
- *DF-41*: ICBM
- *JL-1*: SLBM IRBM

- *JL-2*: SLBM ICBM
- *B-611*: SRBM
- *P-12*: TBM SSM

France

- *M45*: SLBM
- *M51*: SLBM
- *Pluton*: SRBM

India

- Prithvi I: SRBM
- Prithvi II: SRBM
- Prithvi III: MRBM
- Agni I: SRBM
- Agni II: MRBM
- Agni III: IRBM (Agni III (A), Agni III (B), Agni III (3C), Agni III (SLBM))
- Agni V: ICBM (under development)
- Sagarika: SLBM
- Shaurya: MRBM (Quasi-ballistic missile)
- Dhanush: ShipLBM

Iran

- *Shahab-1*: SRBM
- *Shahab-2*: SRBM
- *Shahab-3*: MRBM
- *Zelzal-1*: SRBM
- *Zelzal-2*: SRBM
- *Zelzal-3*: SRBM
- *Fajr-3*: MRBM
- *Sejjil-1*: MRBM
- *Sejjil-2*: MRBM
- *Fateh-110*: SRBM
- *Ashoura*: MRBM
- *Ghadr-110*: MRBM

Israel

- *Jericho I*: SRBM
- *Jericho II*: MRBM
- *Jericho III*: IRBM

Iraq

- *Al Abbas*:
- *Al Hijarah*:
- *Al Hussein*:
- *Al Hussein II*:
- *Al Samoud*:
- *Al Samoud II*:

Nazi Germany

North Korea

- *Hwasong-5*: SRBM
- *Hwasong-6*: SRBM
- *Rodong-1*: MRBM
- *Rodong-2*: MRBM
- *Musudan*: IRBM
- *Taepodong-1*: IRBM
- *Taepodong-2*: ICBM

Pakistan

- *Hatf-I*: SRBM
- *Abdali-I*: SRBM
- *Ghaznavi*: SRBM
- *M-11*: SRBM
- *Shaheen-I*: SRBM
- *Ghauri-I*: MRBM
- *Ghauri-II*: MRBM
- *Shaheen-II*: IRBM
- *Ghauri-III*: IRBM
- *Shaheen-III*: IRBM

Soviet Union/Russia

- *Scud*:
- *SS-18 missile*: ICBM
- *SS-24 missile*: ICBM
- *RT-2UTTH Topol M*: ICBM
- *SS-N-23*: SLBM
- R7 Semyorka / 8K71 / SS-6 Sapwood
- R-16 SS-7 Saddler
- R-9 Desna / SS-8 Sasin
- R-36 SS-9 Scarp
- R-36M2 Voevoda / SS-18 Satan
- UR-100 8K84 / SS-11 Sego
- MR-UR-100 Sotka / 15A15/ SS-17 Spanker
- UR-100N 15A30 / SS-19 Stiletto
- RT-2 8K98 / SS-13 Savage
- RT-23 Molodets / SS-24 Scalpel
- RT-2PM Topol / 15Zh58 / SS-25 Sickle
- RT-2UTTKh Topol M / SS-27
- RS-24: MIRV-equipped. Expected to service in December 2009.

South Korea

- *Hyunmoo I*: SRBM
- *Hyunmoo II*: SRBM

Turkey

- *J-600T Yýldýrým I*: SRBM
- *J-600T Yýldýrým II*: SRBM

United States

- *Atlas*: ICBM
- *Titan*: ICBM
- *Minuteman*: ICBM
- *Peacekeeper*: ICBM
- *Polaris*: SLBM

- *Poseidon*: SLBM
- *Trident* SLBM
- *Skybolt* Air-Launched Ballistic Missile (ALBM)

Ballistic Missile Submarines

Specific types of ballistic missile submarines (SSBN) include:

United States

- *Ohio* class
- *Benjamin Franklin* class
- *James Madison* class
- *Lafayette* class
- *Ethan Allen* class

Russia

- *Borei* class
- *Typhoon* class
- *Delta* class

United Kingdom

- *Vanguard* class
- *Resolution* class

France

- *Triomphant* class
- *Redoutable* class

China

- Type 092 (*Xia* class)
- Type 094 (*Jin* class)
- Type 096-rumoured

India

- *Arihant* class-Under-going Trials.

ANTI-SHIP MISSILE

Anti-ship missiles are guided missiles that are designed for use against ships and large boats at sea. Most anti-ship missiles are of the sea-skimming type, and many use a combination of inertial guidance and radar homing. A good number of other anti-ship missiles use infrared homing to follow the heat that is emitted by a ship, and it is also possible for anti-ship missiles to be guided by radio command all the way. The first anti-ship missiles, which were developed and built by Nazi Germany used radio command guidance, and these saw some success in the Mediterranean Theatre in 1943-44, sinking or heavily damaging several ship, such as the cruiser USS *Savannah*. Another type of anti-ship missile uses TV guidance, in which the missile's guidance electronics contains a picture of the target ship, and which by comparing this to the missile's TV image of the ship, homes in on the ship visually.

Various anti-ship missiles ranging from large to smaller ones can be launched from a variety of weapons systems including surface warships (also referred to as ship-to-ship missiles), submarines, bombers, fighter planes, patrol planes, helicopters, shore batteries, land vehicles, and conceivably, even by infantrymen firing shoulder-launched missiles.

A typical acronym for the phrase "anti-ship missile" is ASM, but AShM can also be used to avoid confusion with air-to-surface missiles and anti-submarine missiles.

History

Anti-ship missiles were among the first instances of short-range guided missiles during World War II in 1943-44. The German Luftwaffe used the Fritz X, the Hs 293 and others, launched from its bombers, to deadly effect against some Allied ships in the Mediterranean Sea, such as seriously damaging the U.S. Navy cruiser USS Phoenix off Salerno, Italy. These all used radio command-guidance from the bombardiers of the warplanes that launched them. Some of these hit and either sank or damaged a number of ships, including warships offshore from amphibious landings on western Italy. These radio-controlled missiles were used successfully by the Luftwaffe until the Allied navies developed missile countermeasures-principally radio jamming. The Allies also developed some of their own similar radio-guided AShMs, such as the "Tiny Tim" and the SWOD-9 "Bat", but these saw little to no use in combat.

During the Cold War, the Soviet Union turned to a sea-denial strategy concentrating on submarines, naval mines, and the AShM. One of the first products of the decision was the SS-N-2 "Styx" missile. Further products were to follow, and they were soon sighted on Soviet Air Force's Tu-95 *Bear* and Tu-22 *Blinder* bombers, in the case of the air-launched KS-1 Komet.

In 1967, the Israeli Navy's destroyer *Eilat* was sunk by a *Styx* missile launched by Egyptian missile boats off the Sinai Peninsula.

The Battle of Latakia in 1973 was the scene of the world's first combat between anti-ship missile-equipped missile boats. In this battle, the Israeli Navy destroyed the Syrian warships without suffering any damage, especially by using electronic countermeasures for defence.

Anti-ship missiles were used in the 1982 Falklands War. The British warship HMS *Sheffield*, a 4,820 ton Type 42 Destroyer, was struck by a single air-launched Exocet AShM, and she later sank as a result of the damage that she sustained. The container ship *Atlantic Conveyor* was also sunk by an Exocet missile, and also the HMS *Glamorgan* was damaged. The *Glamorgan* was struck by an MM38 missile launched from an improvised trailer-based launcher taken from the Argentinean Navy destroyer ARA *Comodoro Seguí* by Navy technicians., but she was able to take evasive maneuvers that lessened her damage.

In 1987, a U.S. Navy guided-missile frigate, the USS *Stark*, was hit by an Exocet anti-ship missile fired by an Iraqi *Mirage F-1* fighter plane. The USS *Stark* was damaged, but she was able steam to a friendly port for temporary repairs. The next year, ASMs were fired by both American and Iranian forces in Operation Praying Mantis in the Persian Gulf. During this naval battle, several Iranian warships were hit by American ASMs (and by the U.S. Navy's *Standard* missiles-SAMs which were doing double-duty in the anti-ship role). Also, in October 1987, the *Sungari*, an American-owned tanker steaming under the Liberian flag, and also a Kuwaiti tanker steaming under the American flag, the *Sea Isle City*, were hit by Iranian HY-2 missiles.

During Operation Praying Mantis, the U.S. Navy hit the Iranian Navy light frigate IS *Sahand* with three Harpoon missiles, four AGM-123 Skipper rocket-propelled bombs, a Walleye laser-guided bomb, and several 1,000 lb "iron bombs". Despite the large number of munitions and successful hits, the 1,540 ton IS *Sahand* did not sink until fire reached her ammunition magazine, causing it to detonate, blowing the entire figate to bits. However, in the same engagement, American warships fired three *Standard* missiles at an Iranian Navy corvette. This corvette had such a low profile above the water that a Harpoon missile that arrived several minutes later could not lock on to it with their targeting radars.

THREAT POSED

Anti-ship missiles are the bane of the modern naval surface combatant. Unlike the ground-combatant, who has the advantage of concealment, terrain, and, fundamentally, ground beneath his feet, the naval surface combatant is alone, aboard a warm boat, easily distinguishable from the cold water that surrounds her, said boat being packed to the gills with men, weaponry, and explosives, sailing on a flat, relatively featureless expanse of ocean, which offers concealment and shelter to none, and is (eventually) naturally deadly to human life. As this is the case, threats that would merely slow down the ground combatant—such as guided missiles—are a much greater threat to the naval combatant. Possessing a speed and an agility that naval platforms cannot forseeably match, as well as computerized "smart" guidance systems and a heavy payload of high-explosive, the modern anti-ship missile, once it has acquired its target, is an enemy that the target ship cannot usually run from, hide from, physically avoid, or absorb.

Therefore, to counter the threat posed, the modern surface combatant has to either avoid being acquired by a platform possessing anti-ship missiles in the first place, has to destroy the enemy anti-ship-missile-carrying weapons system before it can launch any of its anti-ship missiles, or has to have active defence systems capable of deceiving or destroying the anti-ship missile prior to the anti-ship missile hitting its target. Modern navies have spent thousands, if not millions of man-years considering and responding to the threat of anti-ship missiles since World War II, and the multiple, layered, computerized, active and passive defence systems that they employ on board their surface combatants are extremely effective against almost all anti-ship missiles, with certain exceptions.

The first layer of anti-missile missile defence by a modern, fully-equipped Aircraft Carrier Task Force is always the long-range missile-carrying fighter planes of the aircraft carrier herself. This is a capability that only the U.S. Navy has now, with its long-range, supersonic, F/A-18 Hornet fighter planes, and formerly with the F-14 Tomcat fighters with their very long-range Phoenix missiles. Several of these fighters are kept on combat air patrol 24 hours a day, seven days a week when at sea, and many more are put aloft in dangerous situations, such as during wartime or the threat of war.

These fighters patrol up to hundreds of miles away from the Carrier Task Force, and they are equipped with excellent airborne radar systems. When spotting a threatening anti-ship missile, these very fast jet fighters can approach them and shoot them down with their medium-range AMRAAM missiles or their shorter-range Sidewinder missiles. For the anti-ship missiles that evade these, the fighters are also capable of closing in on them and shooting at them with their 20 mm rapid-fire cannons.

However, some AShM's might "leak" past the Carrier Task Force's fighter-plane defenses, and also, many naval warships are not members of Carrier Task Forces. For these situations, there are more layers of missile defence closer-in or for the protection of other warships in other fleets and other navies, as follows.

For example, the U.S. Navy has developed the computerized, automatic AEGIS anti-aircraft/ anti-cruise-missile/ anti-ballistic missile naval defence system, which is said to be able to track, engage, and destroy massive, though finite, quantities of incoming missiles (all at the same time) using agile long-range and short-range surface-to-air missiles. Any missiles that leak through the AEGIS system can then be deceived using electronic countermeasures or decoys, or shot down by short-range anti-missile missiles, such as the NATO *Sea Sparrow* missile system carried by some warships or the *Rolling Airframe Missile* carried by others. They can also be shot at by the warship's 5-inch, multipurpose naval guns, or be shot to pieces by a last-ditch close-in weapon system, such as the *Phalanx* CIWS or the *Goalkeeper*

CIWS. Russia (and the former Soviet Union), various European nations, and the People's Republic of China have developed and deployed similar systems.

However, even as effective as these naval air defence systems are, they only retain their effectiveness as long as they still have ammunition. And, even as expensive as the most-effective, modern anti-ship missiles are, they still remain extremely cost-effective, and they do not lose this cost-effectiveness when launched in their most dangerous threat modality-namely, in massive, defence-saturation-level quantities-since the replacement cost of a single *Nimitz*-class supercarrier, not to mention her irreplaceable crewmen, pilots, and aircraft on board, is *far in excess* of even one thousand of the most modern anti-ship missiles available, a quantity that, if they could be launched en masse at one target (and they cannot), would surely devastate even the most well-defended aircraft carrier that any sea-faring power could conceivably deploy.

As such, navies place a high premium on defending against anti-ship missiles, as even a handful getting through ship-based defenses could badly hurt an entire Naval Task Force.

Current Threats and Vulnerabilities

To counter these defence systems, countries like Russia are developing or deploying very low flying missiles (about five meters above sea level) that slowly cruise at a very low level to within a short range of their target and then, at the point when radar detection becomes inevitable, initiate a supersonic, high-agility sprint (potentially with anti-aircraft missile detection and evasion) to close the terminal distance. Missiles, such as the SS-N-27 Sizzler, that incorporate this sort of threat modality are regarded by U.S. Navy analysts as potentially being able to penetrate current U.S. Navy defensive systems.

MERCHANT VESSEL

A merchant vessel is a ship that transports cargo and passengers during peace time. During wars, the same ships are auxiliaries to the navies of their respective countries, and are called upon to deliver military personnel and materiel. Most countries of the world operate fleets of merchant ships. However, due to the high costs of operations, today these fleets are in many cases sailing under the flags of nations that specialize in providing manpower and services at favourable terms. Such flags are known as "flags of convenience". Currently, Liberia and Panama are particularly favoured. Ownership of the vessels can be by any country, however.

The Greek-owned fleet is the largest in the world. Today, the Greek fleet accounts for some 16 per cent of the world's tonnage; this makes it currently the largest single international merchant fleet in the world, albeit not the largest in history.

In English, "Merchant Navy" without further clarification is used to refer to the British Merchant Navy; the United States merchant fleet is known as the United States Merchant Marine. Merchant ships names are prefixed by which kind of vessel they are: MV = Motor Vessel, SS = Steam Ship, MT = Motor Tanker or Motor Tug Boat, MSV = Motor Stand-by Vessel, MY = Motor Yacht, RMS = Royal Mail Ship, RRS = Royal Research Ship, SV = Sailing Vessel although these can be sub coded as type of sailing vessel. Merchant ships may be divided into several categories, according to their purpose and/or size.

Dry Cargo Ships

A cargo ship or freighter is any sort of ship or vessel that carries cargo, goods, and materials from one port to another. Thousands of cargo carriers ply the world's seas and oceans each year; they handle the bulk of international trade. Cargo ships are usually specially designed for the task, often being equipped with cranes and other mechanisms to load and unload, and come in all sizes.

Dry cargo ships today are mainly bulk carriers and container ships. Bulk carriers or bulkers are used for the transportation of homogeneous cargo such as coal, rubber, copra, tin, and wheat. Container ships are used for the carriage of miscellaneous goods.

Bulk Carriers

A bulk carrier is ocean-going vessel used to transport bulk cargo items such as iron ore, bauxite, coal, cement, grain and similar cargo. Bulk carriers can be recognized by large box-like hatches on deck, designed to slide outboard or fold fore-and-aft to enable access for loading or discharging cargo. The dimensions of bulk carriers are often determined by the ports and sea routes that they need to serve, and by the maximum width of the Panama Canal. Most lakes are too small to accommodate bulk carriers, but a large fleet of lake freighters has been plying the Great Lakes and St. Lawrence Seaway of North America for over a century.

CONTAINER SHIPS

Container ships are cargo ships that carry all of their load in truck-size containers, in a technique called containerization. They form a common means of commercial intermodal freight transport.

TANKERS

Tankers for the transport of fluids, such as crude oil, petroleum products, liquefied petroleum gas, liquefied natural gas and chemicals, also vegetable oils, wine and other food-the tanker sector comprises one third of the world tonnage.

Tankers can range in size from several hundred tons, designed for servicing small harbours and coastal settlements, to several hundred thousand tons, with these being designed for long-range haulage. A wide range of products are carried by tankers, including:

- hydrocarbon products such as oil, LPG, and LNG
- Chemicals, such as ammonia, chlorine, and styrene monomer
- fresh water
- wine.

Different products require different handling and transport, thus special types of tankers have been built, such as "chemical tankers" and "oil tankers". "LNG carriers" as they are typically known, are a relatively rare tanker designed to carry liquefied natural gas.

Among oil tankers, supertankers were designed for carrying oil around the Horn of Africa from the Middle East; the FSO *Knock Nevis* being the largest vessel in the world. Knock Nevis was formerly the ULCC "Jahre Viking". The supertanker Jahre Viking

(Seawise Giant), or as it is better known today as Knock Nevis has a deadweight of 565 thousand metric tons and length of about 500 meters. The use of such large ships is in fact very unprofitable, due to the inability to operate them at full cargo capacity; hence, production supertankers has currently ceased. Today's largest oil tankers in comparison by gross tonnage are TI Europe, TI Asia, TI Oceania, which are the largest sailing vessels today. But even with their deadweight of 441,585 metric tons, sailing as VLCC most of the time, they do not use more than 70% of their total capacity.

Apart from pipeline transport, supertankers are the only method for transporting large quantities of oil, although such tankers have caused large environmental disasters when sinking close to coastal regions, causing oil spills. See *Exxon Valdez, Braer, Prestige, Torrey Canyon, Erika,* for examples of tankers that have caused oil spills.

Specialized Ships

Specialized ships, e.g. for heavy lift goods or refrigerated cargo (Reefer ships), roll-on/roll-off cargo (RoRo) ships for vehicles and wheeled machinery. These ships are not very well developed, except those used as car carriers. Only this sector of Maritime Industry is well developed. Largest roll-on/roll-off cargo (RoRo) ships are Sunbelt Spirit, Liberty (ex-Faust), Phoenix Leader, Aquamarine ACE. They have a capacity of about 6 to 9 thousand units.

Coasters

Coasters, smaller ships for any category of cargo which are normally not on ocean-crossing routes, but in coastwise trades. Coasters are shallow-hulled ships used for trade between locations on the same island or continent. Their shallow hulls mean that they can get through reefs where seagoing ships usually cannot (seagoing ships have a very deep hull for supplies and trade etc.).

Passenger Ships

A passenger ship is a ship whose primary function is to carry passengers. The category does not include cargo vessels which have accommodations for limited numbers of passengers, such as the ubiquitous twelve-passenger freighters once common on the seas in which the transport of passengers is secondary to the carriage of freight. The type does however include many classes of ships which are designed to transport substantial numbers of passengers as well as freight. Indeed, until recently virtually all ocean liners were able to transport mail, package freight and express, and other cargo in addition to passenger luggage, and were equipped with cargo holds and derricks, kingposts, or other cargo-handling gear for that purpose. Modern cruiseferries have car decks for lorries as well as the passenger's cars. Only in more recent ocean liners and in virtually all cruise ships has this cargo capacity been suppressed.

Cruise Ships

A cruise ship or a cruise liner is a passenger ship used for pleasure voyages, where the voyage itself and the ship's amenities are considered an essential part of the experience. Cruising has become a major part of the tourism industry, with millions of passengers each year as of 2008. The industry's rapid growth has seen nine or more newly built ships catering to a North American clientele added every year since 1978, as well as others servicing European clientele. Smaller markets such as the Asia-Pacific region are generally serviced by older tonnage displaced by new ships introduced into the high growth areas. Cruise ships operate on a mostly set roundabout course or round trips (i.e. they tend to return to their originating port) whereas ocean liners are defined by actually doing ocean-crossing voyages, which may not lead back to the same port for years.

Ferries

A ferry is a form of transportation, usually a boat or ship, but also other forms, carrying passengers and sometimes their vehicles. Ferries are also used to transport freight and even railroad cars. Most ferries operate on regular, frequent, return services. A foot-passenger ferry with many stops, such as in Venice, is sometimes called a waterbus or water taxi.

Ferries form public transport systems of many waterside cities, allowing direct transit between points at a capital cost much lower than bridges or tunnels.

7

Indian Navy

The Indian Navy is the naval branch of the armed forces of India. It currently has approximately 56,000 personnel on active duty, including 5,000 members of the naval aviation branch, 2,000 marine commandos and 1,000 Sagar Prahari Bal soldiers, making it the world's sixth largest navy. The Indian Navy currently operates more than 155 vessels, including the aircraft carrier INS *Viraat*, along with operational jet fighters.

Though the primary objective of the navy is to secure national maritime borders, India also uses its navy to enhance its international relations through joint exercises, port visits and humanitarian missions, including disaster relief. In recent years, the Indian Navy has undergone extensive modernization and expansion with an intention to increase its Role

The Indian Navy sees several principal roles for itself:

- In conjunction with other armed forces of the union, act to deter or defeat any threats or aggression against the territory, people or maritime interests of India, both in war and peace;
- Project influence in India's maritime area of interest, to further the nation's political, economic and security objectives;
- In cooperation with the Indian Coast Guard, ensure good order and stability in India's maritime zones of responsibility.
- Provide maritime assistance (including disaster relief) in India's maritime neighbourhood

- To play a key role as part of 'a pluralistic security order' for a better world.

Indo-Pakistan Wars

The Navy has been involved in two wars with Pakistan. While its activity in the Indo-Pakistani War of 1965 largely involved patrolling of the coast, it played a significant role in the bombing of Karachi harbour in the 1971 war. The name given to the attack was *Operation Trident*, which was launched on December 4. Owing to its success, it has been celebrated as Navy Day ever since. The attack was followed by *Operation Python* before the center of conflict shifted to the eastern India-Pakistan border and the Bay of Bengal. To show solidarity with its ally Pakistan, the United States sent Task Force 74 led by the *USS Enterprise* into the Bay of Bengal. A task force led by *INS Vikrant* was stationed to counter the *Enterprise* task force; Soviet Navy submarines also trailed the U.S. task force. A confrontation was averted when the U.S. task force moved towards South East Asia, away from the Indian Ocean.

Type of Vessel	Indian Navy losses	Pakistan Navy losses
Destroyers	Nil	2, PNS Khaibar and Shahjahan*(damaged)
Frigates	1, INS Khukri**	Nil
Submarines	Nil	1, PNS Ghazi
Minesweeper	Nil	1, PNS Muhafiz
Navy Aircraft	1, (Alize)	Nil
Patrol boats and Gunboats	Nil	7 Gunboats and 3 patrol boats
Merchant Navy and others	Nil	11 (including one US ammunition ship)
Loss on land	Nil	Missile attack on Karachi harbour and oil installations.

*PNS Shahjahan was presumably damaged beyond repair.

The sinking of the Pakistani Navy's lone long-range submarine *PNS Ghazi* under unexplained circumstances enabled an easy Indian blockade of East Pakistan.. The missile boats *INS Nirghat* and *INS Nipat* each sank a destroyer; the *INS Veer* destroyed a minesweeper. The naval aircraft, Sea Hawks and Alizés, operating from the *Vikrant* were also instrumental in sinking many gunboats and merchant navy vessels. There was one major casualty, the frigate *Khukri* (sunk by the *PNS Hangor*), while the *Kirpan* was damaged in the western sector of conflict. Ultimately, the naval blockade of Karachi Port and the complete blockade of East Pakistan's ports were successful in cutting Pakistani troops off from reinforcements, supplies, and evacuation routes. These actions proved decisive in India's victory in the war.

Operation Cactus

In 1988, the Indian Navy joined the Indian Air Force in successfully thwarting a coup attempt by PLOTE in the Maldives. A naval maritime reconnaissance aircraft detected a vessel hijacked by PLOTE rebels. One of the hostages on-board included a senior Maldivian minister and *Operation Cactus* was launched to secure the vessel. After military intervention by INS *Godavari* and Indian marine commandos, the rebels surrendered.

1999-2001 Operations

During the 1999 Kargil conflict between India and Pakistan, the Western and Eastern fleets were deployed in the Northern Arabian Sea, as a part of *Operation Talwar*. The intent was to safeguard India's maritime assets from a potential Pakistani naval attack, as also to deter Pakistan from escalating to a full-scale war by blocking India's naval sea-trade routes. Indian Navy's aviators and commandos also fought along side Indian Army personnel during the Kargil War. The Indian Navy was a part of the joint forces exercises, Operation Parakram, during the 2001–2002 India–Pakistan standoff. More than a dozen warships were deployed. Later in 2001, the Indian Navy provided escort to United States warships traveling through the Strait of Malacca to take part in Operation Enduring Freedom.

Disaster Relief

2004 Indian Ocean earthquake

During the 2004 Indian Ocean earthquake crisis, the Indian Navy deployed 27 ships, 19 helicopters, 6 naval aircraft and over

5000 Naval personnel in disaster relief operations. These deployments were a part of various area-specific relief operations including *Operation Madath* in the Indian states of Andhra Pradesh and Tamil Nadu, *Operation Sea Waves* in the Andaman and Nicobar Islands, *Operation Castor* in Maldives, *Operation Rainbow* in Sri Lanka and *Operation Gambhir* in Indonesia. This was one of the largest relief mobilizations that the Indian Navy had undertaken. Indian Naval groups were able to start large scale rescue operations in neighboring countries within 12 hours from the time of the tsunami, and was the first foreign navy to reach the affected areas.

The quick deployment of forces during relief operations was a testing ground for the Navy's amphibious, as well as force projection capabilities. Deficiencies in the response led to modernization of the naval forces after the tsunami, including the acquisition of Landing Platform Docks (LPD) like the INS *Jalashwa* (formerly the USS *Trenton*), as well as smaller amphibious vessels.

Operation Sukoon

During the 2006 Israel-Lebanon conflict, the Indian Navy evacuated 2,286 Indian nationals and expatriates, including 436 Sri Lankan and 69 Nepali citizens, from war-torn Lebanon. This operation was named *Operation Sukoon*, meaning "Peace and tranquility". In the year 2006, ten naval doctors from India served for 102 days on USNS *Mercy* and conducted about 10 medical camps in Philippines, Bangladesh, Indonesia and East Timor. Indian Navy has also provided relief materials to survivors of cyclones in Bangladesh and Myanmar. Two ships from the Indian Navy carried the first international aid material for the victims of Cyclone Nargis in Myanmar.

Anti-piracy Operations

In October 1999, a coordinated effort by the Indian Navy and the Indian Coast Guard led to the release of a hijacked Japanese cargo ship, MV *Alondra Rainbow*, from pirates.

Piracy off the coast of Somalia has caused significant concerns in India as most of its sea-trade routes pass through the region. The Indian Navy responded to these concerns by deploying the frigate INS *Tabar* in the Gulf of Aden in October 2008. Within a month of its deployment, the *Tabar* had prevented attempts by pirates to board two cargo ships and also destroyed a pirate "mother ship".

As of November 11, 2008, the frigate had escorted 35 ships safely through the pirate-infested region. The pirates have hijacked a fishing trawler from Thailand and made it their mothership. There were also reports of India deploying destroyer INS *Mysore* to augment the frigate INS *Tabar* in anti-piracy operations. On November 21, 2008 India was granted permission to enter Somalian territorial waters to intercept suspected pirate vessels. 23 pirates were arrested by Indian Navy while attempting to hijack a merchant ship near the Gulf of Aden. Anti-piracy patrols were carried out after a request was made by the Seychelles government, resulting in the arrest of nine pirates. A further ship has been send to give a boost to anti-piracy operations. While preventing a pirate attack on a Liberian vessel MV Maud, two pirates were killed and the remaining six were apprehended. On December 07, 2009, the Indian Navy successfully repulsed a pirate attack on a US-owned tanker in the Gulf of Aden off Somalia coast. The Indian Navy was awarded by the U.N for anti-piracy operations in the Gulf of Aden.

The Commander of the Navy is the Chief of Naval Staff (CNS). Effective August 31 2009, Vice Admiral Nirmal Kumar Verma, who was fomerly the Eastern Naval Commander at Visakhapatnam, assumed responsibility as the head of Navy from incumbent Admiral.

While the provision for the rank of Admiral of the Fleet exists, it is primarily intended for major wartime use and honour. No officer of the Indian Navy has yet been conferred this rank. (Both the Army and Air Force have had officers who have been conferred with the equivalent rank-Field Marshals Sam Manekshaw and Cariappa of the Army and Marshal of the Indian Air Force (MIAF) Arjun Singh.)

Organization

The Indian Navy is divided into the following broad categories:

- Administration
- Logistics and Material

- Training
- The Fleets
- The Naval Aviation
- The Submarine Arm

Commands: The Indian Navy operates four Commands. Each Command is headed by a Flag Officer Commanding-in-Chief in the rank of Vice Admiral.

Commands	HQ Location	Current FOC-in-C
Western Naval Command	Mumbai	Vice Admiral Vinod Bhasin
Eastern Naval Command	Visakhapatnam	Vice Admiral Anup Singh
Southern Naval Command	Kochi	Vice Admiral K N Sushil
Far Eastern Naval Command	Port Blair	Vice Admiral Vijay Shankar

The Far Eastern command, a joint Navy, Army and Air force command was set up in the Andaman and Nicobar Islands in 2001 as a strategic area of defence. It was created to safeguard India's strategic interests in Southeast Asia and the Strait of Malacca. The Indian Navy plays a major role in patrolling the area with the Indonesian Navy, Royal Malaysian Navy and Royal Thai Navy. India and Australia signed an agreement to provide maritime security in the Asia Pacific region.

Bases

In 2005, the Indian Navy commissioned *INS Kadamba* at Karwar, 100 km from Goa. This is the third operational naval base after Mumbai and Vishakapatnam and the first to be controlled exclusively by the Navy. (The other bases share port facilities with civilian shipping, but this one is for purely naval use.) Built under Phase I of the multi-billion dollar 'Project Seabird', it is the largest naval base in the region. Asia's largest Naval academy INS Zamorin, was inaugurated at Ezhimala, in January 2009 by the Prime Minister of India.

Another naval base is being planned for the eastern shores, near Vishakapatnam at a cost of USD 350 million. The base, which will be located fifty km south of Vishakapatnam in Rambilli Mandal, will have comprehensive anti-aircraft, anti-submarine and amphibious capability.

The Indian Navy is setting up a Naval Station in Madagascar, to monitor and patrol the coast of Mozambique as well as the Southern Indian Ocean. The Indian Navy also has berthing rights in Oman.

Marine Commando Force

The Marine Commando Force (MCF), also known as *MARCOS*, is a special forces unit that was raised by the Indian Navy in 1987 for direct action, special reconnaissance, amphibious warfare and counter-terrorism. In 1988, the MARCOS successfully rescued several hostages, including Maldives' then-Minister of Education, aboard a ship hijacked by PLOTE mercenaries during Operation Cactus.

The MARCOS are also deployed to prevent infiltration through the Jhelum and Wular Lake and are involved in covert counter-terrorism operations in and around lakes and rivers in Jammu and Kashmir.

The MARCOS were also involved in the rescue mission of hostages captured by the terrorists in Taj Mahal Palace & Tower luxury hotel in Mumbai as part of a large terrorist attack in Mumbai metropolis in November 2008.

SHIPS

The names of all commissioned ships (and Naval Bases) of the Indian Navy are prefixed with the letters INS, designating *Indian Naval Ship* or *Indian Navy Station*. The fleet of the Indian Navy is a mix of domestic built and foreign vessels and is expanding with new inductions. India often build destroyers, frigates and corvettes.

Destroyers

The Indian Navy currently operates the *Delhi* and *Rajput* class guided-missile destroyers. The next-generation, *Kolkata* class vessels are expected to be commissioned starting in 2012.

Frigates

The guided-missile frigates currently in service are the *Talwar* class, *Brahmaputra* class and *Godavari* class. The *Nilgiri class* (variants of the British Leander class) vessels have all been decommissioned. The 3 *Advanced Talwar* class frigates (Krivak IV) are also scheduled for delivery by 2012. The next-generation *Shivalik* class vessels, which will have a lot of stealth features incorporated into them are planned for commissioning in 2010.

Corvettes

The Indian Navy currently operates the *Kora, Khukri, Veer* and *Abhay* class corvettes. The next-generation Project 28 and Project 28A class of corvettes are expected to be commissioned starting in 2012.

Amphibious Warfare Vessels

The Indian Navy has an Amphibious transport dock of the Austin class, re-christened as INS Jalashwa in service.

Aircraft Carriers

The Indian Navy presently has one aircraft carrier in active service — INS *Viraat.* The carrier is planned for decommissioning after the induction of the first domestically built *Vikrant* class aircraft carrier. The Indian Navy will also induct the Russian-built INS *Vikramaditya* in 2014.

SUBMARINES

Diesel Submarines

The Indian Navy currently maintains a fleet of diesel-electric submarines, primarily of the Sindhughosh and Shishumar classes. India signed a deal for six Scorpène class submarines with MESMA air-independent propulsion and construction has begun. These submarines will join the Indian Navy from 2012 onwards. The Indian Navy may arm its *Kilo* class submarine fleet with the BrahMos cruise missiles after successfully completing test launches from the submarine. India will issue request for proposals for another six submarines in financial year 2008-09.

Unmanned Submarines

The National Institute of Oceanography has developed the Autonomous Underwater Vehicle (AUV) that has applications in the field of Oceanographic research. Also an Autonomous Surface Vehicle (ASV) has been developed.

Nuclear Powered Submarines

In January 1988, India leased for three years an ex-Soviet Charlie class nuclear powered guided missile submarine with eight Ametist (SS-N-7 Starbright) anti-shipping missile launchers. In the Indian Navy, the vessel was christened INS *Chakra*, and the submarine was manned by an Indian crew. Upon expiration of the ship leasing term in 1991, the submarine was returned to Russia and joined the Pacific Fleet of the Russian Navy. India's indigenously designed and built nuclear-powered ballistic missile submarines of the Arihant class are expected to be commissioned starting in 2011. The lead vessel of the class, INS Arihant, was launched for sea-trials on July 26, 2009 in Visakhapatnam.

Planned Acquisitions

The Navy is purchasing from Russia the Kiev class aircraft carrier *Admiral Gorshkov* (INS *Vikramaditya*), which will be delivered to India by 2012. The Indian Navy is also negotiating with Russia for the acquisition of further *Advanced Talwar* class frigates, and six conventional submarines.

India started a program in 1985 to develop indigenous technologies for building a nuclear-powered submarine, known as the Advanced Technology Vessel (ATV) project.The first Advanced Technology Vessel is called INS Arihant, was launched on July 26, 2009.

The hull for the vessel has been built by Larsen & Toubro at its A naval version of a nuclear reactor has been developed at the Indira Gandhi Centre For Atomic Research, Kalpakkam and will be deployed on the submarine's hull after miniaturization. The Prototype Testing Centre (PTC) will be used to test the submarine's turbines and propellers. A similar facility is operational at Vishakapatnam to test the main turbines and gear box. Once the vessel is completed, it may be equipped with K-15 as well as

Sagarika/Agni-III ballistic missiles and advanced Indian made sonar systems. According to defence sources, the ATV is expected to be commissioned in 2010. Each unit will cost one billion U.S. dollars. Government has given approval for constructing the follow on SSBN's which will be larger than the Arihant class submarines. Approval has also been given for the construction of SSN's which will escort the SSBN's.

India is reportedly paying two billion dollars for the completion of two Akula-II class submarines which were 40-60% completed. Three hundred Indian Navy personnel are being trained in Russia for the operation of these submarines. India has finalized a deal with Russia, in which at the end of the lease of these submarines, it has an option to buy them. According to report, the first submarine will be commissioned into the Indian Navy in September, 2009. The first submarine will be named INS Chakra, it is currently undergoing trials in the Pacific ocean.

AIRCRAFT

The naval air-arm is an important component of the Indian Navy. The Indian Navy air arm consists of Sea Harrier jets that operate from the aircraft carrier INS *Viraat* and also from INS *Jalashwa*. Recently, the Harriers were modernized for Beyond Visual Range missile capability. The Kamov-31 provide the Airborne Early Warning cover for the fleet. In the anti-submarine role the Sea King, Ka-28 and the domestic built HAL Dhruv are used. The MARCOS use Sea King and HAL Dhruv helicopters while conducting operations. Reconnaissance operations are carried out by Tupolev 142, Ilyushin 38, Dornier Do 228 aircraft, as well as HAL Chetak helicopters. The Aircraft used for carrying out roles of a strategic bomber and as a maritime strike are carried out by 4(3 more on order) Tupolev Tu-22M, which is also capable of performing reconnaissance missions. The UAV arm consists of around 30 UAVs like Heron and Searcher-IIs that are operated from ships and shore for better surveillance. The Indian Navy also maintains a four aircraft aerobatic display team, the *Sagar Pawan*. The Sagar Pawan team will be replacing their present Kiran HJT-16 aircraft with the newly developed HJT-36 aircraft. The Indian Navy has also placed an order for 8 P-8I Poseidon long-range maritime reconnaissance (LRMR) aircraft.

In January 2004, the Indian Navy signed a contract for the delivery of 12 MiG-29K and 4 MiG-29KUB which will be operated from INS *Vikramaditya*. The first MiG-29KUB manufactured for the Navy took to the skies in May 2008. The first four aircraft were delivered to India in February 2009. There were also reports that the Indian Navy would purchase an additional 30 MiG-29Ks and-KUBs for the Indigenous Aircraft Carrier.

The Indian Air Force also has a maritime strike role, providing support to the Indian Navy. It operates SEPECAT Jaguar and Sukhoi Su-30MKI Aircraft in this role. The Jaguars are armed with the Sea Eagle missile, which will be replaced with the Harpoon missile. Su-30MKI and the Il-38 will be armed with the air-launched version of the Brahmos cruise missile.

WEAPON SYSTEMS

The Indian Navy uses modern technology and weapon systems, most of which are imported from foreign countries. Others, like the BrahMos supersonic cruise missiles, are jointly developed with Russia-a major stride in defence research. There are reports on the joint development by India and Israel of the Barak-II missile system, an improved, longer range version of the Barak-I air defence missile which is operational on Indian Navy ships. The Barak-I is used on most of the main ships of the Indian Navy. The Indian Navy's nuclear deterrence capability is based on *Sukanya* class ships armed with the *Dhanush* ballistic missiles that has a range of 350 km.

India has a number of foreign made cruise missile systems, including the Klub SS-N-27. It also has its own Nirbhay cruise missile systems under development. The Sagarika (Oceanic) submarine launched ballistic missile (SLBM), which has a range of at least 700 km (some sources claim 1000 km) forms part of India's nuclear triad. Another successful program has been the adaptation of the Yakhont anti-ship missile system into the BrahMos by the NPO and the DRDO. The BrahMos has been tailored to Indian needs and uses a large proportion of Indian-designed components and technology, including its fire control systems, transporter erector launchers, and its onboard navigational attack systems. The successful test of Brahmos from

INS Rajput (D51) provides Indian Navy with precision land attack capability.

Electronic Warfare and Systems Management

DRDO and the Indian Navy. The system comprises a family of electronic warfare suites, such as Ajanta and Ellora, for use on different naval platforms capable of intercepting, detecting, and classifying pulsed, carrier wave, pulse repetition frequency agile, frequency agile and chirp radars. The systems employ a modular approach facilitating deployment on various platforms like helicopters, vehicles, and small ships. Certain platforms, apart from ESM (electronic support measures), have ECM (electronic countermeasure) capabilities. Advanced technologies like multiple-beam phased array jammers are employed in the system for simultaneous handling of multiple threats.

The Indian Navy also relies on information technology to face the challenges of the 21st century. The Indian Navy is implementing a new strategy to move from a platform centric force to a network-centric force by linking all shore-based installations and ships via high-speed data networks and satellites. This will help in increased operational awareness. The network is referred to as the Navy Enterprise Wide Network (NEWN). The Indian Navy has also provided training to all its personnel in Information Technology (IT) at the Naval Institute of Computer Applications (NICA) located in Mumbai. Information technology is also used to provide better training, like the usage of simulators and for better management of the force

Fleet Reviews

The President of India is entitled to inspect his fleet, as he is the supreme commander of the Indian Armed Forces. The first President's fleet review by India was hosted by Dr. Rajendra Prasad on October 10, 1953. President's reviews usually take place once in the President's term. In all, nine fleet reviews have taken place, the most recent being in February 2006, when President Dr. APJ Abdul Kalam took the review The Indian Navy also conducted an International fleet review named *Bridges of Friendship* in February 2001 in Mumbai. Many ships of friendly Navies from all around the world participated, including two from the U.S. Navy. Once in two years navies from the Indian Ocean region meet at the Andaman and Nicobar Islands and the event is named as *MILAN* (Sanskrit: Get together)

NAVAL EXERCISES AND COOPERATION

India often conducts naval exercises with other friendly countries designed to increase naval interoperability and also to strengthen cooperative security relationship. Some such exercises take place annually like the *Varuna* with the French Navy, *Konkan* with the Royal Navy (UK), *Indra* with Russian Navy, *Malabar* with the U.S. Navy and *Simbex* with the Republic of Singapore Navy. The Indian Navy also conducted exercise with the People's Liberation Army Navy in 2003 and will send ships to the South China Sea to participate in the fleet review. In 2007, the *TROPEX* (Theatre-level Readiness Operational Exercises) was held during which Indian Navy experimented the doctrine of influencing a land and air battle to support the Indian Army and the Indian Air Force. Apart from the Indian Ocean, India has steadily gained influence in the Pacific Ocean. In 2007, Indian Navy conducted naval exercise with Japan Maritime Self-Defence Force and U.S Navy in the Pacific and also signed an agreement with Japan in October 2008 for joint naval patrolling in the Asia-Pacific region Naval aircraft from Indian and US Navy flying in formation over Indian Navy aircraft carrier *INS Viraat* during Malabar 2007.

India has also held naval exercise with Vietnam, Philippines and New Zealand.. In 2007, India and South Korea decided to conduct annual naval exercise. and India participated in the South Korean international fleet review. In addition, Indian Navy will also be increasing naval cooperation with other allies, particularly with Germany and Arab states of the Persian Gulf including Kuwait, Oman, Bahrain and Saudi Arabia. India held the first Indian Ocean Naval Symposium (IONS) with an objective to provide a forum for all the littoral nations of the Indian Ocean to cooperate on mutually agreed areas for better security in the region. The Indian Navy is increasingly used in international diplomacy. Since 2000, the Indian naval ships have made port calls in Israel, Turkey, Egypt, Libya, Greece, Oman, Thailand, Indonesia, Australia, New Zealand, Tonga, South Africa,Kenya,

Qatar, Oman, United Arab Emirates, Bahrain, Kuwaitz and other countries in 2005-2007.

The first Atlantic Ocean deployment of the Indian Navy happened in 2009. During this deployment, the Indian Naval fleet will conduct exercise with the French, German, Russian and British Navies.

Exploration

The Indian Navy regularly conducts adventure expeditions. The sailing ship and training vessel INS *Tarangini* began circumnavigating the world on 23 January 2003, intending to foster good relations with various other nations; she returned to India in May of the following year after visiting 36 ports in 18 nations. INS Tarangini returned to port, after a ten month long overseas voyage named Lokayan 07. Lt. Cdr. M.S. Kohli led the Indian Navy's first successful expedition to Mount Everest in 1965; the Navy's ensign was again flown atop Everest on 19 May 2004 by a similar expedition. Another Navy team also successfully scaled Everest from the north face, the technically more challenging route. The expedition was led by Cdr Satyabrata Dam, belonging to the elite submarine arm. Cdr. Dam is a mountaineer of international repute and has climbed many mountains including the Patagonias, the Alps among others. This team's record is unmatched by any other navy. The Navy was also the first to send a submariner to summit Everest.

An Indian Navy team comprising 11 members successfully completed an expedition to the Arctic pole. To prepare, they first travelled to Iceland, where they attempted to summit a peak. The team next flew to eastern Greenland; in the Kulusuk and Angmassalik areas, they used Inuit boats to navigate the region's ice-choked fjords. They crossed northward across the Arctic Circle, reaching seventy degrees North on skis. The team scaled an unnamed peak of height 11,000 feet and named it "Indian Peak"

The Indian Naval ensign first flew in Antarctica in 1981. The Indian Navy succeeded in Mission Dakshin Dhruv 2006 by traversing to the South Pole on skis. With this historic expedition, they have set the record for being the first military team to have successfully completed a ski traverse to the Geographic South

Pole. Also, three of the ten member team-the expedition leader-Cdr. Satyabrata Dam, leading medical assistants Rakesh Kumar and Vikas Kumar are now amongst the few people in the world to have visited the two poles and summited Mt. Everest. Indian Navy became the first organization to reach the poles and Mt.Everest A solo circumnavigation voyage named 'Sagar Parikrama' is underway by Cdr. Dilip Donde.

Ongoing Expansion

In 2004, India bought the Russian aircraft carrier, *Admiral Gorshkov* for the equivalent of US$1.5 billion. It will cost an additional US$1.5 billion to refit, and is expected to join the Indian Navy in 2012 as INS *Vikramaditya*. A further US$700 million will be spent to purchase 12 single-seat MiG-29K and four dual-seat MiG-29KUB fighters, six Kamov-31 attack and reconnaissance anti-submarine helicopters; also included are training facilities for pilots and technical staff, delivery of simulators and spare parts, and establishment and maintenance of Indian Navy facilities. Upgrades include removing missiles from the carrier foredeck to make way for a 14.3-degree ski-jump. The Mig-29's will be delivered to the Indian Navy in 2009.

In April 2007, India began construction of a 40,000 tonne *Vikrant* class aircraft carrier at a cost of $800 million and scheduled to operate 30 aircraft, including Naval LCA, MiG-29K, and Sea Harrier combat aircraft, as well as HAL Dhruv, Ka-31, and Sea King Mk.42 helicopters. Four turbine engines will power the ship. The carrier is being constructed by state-run Cochin Shipyard Limited. and will be commissioned by 2012-13. The Indian Minister of State for Defence, Pallam Raju, went on record in September 2006 stating that the aircraft carrier is likely to be commissioned by 2011. There are plans to build more aircraft carriers domestically.

The Indian Navy is currently undergoing rapid expansion and modernisation. Yantar, a plant in Kaliningrad, Russia, was awarded a US$1.56 billion contract to build three additional 1135.6 frigates. The increased price is due to more sophisticated armaments such as BrahMos cruise missiles. The Navy has government approval for an additional eight warships. The Indian Navy has signed a deal with Boeing to supply eight P-8 Poseidon

Anti Submarine Warfare/Maritime Surveillance Aircraft. The first aircraft will be delivered 4 years after the signing of the contract, that is 2012.

FUTURE PROSPECTS

India is expected to spend about US$40 billion on military modernization from 2008 to 2013.f A major chunk of those purchases were made for the Indian Navy. Work on the third aircraft carrier is to start in 2010 and will be inducted into the Navy by 2017. Order has been placed for seven Project 17A class frigates. India is currently focusing on expanding its submarine fleet. Also newer technology like the Unmanned Underwater Vehicle (UUV) is being developed for the Indian Navy.

After ordering six Scorpene submarines as part of Project 75, Indian Navy is now on the look out for six next-generation submarines in a project worth over Rs 30,000 crore. These six diesel-electric submarines built in India under Project-75I, will be equipped with air-independent propulsion boosting their operational capabilities and will have high degree of stealth, land-attack capability and ability to incorporate futuristic technologies. RFI has been issued to Rosoboronexport, French (Armaris), HDW and other firms, two rounds of discussions have already taken place. The RFP or global tender will be issued in late-2008 or early-2009.

The RFP (request for proposal) for six MRMR aircraft with anti-submarine warfare (ASW) capabilities was issued on July 11, 2008 to Italian Alenia Aeronautica's ATR-72-500MP aircraft, Brazilian Embraer P-99, French Dassault's Falcon 900DX and Russian Antonov-72P. The contract is expected to be signed by June 2009 and deliveries to begin by 2012. The contract is estimated to cost Rs. 1,600 crore. The Navy is also planning to induct more UAVs. The India-Israel joint venture to convert the Chetak helicopters into unmanned UAV's that can operate from ships is progressing steadily. All these will be linked with space-based reconnaissance systems. On January 13, 2009, India has issued a request for proposals (RFPs) for six Medium Range Maritime Reconnaissance (MRMR) aircraft. The new aircraft, which will replace the aging fleet of 10 Islander aircraft in service, are to be equipped with an Airborne Early Warning system. The Indian Coast Guard has an additional requirement for six MRMRs without an Airborne Early Warning system. The MRMR is required to have a range of 500 nautical miles and an endurance of 6 hours. Aircraft competing for the order include a variant of Boeing's P-8I, and possibly the turboprop ATR-72MP, EADS C-295, Dassault's Falcon 900MPA and Embraer P-99A platforms. For the Coast Guard RFP, contenders could be the ATR-42MP, C-295 or CN-235MP.

Indian Navy has issued a tender for procurement of 16 advanced, multi-role naval helicopters to AgustaWestland, EADS and Sikorsky. The order is likely to be expanded to 60 helicopters. The helicopters will be equipped with anti-ship and anti-submarine warfare equipment including cruise missiles and torpedoes, and also be capable of being refuelled in flight. The type will operate from both naval vessels and land bases.

Global bids has been floated to acquire eight mine countermeasure vessels (MCMVs), to replace the twelve Pondicherry class ocean minesweepers in service. France's DCN International, Fincantieri of Italy, Izar of Spain, Kangnam Shipbuilding Co. of South Korea and Northrop Grumman of the U.S have been invited to participate in the bidding process. Six of the craft will be produced at Goa shipyard under transfer of technology.

With the recent and ongoing upgrades and inductions, independent analysts expect that the Indian Navy may soon become a blue-water navy. India's navy is already the most powerful in the region, and with further upgrades in the future, aims to control the Indian Ocean Region, from the coast of East Africa to Australia.f India is also the only Asian navy to regularly operate aircraft carriers.

The aim is to have a total of three Aircraft carriers resulting in two fully operational Carrier battle groups and an additional Aircraft carrier eventually in refit making India an operating Blue-water navy.

The ambitious long term plan that was recently revealed shows a road-map to blue water navy with six aircraft carriers.

SAGARIKA (MISSILE)

Sagarika is a nuclear-capable submarine-launched ballistic missile with a range of 750 kilometres (466 mi).

Overview

Sagarika has a length of 10 metres (33 ft), diameter of 0.74 metres (2 ft 5 in), weighs 17 tonnes (17 LT; 19 ST) and can carry a payload of up to 500 kilograms (1,102 lb). Sagarika was developed at the DRDO's missile complex in Hyderabad. This missile will form part of the triad in India's nuclear deterrence, and will provide retaliatory nuclear strike capability.

Development

The development of this missile (under the title Project K-15 started in 1991. The Indian government first confirmed Sagarika's development seven years later (1998), when the then Defence Minister, George Fernandes, announced it during a press conference. The development of the underwater missile launcher, known as Project 420 (P420), was completed in 2001 and handed over to the Indian Navy for trials. The missile launcher is developed at Hazira in Gujarat. The scientists who developed the missile were felicitated by the Prime Minister of India, Dr. Manmohan Singh.

Testing

The missile was successfully test fired six times, and tested to its full range up to three times. The tests of February 26, 2008 was conducted from a submerged pontoon off the coast of Vishakhapatnam. A land-based version of the K-15 Sagarika was successfully test-fired on November 12, 2008

Induction

The Indian Navy plans to introduce the missile into service by the end of 2010. Sagarika missile is being integrated with India's nuclear-powered Arihant class submarine that began sea trials on the 26th of July 2009. India also successfully developed a land variant of Sagarika, known as Shaurya which can be stored in underground silos for longer time and can be launched using gas canisters as booster.

SHAURYA MISSILE

The Shaurya missile (Sanskrit: *Valour*) is a canister launched hypersonic surface-to-surface tactical missile developed by the Indian Defence Research and Development Organization (DRDO) for use by the Indian Armed Forces. It has a range of between 600-700 km and is capable of carrying a payload of one-tonne conventional or nuclear warhead It can hit targets deep inside Pakistan and China. The Shaurya missile provides India with a significant second strike capability

DESCRIPTION

The Shaurya missile is speculated to be the land version of the under-water Sagarika K-15 missile, although DRDO officials have reportedly denied its connection with the K-15 program Similar to the BrahMos, Shaurya is stored in a composite canister, which makes it much easier to store for long periods without maintenance as well as to handle and transport. It also houses the gas generator to eject the missile from the canister before its solid propellant motors take over to hurl it at the intended target.

Shaurya missiles can remain hidden or camouflaged in underground silos from enemy surveillance or satellites till they are fired from the special storage-cum-launch canisters. DRDO scientists admit that given Shaurya's limited range at present, either the silos will have to be constructed closer to India's borders or an extended range version will have to be developed. The Shaurya system will require some more tests before it becomes fully operational in two-three years. Moreover, defence scientists say the high-speed, two-stage Shaurya has *high maneuverability* which also makes it *less vulnerable* to existing anti-missile defence systems. Shaurya can reach a velocity of Mach 6 even at low altitudes. On November 12, even before the missile crossed a distance of 300 km, it reached a velocity of Mach 5, heating up its surface to 700{+0} Celsius. The missile performed rolls to spread the heat uniformly on its surface. Its flight time is 500 seconds to 700 seconds. with its high-performance navigation and guidance systems, efficient propulsion systems, state-of-the-art control technologies and canisterised launch. It can be easily transported by road. The missile, encased in a canister, is mounted on a single vehicle, which has only a driver's cabin, and the vehicle itself is the launch platform. This "single vehicle solution" reduces its signature – it cannot be easily detected by satellites – and makes its deployment easy. The gas generator, located at the bottom of the canister, fires for about a second and a half. It produces high pressure gas, which expands and ejects the missile from the tube. The missile has six motors; the first one is the motor in the gas generator. The centerpiece of a host of new technologies incorporated in Shourya is its ring laser gyroscope and accelerometer. The ring laser gyroscope was made by the Research Center Imarat (RCI) based in Hyderabad

First test

The missile was first test fired on November 12, 2008. The missile was launched from an underground facility with an in-built canister from Complex-3 of the Integrated Test Range at Chandipur

The Shaurya missile (Sanskrit: *Valour*) is a canister launched hypersonic surface-to-surface tactical missile developed by the Indian Defence Research and Development Organization (DRDO) for use by the Indian Armed Forces. It has a range of between 600-700 km and is capable of carrying a payload of one-tonne conventional or nuclear warhead. It can hit targets deep inside Pakistan and China. The Shaurya missile provides India with a significant second strike capability.

Description

The Shaurya missile is speculated to be the land version of the under-water Sagarika K-15 missile, although DRDO officials have reportedly denied its connection with the K-15 program. Similar to the BrahMos, Shaurya is stored in a composite canister, which makes it much easier to store for long periods without maintenance as well as to handle and transport. It also houses the gas generator to eject the missile from the canister before its solid propellant motors take over to hurl it at the intended target.

Shaurya missiles can remain hidden or camouflaged in underground silos from enemy surveillance or satellites till they are fired from the special storage-cum-launch canisters. DRDO scientists admit that given Shaurya's limited range at present, either the silos will have to be constructed closer to India's borders or an extended range version will have to be developed. The Shaurya system will require some more tests before it becomes fully operational in two-three years. Moreover, defence scientists say the high-speed, two-stage Shaurya has *high maneuverability* which also makes it *less vulnerable* to existing anti-missile defence systems. Shaurya can reach a velocity of Mach 6 even at low altitudes. On November 12, even before the missile crossed a distance of 300 km, it reached a velocity of Mach 5, heating up its surface to 700{+0} Celsius. The missile performed rolls to spread the heat uniformly on its surface. Its flight time is 500 seconds to 700 seconds. with its high-performance navigation and guidance systems, efficient propulsion systems, state-of-the-art control technologies and canisterised launch. It can be easily transported by road. The missile, encased in a canister, is mounted on a single vehicle, which has only a driver's cabin, and the vehicle itself is the launch platform. This "single vehicle solution" reduces its signature – it cannot be easily detected by satellites – and makes its deployment easy. The gas generator, located at the bottom of the canister, fires for about a second and a half. It produces high pressure gas, which expands and ejects the missile from the tube. The missile has six motors; the first one is the motor in the gas generator. The centerpiece of a host of new technologies incorporated in Shourya is its ring laser gyroscope and accelerometer. The ring laser gyroscope was made by the Research Center Imarat (RCI) based in Hyderabad.

First Test

The missile was first test fired on November 12, 2008. The missile was launched from an underground facility with an inbuilt canister from Complex-3 of the Integrated Test Range at Chandipur.

8

Types of Navy in Difference Countries

FRENCH NAVY

The French Navy, officially the Marine nationale (*National Navy*) and often called La Royale is the maritime arm of the French military. It consists of a full range of vessels, from patrol boats to guided missile frigates, and operates one nuclear aircraft carrier and ten nuclear submarines (four of which are submarine-launched ballistic missile–capable (SNLEs)). The motto of the French Navy is *Honneur, Patrie, Valeur, Discipline* ("Honour, Fatherland, Valour, Discipline"). These words are found on the deck of every ship of the Navy.

History

The French navy is affectionately known as *La Royale* ("the Royal"). The reason is not well known; some theorise that it is for its traditional attachment to the French monarchy, some others said that before to be named "nationale", the Navy had be named "royale" or simply because of the location of its headquarters, "rue Royale" in Paris. The navy did not sport the royal titles common with other European navies like the British Royal Navy.

Middle Ages

The history of the French Navy goes back to the Middle Ages, when it was defeated by the English at the Battle of Sluys and, with Castilian help, managed to beat the English at the Battle of La Rochelle.

Colbert

The Navy became a consistent instrument of national power around the seventeenth century with Louis XIV. Under the tutelage of the "Sun King," the French Navy was well financed and equipped, managing to score several early victories in the Nine Years War against the Royal Navy and the Dutch Navy. Financial troubles, however, forced the navy back to port and allowed the English and the Dutch to regain the initiative. Before the Nine Years War, in the Franco-Dutch War, it managed to score a decisive victory over a combined Spanish-Dutch fleet at the Battle of Palermo.

18th Century

The eighteenth century saw the beginning of Royal Navy domination, which managed to inflict a number of significant defeats on the French. However, the French Navy continued to score various successes, as in the campaigns led in the Atlantic by Picquet de la Motte. In 1766, Bougainville led the first French circumnavigation

During the American War of Independence the French Navy played a decisive role in supporting the American side. In a very impressive effort, the French under de Grasse managed to defeat a British fleet at the Battle of the Chesapeake in 1781, thus ensuring that the Franco-American ground forces would win the ongoing Battle of Yorktown.

In India, Suffren waged campaigns against the British (1770-1780), successfully contending for supremacy against Vice-Admiral Sir Edward Hughes. The French Revolution, in eliminating numerous officers of noble lineage (among them, Charles d'Estaing), all but crippled the French Navy. Efforts to make it into a powerful force under Napoleon I were dashed by the death of Latouche Tréville in 1804, and the Battle of Trafalgar in 1805, where the British all but annihilated a combined Franco-Spanish fleet. The disaster guaranteed British naval domination until World War II.

In 1810 the French Navy achieved an important victory against the British during the Napoleonic Wars, was the Battle of Grand Port, a frigate action in the Indian Ocean won by Admiral Duperré.

19th century Revival

Abel Aubert Dupetit Thouars taking over Tahiti on 9 September 1842. July Monarchy.

Global Interventions

In a speech in 1852, Napoleon III famously proclaimed that "The Empire means peace" (*"L'Empire, c'est la paix"*), but actually he was thoroughly determined to follow a strong foreign policy to extend France's power and glory. Around that time, the French Navy was involved in a multitude of actions around the world.

Oceania (July Monarchy)

In 1842, the French Navy took over Tahiti under Admiral Abel Aubert Dupetit Thouars. French activity in those parts would continue throughout the 19th century, as his nephew Abel-Nicolas Bergasse Dupetit Thouars went on pacifying the Marquesas Islands in 1880.

The Crimean War

Napoleon III's challenge to Russia's claims to influence in the Ottoman Empire led to France's successful participation in the Crimean War (March 1854–March 1856). During this war Napoleon successfully established a French alliance with Britain, which continued after the war's close.

CONQUEST OF COCHIN CHINA

Napoleon III took the first steps to establishing a French colonial influence in Indochina. He approved the launching of the Cochinchina Campaign in 1858 to punish the Vietnamese for their mistreatment of French Catholic missionaries and force the court to accept a French presence in the country. An important factor in his decision was the belief that France risked becoming a second-rate power by not expanding its influence in East Asia. Also, the idea that France had a civilising mission was spreading. This eventually led to a full-out invasion in 1861. By 1862 the war was over and Vietnam conceded three provinces in the south, called by the French Cochin-China, opened three ports to French trade, allowed free passage of French warships to Cambodia (which led to a French protectorate over Cambodia in 1867), allowed freedom of action for French missionaries and gave France a large indemnity for the cost of the war. The French frigate *Guerrière* commanded by Admiral Roze was the lead ship in the French Campaign against Korea, 1866. Here the ship is photographed in Nagasaki harbour, circa 1865.

Second Opium War

In China, France took part in the Second Opium War along with Great Britain, and in 1860 French troops entered Beijing. China was forced to concede more trading rights, allow freedom of navigation of the Yangzi river, give full civil rights and freedom of religion to Christians, and give France and Britain a huge indemnity. This combined with the intervention in Vietnam set the stage for further French influence in China leading up to a sphere of influence over parts of Southern China.

Mexico

The French Navy conducted a successful blockade of Mexico in the Pastry War of 1838. It was then heavily involved in French intervention in Mexico (January 1862–March 1867). Napoleon III, using as a pretext the Mexican Republic's refusal to pay its foreign debts, planned to establish a French sphere of influence in North America by creating a French-backed monarchy in Mexico, a project which was supported by Mexican conservatives tired of the anti-clerical Mexican republic.

Korea

In 1866, French Navy troops made an attempt to colonise Korea, during the French campaign against Korea. The French Navy also had a significant presence in Japan with the Bombardment of Shimonoseki in 1863. In 1867-1868, some level of presence in Japan was maintained around the actions of French Military Mission to Japan, and the subsequent Boshin war.

Sino-French War

The projection of French naval power in the Far East reached a peak in the first half of the 1880s. The Far East Squadron (*escadre de l'Extrême-Orient*), an exceptional naval grouping of two (subsequently three) naval divisions under the command of Admiral Amédée Courbet created for the duration of the Sino-French War (August 1884 to April 1885), saw considerable action during the war along the China Coast and in the seas around Formosa (Taiwan). Besides almost obliterating China's Fujian Fleet at the Battle of Fuzhou (23 August 1884), the squadron took part in the bombardment and landings at Jilong (Keelung) and Danshui (Tamsui) (5 and 6 August 1884 and 1 to 8 October 1884), the blockade of Formosa (October 1884 to April 1885), the Battle of Shipu (14 February 1885), the so-called Battle of Zhenhai (1 March 1885), the Pescadores Campaign (March 1885) and the 'rice blockade' of the Yangzi River (March to June 1885).

Technological innovations (19th century)

In the nineteenth century, the navy recovered and became arguably the second finest in the world after the Royal Navy, albeit very much smaller. The French Navy, eager to challenge British naval supremacy, took a leadership role in many areas of warship development, with the introduction of new technologies.

- France led the development of shell guns for the Navy, with its invention by Henri-Joseph Paixhans
- In 1850, *Le Napoléon* became the first steam-powered battleship in history.
- *La Gloire* became the first seagoing ironclad in history when she was launched in 1859.
- In 1863, the French Navy launched *Plongeur*, the first submarine in the world to be propelled by mechanical power.
- In 1876, the *Redoutable* became the first steel-hulled warship ever.
- In 1887, the *Dupuy de Lôme* became the world's first armoured cruiser.

The French Navy also became an active proponent of the "*Jeune École*" doctrine, calling for small but powerful warships using torpedoes and shell guns to attack the British fleet. French warship construction proved attractive to the newly industrialising Japan, when the French engineer Émile Bertin was invited to assist in warship design for the Imperial Japanese Navy.

20th century

The development of the French Navy slowed down in the beginning of 20th century as the naval arms race between Germany and Great Britain grew in intensity. As a result, it was outnumbered not only by the Royal Navy but also by the German and US Navies, which were also technically superior. It was late to introduce new battleships-dreadnoughts and light cruisers and it entered World War I with relatively few modern vessels.

The Entente Cordiale ended the period in which Britain was seen as a potential enemy, reducing the need for a strong navy. Although there was no formal military alliance, there was a de facto agreement that France would play a leading role in the Mediterranean and Britain would protect the Northern coast of France against a possible German attack.

During the war, the main French effort was on land, so not many new warships were built. Despite it, it performed well in World War I. The main operation of the French Navy was Dardanelles Campaign. Most significant losses during the war were four pre-dreadnought battleships.

A number of major ships of the French Navy at the outbreak / end of World War:

- dreadnought battleships: 4/7
- pre-dreadnought battleships: 17/13
- armoured cruisers: 22/18
- protected cruisers: 13/12
- destroyers: 35/42 (displacement over 500 tons)
- torpedo boats: 180/164
- submarines: 50/61

The First proto-aircraft Carrie

The invention of the seaplane in 1910 with the French *Le Canard* led to the earliest development of ships designed to carry aeroplanes, albeit equipped with floats. In 1911 appears the French Navy *La Foudre*, the first seaplane carrier. She was commissioned as a seaplane tender, and carried float-equipped planes under hangars on the main deck, from where they were lowered on the sea with a crane. *La Foudre* was further modified in November 1913 with a 10 metre flat deck to launch her seaplanes.

FLEET CONSTRUCTION BETWEEN THE WORLD WARS

After the World War I, the French Navy remained the 4th largest in the world, after the British, US and Japanese navies, but the Italian Navy, considered as the main enemy, was close. This order of fleets, with the French Navy equal to the Italian Navy, was sanctioned by the 1922 Washington Naval Treaty. Every naval fleet consists of a variety of ships of different sizes, and no fleet has enough resources to make every vessel supreme in its class. Nonetheless, different countries strive to excel in particular classes. Between the world wars, the French fleet was remarkable in its building of small numbers of ships that were "over the top" with relation to their equivalents of other powers. For example, the French chose to build "super-destroyers" which were deemed during the Second World War by the Allies as the equivalent of light cruisers.

The *Le Fantasque* class of destroyer is still the world's fastest class of destroyer. The *Surcouf* submarine was the largest and most powerful of its day. The *Dunkerque* class battleships, designed specially to fight the German so-called pocket battleships, were, in spite of their relatively small size, very well-balanced designs and precursors of a new fast battleship generation in the world. The *Richelieu* class full-size battleships are considered by some experts as the most successful battleships, built under displacement limits of Washington Treaty in the world.

In spite of proposals of the French inventor Clément Ader in 1909 to build a ship with a flat deck to operate aeroplanes at sea, similar to modern aircraft carriers, the French Navy built its first aircraft carrier only in 1920s and did not go further in developing aircraft carriers before World War II. In 1920, Paul Teste achieved the first carrier landing of the history of the French Navy, aboard the *Béarn*. Major ships of the French Navy at the beginning of German attack in May 1940:

Submarine *Surcouf,* at the beginning of World War II, the largest submarine in the world.

- modern battleships: 2

- old battleships-dreadnoughts: 5 (*Bretagne, Provence, Lorraine, Paris and Courbet*)
- aircraft carriers: 1 (*Béarn*, and one planned)
- seaplane carriers: 1
- heavy cruisers: 7
- light cruisers: 11
- big destroyers: 32 (*Contre-Torpilleurs*)
- destroyers: 38
- submarines: 77 (and two dozen in various stages of completion)
- sloops and escorts: 65 (with over twenty in various stages of completion and several in reserve)

Apart from these, there was one modern battleship advanced in construction; the second battleship, one aircraft carrier, numerous submarines and several destroyers were in different stages of construction.

Second World War

At the outset of the war, the French Navy was involved in a number of operations against the Axis Powers, participating in the Battle of the Atlantic, the Allied campaign in Norway, the Dunkirk evacuation and, briefly, the Battle of the Mediterranean. However, Pétain's armistice terms completely changed the situation: the French fleet immediately withdrew from the fight.

The British perceived the French fleet under the Vichy government as a potentially lethal threat. This threat would be made all the more real should the French somehow become formal enemies or, more likely, should the German Navy (*Kriegsmarine*) gain control of French vessels. It was essential that the French Navy be put out of action. Some vessels were in British-controlled ports in Britain or Egypt. Many ships were easily persuaded to re-join the Allies as part of the Free French Navy (*Forces navales françaises libres*, FNFL) because of General de Gaulle's growing influence.

However, the bulk of the French fleet remained in Mers-el-Kebir or Dakar. The Royal Navy delivered an ultimatum to the non-Free French fleet at Mers-el-Kebir. On 3 July 1940, the British opened fire and sank or damaged much of the fleet when agreement proved impossible (Operation Catapult). In September, an attempt to take Vichy-held Dakar ended with the Battle of Dakar and a victory for the Vichy forces. In addition, the Allied attack on Dakar led directly to the Vichy bombing of Gibraltar. These actions soured Anglo-French relations, but did not inhibit further defections to the Allies. The subsequent Battle of Gabon, the Syria-Lebanon Campaign, and the Battle of Madagascar ended in Vichy defeats

During Operation Torch in November 1942, the Allies invaded French North Africa and the Vichy forces quickly turned sides. In response, the Germans launched Case Anton and occupied the Vichy-held portion of Metropolitan France. The German occupation included the French naval port of Toulon where the main part of the surviving French fleet lay. This was a major German objective and forces under SS command had

Light cruiser *Georges Leygues* provided fire support during Normandy and French Riviera landings.

been detailed to capture them (Operation *Lila*). This eventually resulted in French sailors sinking their own ships to save them from falling into German hands (scuttling of the French fleet in Toulon). No French capital ships and few others were taken in reparable condition. A few ships fled Toulon and joined the Allies. Five submarines tried to escape. Three of them were successful, the *Casabianca*, Glorieux and Marsouin. Following "Torch", remnants of the French Navy moved to the Allies, including ships interned in Egypt, and then there were French FNFL warships supporting the Allied landings in Normandy and southern France (Operation Dragoon).

The conquest of the European harbours put an end to the combat operations of the Navy, which spent the rest of the war clearing mines and repairing port installations. On the Pacific theatre, the French Navy was present until the Japanese capitulation ; *Richelieu* was present at the Japanese instrument of surrender. At the end of the war, the weight of the French navy was 400,000 tonnes (800,000 in May 1940).

The French navy ships *Béarn, Fantasque, Triomphant, Duquesne, Tourville,* and *Emile Bertin* helped transport the French Far East

Expeditionary Corps to French Indochina in 1946.

The French Navy Today

As of 2006, the French Navy is the largest naval employer in Western Europe, including, among other things, the Marseille Marine Fire Battalion. The chief of the naval staff is Admiral Pierre-François Forissier.

Branches

The Navy is organised in five branches:

- The *"Force d'Action Navale"* ("Naval Action Force"), surface fleet
- The *"Forces Sous-marines"* ("Submarine forces"), strategic nuclear deterrent fleet based at Île Longue
- The *"Aviation Navale"* ("Naval air force"), ground and sea-based planes and helicopters
- The *"Fusiliers Marins"* ("Naval fusiliers", ground forces used to secure naval installations) and *"Commandos de Marine"* (amphibious assault and other special operations), collectively known as FORFUSCO.
- The *"Gendarmerie maritime"*, police operations and coast guard

Note that the *Troupes de Marine* ("Naval Troops"), which comprise the *Régiments d'Infanterie de Marine* (the famous elite *RIMa*) are the modern name of the *Troupes Coloniales* ("Colonial Troops"), and are not part of the Navy, but of the Army.

Ships

French naval doctrine calls for two aircraft carriers, but the French only have one, the *Charles de Gaulle*. The order for the Future French aircraft carrier based on the design of the British Queen Elizabeth class aircraft carrier (under construction as of 2009) has been delayed several times for budgetary reasons, priority being given to the more easily exportable FREMM project; the decision on whether to build the second carrier has now been delayed until 2012. The navy is in the midst of major technological and procurement changes; newer submarines have been ordered as well as new jet fighters, the Dassault Rafales.

- 1 aircraft carrier (*Charles de Gaulle*),
- 1 helicopter cruiser (*Jeanne d'Arc*)
- 2 amphibious assault ships of the The *Mistral* type
- 2 Landing Platform Dock of the *Foudre* type
- 13 destroyers (officially classified as frigates)
- 11 frigates
- 9 corvettes (classified as "aviso")
- 4 ballistic missile submarines
- 6 nuclear attack submarines.

AIRCRAFT

Currently (2009) aircraft in service are :

Shipborne aircraft

- 41 Super Etendard (11F,17F)
- 28 Rafales (12F)
- 3 E-2 Hawkeye (4F)

Maritime patrol aircraft

- 22 Atlantique 2 (21F,23F)

Surveillance aircraft

- 5 Falcon 200 "Gardian" (25F)
- 4 Falcon 50 M (24F)

Support and training

- 6 Falcon DA 10 (57S)
- 11 Xingu (24F,28F)
- 7 Cap 10 (50S)
- 9 MS88 Rallye (50S)

HELICOPTERS

ASW

- 26 HAS.2 Lynx (31F,34F)

ASuW

- 16 AS 365 Panther (36F)

Rescue

- 11 SA 365 Dauphin (35F)
- 8 SA 321 Super-Frelon (32F)

Support and training

- 26 SA 3160 Alouette III (35F,22S)

Bases

As of 2009, the naval bases in use are :

- Toulon, home of the Force d'action navale, the *Charles de Gaulle*, the tactical nuclear submarines, of a large part of the surface fleet and the special commando of combat swimmer : the commando Hubert.
- Brest, home of the part of the surface fleet tasked to protect the FOST, the mine warfare force, the GEAOM (Training Squadron for Naval Officers), hydrographic and oceanographic fleet and a flotilla of patrol boats, intervention tugs, and training ships.
- Ile Longue (near Brest) home of the strategic nuclear arm of the fleet (FOST).
- Cherbourg, home of a flotilla of patrol craft, intervention tug and a mine clearance diving unit with support ship *Vulcain* (M611)..

Regional presence bases :

- Fort de France, with surveillance frigate *Ventôse* (F733) and BATRAL *Francis Garnier*.
- Degrad des Cannes, harbours patrol vessels *La Capricieuse* (P684) and *L'Audacieuse* (P682).
- Port des Galets, hosts the fleet of patrol boats who police the large Southern EEZ, notably surveillance frigates, *Floréal* (F 730) and *Nivôse* (F 732), Austral patrol boat *Albatros* (P681), BATRAL *La Grandière* (L9034) and patrol vessels *La Boudeuse* (P683) and *La Rieuse* (P690).
- Nouméa, with surveillance frigate *Vendémiaire* (F734), BATRAL *Jacques Cartier* (L9033) and patrol vessels *La Glorieuse* (P686) and *La Moqueuse* (P688).

- Papeete, with surveillance frigate *Prairial* (F731), BATRAL *Dumont d'Urville* (L9032), high sea tug *Revi* (A635), patrol vessels *La Railleuse* (P689), *La Tapageuse* (P691) and *Jasmin* (P723).
- Abu Dhabi, United Arab Emirates's first foreign forces deployed on its soil
- Dakar, harbours the landing craft *Sabre*, support of the temporarily deployed ships (6 ships in 2007).
- Djibouti the home port of the flagship of ALINDIEN, the French naval task force in the Indian Ocean, with Command and Replenishement Tanker *Var* (A608), 2 stationed frigates detached from Toulon, a detachment of commandos (commando Arta) supported by landing craft *Dague* (L9052).

Metropolitan France

- BAN Landivisiau 4F,23F,24F
- BAN Lann-Bihoue 4F,23F,24F
- BAN Lanvéoc-Poulmic 32F,34F,22S,50S
- BAN Nîmes-Garons 21F,28F
- BAN Hyères 31F,35F,36F,57S

Overseas Departments and Territories

Other establishments:

- Aspretto
- Bayonne, home of three patrol ships and craft for surveillance duty of the missile launch range of Biscarosse.
- Lorient, headquarter of FORFUSCO, naval fusiliers college, training center, commando units "Jaubert", "Kieffer", "de Montfort", "de Penfentenyo", "Trepel" and the "ECTLO".
- Marseille, the fire department of Marseille is a part of the French Navy: the Marseille Marine Fire Battalion.
- Dzaoudzi

Future Developments

The French Navy is undertaking a significant reinforcement, both in modernising and in number, under the *Projet de loi de programmation militaire 2003–2008* ("Military programme law project 2003–2008"), which notably calls for:

- Two *Horizon* frigates (the *Forbin* and *Chevalier Paul*) that are now fitting out;
- 11 FREMM multipurpose frigates—eight have so far been ordered, the first of which is due to be delivered in 2012.
- Six nuclear attack submarines of the *Barracuda* class—the first commissioning (the *Suffren*) being expected for 2017.
- On 18 April 2009, construction of 3rd *Mistral* class amphibious assault ship was started. A fourth ship may also be built.
- Four L-Cat (CNIM's new Landing craft) were also ordered.
- A second aircraft carrier, the Future French aircraft carrier. This project appears delayed almost indefinitely as of late 2008.
- New models of the successful Exocet missile
- MBDA Aster and SYLVER launcher systems for anti-missile and anti-air defence
- Cruise missiles-the surface naval or submarine *SCALP EG*

NAVAL REACTORS

Naval Reactors (often abbreviated to NR) is an umbrella term for the U.S. government office that has comprehensive responsibility for the continued safe and reliable operation of the United States Navy's nuclear propulsion program. A single entity, it has authority and reporting responsibilities within both the Department of the Navy and the U.S. Department of Energy.

HISTORY

Soon after his U.S. Navy service during World War II, Admiral Hyman G. Rickover became an early convert to the idea of nuclear marine propulsion. Assigned to the Bureau of Ships in September 1947, Rickover received training in nuclear power at Oak Ridge, Tennessee, and worked with the bureau to explore the possibility of nuclear ship propulsion. In February 1949 he received an assignment to the Division of Reactor Development, U.S. Atomic Energy Commission and then assumed control of the Navy's effort as Director of the Naval Reactors Branch in the Bureau of Ships.

As noted above, the office was originally a joint activity of the U.S. Atomic Energy Commission (AEC) and the U.S. Navy's Bureau of Ships. When the AEC was abolished, Naval Reactors became a joint effort of the Navy and the Energy Research and Development Administration, which partly replaced the AEC. In 1977, ERDA was combined with the Federal Energy Administration to form the US Department of Energy. On the Navy side of the organization, the Bureau of Ships has given way since the 1950s to the Naval Sea Systems Command, within which NR is Code 08, usually abbreviated NAVSEA-08.

Within seven years of its inception, the organization that developed out of this concept would put into operation the nation's first power reactor (the *Nautilus* prototype). The following four years would see three more nuclear submarines and two reactor plant prototypes operating and another seven ships and two prototypes being built. To date, more reactors have been built and safely operated by the NR program than any other U.S. program.

Current and Past Directors

1949 to February 1, 1982, Admiral Hyman G. Rickover

February 1, 1982 to Oct. 22, 1988, Admiral Kinnaird R. McKee

Oct. 22, 1988 to Sep 27, 1996: Admiral Bruce DeMars

Sep 27, 1996 to Nov 5, 2004: Admiral Frank "Skip" Bowman, USN

Nov 5, 2004 to Present : Admiral Kirkland H. Donald, USN

Management and Personnel Principles

Many books (including those referenced below) and articles have been written about core NR management principles such as attention to detail and adherence to rigidly-defined standards and specifications, as well as the organization's unique (for government) personnel practices. NR staff and alumni (including Admiral Rickover himself) have often been called by Congress, the President and other government agencies to provide expert opinion and management support to other important government programs, most notably the large scale reviews following the destruction of the Space Shuttles *Columbia* and *Challenger*. NR alumni have also founded or led numerous corporate and industrial organizations, for example MPR Associates, Inc., founded by three of Admiral Rickover's leading technical managers in NR's early days.

NR originally recruited the majority of its personnel from three sources: the Navy Engineering Duty Officer (EDO) community, other government technology programs and the submarine force. At that time, these selectees from other agencies and programs comprised the "cream" of the available crop. These personnel had been highly successful in their respective fields, whether in naval engineering and construction, in atomic energy laboratories or in submarines. NR attempted to "skim the cream" from those already competitive sources. The importance of this effort, to select only from the "cream of the crop," cannot be overestimated. In addition, it is believed that insight can be gained from evaluating the education, training and qualification programs at NR; programs considered by many to have made a lasting contribution to the field of nuclear safety.

It is sometimes assumed that the comprehensive personnel management system developed by NR was, somehow, readily available at the outset. This was not the case, either as regards selection or the education, training and qualification areas. The system as it exists today was built through vision, will, and persistence. In addition, it drew upon a number of already competitive Navy education programs (e.g., Naval Academy and the Naval Reserve Officer Training Corps (NROTC)). A number of obstacles had to be overcome to reach the point where it is today; maintaining such a system requires unremitting top management attention to keep further obstacles from arising and old ones from resurfacing.

NUCLEAR MARINE PROPULSION

A nuclear fuel element for the cargo ship NS *Savannah*. The element contains four bundles of 41 fuel rods. The uranium oxide is enriched to 4.2 and 4.6 percent of U-235

Power Plants

The majority of marine reactors are of the pressurized water, although the Soviets designed and fielded warships powered with liquid metal cooled reactors. Marine-type reactors which differ from commercial reactors producing electricity in that:

- marine reactors are compact but have high power density, i.e. they produce significant power in a small volume, however the total amount of power produced in a marine reactor is small (hundreds of MWt) compared to a commercial power reactor (thousands of MWt).
- the fuel used is typically of higher enrichment; some run on low-enriched uranium (requiring frequent refuelings), others run on highly enriched uranium (greater than 20% U-235, varying to over 96% in U.S. submarines (They do not need to be refueled as often and are quieter in operation from smaller coreto between 30–40% in Russian submarines to lower levels in some others),
- the fuel is not ceramic UO_2 (uranium oxide) but a metal-zirconium alloy (circa 15% U with 93% enrichment, or more U with lower enrichment),
- marine reactors are designed for long core life, enabled by the relatively high enrichment of the uranium and by incorporating a "burnable poison" in the cores which is progressively depleted as fission products and minor actinides accumulate; the two effects cancel each other out. One of the technical difficulties is the creation of a fuel which will tolerate the very large amount of radiation damage. It is known that during use the properties of nuclear fuel change; it is quite possible for fuel to crack and for fission gas bubbles to form.

Long-term integrity of the compact reactor pressure vessel is maintained by providing an internal neutron shield. (This is in contrast to early Soviet civil PWR designs where embrittlement occurs due to neutron bombardment of a very narrow pressure vessel.)

The Russian, U.S. and British navies rely on steam turbine propulsion, while the French and Chinese use the turbine to generate electricity for propulsion (turbo-electric propulsion). Most Russian submarines as well as most American aircraft carriers since CVN-65 are powered by two reactors (although *Enterprise* has eight). U.S., British, French and Chinese submarines are powered by one.

Decommissioning nuclear-powered submarines has become a major task for US and Russian navies. After defuelling, U.S. practice is to cut the reactor section from the vessel for disposal in shallow land burial as low-level waste. In Russia, the whole vessels, or the sealed reactor sections, typically remain stored afloat, although a new facility near Sayda Bay is beginning to provide storage in a concrete-floored facility on land for some submarines in the Far North.

Russia is well advanced with plans to build a floating nuclear power plant for their far eastern territories. The design has two 35 MWe units based on the KLT-40 reactor used in icebreakers (with refueling every four years). Some Russian naval vessels have been used to supply electricity for domestic and industrial use in remote far eastern and Siberian towns.

HISTORY

MILITARY

Under the direction of Admiral Hyman G. Rickover, the design, development and production of nuclear marine propulsion plants started in the USA in the 1940s, with the first test reactor being started up in 1953. The first nuclear-powered submarine, USS Nautilus (SSN-571), put to sea in 1955. Much of the early development work on naval reactors was done at the Naval Reactor Facility on the campus of the Idaho National Laboratory

The Soviets were also involved in the production of a nuclear submarine. They produced the November class, the first of which, K-3 "Leninskiy Komsomol", was underway under nuclear power on July 4, 1958.

The large amounts of power produced by an air-independant nuclear reactor marked the transition of submarines from slow vessels required to surface often, to warships capable of sustaining 20-25 knots (37-46 km/h) submerged for many weeks.

Nautilus led to the parallel development of further *Skate*-class submarines, powered by single reactors, and a cruiser, USS Long Beach (CGN-9), in 1961, powered by two reactors. The aircraft carrier USS *Enterprise*, commissioned in 1962, is powered by eight reactor units.

By 1962 the United States Navy had 26 nuclear submarines operational and 30 under construction. Nuclear power had revolutionized the Navy. The technology was shared with the United Kingdom, while French, Soviet, Indian and Chinese developments proceeded separately.

After the *Skate*-class vessels, reactor development proceeded and in the USA a single series of standardized designs was built by both Westinghouse and General Electric, one reactor powering each vessel. Rolls Royce built similar units for Royal Navy submarines and then developed the design further to the PWR-2 (pressurized water reactor). The largest nuclear submarines ever built are the 26,500 tonne Russian *Typhoon* class.

Civil

Development of nuclear merchant ships began in the 1950s, but has not generally been commercially successful. The US-built NS *Savannah*, was commissioned in 1962 and decommissioned eight years later. It was a technical success, but not economically viable. The German-built *Otto Hahn* cargo ship and research facility sailed some 650,000 nautical miles (1,200,000 km) on 126 voyages in 10 years without any technical problems. However, it proved too expensive to operate and was converted to diesel. The Japanese *Mutsu* was the third civil vessel. It was dogged by technical and political problems and was an embarrassing failure. All three vessels used reactors with low-enriched uranium fuel.

The fourth nuclear merchant ship, *Sevmorput*, operates successfully in the specialised environment of the Northern Sea Route. Recently there has been renewed interest in nuclear propulsion, and some proposals have been drafted. For example, the cargo coaster is a new design for a nuclear cargo ship. Using the new micro nuclear reactors, other existing cargo ships could potentially be converted to nuclear propulsion as well.

When the Arktika class NS *50 Let Pobedy* was put into service in 2007, it became the world's largest icebreaker.

Nuclear propulsion has proven both technically and economically feasible for nuclear powered icebreakers in the Soviet

Arctic. The power levels and energy required for icebreaking, coupled with refueling difficulties for other types of vessels, are significant factors. The Soviet icebreaker *Lenin* was the world's first nuclear-powered surface vessel and remained in service for 30 years (new reactors were fitted in 1970). It led to a series of larger icebreakers, the 23,500 ton *Arktika* class, launched from 1975. These vessels have two reactors and are used in deep Arctic waters. NS *Arktika* was the first surface vessel to reach the North Pole.

For use in shallow waters such as estuaries and rivers, shallow-draft *Taymyr* class icebreakers with one reactor are being built in Finland and then fitted with their nuclear steam supply system in Russia. They are built to conform with international safety standards for nuclear vessels.

NAVAL NUCLEAR ACCIDENTS

United States

- USS *Thresher* (SSN-593) (sank, 129 killed)
- USS *Scorpion* (SSN-589) (sank, 99 killed)

Both sank for reasons unrelated to their reactor plants and still lie on the Atlantic sea floor.

Russian or Soviet

- Komsomolets K-278 (sank, 42 killed)
- Kursk K-141 (sank, 118 killed)
- K-8 (loss of coolant) (sank after fire, 52 killed)
- K-11 (two refueling criticalities)
- K-19 (two loss of coolant accidents, 27 killed due to one accident)
- K-27 (scuttled)
- K-116 (reactor accident)
- K-122 (reactor accident)
- K-123 (loss of coolant)
- K-140 (power excursion)
- K-159 (radioactive discharge) (sank recently, 9 killed)
- K-192 (loss of coolant)

- K-219 (sank after collision, 6 killed)
- K-222 (uncontrolled startup)
- K-431 (refueling criticality, 10 killed)
- K-320 (uncontrolled startup)
- K-429 (sank twice, 16 killed)
- The Soviet icebreaker Lenin is also rumored to have had a nuclear accident.

While not all of these were reactor accidents, they have a major impact on nuclear marine propulsion and the global politics because they happened to nuclear vessels. Many of these accidents resulted in the sinking of the boat containing nuclear weapons on board, which remain there to this day.

NUCLEAR POWERED ICEBREAKER

A nuclear powered icebreaker is a purpose-built ship for use in waters continuously covered with ice. Icebreakers are ships capable of cruising on ice-covered water by breaking through the ice with their strong, heavy, steel bows. Nuclear powered icebreakers are far more powerful than their diesel powered counterparts, and have been constructed by Russia primarily to aid shipping in the frozen Arctic waterways in the north of Siberia.

During the winter, the ice along the northern seaways varies in thickness from 1.2 to 2.0 metres (3.9 to 6.5 feet). The ice in central parts of the Arctic Ocean is on average 2.5 metres (8.2 ft) thick. Nuclear-powered icebreakers can force through this ice at speeds up to 10 knots (19 km/h, 12 mph). In ice-free waters the maximum speed of the nuclear-powered icebreakers is as much as 21 knots (35 km/h, 24 mph).

Uses of Nuclear-powered Icebreakers

The nuclear ice breakers of the *Arktika* design are used to force through the ice for the benefit of cargo ships and other vessels along the northern seaway. The northern seaway comprises the eastern part of the Barents Sea, the Petchora Sea, the Kara Sea, the Laptev Sea and the Eastern Siberian Sea to the Bering Strait. Important ports on the northern seaway are, among others, Dikson, Tiksi, and Pevek.

Two nuclear-powered icebreakers, NS *Vaigach* and NS *Taimyr*, have been built for shallow waters and are usually used on the river Yenisei to Dikson, where they break through the ice followed by cargo ships with lumber from Igarka and cargo ships with ore and metals from the Norilsk Company's port Dudinka. These nuclear powered icebreakers can also be used as fireboats.

The icebreakers have also been used for a number of scientific expeditions in the Arctic. On August 17, 1977, the NS *Arktika* was the first surface vessel in the world to reach the North Pole. Since 1989, some icebreakers have been used for Arctic tourism cruises.

Russian Nuclear Icebreakers

In all, ten civilian nuclear powered vessels have been built in Russia. Nine of these are icebreakers, and one is a container ship with an ice-breaking bow. All nuclear-powered icebreakers of the NS Arktika design have been built at the Admiralty Shipyard in St. Petersburg. The NS Vaigach and NS Taimyr were built at the Helsinki New Shipyard in Finland and then brought to Russia for installation of the reactors and steam propulsion systems.

Lenin Class

At its launch in 1957 the icebreaker NS *Lenin* was both the world's first nuclear powered surface ship and the first nuclear powered civilian vessel. *Lenin* was put into ordinary operation in 1959. *Lenin* had two nuclear accidents, the first in 1965, and the second in 1967.

The second accident resulted in one of the three OK-150 reactors being damaged beyond repair. All three reactors were removed, and replaced by two OK-900 reactors; the ship returned to service in 1970. The *Lenin* was taken out of operation in November 1989 and laid up at Atomflot, the base for nuclear powered icebreakers, in the Murmansk Fjord. Conversion to a museum ship was scheduled to be completed during 2005.

Arktika Class

Arktika class icebreakers are the bulk of the Russian nuclear icebreaker fleet; six of Russia's ten nuclear civilian ships are Arktikas. Since they have been built over a period of thirty years, there is a fair bit of variation between ships of the class; thus specifications are listed as a range of values. In general, the newer ships are larger, faster, and require smaller crews.

Specifications:

- Length: 148 m to 159 m (approximately 136 m at the waterline)
- Beam: 30 m (28 m at the waterline)
- Draft: approximately 11.08 m.
- Height (keel to masthead): approximately 55 m
- Displacement: 23,000 to 25,000 tons
- Maximum speed: 18 to 22 knots
- Cruising speed: approximately 18 to 20 knots
- Crew: 138 to over 200
- Passengers: approximately 100
- Reactors: 2 OK-900A, 171 megawatt each
- Propulsion: 3 propellers totalling approximately 75,000 hp
- Maximum Ice Thickness: 2 to 2.8 m
- Endurance: 7.5 months at sea, 4 years between refuelings

Arktika-class icebreakers have a double hull, with the outer hull being approximately 48 mm thick at the ice-breaking areas and 25 mm thick elsewhere. There is water ballast between the inner and outer hulls which can be shifted to aid icebreaking. Icebreaking is also assisted by an air bubbling system which can deliver 24 m^3/s of water from jets 9 m below the surface. Some ships have polymer coated hulls to reduce friction. Arktika-class ships can break ice while making way either forwards or backwards. These ships must cruise in cold water, in order to cool their reactors. As a result, they cannot pass through the tropics to undertake voyages in the Southern Hemisphere. Although they have two reactors, normally only one is used to provide power, with the other being maintained in systems can include navigation, telephone, fax, and email capabilities.

Most nuclear powered icebreakers in the Russian service today have a swimming pool, a sauna, a cinema, and a gymnasium. In the restaurants a standby mode. Some ships carry one or two helicopters and several Zodiac boats. Radio and satellite aboard there is a bar and facilities for live music performances. Some also have a library and at least one has a volleyball court.

Individual Ships

The NS *Arktika* and NS *Sibir* ("Siberia") are presently not in operation but are stationed at Atomflot for extensive repair. Among other things, the nuclear reactors and turbine generators are to be upgraded as these do not satisfy the safety standards established for newer nuclear powered icebreakers. The *Arktika*'s reactors have operated for over 150,000 hours, and research is underway to determine if they can be refitted to yield another 25,000 to 50,000 hours of service.

Neither the NS *Arktika*, nor the NS *Sibir* might ever come into operation again due to the operational economics. Unless there is a significant increase of transport in the Arctic it will not be profitable to operate all six Arktika-class icebreakers. It is to be expected that the oldest icebreakers would be the first ones to be taken out of operation.

The NS *Rossiya* ("Russia") carries two helicopters. *Rossiya* was used to transport an expedition of around 40 West Germans to the North Pole in the Summer of 1990; this may have been the first non-communist charter of a nuclear icebreaker. *Rossiya* was in refit as of December 2004.

The NS *Sovetskiy Soyuz* ("Soviet Union") was trapped in ice for three days in 1998. In 2004, it was one of three icebreakers used for an Arctic ice core expedition intended to research climate change and global warming. One tourism operator lists it as being possibly used for North Pole cruises.

The NS *Yamal* is mostly used for tourism and scientific expeditions. It has 50 passenger cabins and suites, and carries one helicopter. The crew is 150, including 50 officers and engineers. *Yamal* was the 12th surface ship ever to reach the North Pole.

The NS *50 Lyet Pobyedi* ("50 Years of Victory") is the final *Arktika* class ship. It was launched from the shipyard at Saint Petersburg on December 29, 1993 as the NS *Ural*, and delivered to Murmansk in 1994. It was later renamed and not actually completed and commissioned until 2006 due to funding delays. The crew is expected to normally number 138 persons. It has an environmental waste processing module added to the hull which accounts for 9 m of the ship's 159 m length; this makes it the largest of the *Arktika* class and the largest nuclear powered icebreaker in the world. It carries two Ka-32 helicopters. It entered service on April 2, 2007.

Taimyr Class

Taimyr is also sometimes spelled *Taymyr* in English, and *Vaigach* is sometimes spelled *Vayguch*. The ships were built at the Helsinki New Shipyard in Finland by Wärtsilä. The nuclear reactors were installed at the Leningrad Baltic Shipyard in the Soviet Union after delivery from Finland.

Taimyr class specifications:

- Length: 150.2 m (*Taimyr*), 151.8 m (*Vaiguch*)
- Beam: 29.2 m
- Draft: 8.0 m
- Height: 15.2 m keel to main deck, 8 stories from main deck to bridge
- Displacement: 20,000 tons
- Speed: 18.5 knots
- Crew: 120 to 138
- Reactors: One KLT-40M reactor producing 135 MW
- Propulsion: 3 propellers totalling 52,000 hp

The bow hull plating is approximately 32 mm thick. As of December 2004, both vessels were undergoing refitting.

Future Icebreakers

Russia is planning to start building new icebreakers after 2010. In June 2008 the head of the state nuclear corporation Rosatom, Sergei Kiriyenko, said "It is important to not only use the existing fleet of icebreakers, but also to build new ships, and the first nuclear icebreaker of a new generation will be built by 2015. This should be an icebreaker capable of moving in rivers and seas," he said. He went on saying that the Iceberg Design Bureau in St. Petersburg would prepare the design of the icebreaker by 2009.

INFRASTRUCTURE

Support facilities include the fuel transports *Imandra* and *Lotta* which are used for refuelling and spent fuel. The *Volodarsky* is used for storage of solid waste; it can hold 300 cubic meters. *Serebryanka* is a tanker used for liquid waste which can hold 1000 cubic meters of material. The *Rosta-1* boat is used for radiation monitoring and control, including sanitization of workers.

A third fuel vessel, *Lepse,* is filled with spent nuclear fuel elements, many of them damaged and thus difficult to handle. The vessel was used for illegal dumping of nuclear waste in the Barents and Kara Seas during the period 1963-1984. During a dumping operation in 1984, *Lepse* encountered very rough seas, and high-level reactor waste mixed with water was splashed all over the inside of the cargo compartment. The contamination was so severe that the crew were forced to immediately return to port at the Atomflot harbor with most of the nuclear waste still in the hold. The ship was immediately recognized as being far too dangerous to decontaminate and return to service, and has been essentially abandoned with a cargo hold full of leaking spent reactor fuel vessels, in the harbor for over 15 years. It forms one of the world's most difficult and potentially dangerous nuclear waste disposal problems; an accident there could release more radiation than the Chernobyl catastrophe into the immediate vicinity of MurmanskA small crew monitors the ship on a constant basis while Russia tries to raise the money and perform the research needed for safe disposal.

In all, about 2,000 people work aboard the icebreakers, the nuclear powered container ship, and aboard the service and storage ships stationed at the Atomflot harbour. The crew on the civil nuclear powered vessels receive special training at the Makarov college in St. Petersburg, Russia.

Icebreakers generally try to navigate paths with the least possible ice in order to make speedier progress and to help ensure that they do not become trapped in ice too thick for them to break. In the 1970s and 1980s, land-based aircraft would observe and map the ice to help with course plotting. Over time, most of this work has been taken over by satellite surveillance systems, sometimes aided by the helicopters carried by the icebreakers.

ARCTIC TOURISM

Since 1989 the nuclear powered icebreakers have also been used for tourist purposes carrying passengers to the North Pole. Each participant pays up to US$ 25,000 for cruises lasting three weeks. The NS *Sibir* was used for the first two tourist cruises in 1989 and 1990. In 1991 and 1992, the tourist trips to the North Pole were undertaken by NS *Sovyetski Soyuz*. During the summer of 1993 the NS *Yamal* was used for three tourist expeditions in the Arctic. The NS *Yamal* has a separate accommodation section for tourists. The NS *50 Let Pobedy* contains an accommodation deck customised for tourists.

Quark Expeditions has chartered the nuclear-powered icebreaker "50 Years of Victory" for expeditions to the North Pole in 2008. The vessel's maiden voyage to the North Pole embarks in Murmansk, June 24, 2008. The ship will carry 128 guests in 64 cabins in 5 categories. "50 Years of Victory" will complete a total of 3 expeditions to the North Pole in 2008 for the polar adventure company.

BLUE-WATER NAVY

The term blue-water navy is a colloquialism used to describe a maritime force capable of operating across the deep waters of open oceans. While what actually constitutes such a force remains undefined, there is a requirement for the ability to exercise sea control at wide ranges. The term used in the United Kingdom is expeditionary.

CAPABILITIES OF A BLUE-WATER NAVY

*"Blue-water" (high seas) naval capability*means that a fleet is able to operate on the "high seas." While traditionally a distinction was made between the coastal brown-water navy (operating in the littoral zone to 200 nautical miles (370 km)) and a seagoing blue-water navy, a new term "green-water navy" has been created by the U.S. NavyGreen-water navy appears to be equivalent to a brown-water navy in older sources. The term *brown-water navy* appears to have been reduced in U.S. Navy parlance to a riverine force. In modern warfare blue-water navy implies self-contained force protection from sub-surface, surface and airborne threats

and a sustainable logistic reach, allowing a persistent presence at range. In some maritime environments such a defence is given by natural obstacles, such as the Arctic ice shelf.

Few navies can operate as blue-water navies, but "many States are converting green-water navies to blue-water navies and this will increase military use of foreign Exclusive Economic Zones [littoral zone to 200 nautical miles (370 km)] with possible repercussions for the EEZ regime."

As there is no clear definition of a blue-water navy, the status is disputed. Usually it is considered to be strongly linked to the maintenance of aircraft carriers capable of operating in the oceans. "In the early 80s there was a bitter and very public battle fought over whether or not to replace Australia's last aircraft carrier, HMAS *Melbourne*. Senior navy personnel warned without a carrier, Australia would be vulnerable to all types of threat. One ex-Chief of Navy went so far as to claim that Australia "would no longer have a blue-water navy (one capable of operating away from friendly coasts)."

The term blue-water navy should not be mixed up with brown, green and blue water capability or ship. U.S. Navy Chief of Naval Operations Admiral Michael Mullen pointed out in an interview with KQV (Pittsburgh): "We are looking at, in addition to the blue-water ships which I would characterize and describe as our aircraft carriers and other ships that support that kind of capability, we're also looking to develop capability in what I call the green-water and the brown-water, and the brown-water is really the rivers... These are challenges we all have, and we need to work together to ensure that the sea lanes are secure." The capability for blue, green or brown water depends on the vessel's specifications. The vessels of a green-water navy can often operate in blue-water for example. A number of nations have extensive maritime assets but lack the capability to maintain the required sustainable logistic reach. Some of them join coalition task groups in *blue-water* deployments.

While a *blue-water navy* can project sea control power into another nation's littoral, it remains susceptible to threats from less capable forces. Sustainment and logistics at range yield high costs and there may be a saturation advantage over a deployed force through the use of land-based air or surface-to-surface missile assets, diesel-electric submarines, or asymmetric tactics such as Fast Inshore Attack Craft. An example of this vulnerability was the October 2000 USS *Cole* bombing in Aden.

NAVIES DESCRIBED AS BLUE-WATER NAVIES

These are navies that have successfully used the capabilities of their blue-water navies to exercise control at high seas and from there have projected power into other nations' littoral waters.

- The United States Navy maintains eleven Carrier Strike Groups (one centred on USS *Enterprise*, the remainder on *Nimitz* class carriers), of which six are deployed or ready for deployment within 30 days, and two ready for deployment within 90 days under the Fleet Response Plan (FRP). The US Navy also maintains a posture of Continuous At Sea Deterrence (CASD) through the Trident submarine-launched ballistic missiles on *Ohio*-class submarines. It also maintains a continuous deployment of Expeditionary Strike Groups that embark a Marine Expeditionary Unit with an Aviation Combat Element of Landing Helicopter Docks and Landing Helicopter Assault
- The United Kingdom's Royal Navy maintains two task forces concurrently (one based around an aircraft carrier and one based around an Amphibious assault ship). At least one task group is deployed at any one time. There are currently two *Invincible*-class aircraft carriers in operation, with a further one in reserve. The Royal Navy also uses the *Ocean*-class Landing Platform, Helicopter (LPH) as well as the two *Albion*-class amphibious transport docks as the centre of a task group. The Royal Navy maintains a Continuous At Sea Deterrence policy via its *Vanguard*-class ballistic missile submarines utilising Trident missiles. The Royal Navy also supports a number of standing commitments worldwide on a continuous basis.
- The Russian Navy maintains a Carrier Battle Group around *Admiral Kuznetsov* and multiple Surface Action Groups centred around nuclear-powered Large Battle Cruisers of Kirov Class. Russia also maintains a posture of Continuous

At Sea Deterrence (CASD) with its ballistic missile submarine fleet, comparable to United States Navy.

- The French Navy (*Marine Nationale*) has the ability to deploy an aircraft-carrier-based task group and maintains a Continuous At Sea Deterrence included in the Force Océanique Stratégique (Strategic Oceanic Force). France also has a wide range of naval deployments throughout the world

Navies with Limited Blue Water Capabilities

Several other countries maintain navies capable of some "blue water operation". The Italian Navy operates 2 indigenous aircraft carriers, the Spanish Navy operates a single indigenous aircraft carrier, while the Indian Navy operates a British-built aircraft carrier. All 3 of these navies are capable of limited oceanic operations. The Brazilian Navy also owns a French-built carrier but mainly operates in its coastal and regional waters. The Royal Thai Navy owns a Spanish-built carrier that is largely inactive. Many navies, including the Japanese Maritime Self-Defence Force, Republic of Korea Navy, Royal Australian Navy, Canadian Forces Maritime Command, and the People's Liberation Army Navy operate a limited number of ships far from their home waters either alone or in coordination with true "blue water navies". None of these operate aircraft carriers.

BROWN-WATER NAVY

Brown-water navy is a term that originated in the United States Navy, referring to the small gunboats and patrol boats used in rivers. A broader meaning is any naval force that has the capacity to carry out military operations in river or littoral environments.

The term is used in contrast to the terms "green-water navy" and "blue-water navy" At one time, it was common to refer to all non blue-water navies as "brown-water navies". Today blue-water navies are generally defined as being capable of sustained oversea deployment, preferably with aircraft carriers while green-water navies are defined as those with frigates or better, operating in coastal and regional areas. The brown-water navy is generally defined as one with patrol boats operating in rivers, lakes, and littoral regions. Being a brown-water navy does not imply that it lacks offensive capability, as many small littoral-combat ships today are armed with powerful anti-ship missiles.

HISTORY

IN USA

American Civil War

The term *brown-water navy* originated in the American Civil War (1861–1865) As a blueprint for the "strangulation" of the Confederate States of America, Winfield Scott's Anaconda plan called for a two-pronged approach by first blocking the South's harbors and then pushing along the Mississippi River, effectively cutting the Confederate territory in two while also robbing the South of its main artery of transport. The U.S. Navy was assigned the blockade of the seaports, while a new force of gunboats and river ironclads, together with regular army units, would take, or at least lay siege on, the Confederate forts and cities along the Mississippi. In the early days of the war, these boats were built and crewed by the U.S. Army, with the naval officers commanding them being the only direct connection to the U.S. Navy. By the autumn of 1862, the boats and their mission were transferred to the Department of the Navy. Because of the river's murky brown water, the ships that participated in these Mississippi campaigns were quickly referred to as the *brown-water navy*, as opposed to the regular U.S. Navy (which was henceforth referred to as the *deep-water* or *blue-water* navy).

GUNBOAT DIPLOMACY

Save for an occasional river patrol boat, the river ironclad navy was all but abolished at the end of the Civil War. Yet the concept of a river defence force lived on in countries and regions where rivers enabled the US to project its military presence, allowing it to protect its foreign interests abroad. US river boats (gunboats) operated in portions of Chinese rivers (sometimes referred to as the "Asiatic Navy") during the 1920s, such as the gunboat USS *Panay*, which was sunk in 1937 (by Japanese aircraft, prior to WWII). The US Navy during that era was, under the terminology used then, protecting US foreign policy and her citizens abroad via "Gunboat diplomacy". The China gunboat USS *Asheville* (PG-21) was lost in action March 1942.

Vietnam

The first time since the US Civil War, the US Navy formalized the new brown-water Navy in Vietnam. Its primary mission would be to interdict enemy re-supply, and any unauthorized contraband which might contribute to the enemy's war effort. In the beginning, the brown-water navy patrolled the inland waterways, primarily with South Vietnamese river craft (RAG—River Assault Groups) which had been mostly inherited from the French during their war; which in turn, had been received from the US, as military aid, during the French fight against the Viet Minh (Communist-led Vietnamese alliance). As the new fiberglass PBR (Patrol Boat, River), using water jet propulsion, became available, it became the main interdiction vessel for the inland waterways. For close coastal waters during the war, more seaworthy South Vietnamese Navy water craft were used, until replaced by newer US Navy and US Coast Guard patrol vessels, such as the Coast Guard 82-footers, and US Navy Swift Boats (PCF—Patrol Craft Fast, aluminum 50 footers). By the late 1960s, the Swift Boat would commence operations alongside the PBR's in the inland waters, as well as maintaining operations along the coast line. The brown-water navy was a joint venture between the Navy and the Army, modeled after the earlier French Riverine and coastal patrols in the First Indochina War (1945–1954). In the beginning this force consisted of mostly modified surplus US WWII Landing craft (boats), such as the LCMs, LCVPs, LCIs, etc. The only entirely new riverine boat from the French Indochina War had been the French designed STCN (an all steel "V" hulled boat, approximately 40 feet in length, whose design had been influenced by the US LCVP). This particular craft influenced the design of the US Navy's only original riverine boat built for the Vietnam War; the 50 foot all steel hull, aluminum super-structured ASPB (Assault Support Patrol Boat, better known as the "Alpha Boat" The "Alpha" boat was built by the Gunderson Company, in Oregon, USA, and was of reinforced construction, in order to survive exploding mines. As a consequence, the ASPB earned a reputation as the "mine-sweeper" of the riverine forces. Other riverine craft included, along with the aforementioned PBRs, PCFs, and ASPBs, were the Patrol Air Cushion Vehicles (PACVs), Coast Guard 82 footers, and the Monitors (modified LCMs). Together these craft formed a Mobile Riverine Force, that utilized various supporting facilities, such as the Yard Repair Berthing and Messings, advance bases, LSTs, helicopter and seawolf units.

PBR Mk II

The brown-water navy was largely successful in its tactics to combat infiltration and weapons smuggling during its existence between 1965 and 1970. The units were formalized in January 1967 with the 2nd Brigade, 9th Infantry Division arriving under the command of Major General William Fulton. Later that same year, in combination with US Navy Task Force 117 they formed the Mobile Riverine Force. In 1970, for the last time since the US Civil War, the US Navy stood down the last of its brown-water navy units; as they were turned over to the South Vietnamese Government, during the US Navy's phase of Vietnamization.

Iraq War

Although not formalized as a Brown Water Navy by the US Navy, U.S. Marines began patrolling the inland waters of Iraq soon after the beginning of the Iraq War, using a variety of patrol boats. In 2004 the Marines received a new type of fast boat, the small unit riverine craft (SURC), to patrol the waters of the Euphrates River and deny water passage to the insurgents. Beginning in 2006, the Navy established the Riverine Squadrons to assume this task from the Marines. A Riverine Squadron was deployed to Iraq in March 2007 and has been patrolling the waters of the river around the Haditha Dam.

GUNBOAT DIPLOMACY

If foreign policy objectives with the aid of conspicuous displays of military power — implying or constituting a direct threat of warfare, should terms not be agreeable to the superior force.

Origin of the Term

The term comes from the age of warring Colonialism, where

such displays typically involved demonstrations of naval might—gunboats were a prominent type of warship and symbolized an advanced military. A country negotiating with a European power—usually over issues of trade—would notice that a warship or fleet of ships had appeared off its coast. The mere sight of such power almost always had a considerable effect, and it was rarely necessary for such boats to use other measures, such as demonstrations of cannon fire.

A notable and controversial example of gunboat diplomacy was the Don Pacifico Incident in 1850, in which the British Foreign Secretary Lord Palmerston dispatched a squadron of the Royal Navy to blockade the Greek port of Piraeus in retaliation for the harming of a British subject, David Pacifico, in Athens, and the subsequent failure of the government of King Otto to compensate the Gibraltar-born (and therefore British) Pacifico.

The effectiveness of such simple demonstrations of a nation's projection of force capabilities meant that those nations with naval power, especially Britain, could establish military bases (for example, Diego Garcia) and arrange economically advantageous relationships around the world. Aside from military conquest, gunboat diplomacy was the dominant way to establish new trade partners, colonial outposts and expansion of empire.

Those lacking the resources and technological advancements of European empires found that their own peaceable relationships were readily dismantled in the face of such pressures, and they therefore came to depend on the imperial nations for access to raw materials and overseas markets.

The British diplomat and naval thinker James Cable spelled out the nature of gunboat diplomacy in a series of works published between 1971 and 1994. In these, he defined the phenomenon as "the use or threat of limited naval force, otherwise than as an act of war, in order to secure advantage or to avert loss, either in the furtherance of an international dispute or else against foreign nationals within the territory or the jurisdiction of their own state." He further broke down the concept into four key areas:

- Definitive Force: the use of gunboat diplomacy to create or remove a fait accompli.

- Purposeful Force: application of naval force to change the policy or character of the target government or group
- Catalytic Force: a mechanism designed to buy a breathing space or present policy makers with an increased range of options
- Expressive Force: use of navies to send a political message- interestingly this aspect of gunboat diplomacy is undervalued and almost dismissed by Cable.

Gunboat diplomacy comes in contrast to the views held prior to the 18th century influenced by Hugo Grotius, *De Jure Belli ac Pacis*, in which he circumscribed the right to resort to force with what he described as 'temperamenta'.

Modern Contexts

Nimitz class carriers, the most powerful capital ships currently in service, are the exclusive domain of the United States.

Gunboat diplomacy is considered a form of hegemony. As the United States became a military power in the first decade of the 20th century, the Rooseveltian version of gunboat diplomacy, big stick diplomacy, was partially superseded by dollar diplomacy: replacing the big stick with the "juicy carrot" of American private investment. However, during Woodrow Wilson's presidency, conventional gunboat diplomacy did occur, most notably in the case of the U.S. Army's occupation of Veracruz in 1914, during the Mexican Revolution.

Gunboat diplomacy in the post-Cold War world is still based mostly on naval forces, owing to the United States Navy's overwhelming seapower. U.S. administrations have frequently changed the disposition of their major naval fleets to influence opinion in foreign capitals. More urgent diplomatic points were made by the Clinton administration in the Yugoslav wars of the 1990s (in alliance with the United Kingdom's Blair government) and elsewhere, using sea-launched Tomahawk missiles, and E-3 AWACS airborne surveillance aircraft in a more passive display of military presence. The term "gunboat diplomacy" has been superseded in many circles by the more euphemistic "power projection".

Warship

A warship is a ship that is built and primarily intended for combat. Warships are usually built in a completely different way than merchant ships. As well as being armed, warships are designed to withstand damage and are usually faster and more maneuverable than merchant ships. Unlike a merchant ship, a warship typically only carries weapons, ammunition and supplies for its own crew (rather than merchant cargo). Warships usually belong to a navy, though they have sometimes been operated by individuals or companies.

In wartime, the distinction between warships and merchant ships is often blurred. In war, merchant ships are often armed and used as auxiliary warships, such as the Q-ships of the First World War and the armed merchant cruisers of the Second World War. Until the 17th century it was common for merchant ships to be pressed into naval service and not unusual for more than half a fleet to be composed of merchant ships. Until the threat of piracy subsided in the 19th century, it was normal practice to arm larger merchant ships such as Galleons. Warships have also often been used as troop carriers or supply ships, such as by the French Navy in the 18th century or the Japanese Navy during the Second World War.

EVOLUTION OF WARSHIPS

The Age of Galleys

In the time of Ancient Persia, Ancient Greece and the Roman Empire, the most common type of warship was the galley (such as biremes, triremes and quinqueremes), a long, narrow vessel powered by banks of oarsmen and designed to ram and sink enemy vessels, or come alongside the enemy so its occupants could be attacked hand-to-hand. However with the development of catapults in the 4th century BC and the subsequent refinement of its technology enabled the first fleets of artillery equipped warships by the Hellenistic age. With the political unification of the Mediterranean Sea in the 2nd and 1st centuries BC, naval artillery fell out of use. Throughout late antiquity and the Middle Ages until the 16th century, naval warfare relied on the ship itself, used as a ram, the swords of the crew, and various missiles such as bows and arrows and bolts from heavy crossbows fixed on a ship's bulwarks. Naval warfare primarily involved ramming and boarding actions, so warships did not need to be particularly specialized.

The Age of Sail

Naval artillery was redeveloped in the 14th century, but cannon did not become common at sea until the guns were capable of being reloaded quickly enough to be reused in the same battle. The size of a ship required to carry a large number of cannons made oar-based propulsion impossible, and warships came to rely primarily on sails. The sailing man-of-war emerged during the 16th century.

By the middle of the 17th century, warships were carrying increasing numbers of cannon on their broadsides and tactics evolved to bring each ship's firepower to bear in a line of battle. The man-of-war now evolved into the ship of the line. In the 18th century, the frigate and sloop-of-war – too small to stand in the line of battle – evolved to convoy trade, scout for enemy ships and blockade enemy coasts.

Steel, Steam and Shellfire

During the 19th century a revolution took place in the means of propulsion, armament and construction of warships. Steam engines were introduced, at first as an auxiliary force, in the second quarter of the 19th century.

The Crimean War gave a great stimulus to the development of guns. The introduction of explosive shells soon led to the introduction of iron, and later steel, armour for the sides and decks of larger warships. The first ironclad warships, the French *Gloire* and British *Warrior*, made wooden vessels obsolete. Metal soon entirely replaced wood as the main material for warship construction.

From the 1850s, the sailing ships of the line were replaced by steam-powered battleships, while the sailing frigates were replaced by steam-powered cruisers. The armament of warships also changed with the invention of the rotating barbettes and turrets, which allowed the guns to be aimed independently of the direction of the ship and allowed a smaller number of larger guns to be carried.

The final innovation during the 19th century was the development of the torpedo and development of the torpedo boat. Small, fast torpedo boats seemed to offer an alternative to building expensive fleets of battleships.

The Dreadnought Era

Another revolution in warship design began shortly after the turn of the century, when Britain launched the all-big-gun battleship *Dreadnought* in 1906. Powered by steam turbines, she was bigger, faster and more heavily gunned than all existing battleships, which she immediately rendered obsolete. She was rapidly followed by similar ships in other countries.

Britain also developed the first battlecruisers. Mounting the same heavy guns as the Dreadnoughts on an even larger hull, battlecruisers sacrificed armour protection for speed. Battlecruisers were faster and more powerful than all existing cruisers, which they made obsolete, but battlecruisers proved to be much more vulnerable than contemporary battleships.

The torpedo-boat destroyer was developed at the same time as the Dreadnoughts. Bigger, faster and more heavily gunned than the torpedo boat, the destroyer evolved to protect the capital ships from the menace of the torpedo boat.

Second World War

During the lead-up to the Second World War, Germany and Great Britain once again emerged as the two dominant Atlantic sea powers. Germany, under the Treaty of Versailles, had its navy limited to only a few minor surface ships. But clever names, such as "pocket battleships" deceived the British and French commands. They were rudely surprised when ships such as the *Admiral Graf Spee*, *Scharnhorst*, and *Gneisenau* constantly raided the Allied supply lines.

The greatest threat though, was the introduction of the Kriegsmarine's most lethal weapons, the *Bismarck* and *Tirpitz*. The Bismarck was sunk in a wild, short series of sea battles in the north Atlantic, while the Tirpitz caused a bit of a stir before being knocked out by the RAF. The Royal Navy gained dominance of the European theatre by 1943.

Development of the Submarine

The first practical submarines were developed in the late 19th century, but it was only after the development of the torpedo that submarines became truly dangerous (and hence useful). By the end of the First World War submarines had proved their potential. During the Second World War the German Navy's submarine fleet of U-boats almost starved Britain into submission and inflicted huge losses on US coastal shipping. The success of submarines led to the development of new anti-submarine convoy escorts during the First and Second World Wars, such as the destroyer escort. Confusingly, many of these new types adopted the names of the smaller warships from the age of sail, such as corvette, sloop and frigate.

DEVELOPMENT OF THE AIRCRAFT CARRIER

A major shift in naval warfare occurred with the introduction of the aircraft carrier. First at Taranto and then at Pearl Harbor, the aircraft carrier demonstrated its ability to strike decisively at enemy ships out of sight and range of surface vessels. By the end of the Second World War, the carrier had become the dominant warship.

Modern Warships

Modern warships are generally divided into seven main categories, which are: aircraft carriers, cruisers, destroyers, frigates, corvettes, submarines and amphibious assault ships. Battleships encompass an eighth category, but are not in current service with any navy in the world. Only the deactivated American Iowa-class battleships still exist as potential combatants, and battleships in general are unlikely to re-emerge as a ship class without redefinition. The destroyer is generally regarded as the dominant surface-combat vessel of most modern blue water navies. However, it must be noted that the once distinct roles and appearances of cruisers, destroyers, frigates, and corvettes have blurred. Most vessels have come to be armed with a mix of anti-surface, anti-submarine and anti-aircraft weapons. Class designations no longer reliably indicate a displacement hierarchy, and the size of all vessel types has grown beyond the definitions used earlier in the 20th century. Another key differentiation between older and modern vessels is that all modern warships are "soft", without the thick armour and bulging anti-torpedo protection of WWII and older designs.

Most navies also include many types of support and auxiliary vessels, such as minesweepers, patrol boats and offshore patrol vessels.

9

Naval Mine

A naval mine is a self-contained explosive device placed in water to destroy ships or submarines. Unlike depth charges, mines are deposited and left to wait until they are triggered by the approach of or contact with an enemy ship. Naval mines can be used offensively, to hamper enemy ships or lock them into a harbour; or defensively, to protect friendly ships and create "safe" zones. Mines can be laid in many ways: by purpose-built minelayers, refitted ships, submarines, or aircraft—and even by dropping them into a harbour by hand. They can be inexpensive: some variants can cost as little as a thousand United States dollars (USD), although more sophisticated mines can cost millions of USD, be equipped with several kinds of sensors, and deliver a warhead by rocket or torpedo.

Their flexibility and cost-effectiveness make mines attractive weapons to the less powerful belligerent in asymmetric warfare. The cost of producing and laying a mine is usually anywhere from 0.5% to 10% of the cost of removing it, and it can take up to 200 times as long to clear a minefield as to lay it. Parts of some World War II naval minefields still exist, because they are too extensive and expensive to clear; some of these mines might remain dangerous for hundreds of years

There are three main uses of mines: offensive, defensive, and psychological. Offensive mines are placed in enemy waters, outside harbours and in important shipping routes to sink civilian and military ships. Defensive minefields protect a coast from enemy ships and submarines and force them into areas that are easier to defend. Minefields designed for psychological effect are usually placed in trade routes and are used to stop shipping to an enemy nation. They are also spread out thinly, to create a feeling of random minefields in large areas. A single mine along a shipping route can stop shipping for days until the entire area is swept.

International law requires nations to declare when they mine an area, in order to make it easier for civil shipping to avoid the mines. The warnings do not have to be specific; during World War II, Britain declared simply that it had mined the English Channel, North Sea, and French coast. In 1988, an Iranian M-08 mine made a 25-foot (8 m) hole in the hull of the USS *Samuel B. Roberts* (FFG-58), forcing the ship to seek temporary repairs in a dry dock in Dubai, UAE.

HISTORY

The precursor to naval mines was first described by the early Ming Dynasty Chinese artillery officer Jiao Yu, in his 14th century military treatise known as the *Huolongjing*Chinese records tell of naval explosives in the 16th century, used to fight against Japanese pirates (Wokou). This kind of naval mine was loaded in a wooden box, sealed by putty. General Qi Jiguang made several timed, drifting explosives to harass Japanese pirate ships. However, in the *Tiangong Kaiwu* ('The Exploitation of the Works of Nature') treatise, written by Song Yingxing in 1637 AD, it describes naval mines with a rip cord pulled by a hidden ambusher located on the nearby shore which rotated a steel wheellock flint mechanism to produce sparks and ignite the fuse of the naval mine. Although this is the rotating steel wheellock's first use with naval mines, Jiao Yu had described their use for land mines back in the 14th century

The first plan for a sea mine in the West was by Ralph Rabbards, who presented his design to Queen Elizabeth I of England in 1574. The Dutch inventor Cornelius Drebbel was employed in the Office of Ordnance by King Charles I of England to make weapons, including a "floating petard" which proved a failure Weapons of this type were apparently tried by the English at the Siege of La Rochelle in 1627

American David Bushnell invented the first practical mine, for use against the British in the American War of Independence.

It was a watertight keg filled with gunpowder that was floated toward the enemy, detonated by a sparking mechanism if it struck a ship.

In 1812 Russian engineer Pavel Shilling exploded an underwater mine using an electrical circuit. In 1854, during the unsuccessful attempt of the Anglo-French fleet to seize Kronshtadt fortress, British steamships HMS *Merlin* (9 June 1855, the first successful mining in history), HMS *Vulture* and HMS *Firefly* were damaged by underwater explosions of Russian naval mines. More than 1500 naval mines, or *infernal machines,* designed by Moritz von Jacobi and Alfred Nobel were set by Russian naval specialists in the Gulf of Finland during the Crimean War. The mining of *Vulcan* led to the worlds first minesweeping operation during the next 72 hours, 33 mines were swept

In the 19th century, mines were called torpedoes, a name probably conferred by Dennis Fletcher after the torpedo fish, which gives powerful electric shocks. A spar torpedo was a mine attached to a long pole and detonated when the ship carrying it rammed another one. The *H. L. Hunley* used one to sink the USS *Housatonic* on February 17, 1864. A Harvey Torpedo was a type of floating mine towed alongside a ship, and was briefly in service in the Royal Navy in the 1870s. Other "torpedoes" attached to ships or propelled themselves. One such weapon, called the Whitehead Torpedo after its inventor, caused the word "torpedo" to be used for self-propelled underwater missiles rather than static devices.

The next major use of mines was in the Russo-Japanese War in 1904, sinking the Russian battleship *Petropavlovsk,* killing the fleet commander, Admiral Makaroff, and most of the crew. In the course of this conflict the Japanese Navy lost two battleships, four cruisers, two destroyers and a torpedo-boat to offensively laid mines. In May 1905 the Russian minelayer *Amur* laid a minefield off Port Arthur and sank Japan's battleship Hatsuse, a 15,000-ton vessel with 496 crew.

Many early mines were fragile and dangerous to handle, with glass containers filled with nitroglycerin or mechanical devices that activated them upon tipping. Several mine-laying ships were destroyed when their cargo exploded.

During World War I mines were used extensively to defend coasts, coastal travel, ports and naval bases. The Germans laid mines in shipping lanes to sink merchant and naval vessels serving Britain. The Allies targeted the German U-boats in the Strait of Dover and the Hebrides. In an attempt to seal up the northern exits of the North Sea, the Allies developed the Northern Barrage during a period of five months from June almost 70,000 mines were laid spanning the North Sea's northern exits. The total number of mines laid in the North Sea, the British East Coast, Straits of Dover, and Heligoland Bight is estimated at 190,000 and the total number during the whole of WWI was 235,000 sea mines.

During World War II The U-boat fleet, which dominated much of the battle of the Atlantic, was small at the beginning of the war and much of the early action by German forces involved mining convoy routes and ports around Britain. The German submarines also operated in the Mediterranean Sea, in the Caribbean Sea, and along the U.S. coast.

Initially contact mines were employed — meaning that a ship had to physically strike a mine to detonate it — usually tethered at the end of a cable just below the surface of the water. By the beginning of World War II most nations had developed mines that could be dropped from aircraft and floated on the surface, making it possible to lay them in enemy harbors. The use of dredging and nets was effective against this type of mine, but this consumed time and resources, and required harbors to be closed. Contact mines usually hole ships' hulls.

Later some ships survived mine blasts, limping into port with buckled plates and broken backs. This appeared to be due to a new type of mine, detecting ships magnetically and detonating at a distance, causing damage with the shock wave of the explosion. Ships that had successfully run the gauntlet of the Atlantic crossing were sometimes destroyed entering freshly cleared British harbors. More shipping was being lost than could be replaced, and Churchill ordered that the intact recovery of one of these new mines was of the highest priority.

The British experienced a stroke of luck in November 1939. A German mine was dropped from an aircraft onto the mud flats of the Thames estuary during low tide. As if this was not sufficiently good fortune, the land belonged to the army, and a base with men and workshops was at hand. Experts were dispatched from London to investigate the mine. They had some idea that the mines used magnetic sensors, so everyone removed all metal, including their buttons, and made tools of non-magnetic brass. They disarmed the mine and rushed it to labs at Portsmouth, where scientists discovered a new type of arming mechanism. A large ferrous object passing through the Earth's magnetic field will concentrate the field through it; the mine's detector was designed to trigger at the mid-point of a steel-hulled ship passing overhead. The mechanism had an adjustable sensitivity, calibrated in milligauss.

From these data, methods were developed to clear the mines. Early methods included the use of large electromagnets dragged behind ships or below low-flying aircraft (a number of older bombers like the Vickers Wellington were used for this). Both of these methods had the disadvantage of "sweeping" only a small strip. A better solution was found in the "Double-L Sweep using electrical cables dragged behind ships that passed large pulses of current through the seawater. This induced a large magnetic field and swept the entire area between the two ships. The older methods continued to be used in smaller areas. The Suez Canal continued to be swept by aircraft, for instance.

While these methods were useful for clearing mines from local ports, they were of little or no use for enemy-controlled areas. These were typically visited by warships, and the majority of the fleet then underwent a massive degaussing process, where their hulls had a slight "south" bias induced into them which offset the concentration effect almost to zero.

Initially, major warships and large troopships had a copper *degaussing coil* fitted around the perimeter of the hull, energized by the ship's electrical system whenever in suspected magnetic-mined waters. Some of the first to be so-fitted were the carrier HMS *Ark Royal* and the liners RMS *Queen Mary* and RMS *Queen Elizabeth,* which were used as troopships. This was felt to be impracticable for the myriad of smaller warships and merchant vessels, not least due to the amount of copper that would be required. It was found that "wiping" a current-carrying cable up and down a ship' hull temporarily canceled the ships' magnetic signature sufficiently to nullify the threat. This started in late 1939, and by 1940 merchant vessels and the smaller British warships were largely immune for a few months at a time until they once again built up a field. Many of the boats that sailed to Dunkirk were degaussed in a marathon four day effort by degaussing stations.

The Germans had also developed a pressure-activated mine and planned to deploy it as well, but they saved it for later use when it became clear the British had defeated the magnetic system. Since World War II, mines have damaged 14 United States Navy ships, whereas air and missile attacks have damaged four. During the Korean War, mines laid by North Korean forces damaged 11 U.S. naval vessels. During the Iran–Iraq War from 1980 to 1988, the belligerents mined several areas of the Persian Gulf and nearby waters. On April 14, 1988, the USS *Samuel B. Roberts* (FFG-58) struck an Iranian M-08/39 mine in the central Persian Gulf shipping lane, wounding 10 sailors. During the Gulf War, Iraqi naval mines severely damaged USS *Princeton* (CG-59) and USS *Tripoli* (LPH-10).

Types

Naval mines may be classified into two major groups.

Contact mines

The earliest mines were usually of this type. They are still used today, as they are extremely low cost compared to any other anti-ship weapon and are effective, both as a terror weapon and to sink enemy ships. Contact mines need to be touched by the target before they detonate, limiting the damage to the direct effects of the explosion and usually affecting only the single vessel that triggers them. (Read the section on damage below for explanation).

Early mines had mechanical mechanisms to detonate them, but these were superseded in the 1870s by the Hertz Horn (or chemical horn), which was found to work reliably even after the mine had been in the sea for several years. The mine's upper half is studded with hollow lead protuberances, each containing a glass vial filled with sulfuric acid. When a ship's hull crushes the metal horn, it cracks the vial inside it, allowing the acid to run down a tube and into a lead-acid battery which until then contains no acid electrolyte. This energizes the battery, which detonates the explosive. Earlier forms of the detonator used a vial filled with sulfuric acid, surrounded by a mixture of potassium perchlorate and sugar. When the vial was crushed, the acid ignited the perchlorate-sugar mix, and the resulting flame ignited the gunpowder charge.

During World War I the British heavily mined the English Channel and later large areas of the North Sea to prevent German submarines from using it. As the submarine could be at any depth down to the seabed, an American invention, the antenna mine, was widely used. This had a copper wire attached to a buoy that floated above the mine. The top part of the cable connecting the mine to the weight on the seabed was also made of copper. The copper wire was insulated from the steel cable below it. If a submarine's steel hull touched the copper wire, the slight voltage produced because of the contact between two dissimilar metals was amplified and detonated the explosive.

Limpet Mines

Limpet mines are a special form of contact mine which are attached to the target by magnets and left, and are so named because of the superficial similarity to the limpet, a mollusk.

Moored Contact Mines

Generally, this mine type is set to float just below the surface of the water or as deep as five meters. A steel cable connecting the mine to an anchor on the seabed prevents it from drifting away. The explosive and detonating mechanism is contained in a buoyant metal or plastic shell. The depth below the surface at which the mine floats can be set so that only deep draft vessels such as aircraft carriers, battleships or large cargo ships are at risk, saving the mine from being used on a less valuable target. In littoral waters it is important to ensure that the mine does not become visible when the sea level falls at low tide, so the preset cable length is adjusted to take account of tides. Even at the time of the Second World War there were mines which could be moored in 300-metre-deep water.

Floating mines typically have a mass of around 200 kg, including 80 kg of explosives e.g. TNT, minol or amatol.

During WWII mine traps were used for blocking port entrances. Two floating mines were anchored some distance apart on either side of a shipping channel, linked by a chain. When a deep draft vessel passed through the trap it would pull the chain along with it, dragging the mines onto the sides of the ship; the resulting double explosion often sank it. This system was not used extensively, but proved effective in blocking ports.

Drifting Contact Mines

Drifting mines were occasionally used during World War I and World War II. However, they were more feared than effective. Sometimes floating mines break from their moorings and become drifting mines; modern mines are designed to deactivate in this event. After several years at sea, the deactivation mechanism might not function as intended and the mines may remain live. Admiral Jellicoe's British fleet did not pursue and destroy the outnumbered German High Seas Fleet when it turned away at the Battle of Jutland because he thought they were leading him into a trap: he believed it possible that the Germans were either leaving floating mines in their wake, or were drawing him towards submarines, although neither of these was the case.

Churchill promoted "Operation Royal Marine" in 1940 and again in 1944 where floating mines were put into the Rhine in France to float down the river, becoming active after a time calculated to be long enough to reach German territory.

After World War I the drifting contact mine was banned, but was occasionally used during World War II. The drifting mines were much harder to remove than tethered mines after the war, and they caused about the same damage to both sides.

Bottom Contact Mines

A bottom contact mine is the simplest form of mine. It is merely an explosive charge with some form of fuze fitted lying on the seafloor. They have been used against submarines, as submarines sometimes lie on the seafloor to reduce their acoustic signature. They are also used to prevent landing craft from reaching the shore and were a major obstacle during the D-Day landings. The Germans used antitank mines here with minor modifications to make them more reliable underwater, attaching the mines to the front of many of the obstacles seen in photos of the landing.

These mines usually weighed 2 to 50 kg, including 1 to 40 kg of explosives (TNT or hexatonal).

Remotely Controlled Mines

Frequently used in combination with coastal artillery and hydrophones, controlled mines (or command detonation) mines can be in place in peacetime, which is a huge advantage in blocking important shipping routes. The mines can usually be turned into "normal" mines with a switch (which prevents the enemy from simply capturing the controlling station and deactivating the mines), detonated on a signal or be allowed to detonate on their own. The earliest ones were developed around 1812 by Robert Fulton. The first remotely controlled mines were moored mines used in the American Civil War, detonated electrically from shore. They were considered superior to contact mines because they did not put friendly shipping at risk. Modern examples usually weigh 200 kg (440 lb), including 80 kg (175 lb) of explosives (TNT or hexatonal).

Influence Mines

These mines are triggered by the influence of a ship or submarine, rather than direct contact. Such mines incorporate electronic sensors designed to detect the presence of a vessel and detonate when it comes within the blast range of the warhead. The fuzes on such mines may incorporate one or more of the following sensors: magnetic, passive acoustic or water pressure displacement caused by the proximity of a vessel.

First used during the Second World War, the sophistication of influence mine fuzes has increased considerably over the years as first transistors and then microprocessors have been incorporated into designs. Simple magnetic sensors have been superseded by total-field magnetometers. Whereas early magnetic mine fuzes would respond only to changes in a single component of a target vessel's magnetic field, a total field magnetometer responds to changes in the magnitude of the total background field (thus enabling it to better detect even degaussed ships). Similarly, the original broadband hydrophones of 1940s acoustic mines (which operate on the integrated volume of all frequencies) have been replaced by narrow-band sensors which are much more sensitive and selective. Mines can now be programmed to listen for highly specific acoustic signatures (e.g. a gas turbine powerplant and/or cavitation sounds from a particular design of propellor) and ignore all others. The sophistication of modern electronic mine fuzes incorporating these Digital Signal Processing capabilities makes it much more difficult to detonate the mine with electronic countermeasures because several sensors working together (e.g. magnetic, passive acoustic and water pressure) allow it to ignore signals which are not recognised as being the unique signature of an intended target vessel.

Modern influence mines such as the BAE Stonefish are computerised, with all the programmability that this implies e.g. the ability to quickly load new acoustic signatures into fuzes, or program them to detect a single, highly distinctive target signature. In this way, a mine with a passive acoustic fuze can be programmed to ignore all friendly vessels and small enemy vessels, only detonating when a very large enemy target passes over it. Alternatively, the mine can be programmed specifically to ignore all surface vessels regardless of size and exclusively target submarines.

Even as far back as the Second World War it was possible to incorporate a "ship counter" facility into mine fuzes e.g. set the mine to ignore the first two ships to pass over it (which could be mine-sweepers deliberately trying to trigger mines) but detonate when the third ship passes overhead—which could be a high-value target such as an aircraft carrier or oil tanker. Even though modern mines are generally powered by a long life lithium battery, it is important to conserve power because they may need to remain active for months or even years. For this reason, most influence mines are designed to remain in a semi-dormant state until an unpowered (e.g. deflection of a magnetic compass needle) or low-powered sensor detects the possible presence of a vessel, at which point the mine fuze powers up fully and the passive acoustic sensors will begin to operate for some minutes. It is possible to program computerised mines to delay activation for days or weeks after being laid; similarly, they can be programmed to self-destruct or render themselves safe after a preset period of time, e.g., 12 days or 12 months. Generally, the more sophisticated the mine design, the more likely it is to have some form of anti-handling device fitted in order to hinder clearance by divers or remotely piloted submersibles.

Moored Mines

The moored mine is the backbone of modern mine systems. They are deployed where water is too deep for bottom mines. They can use several kinds of instruments to detect an enemy, usually a combination of acoustic, magnetic and pressure sensors, or more sophisticated optical shadows or electro potential sensors. These cost many times more than contact mines. Moored mines are effective against most kinds of ships. As they are cheaper than other anti-ship weapons they can be deployed in large numbers, making them useful area denial or "channelizing" weapons. Moored mines usually have lifetimes of more than 10 years, and some almost unlimited. These mines usually weigh 200 kg (440 lb), including 80 kg (175 lb) of explosives (hexatonal). In excess of 150 kg (330 lb) of explosives the mine becomes inefficient, as it becomes too large to handle and the extra explosives add little to the mine's effectiveness.

Bottom Mines

Bottom mines are used when the water is no more than 60 meters (180 ft) deep or when mining for submarines down to around 200 meters (660 ft). They are much harder to detect and sweep, and can carry a much larger warhead than a moored mine. Bottom mines commonly use pressure sensitive exploders, which are less sensitive to sweeping. These mines usually weigh between 150 and 1,500 kilograms (330 to 3,300 pounds), including between 125 and 1,400 kg (275 to 3,090 pounds) of explosives.

Unusual Mines

Several specialized mines have been developed for other purposes than the common minefield. The anti sweep mine is a very small mine (40 kg warhead) with as small a floating device as possible. When the wire of a mine sweep hits the mine, it "sinks", letting the sweep wire drag along the anchoring wire of the mine until the sweep hits the mine. That detonates the mine and cuts the sweeping wire. They are very cheap and usually used in combination with other mines in a minefield to make sweeping more difficult.

Rocket Mine

A Russian invention, the rocket mine is a bottom distance mine that fires a homing high-speed rocket (not torpedo) upwards towards the target.It is intended to allow a bottom mine to attack surface ships as well as submarines from a greater depth.

Torpedo Mine

The torpedo mine is a self-propelled variety, able to lie in wait for a target and then pursue it e.g. the CAPTOR mine. Other designs such as the Mk 67 Submarine Launched Mobile Mine (which is based on a Mark 37 torpedo) are capable of swimming as far as 10 miles through or into a channel, harbor, shallow water area and other zones which would normally be inaccessible to craft laying the device. After reaching the target area they sink to the sea bed and act like conventionally laid influence mines. Generally, torpedo mines incorporate computerised acoustic and magnetic fuzes. The U.S. Mark 24 "mine", code-named FIDO, was actually an ASW homing torpedo. The mine designation was disinformation to conceal its function.

Bouquet Mine

The bouquet mine is a single anchor attached to several floating mines. It is designed so that when one mine is swept/detonated, another takes its place. It is a very sensitive construction and lacks reliability. The ascending mine is a floating distance mine that may cut its mooring or in some other way float higher when it detects a target It lets a single floating mine cover a much larger depth range.

Nuclear Mine

During the Cold War a number of tests were conducted with

naval mines fitted with tactical nuclear warheads. These weapons were experimental and never went into production This comprises two moored, floating contact mines which are tethered together by a length of steel cable or chain. Typically, each mine is situated approximately 60 feet (18 m) away from its neighbour, and each floats a few metres below the surface of the ocean. When the target ship hits the steel cable, the mines on either side are drawn down the side of the ship's hull, exploding on contact. In this manner it is almost impossible for target ships to pass safely between two individually moored mines. Daisy-chained mines are a very simple concept which was used during the Second World War.

Dummy Mine

Plastic drums filled with sand or concrete are periodically rolled off the side of ships as real mines are laid in large minefields. These inexpensive false targets (designed to be of a similar shape and size as genuine mines) are intended to slow down the process of mine clearance: a mine-hunter is forced to investigate each suspicious sonar contact on the sea bed, whether it is real or not.

Mine Laying

Historically several methods were used to lay mines. During the First and Second World Wars, the Germans used U-boats to lay mines around the UK. In the Second World War, aircraft came into favour for mine laying with the one of largest such examples being the mining of the Japanese sea routes in Operation Starvation. Laying a minefield is a relatively fast process with specialized ships, which is still today the most common method. These minelayers can carry several thousand mines and manoeuvre with high precision. The mines are dropped at a predefined interval into the water behind the ship. Each mine is recorded for later clearing, but it is not unusual for these recordings to be lost together with the ships. Therefore many countries demand that all mining operations shall be planned on land and records kept so the mines can later be recovered more easily.

Other methods to lay minefields include:

- Converted merchant ships-rolled or slid down ramps

- Aircraft-descent to the water is slowed by a parachute
- Submarines-launched from torpedo tubes or deployed from specialized mine racks on the sides of the submarine
- Combat boats-rolled off the side of the boat
- Camouflaged boats-masquerading as fishing boats
- Dropping from the shore-typically smaller, shallow-water mines
- Attack divers-smaller shallow-water mines

In some cases, mines are automatically activated upon contact with the water. In others, a safety lanyard is pulled (e.g. one end attached to the rail of a ship, aircraft or torpedo tube) which starts an automatic timer countdown before the arming process is complete. Typically, the automatic safety-arming process takes some minutes to complete. This is in order to give the people laying the mines sufficient time to move out of its activation/blast zone.

AERIAL MINING IN WORLD WAR II

Germany

In the 1930s, Germany had experimented with the laying of mines by aircraft; it became a crucial element in their overall mining strategy. Aircraft had the advantage of speed, and they would never get caught in their own minefields. German mines held a large 1,000 lb. (450 kg) explosive charge. From April to June 1940, the Luftwaffe laid 1,000 mines in British waters. Soviet ports were mined, as was the Arctic convoy route to Murmansk. The Heinkel He 115 could carry two medium or one large mine while the Heinkel He 59, Dornier Do 18, Junkers Ju 88 and Heinkel He 111 could carry more.

Soviet Union

The USSR was relatively ineffective in its use of naval mines in WWII in comparison with its record in previous wars.Small mines were developed for use in rivers and lakes, and special mines for shallow water. A very large chemical mine was designed to sink through ice with the aid of a melting compound. Special aerial mine designs finally arrived in 1943-1944, the AMD-500 and

AMD-1000. Various Soviet Naval Aviation torpedo bombers were pressed into the role of aerial mining in the Baltic Sea and the Black Sea, including Ilyushin DB-3s, Il-4s and Lend Lease Douglas Boston IIIs.

UNITED KINGDOM

In September 1939, the UK announced the placement of extensive defensive minefields in waters surrounding the Home Islands. Offensive aerial mining operations began in April 1940 when 38 mines were laid at each of these locations: the Elbe River, the port of Lübeck and the German naval base at Kiel. In the next 20 months, mines delivered by aircraft sank or damaged 164 Axis ships with the loss of 94 aircraft. By comparison, direct aerial attacks on Axis shipping had sunk or damaged 105 vessels at a cost of 373 aircraft lost. The advantage of aerial mining became clear. The United Kingdom geared up for mining; a total of 48,000 aerial mines were laid by the Royal Air Force (RAF) in the European Theatre during World War II.

UNITED STATES

The United States's early aerial mining efforts used smaller aircraft that are unable to carry many mines. Using TBF Avenger torpedo bombers, the US Navy mounted a direct aerial mining attack on enemy shipping in Palau on 30 March 1944 in concert with simultaneous conventional bombing and strafing attacks. The dropping of 78 mines stopped 32 Japanese ships from escaping Koror harbor; the combined operation sank or damaged 36 ships.Two Avengers were lost; their crews were recovered. The mines brought port usage to a halt for 20 days; further mine-laying in the area contributed to the Japanese abandoning Palau as a base.

As early as 1942, American mining experts such as Naval Ordnance Laboratory scientist Dr. Ellis A. Johnson, Commander, Naval Reserve, suggested massive aerial mining operations against Japan's "outer zone" (Korea and northern China) as well as the "inner zone", their home islands. First, aerial mines would have to be developed further and manufactured in large numbers. Second, laying the mines would require a sizable air group. The US Army Air Force had the carrying capacity but considered mining to be the Navy's job. The US Navy lacked suitable aircraft. Johnson set about convincing General Curtis LeMay of the efficacy of very heavy bombers laying aerial mines.

In the meantime, B-24 Liberator, PBY Catalina and other available bomber aircraft took part in localized mining operations in the Southwest Pacific and the China Burma India (CBI) Theaters, beginning with a very successful attack on the Yangon River in February 1943. Aerial minelaying operations involved a coalition of British, Australian and American aircrews, with the RAF and the Royal Australian Air Force (RAAF) carrying out 60% of the sorties and the USAAF and US Navy covering 40%. Both British and American mines were used. Japanese merchant shipping suffered tremendous losses, while Japanese mine sweeping forces were spread too thin attending to far-flung ports and extensive coastlines. Admiral Thomas C. Kinkaid, who directed nearly all RAAF mining operations in CBI, heartily endorsed aerial mining, writing in July 1944 that "aerial mining operations were of the order of 100 times as destructive to the enemy as an equal number of bombing missions against land targets."

Finally, in March 1945, Operation Starvation began in earnest, using 160 of LeMay's B-29 Superfortress bombers to attack Japan's inner zone. Almost half of the mines were the US-built Mark 25 model, carrying 1250 lbs of explosives and weighing about 2,000 lbs. Other mines used included the smaller 1,000 lb Mark 26. 15 B-29s were lost while 293 enemy merchant ships were sunk or damaged. 12,000 aerial mines were laid, a significant barrier to Japan's access to outside resources. Prince Fumimaro Konoe said after the war that the aerial mining by B-29s had been "equally as effective as the B-29 attacks on Japanese industry at the closing stages of the war when all food supplies and critical material were prevented from reaching the Japanese home islands." The United States Strategic Bombing Survey (Pacific War) concluded that it would have been more efficient to combine the United States's effective anti-shipping submarine effort with land-and carrier-based air power to strike harder against merchant shipping and begin a more extensive aerial mining campaign earlier in the war. Survey analysts projected that this would have starved Japan, forcing an earlier end to the war. After the war, Dr. Johnson looked at the Japan inner zone shipping results, comparing the total economic cost of submarine-delivered mines versus air-dropped mines and found that, though 1 in 12 submarine mines connected with the enemy as opposed to 1 in 21 for aircraft mines, the aerial mining operation was about ten times less expensive per enemy ton sunk.

Clearing WWII Aerial Mines

Between 600,000 and 1,000,000 naval mines of all types were laid in World War II. Advancing military forces worked to clear mines from newly-taken areas, but extensive minefields remained in place after the war. Air-dropped mines had an additional problem for mine sweeping operations: they weren't meticulously charted. In Japan, much of the B-29 mine-laying work had been performed at high altitude, with the drifting on the wind of mines carried by parachute adding a randomizing factor to their placement. Generalized danger areas were identified, with only the quantity of mines given in detail. Mines used in Operation Starvation were supposed to be self-sterilizing, but the circuit did not always work. Clearing the mines took so many years that the task was eventually given to the Japan Maritime Self-Defence Force.

For the purpose of clearing all types of naval mines, the Royal Navy employed German crews and minesweepers from June 1945 to January 1948, organised in the German Mine Sweeping Administration, the *GMSA*, which consisted of 27,000 members of the former *Kriegsmarine* and 300 vessels Mine clearing wasn't always successful: a number of ships were damaged or sunk by mines after the war. Two such examples were the Liberty ships *Pierre Gibault* which was scrapped after hitting a mine in a previously-cleared area off the Greek island of Kythira in June 1945 and *Nathaniel Bacon* which hit a minefield off Civitavecchia, Italy in December 1945, caught fire, was beached, and broke in two.

Damage

The damage that may be caused by a mine depends on the "shock factor value", a combination of the initial strength of the explosion and of the distance between the target and the detonation.

When taken in reference to ship hull plating, the term "Hull Shock Factor" (HSF) is used, while keel damage is termed "Keel Shock Factor" (KSF). If the explosion is directly underneath the keel, then HSF is equal to KSF, but explosions that are not directly underneath the ship will have a lower value of KSF.

Direct Damage

Usually only created by contact mines, direct damage is a hole blown in the ship. Among the crew, shrapnel wounds are the most common form of damage. This rarely sinks the ship, but might flood one or two compartments – usually in the bow.

Bubble Jet Effect

The bubble jet effect occurs when a mine detonates in the water some distance away from the ship. The explosion creates a "hole" in the water, and due to the difference in pressure, this sphere will collapse from the bottom. This creates a "pillar" of water that can go over a hundred meters into the air. The damage to the ship is heavy. The water breaks a meter wide hole straight through the ship, flooding one or more compartments, and might break the ship apart. The crew in the areas hit by the pillar are usually killed instantly. Other damage is usually limited.

Shaking Effect

If the mine detonates at a distance from the ship, the change in water pressure causes the ship to resonate. This is frequently the most deadly type of explosion, if it is strong enough. The whole ship is dangerously shaken and everything onboard is tossed around. Engines rip from their beds, cables from their holders, etc. A badly shaken ship usually sinks quickly, with hundreds, or even thousands of small leaks all over the ship and no way to power the pumps. The crew fare no better, as the violent shaking tosses them around.

The resulting gas cavitation and shock-front-differential over the width of the human body will stun or kill the divers.

Countermeasures

Weapons are frequently a few steps ahead of countermeasures, and mines are no exception. In this field the British, with their large seagoing navy, have had the bulk of world experience, and most anti-mine developments, such as de-gaussing and the double-L sweep were British inventions. When on operational missions, such as the recent invasion of Iraq, the US still rely on British and Canadian minesweeping services. The US have worked on some innovative mine hunting countermeasures, such as the use of military dolphins to detect and flag mines. However, they are of questionable effectiveness.

Passive Countermeasures

Ships can be designed to be difficult for mines to detect, to avoid detonating them. This is especially true for minesweepers and mine hunters that work in minefields, where a minimal signature outweighs the need for armour and speed. These ships have hulls of glass fibre or wood instead of steel to avoid magnetic signatures, they use special propulsion systems, such as Voith-Schneider propellers, to limit the acoustic signature. They are built with hulls that produce a minimal pressure signature. These measures create other problems. They are expensive, slow, and vulnerable to enemy fire. Therefore, they need protection. Many modern ships have a mine-warning sonar—a simple sonar looking forward and warning the crew if it detects possible mines ahead. It is only effective when the ship is moving slowly.

A steel-hulled ship can be *degaussed* (more correctly, de-oerstedted or depermed) using a special degaussing station that contains many large coils and induces a magnetic field in the hull with alternating current to demagnetize the hull. This is a rather problematic solution, as magnetic compasses need recalibration and all metal objects must be kept in exactly the same place. Ships slowly regain their magnetic field as they travel through the Earth's magnetic field, so the process has to be repeated every six months.

A simpler variation of this technique, called *wiping*, was developed by Charles F. Goodeve which saved time and resources.

Between 1941 and 1943 the US Naval Gun factory (a division of the Naval Ordinance Laboratory) in Washington D.C. built physical models of all US Naval ships. Three kinds of steel were used in shipbuilding: mild steel for bulkheads, a mixture of mild steel and high tensile steel for the hull, and special treatment steel for armour plate. The models were placed within coils which could simulate the Earth's magnetic field at any location. The magnetic signatures were measured with degaussing coils. The objective was to reduce the vertical component of the combination of the Earth's field and the ship's field at the usual depth of German mines. From the measurements, coils were placed and coil currents determined to minimize the chance of detonation for any ship at any heading at any latitude.

Some ships are built with magnetic inductors, large coils placed along the ship to counter the ship's magnetic field. Using magnetic probes in strategic parts of the ship, the strength of the current in the coils can be adjusted to minimize the total magnetic field. This is a heavy and clumsy solution, suited only to small-to-medium sized ships. Boats typically lack the generators and space for the solution, while the amount of power needed to overcome the magnetic field of a large ship is impractical.

Active Countermeasures

Active countermeasures are ways to clear a path through a minefield or remove it completely. This is one of the most important tasks of any mine warfare flotilla.

Mine Sweeping

A sweep is either a contact sweep, a wire dragged through the water by one or two ships to cut the mooring wire of floating mines, or a distance sweep that mimics a ship to detonate the mines. The sweeps are dragged by minesweepers, either purpose-built military ships or converted trawlers. Each run covers between one and two hundred meters, and the ships must move slowly in a straight line, making them vulnerable to enemy fire. This was exploited by the Turkish army in the Battle of Gallipoli in 1915, when mobile howitzer batteries prevented the British and French from clearing a way through minefields. If a contact sweep hits a mine, the wire of the sweep rubs against the mooring wire until it is cut. Sometimes "cutters", explosive devices to cut the mine's wire, are used to lessen the strain on the sweeping wire. Mines cut free are recorded and collected for research or shot with a deck gun.

Minesweepers protect themselves with an oropesa or paravane instead of a second minesweeper. These are torpedo-shaped towed bodies, similar in shape to a Harvey Torpedo, that are streamed from the sweeping vessel thus keeping the sweep at a determined depth and position. Some large warships were routinely equipped with paravane sweeps near the bows in case they inadvertently sailed into minefields — the mine would be deflected towards the paravane by the wire instead of towards the ship by its wake. More recently, heavy-lift helicopters have dragged minesweeping sleds, as in the 1991 Persian Gulf War.

The distance sweep mimics the sound and magnetism of a ship and is pulled behind the sweeper. It has floating coils and large underwater *drums*. It is the only sweep effective against bottom mines. During the Second World War, RAF Coastal Command used Vickers Wellington bombers fitted with degaussing coils to trigger magnetic mines.

Modern influence mines are designed to discriminate against false inputs and are therefore much harder to sweep. They often contain inherent anti-sweeping mechanisms. For example, they may be programmed to respond to the unique noise of a particular ship-type, its associated magnetic signature and the typical pressure displacement of such a vessel. As a result, a mine-sweeper must accurately guess and mimic the required target signature in order to trigger detonation. The task is complicated by the fact that an influence mine may have one or more of a hundred different potential target signatures programmed into it.

Another anti-sweeping mechanism is a ship-counter in the mine fuze. When enabled, this allows detonation only after the mine fuze has been triggered a pre-set number of times. To further complicate matters, influence mines may be programmed to arm themselves (or disarm automatically—known as *self-sterilization*) after a pre-set time. During the pre-set arming delay (which could last days or even weeks) the mine would remain dormant and ignore any target stimulus, whether genuine or faked.

When influence mines are laid in an ocean minefield, they may have various combinations of fuze settings configured. For example, some mines (with the acoustic sensor enabled) may become active within three hours of being laid, others (with the acoustic and magnetic sensors enabled) may become active after two weeks but have the ship-counter mechanism set to ignore the first two trigger events, and still others in the same minefield (with the magnetic and pressure sensors enabled) may not become armed until three weeks have passed. Groups of mines within this mine-field may have different target signatures which may or may not overlap. The fuzes on influence mines allow many different permutations, which complicates the clearance process. Mines with ship-counters, arming delays and highly specific target signatures in mine fuzes can falsely convince a belligerent that a particular area is clear of mines or has been swept effectively because a succession of vessels have already passed through safely.

Mine Hunting

Mine hunting is very different from sweeping, although some minehunters can do both tasks. Mines are hunted using sonar, then inspected and destroyed either by divers or ROVs (remote controlled unmanned mini submarines). It is slow, but also the most reliable way to remove mines. Mine hunting started during the Second World War, but it was only after the war that it became truly effective. Sea mammals (mainly the Bottlenose Dolphin) have been trained to hunt and mark mines, most famously by the U.S. Navy Marine Mammal Program. Mine-clearance dolphins were deployed in the Persian Gulf during the Iraq War in 2003. The Navy claims that these dolphins were effective in helping to clear more than 100 antiship mines and underwater booby traps from Umm Qasr Port.

French naval officer Jaçques Yves Cousteau's Undersea Research Group was once involved in mine-hunting operations: They removed or detonated a variety of German mines, but one particularly defusion-resistant batch—equipped with acutely sensitive pressure, magnetic, and acoustic sensors and wired together so that one explosion would trigger the rest — was simply left undisturbed for years until corrosion would (hopefully) disable the mines.

Mine Breaking

A more drastic method is simply to load a cargo ship with cargo that makes her less vulnerable to sinking (wood for example) and drive her through the minefield, letting the ship to be protected follow the same path. This method was employed by the German Kriegsmarine during WWII, using converted ships known as *Sperrbrecher* ("barrage breaker"). Alternatively, a shallow draught vessel can be steamed through the minefield at high speed to generate a pressure wave sufficient to trigger mines, with the minesweeper moving fast enough to be sufficiently clear of the pressure wave so that triggered mines do not destroy the ship itself. These techniques are the only way to sweep pressure mines. The technique can be simply countered by use of a ship-counter, set to allow a certain number of passes before the mine is actually triggered. Modern doctrine calls for ground mines to be hunted rather than swept.

SEEHUND ROVS OF THE GERMAN NAVY USED FOR MINESWEEPING/BREAKING

An updated form of mine breaking is the use of small unmanned ROVs that simulate the acoustic and magnetic signatures of larger ships and are built to survive exploding mines. Repeated sweeps would be required in case one or more of the mines had its "ship counter" facility enabled i.e. were programmed to ignore the first 2, 3, or even 6 target activations.

NUCLEAR NAVY

Nuclear navy, or nuclear powered navy consists of ships powered by relatively small onboard nuclear reactors known as naval reactors. The concept was revolutionary for naval warfare when first proposed, as it meant that these vessels did not need to stop for fuel like their conventional counterparts, being limited only by crew endurance and supplies.

Nuclear-powered Aircraft Carriers

The United States Navy has by far the most nuclear-powered aircraft carriers, with 11 in service. France's latest aircraft carrier, the FS *Charles de Gaulle*, is nuclear powered. The United Kingdom rejected nuclear power early in the development of its *Queen Elizabeth*-class aircraft carriers on cost grounds. As currently envisaged, France's new aircraft carrier would also be conventionally powered.

Nuclear-powered Submarines

The United States Navy operates the largest fleet of nuclear submarines.Only the United States Navy, the Royal Navy of the United Kingdom, and France's *Marine Nationale* field an all-nuclear submarine force. By 1989, there were over 400 nuclear-powered submarines operational or being built Some 250 of these submarines have now been scrapped and some on order cancelled, due to weapons reduction programs. Russia and the United States had over one hundred each, with the United Kingdom and France fewer than twenty each and China six. The Indian Navy launched their first indigenous *Arihant* class nuclear-powered submarines on July 26, 2009.India is also reported to be leasing two additional nuclear submarines from Russia. Nuclear-powered submarines can stay submerged for up to 400 days if the vessel is fully loaded.

Other Nuclear-powered Vessels

The United States no longer has nuclear cruisers, but they are still in use by Russia, the largest of which are the *Kirov*-class battle cruisers. Russia also has eight nuclear icebreakers in service or under construction.

The United States Navy

The U.S. Navy has accumulated over 5,400 "reactor years" of accident-free experience, and operates more than 80 nuclear-powered ships

Admiral Hyman G. Rick over

Admiral Hyman G. Rickover, (1900–1986), of the United States Navy, known as "father of the nuclear navy" was an electrical engineer by training, and was the primary architect who implemented this daring concept, and believed that it was the natural next phase for the way military vessels could be propelled and powered. The challenge was to reduce the size of a nuclear reactor to fit onboard a ship or submarine, as well as to encase it sufficiently so that radiation hazards would not be a safety concern.

Soon after World War II, Rickover was assigned to the Bureau of Ships in September 1947 and received training in nuclear power at Oak Ridge, Tennessee. In February 1949 he received an assignment to the Division of Reactor Development, U.S. Atomic Energy Commission and then assumed control of the United States Navy's effort as Director of the Naval Reactors Branch in the Bureau of Ships. This dual role allowed him to lead the efforts to develop the world's first nuclear-powered submarine, USS *Nautilus* (SSN 571), which was launched in 1954. As Vice Admiral, from 1958, for three decades Rickover exercised tight control over the ships, technology, and personnel of the nuclear navy, even interviewing every prospective officer for new nuclear powered navy vessels.

Philip Abelson

Leading nuclear physicist Philip Abelson (1913–2004) turned his attention under the guidance of Ross Gunn to applying nuclear power to naval propulsion. Their early efforts at Naval Research Laboratory (NRL) provided an early glimpse at what was to become the nuclear Navy.

ROYAL NAVY

The Royal Navy of the United Kingdom is the oldest of HM Armed Forces (and is therefore known as the Senior Service). From the beginning of the 18th century until well into the 20th century it was the most powerful navy in the world, playing a key part in establishing the British Empire as the dominant world power from 1815 until the early 1940s. In World War II the Royal Navy operated almost 900 ships. During the Cold War it was transformed into a primarily anti-submarine force, hunting for Soviet submarines, mostly active in the GIUK gap. With the collapse of the Soviet Union, its role for the 21st century has returned to focus on global expeditionary operations.

The Royal Navy is a blue water navy and the second-largest navy of the NATO alliance, in terms of the combined displacement approx. 450,000 long tons (460,000 t) (950,000 long tons (970,000 t) including RFA) after the United States Navy. As of 2010 there were 88 commissioned ships in the Royal Navy, including aircraft carriers, a helicopter carrier, landing platform docks, ballistic missile submarines, nuclear fleet submarines, guided missile destroyers, frigates, mine counter-measures and patrol vessels. Twenty-two vessels of the Royal Fleet Auxiliary (RFA) also contribute to the Royal Navy's order-of-battle. The Royal Navy's ability to project power globally is considered second only to the U.S. Navy. The Royal Navy maintains the United Kingdom's nuclear weapons.

The Royal Navy is a constituent component of the Naval Service, which also comprises the Royal Marines, Royal Naval Reserve and Royal Marines Reserve. As of April 2009 the Royal Navy numbered approximately 39,100 Regular personnel of whom 7,500 were in the Royal Marines; in addition, there were 3,600 Volunteer Reserve personnel, giving a total of 42,700 personnel. This makes the Royal Navy the largest navy in the European Union given the combined total of ships, aircraft and personnel.

The Royal Navy is also supported by the Royal Fleet Auxiliary, a civilian logistical support fleet which is owned and operated by the Ministry of Defence as part of the British Merchant Navy.The RFA primarily serves to replenish Royal Navy warships at sea, but also augments the Royal Navy's amphibious warfare capabilities through its four Bay-class LSDs (Landing Ship Dock).

HISTORY

The Development of England's Navy 900–1500

While the early Anglo-Saxon kingdoms certainly engaged in naval warfare and occasional specific instances of troops being transported by sea are known, the earliest surviving references to them fighting at sea come from the period of Viking raids in the 9th century. Under Aethelwulf of Wessex and his son Alfred the Great, who instituted a programme of building large warships on a new design, battles were fought at sea against marauding Danes. The basis of naval organisation at this time is unclear, but the strength of its fleets, perhaps supported by levies on landholding, was an important element in the power of the united Kingdom of England which emerged in the 10th century.

At one point Aethelred II had an especially large fleet built by a national levy of one ship for every 310 hides of land, but it is uncertain whether this was a standard or exceptional model for raising fleets. During the period of Danish rule in the 11th century a standing fleet was maintained by taxation, and this continued for a time under the restored English regime of Edward the Confessor, who frequently commanded fleets in person. When the Norman invasion was imminent, King Harold assembled a large fleet to prevent Duke William from crossing the Channel, but he was forced to dismiss his ships when their supplies ran out and the Normans were able to cross unopposed and defeat Harold at the Battle of Hastings.

English naval power seems to have declined as a result of the Norman conquest. Medieval fleets, in England as elsewhere, were almost entirely composed of merchant ships enlisted into naval service in time of war. From time to time a few 'king's ships' owned by the monarch were built for specifically warlike purposes, but unlike some European states England did not maintain a small permanent core of warships in peacetime. England's naval organisation was haphazard and the mobilisation of fleets when war broke out was slow

With the Viking era at an end, and conflict with France largely confined to the French lands of the English monarchy, England faced little threat from the sea during the 12th and 13th centuries, but in the 14th century the outbreak of the Hundred Years War dramatically increased the French menace. Early in the war French plans for an invasion of England were thwarted when their fleet was destroyed by Edward III in the Battle of Sluys in 1340. Major fighting was thereafter confined to French soil and England's naval capabilities sufficed to transport armies and supplies safely to their continental destinations.

However, while subsequent French invasion schemes came to nothing, England's naval forces were unable to prevent frequent raids on the south coast ports by the French and their Genoese and Castilian allies, which were finally halted only by the occupation of northern France by Henry V.

1500–1707

The standing Navy Royal, with its own secretariat, dockyards and a permanent core of purpose-built warships, was created in the 16th century during the reign of Henry VIII. By the time of

Henry's death in 1547 his fleet had grown to 58 vessels, although armed merchantmen owned by private individuals still comprised a large proportion of war-fleets. Under Elizabeth I England became involved in a war with Spain, which saw privately-owned ships combining with the Navy Royal in highly profitable raids against Spanish commerce and colonies.

In 1588 Philip II of Spain sent the Spanish Armada against England in order to end English support for Dutch rebels, to stop English corsair activity and to depose the Protestant Elizabeth I. The Spaniards sailed from Lisbon, planning to escort an invasion force from the Spanish Netherlands but the plan failed due to maladministration, logistical errors, English harrying, blocking actions by the Dutch, and bad weather.

During the early 17th century England's relative naval power deteriorated and a new threat emerged from the slaving raids of the Barbary corsairs, which the Navy had little success in countering. Charles I undertook a major programme of warship building, creating a small force of ships of unprecedented size and power, but his methods of fund-raising to finance this fleet contributed to the outbreak of the English Civil War. In the wake of this conflict, the king's execution and the abolition of the monarchy, the new Commonwealth of England, isolated and threatened from all sides, dramatically expanded the Navy, which became the most powerful in the world.

The new regime's introduction of Navigation Acts, providing that all merchant shipping to and from England or her colonies should be carried out by English ships, led to war with the Dutch Republic. In the early stages of this First Anglo-Dutch War (1652–1654), the superiority of the large, heavily armed English ships was offset by superior Dutch tactical organisation and the fighting was inconclusive.

English tactical improvements resulted in a series of crushing victories in 1653 at Portland, the Gabbard and Scheveningen, bringing peace on favourable terms.. This was the first war fought largely, on the English side, by purpose-built, state-owned warships. As a result of their defeat in this war, the Dutch transformed their navy on the English model, and the Second Anglo-Dutch War (1665–1667) was a closely fought struggle between evenly-matched opponents, with a crushing English victory at Lowestoft (1665) countered by Dutch triumph in the epic Four Days Battle (1666). The war was ended not by fighting but finance, as in 1667 the restored royal government of Charles II was forced to lay up the fleet in port for lack of money to keep it at sea, while negotiating for peace. Disaster followed, as the Dutch fleet mounted the Raid on the Medway, breaking into the base at Chatham and capturing or burning many of the Navy's largest ships at their moorings. In the Third Anglo-Dutch War (1672–1674), Charles II allied with Louis XIV of France against the Dutch, but the combined Anglo-French fleet was fought to a standstill in a series of inconclusive battles, while the French invasion by land was warded off.

During the 1670s and 1680s the Navy succeeded in permanently ending the threat to English shipping from the Barbary corsairs, inflicting defeats which induced the Barbary states to conclude peace treaties which would long endure. Following the Glorious Revolution, England joined the European coalition against Louis XIV in the War of the Grand Alliance (1688–1697), and combined with the Dutch against the French navy, which had grown rapidly to become the world's largest. The allied fleet was defeated at Beachy Head (1690), but victory at Barfleur-La Hogue (1691) was a turning-point marking the end of France's brief pre-eminence at sea and the beginning of an enduring English, later British, supremacy. In the course of the 17th century the Navy completed the transition from a semi-amateur Navy Royal fighting in conjunction with private vessels into a fully professional, national institution, a Royal Navy. Its financial provisions were gradually regularised, it came to rely purely on dedicated warships, phasing out the use of armed merchantmen, and it developed a professional officer corps with a defined career structure, superseding the earlier mixture of 'tarpaulins' (merchant captains and others who had risen from the ranks of ordinary seamen) and 'gentlemen' (aristocratic soldiers without prior maritime experience, appointed to positions of command on the basis of social status). Under the Acts of Union in 1707 the three-ship Royal Scots Navy merged with that of England to create a British Royal Navy.

DEVELOPMENT OF THE UNITED KINGDOM'S NAVY 1707–1815

Throughout the 18th and 19th centuries the Royal Navy was the largest in the world, but until 1805 its forces were repeatedly matched or exceeded in numbers by a combination of enemies. Despite this it was able to maintain an almost uninterrupted ascendancy over its rivals through superiority in financing, tactics, training, organisation, social cohesion, hygiene, dockyard facilities, logistical support and, from the middle of the 18th century, warship design and construction

During the War of the Spanish Succession (1702–1714), the Navy operated in conjunction with the Dutch against the navies of France and Spain. Naval operations in European waters focused on the acquisition of a Mediterranean base, contributing to a long-lasting alliance with Portugal in 1703 and the capture of Gibraltar (1704) and Minorca (1708), which were both retained by Britain after the war, and on supporting the efforts of Britain's Habsburg allies to seize control of Spain and its Mediterranean dependencies from the Bourbons. French naval squadrons did considerable damage to English and Dutch commercial convoys during the early years of the war, but a devastating victory over France and Spain at Vigo (1702), further successes in battle, and the scuttling of the entire French Mediterranean fleet at Toulon in 1707 virtually cleared the Navy's opponents from the seas for the latter part of the war. Naval operations also enabled the conquest of the French colonies in Nova Scotia and Newfoundland. While the Habsburgs ultimately failed to conquer Spain, with the Navy's help they had acquired its Italian territories, and in the War of the Quadruple Alliance (1718–20), the Navy helped frustrate a Bourbon attempt to regain these possessions, smashing a Spanish fleet at Cape Passaro (1718)

After a period of relative peace, the Navy became engaged in the War of Jenkin's Ear (1739–1742) against Spain, and then the wider War of the Austrian Succession (1744–1748), again pitting Britain against France. Naval fighting in this war, which for the first time included major operations in the Indian Ocean, was largely inconclusive, the most significant event being the failure of an attempted French invasion of England in 1744The subsequent

Seven Years War (1755–1763) saw the Navy conduct amphibious campaigns which brought about the conquest of the remainder of French Canada and the capture of a number of French islands in the Caribbean, while facilitating the capture of the French possessions in India. A new French attempt to invade Britain was thwarted by victories at Lagos and the extraordinary Battle of Quiberon Bay in 1759. Once again the French navy was effectively eliminated from the war, abandoning major operations In 1762 the resumption of hostilities with Spain led to the British capture of Havana, along with a Spanish fleet sheltering there, and Manila.

In the American Revolutionary War, the small Continental Navy of frigates fielded by the rebel colonists was obliterated with ease, but the entry of France, Spain and the Netherlands into the war against Britain produced a combination of opposing forces which deprived the Navy of its position of superiority for the first time since the 1690s, briefly but decisively. The war saw a series of indecisive battles in the Atlantic and Caribbean, in which the Navy failed to achieve the conclusive victories needed to secure the supply lines of British forces in North America and cut off the colonial rebels from outside support. The most important operation of the war came in 1781 when in the Battle of the Chesapeake the British fleet failed to lift the French blockade of Lord Cornwallis's army, resulting in Cornwallis's surrender in the Battle of Yorktown. Although this disaster effectively concluded the fighting in North America, it continued in the Indian Ocean, where the French were prevented from re-establishing a meaningful foothold in India, and in the Caribbean. Victory there in the Battle of the Saintes in 1782 and the relief of Gibraltar later the same year symbolised the restoration of British naval ascendancy, but this came too late to prevent the independence of the Thirteen Colonies.

The Napoleonic Wars (1793–1801, 1803–1814 and 1815) saw the Royal Navy reach a peak of efficiency, dominating the navies of all Britain's adversaries, which spent most of the war blockaded in port. The Navy achieved an emphatic early victory at the Glorious First of June (1794), and gained a number of smaller victories while supporting abortive Royalist efforts to regain control of France. In the course of one such operation the majority of the French Mediterraean fleet was captured or destroyed during a short-lived occupation of Toulon in 1793 The military successes of the French Revolutionary regime brought the Spanish and Dutch navies into the war on the French side, but in 1797 the British inflicted a defeat on Spain at Cape St Vincent and crushed the Dutch at Camperdown; two years later the remainder of the Dutch fleet surrendered to an Anglo-Russian landing force at Den Helder The British Mediterranean fleet under Nelson failed to intercept Napoleon Bonaparte's 1797 expedition to invade Egypt, but annihilated his fleet at the Battle of the Nile, leaving his army isolated. Two major mutinies at the Spithead and the Nore in 1797, were potentially very dangerous for Britain, because at the time the country was at risk of a French invasion. The emergence of a Baltic coalition opposed to Britain led to an attack on Denmark, which lost much of its fleet in the Battle of Copenhagen (1801) and came to terms with Britain.

During these years the Navy also conducted amphibious operations which captured most of the French Caribbean islands and the Dutch colonies at the Cape of Good Hope and Ceylon and in the Dutch East Indies, but all of these gains except Ceylon and Trinidad were returned following the Peace of Amiens in 1802, which briefly halted the fighting. War resumed in 1803 and Napoleon, now ruling France as emperor, attempted to assemble a large enough fleet from the French and Spanish squadrons blockaded in various ports to cover an invasion of England. The Navy frustrated these efforts and, following the abandonment of the invasion plan, the combined Franco-Spanish fleet which had been gathered was smashed by Nelson in the Battle of Trafalgar (1805). This victory marked the culmination of decades of developing British naval dominance, and left the Navy in a position of uncontested hegemony at sea which endured until the early years of the twentieth century.

After Trafalgar, large-scale fighting at sea was limited to the destruction of small, fugitive French squadrons at Cape Ortegal, San Domingo and the Basque Roads, and amphibious operations which again captured the colonies which had been restored at Amiens, along with France's Indian Ocean base at Mauritius. In 1807 French plans to seize the Danish fleet led to a pre-emptive British attack on Copenhagen, resulting in the surrender of the entire Danish navy. The impressment of British and American sailors from American ships contributed to the outbreak of the War of 1812 (1812–1814) against the United States, in which the naval fighting was largely confined to commerce raiding and single-ship actions. In the later years of the war the French devoted great effort to rebuilding their navy, but the scattered force of hastily-built, often unseaworthy ships and inexperienced and demoralised crews they produced was incapable of challenging British control of the sea and remained under blockade until the fighting ended in 1814, while the brief renewal of war after Napoleon's return to power in 1815 did not bring a resumption of naval combat.

1815-1914

Between 1815 and 1914 the Navy saw little serious action, owing to the absence of any opponent strong enough to challenge its dominance. It succeeded in maintaining the huge advantage it had built up over all potential rivals despite the comprehensive transformation of naval warfare brought about by steam propulsion, metal ship construction and high-explosive munitions, which required the complete replacement of war fleets. Thanks to British leadership in the Industrial Revolution, the country enjoyed unparalleled shipbuilding capacity and financial resources, which ensured that no rival could take advantage of the potential of these revolutionary changes to negate the British advantage in ship numbers. The Navy was thus able to preserve a numerical dominance based on the 'two power standard', which stipulated that it should remain larger than its two most powerful competitors combined.

During the 19th century the Royal Navy enforced a ban on the slave trade, acted to suppress piracy, and continued to map the world. To this day, Admiralty charts are maintained by the Royal Navy. Royal Navy vessels on surveying missions carried out extensive scientific work. Charles Darwin travelled around the world on HMS *Beagle*, making scientific observations which led him to propose the idea of evolution.

The end of the 19th century saw structural changes brought about by the First Sea Lord (Chief of Staff) Jackie Fisher who retired, scrapped, or placed into reserve many of the older vessels, making funds and manpower available for newer ships. He also oversaw the development of HMS *Dreadnought*, the first all-big-gun ship and one of the most influential ships in naval history. This ship rendered all other battleships then existing obsolete, and unlike the more dramatic technological revolutions of the 19th century it brought a serious challenge to British naval hegemony. The industrial and economic development of Germany had by this time overtaken Britain, enabling it to compete in warship building, and a politically charged and expensive arms race ensued. Britain emerged from this contest triumphant, in as much as it was able to maintain a substantial numerical advantage over Germany, but for the first time since 1805 another navy now existed with the capacity to challenge the Royal Navy in battle. During these years, British supremacy was also undermined by the development of submarines, which made it possible for commerce raiders to bypass a dominant surface fleet.

1914–1945

During the two World Wars, the Royal Navy played a vital role in keeping the United Kingdom supplied with food, arms and raw materials and in defeating the German campaigns of unrestricted submarine warfare in the first and second battles of the Atlantic.

During this period, relations between the Royal Navy and the separate navies of the Dominions—the Royal Australian Navy (established as a separate service in 1901), the Royal Canadian Navy (1910), the Royal New Zealand Navy (1941) and the South African Navy (1922)—were very close. Officers were frequently transferred between them and the RN, and many ships belonging to Dominion navies served in British fleets and flotillas. The Dominion navies were frequently regarded as branches of the RN, and Dominion governments often did little to contradict this impression.

During the First World War most of the Royal Navy's strength was deployed at home in the Grand Fleet. Their primary aim was to draw the Hochseeflotte (the German "High Seas Fleet") into an engagement. No decisive victory ever came though. The Royal

Navy and the Kaiserliche Marine fought many engagements including the Battle of Heligoland Bight, and the Battle of Jutland. Although it suffered heavier losses than the Hochseeflotte it did succeed in preventing the German Fleet from putting to sea in the latter stages of the War

In the inter-war period the Royal Navy was stripped of much of its power. The Washington Naval Treaty of 1922, together with severe financial constraints during the immediate post-war period and the Great Depression, forced the Admiralty to scrap some capital ships and to cancel plans for new construction. The London Naval Treaty of 1930 deferred new capital ship construction until 1937 and reiterated construction limits on cruisers, destroyers and submarines. In 1931 Britain was forced off the gold standard by the worsening economic conditions; in 1932 she revoked her involvement in free trade, and the Invergordon Mutiny took place over a proposed 25% pay cut which was eventually reduced to 10%. As international tensions increased in the mid-1930s the Second London Naval Treaty of 1935 failed to halt the development of a naval arms race and by 1938 treaty limits were effectively ignored. The rearmament of the Royal Navy was well under way by this point; the Royal Navy had begun construction of the *King George V* class and several aircraft carriers including *Ark Royal*. In addition to new construction several existing old battleships, battlecruisers and heavy cruisers were reconstructed, and anti-aircraft weaponry reinforced. New technologies such as ASDIC, Huff-Duff and hydrophones were developed, and the Fleet Air Arm was reintroduced in 1937. However, around this time the Imperial Japanese Navy and the United States Navy began to surpass the Royal Navy in power.

During the early phases of World War II the Royal Navy provided critical cover during British evacuations from Dunkirk. At the Battle of Taranto Admiral Cunningham commanded a fleet that launched the first all-aircraft naval attack in history. Later Cunningham was determined that as many Commonwealth soldiers as possible should be evacuated after their defeat on Crete. When army generals feared he would lose too many ships, he famously said, "It takes three years to build a ship; it takes three centuries to build a tradition".

The Royal Navy suffered huge losses in the early stages of the war including HMS *Hood* to the *Bismarck*, and HMS *Repulse* and HMS *Prince of Wales* of Force Z during the fall of Singapore. There were, however, early successes against enemy surface ships, in particular off Norway. As well as providing cover in operations, it was also vital in guarding the sea lanes that enabled British forces to fight in remote parts of the world such as North Africa, the Mediterranean and the Far East. Naval supremacy in the Atlantic was vital to the amphibious operations carried out, such as the invasions of Northwest Africa, Sicily, Italy, and Normandy. During the war however, it became clear that aircraft carriers were the new capital ships of naval warfare, and that Britain's former naval superiority in terms of battleships had become irrelevant. Though Britain was an early innovator in aircraft carrier design and in many naval technologies, it did not have the resources to pursue this in the post-war period.

Postwar Period and Early 21st Century

After World War II the decline of the British Empire and the economic hardships in Britain at the time forced the reduction in the size and capability of the Royal Navy. The increasingly powerful U.S. Navy took on the former role of the Royal Navy as global naval power. However, the threat of the Soviet Union and British commitments throughout the world created a new role for the Navy.

The 1960s saw the peak of the Royal Navy's capabilities in the post-war era. The two Audacious class fleet carriers HMS *Ark Royal*, HMS *Eagle*, the rebuilt HMS *Victorious* and the four Centaur class light carriers gave the Royal Navy the most powerful carrier fleet outside the United States. The navy also had a large fleet of frigates and destroyers. New, more modern units like the County-class destroyers and *Leander*-class frigates also began to enter service in the 1960s.

HMS *Dreadnought*, the Royal Navy's first nuclear submarine, was launched in the 1960s. The navy also received its first nuclear weapons with the introduction of the first of the Resolution class submarines and later became responsible for the maintenance of the UK's entire nuclear deterrent.

The Navy began plans to replace its fleet of aircraft carriers in the mid-1960s. A plan was drawn up for 3 large aircraft carriers each displacing about 60,000 tons; the plan was designated CVA-01. These carriers would be able to operate the latest aircraft that were coming into service, and would keep the Royal Navy's place as a major naval power.

However, the new Labour government that came into power in the mid-1960s was determined to cut defence expenditure as a means to reduce public spending, and in the 1966 Defence White Paper the project was cancelled.

After this the navy began to fall in size and by 1979 the last fleet carrier, HMS *Ark Royal*, was scrapped. The navy was forced to make do with three much smaller *Invincible*-class aircraft carriers, and the fleet was now centred around anti-submarine warfare in the north Atlantic as opposed to its former position with world wide strike capability.

The most important operation conducted predominantly by the Royal Navy after the Second World War was the 1982 defeat of Argentina in the Falkland Islands War. Despite losing four naval ships and other civilian and RFA ships the Royal Navy proved it was still able to fight a battle 8,345 miles (12,800 km) from Great Britain. HMS *Conqueror* is the only nuclear-powered submarine to have engaged an enemy ship with torpedoes, sinking the Argentine cruiser ARA *General Belgrano*. The war also underlined the importance of aircraft carriers and submarines and exposed the weaknesses of the service's late 20th century dependence on chartered merchant vessels.

The Royal Navy also took part in the Gulf War, the Kosovo conflict, the Afghanistan Campaign, and the 2003 Iraq War, the last of which saw RN warships bombard positions in support of the Al Faw Peninsula landings by Royal Marines. In August 2005 the Royal Navy rescued seven Russians stranded in a submarine off the Kamchatka peninsula. The Navy's Scorpio 45 remote-controlled mini-sub freed the Russian submarine from the fishing nets and cables that had held it for three days. The Royal Navy was also involved in an incident involving Somali pirates in November 2008, after the pirates tried to capture a civilian vessel.

THE ROYAL NAVY TODAY

Personnel

The Royal Navy has approximately 39,000 personnel on active duty as of 1 June 2009.of which 34,400 are trained. This also includes active duty Royal Marine personnel. Before the Falklands War in 1982 Defence Secretary John Nott had advocated and initiated a series of cutbacks to the NavyThe Falklands War though, proved a need for the Royal Navy to regain an expeditionary and littoral capability which, with its resources and structure at the time, would prove difficult. At the end of the Cold War at the beginning of the 1990s the Royal Navy was a force focused on blue water anti-submarinewarfare. Its purpose was to search for and destroy Soviet submarines in the North Atlantic, and to operate the nuclear deterrent submarine force.

UK foreign policy after the end of the Cold War has given rise to a number of operations which have required an aircraft carrier to be deployed globally such as the Adriatic, Peace Support Operations in Bosnia and Herzegovina and Kosovo, Sierra Leone, the Persian Gulf. Destroyers and frigates have been deployed against piracy in the Malacca Straits and Horn of Africa. Consequently in the 1990s the navy began a series of projects to modernise the fleet and convert it from a North Atlantic-based anti-submarine force to an expeditionary force. This has involved the replacement of much of the Fleet and has seen a number of large procurement projects.

Large Fleet Units

Two *Queen Elizabeth*-class aircraft carriers which have been ordered are to be a new generation of aircraft carrier to replace the three *Invincible* class aircraft carriers. The two vessels are expected to cost £3.9 billion, will displace 65,000 tons and, although as of 2010 somewhat delayed, are planned to enter service from around 2016. They will be STOVL aircraft carriers, operating the STOVL variant of the F-35 Lightning II, which is planned for both the Fleet Air Arm and the Royal Air Force to replace the Harrier. A helicopter carrier designed from the *Invincible* class aircraft carriers, HMS *Ocean*, complements the aircraft carrier force.

The introduction of the four vessels of the *Bay* class of landing ship dock into the Royal Fleet Auxiliary in 2006 and 2007, and the two *Albion* class landing platform docks gave the Royal Navy a significantly-enhanced amphibious capability. In November 2006 First Sea Lord Admiral Sir Jonathon Band said, "These ships represent a major uplift in the Royal Navy's war fighting capability.

Escort Units

The escort fleet, in the form of frigates and destroyers, is the traditional workhorse of the Navy, and is also being updated. The 2009 fleet of five and 1 in reserve Type 42 destroyers are to be replaced with the much larger Type 45 destroyer class.

Six Type 45 destroyers are under construction or waiting to enter service as of 2009. Under the terms of the original contract the Navy was to order twelve vessels, but only the six will be constructed The main role of the Type 45 destroyer is anti-air warfare; in order to fulfil this role, it will be equipped with the Sea Viper (formerly known as PAAMS) integrated anti-aircraft system which will fire Aster 15 and Aster 30 missiles. The Type 45 will operate the highly sophisticated Sampson radar system that will be fully integrated into the PAAMS system.

The last frigate to enter service was the Type 23 frigate, HMS *St Albans*. On 21 July 2004, in the Delivering Security in a Changing World review of defence spending, Defence Secretary Geoff Hoon announced that three frigates of the fleet of sixteen would be paid off as part of a continuous cost-cutting strategy. Several designs have been created for a new generation frigate such as the Future Surface Combatant, but these concepts have not yet obtained Main Gate approval. The remaining fleet of four batch 3 Type 22 frigates, the Type 23 frigate's predecessor, are in service to complement the Royal Navy's fleet of destroyers.

Submarines are currently under construction or awaiting to enter service, with a further three or four planned depending on costs. The first, HMS *Astute* is due to enter service in 2009These submarines are much larger than their predecessors, the *Trafalgar* class and are expected to displace 7,800 tons submerged All seven *Trafalgar* class submarines are currently in service, with one *Swiftsure*-class submarine, the *Trafalgar* class's predecessor, also still in service. In December 2006, plans were unveiled for a new class of four ballistic missile submarines to replace the *Vanguard*-class submarine, which is due to be replaced by 2024. This new class will mean that the United Kingdom will maintain a nuclear ballistic missile submarine fleet and the ability to launch nuclear weapons.

Other Vessels

At the beginning of the 1990s the Royal Navy had two classes of Offshore Patrol vessel, the Island class, and the larger Castle class. However, in 1997 a decision was taken to replace them. An order for three much larger offshore patrol vessels, the *River* class was placed in 2001. Unusually, the three River class ships are owned by Vosper Thorneycroft, and leased to the Royal Navy until 2013. This relationship is defined by a ground-breaking Contractor Logistic Support] contract which contracts the ships' availability to the RN, including technical and stores support. A modified River class vessel, HMS *Clyde,* was commissioned in July 2007 and became the Falkland Islands guardship. The Royal Navy also has the *Sandown*-class minehunter and the *Hunt* class mine countermeasure vessel. The Hunt class of 8 vessels are mine countermeasure vessels that combine the separate role of the traditional minesweeper and that of the active minehunter in one hull. When needed they take on the role of offshore patrol vessels. The Royal Navy has a mandate to provide support to the British Antarctic Survey (BAS), which comes in the form of the dedicated Antarctic Patrol Ship HMS *Endurance*. The four *Hecla* class vessels were replaced by the survey vessel HMS *Scott* which surveys the ocean floor. HMS *Roebuck* meanwhile, surveys the UK continental shelf or other shallow waters in support of the larger vessels. The other survey vessels of the Royal Navy are the two multi-role ships of the *Echo* class which came into service in 2002 and 2003.

CURRENT ROLE

The current role of the Royal Navy (RN) is to protect British interests at home and abroad, executing the foreign and defence policies of Her Majesty's Government through the exercise of military effect, diplomatic activities and other activities in support of these objectives. The RN is also a key element of the UK contribution to NATO, with a number of assets allocated to NATO tasks at any time. These objectives are delivered via a number of core capabilities:

The F-35 will replace the Harrier aboard the Queen Elizabeth class aircraft carriers, which will replace the Invincible class aircraft carriers.

- Maintenance of the UK Nuclear Deterrent through a policy of *Continuous at Sea Deterrence.*
- Provision of two medium scale maritime task groups with organic air assets.
- Delivery of the UK Commando force.
- Contribution of assets to Joint Force Harrier.
- Contribution of assets to the Joint Helicopter Command.
- Maintenance of standing patrol commitments.
- Provision of Mine Counter Measures capability to UK and allied commitments.
- Provision of Hydrographic and meteorological services deployable worldwide.
- Protection of the UK and EU's Exclusive Economic Zone.

Current Deployments

The Royal Navy is currently deployed in many areas of the world, including a number of standing Royal Navy deployments. These include several home tasks as well as overseas deployments. The Royal Navy is deployed in the Mediterranean as part of standing NATO deployments including mine countermeasures and NATO Maritime Group 2 and also has the Royal Navy Cyprus Squadron. In both the North and South Atlantic Royal Naval vessels are patrolling. There is always a Falkland Islands Patrol Vessel on deployment, currently the new vessel HMS *Clyde*. The Royal Navy is also deployed in the Middle East to provide "maritime security and surveillance in the Northern Persian Gulf.

COMMAND, CONTROL AND ORGANISATION

The head of the Royal Navy is the Lord High Admiral, a position which has been held by the Sovereign since 1964 (the Sovereign being the overall head of the Armed Forces).

The professional head of the Naval Service is the First Sea Lord, an Admiral and member of the Defence Council. The Defence Council delegates management of the Naval Service to the Admiralty Board, chaired by the Secretary of State for Defence, which directs the Navy Board, a sub-committee of the Admiralty Board comprising only Naval Officers and Ministry of Defence (MOD) civil servants. These are all based in MOD Main Building in London, where the First Sea Lord, also known as the Chief of the Naval Staff, is supported by the Naval Staff Department.

Senior Leadership

As of July 2009, the following persons were in office:

- Lord High Admiral: Queen Elizabeth II.
- Naval members of the Admiralty Board:
  - First Sea Lord: Admiral Sir Mark Stanhope, *based in MOD Main Building*
  - Commander-in-Chief Fleet: Admiral Sir Trevor Soar
  - Second Sea Lord: Vice Admiral Alan Massey CBE ADC
  - Assistant Chief of the Naval Staff: Rear Admiral R. G. Cooling
  - Controller of the Navy: Rear Admiral Paul Lambert
  - Naval Member for Logistics: Rear Admiral Amjad Hussain

Fleet Command

Full command of all deployable fleet units (including the Royal Marines and the Fleet Auxiliary) is the responsibility of Commander-in-Chief Fleet (CINCFLEET), with a Command Headquarters at HMS *Excellent* in Portsmouth and an Operational Headquarters at Northwood, Middlesex. The latter is co-located with the Permanent Joint Headquarters of the United Kingdom's armed forces, and a NATO Regional Command, Allied Maritime Component Command Northwood (AMCCN). CINCFLEET is also Commander AMCCN. The purpose of CINCFLEET is to provide ships and submarines and commando forces at readiness to conduct military and diplomatic tasks as required by the UK government, including the recruitment and training of personnel.

- Commander-in-Chief Fleet Headquarters:f
  - o Deputy CINC and Chief of Staff: Vice Admiral Paul Boissier, *(based in HMS* Excellent, *commands the Headquarters).*
  - o Chief of Staff (Capability): Major General Garry Robison
  - o Commander Operations: Rear Admiral Mark Anderson *(based at Northwood, also Rear Admiral Submarines and Commander Submarine Allied Forces North (NATO)).*
  - o Commander UK Maritime Forces: Rear Admiral Peter Hudson *(deployable Force Commander responsible for Maritime Battle Staffs; UK Task Group, UK Amphibious Task Group, UK Maritime Component Command).*
  - o Commander UK Amphibious Force: Major General Andy Salmon OBE, also the Commandant General Royal Marines
  - o Flag Officer Scotland, Northern England and Northern Ireland: Rear Admiral Martin Alabaster
  - o Flag Officer Sea Training: Rear Admiral C. A. Snow

Second Sea Lord and Commander-in-Chief Naval Home Command Headquarters

  - o Vice Admiral Sir Alan Massey KCB CBE
  - o Chief of Staff (Personnel)/Naval Secretary: Rear Admiral C. P. R. Montgomery CBE
  - o Director General Naval Chaplaincy Services: The Venerable J. Green OHC

Locations

The Royal Navy currently operates three *bases* in the United Kingdom where commissioned ships are based; Portsmouth, Clyde and Devonport, Plymouth — Devonport is the largest operational naval base in the UK and Western Europe. Each base hosts a Flotilla Command under a Commodore, or in the case of Clyde a Captain, responsible for the provision of Operational Capability using the ships and submarines within the flotilla. 3 Commando Brigade Royal Marines is similarly commanded by a Brigadier and based in Plymouth. Historically the Royal Navy maintained Royal Navy Dockyards around the world. Dockyards of the Royal Navy are harbours where ships are overhauled and refitted. Only four are operating today; at Devonport, Faslane, Rosyth and at Portsmouth. A Naval Base Review was undertaken in 2006 and early 2007, the outcome being announced by Secretary of State, Des Browne the Defence Secretary confirming that all would remain however some reductions in manpower were anticipated.

The academy where initial training for future Royal Navy officers takes place is Britannia Royal Naval College, located on a hill overlooking Dartmouth, Devon. Significant numbers of naval personnel are employed within the Ministry of Defence, Defence Equipment and Support and on exchange with the Army and Royal Air Force. Small numbers are also on exchange within other government departments and with allied fleets eg United States Navy.

Special Forces

The Royal Navy, through the Royal Marines, provides the Special Boat Service (SBS), one of the three Special Forces units within the United Kingdom Special Forces group. The SBS is a maritime Special Forces capability and is an independent force element of the Royal Marines. Based at RM Poole in Poole, Dorset it is made up of 4 operational squadrons and an element of the Royal Marines Reserve which provides individual trained ranks to the regular force. Roles include maritime activities such as covert shore reconnaissance, small boat operations, amphibious raiding and Maritime Counter-Terrorism however the force also conducts traditional land-centric activities. The SBS provides the special forces element of 3 Commando Brigade when deployed.

TITLES AND NAMING

Of the Royal Navy

The British Royal Navy is commonly referred to as the "Royal Navy" both in the United Kingdom and other countries. Navies of Commonwealth of Nations countries where the British monarch is also head of state also include their national name e.g. Royal Australian Navy. Some navies of other monarchies, such as the

Koninklijke Marine (Royal Netherlands Navy) and *Kungliga Flottan* (Royal Swedish Navy), are also called "Royal Navy" in their own language and the French Navy, despite France being a republic since 1870, is often nicknamed *"La Royale"* (literally: The Royal)

Of Ships

Royal Navy ships in commission are prefixed since 1789 with Her Majesty's Ship (His Majesty's Ship), abbreviated to HMS, *e.g.*, HMS *Ark Royal*. Submarines are styled HM Submarine, similarly HMS. Names are allocated to ships and submarines by a naming committee within the MOD and given by class, with the names of ships within a class often being thematic (*e.g.*. the Type 23 class are named after British Dukes) or traditional (*e.g.*, the *Invincible* class all carry the names of famous historic ships). Names are frequently re-used offering a new ship the rich heritage, battle honours and traditions of her predecessors. Often, a particular vessel class will be named after the first ship of that type to be built. As well as a name each ship, and submarine, of the Royal Navy and the Royal Fleet Auxiliary is given a pennant number which in part denotes its role.

CUSTOM AND TRADITION

The Royal Navy has several formal customs and traditions including the use of ensigns and ships badges. Royal Navy ships have several ensigns used when under way and when in port. Commissioned ships and submarines wear the White Ensign at the stern whilst alongside during daylight hours and at the main-mast whilst under way. When alongside, the *Union Jack* (as distinct from the Union Flag, often referred to as the Union Jack) is flown from the jackstaff at the bow, and can only be flown under way either to signal a court-martial is in progress or to indicate the presence of an Admiral of the Fleet on-board (including the Lord High Admiral, the Monarch) The Fleet Review is an irregular tradition of assembling the fleet before the monarch. The first review on record was held in 1400, and the most recent review as of 2009 was held on 28 June 2005 to mark the bi-centenary of the Battle of Trafalgar; 167 ships from many different nations attended with the Royal Navy supplying 67. Another popular tradition of the British Navy is that they play several cricket matches with local teams, and against the Australian Navy in The Ashes.

There are several less formal traditions including service nicknames and Naval slang.The nicknames include "The Andrew" (of uncertain origin, possibly after a zealous press ganger) and "The Senior Service". The RN has evolved a rich volume of slang, known as "Jack-speak". Nowadays the British sailor is usually "Jack" (or "Jenny") rather than the more historical "Jack Tar". Royal Marines are fondly known as "Bootnecks" or often just as "Royals". The current compendium of Naval slang was brought together by Commander A. Covey-Crump and his name has in itself become the subject of Naval slang; Covey Crump A game traditionally played by the Navy is the four-player board game "Uckers". This is similar to Ludo and it is regarded as easy to learn, but difficult to play well.

In Popular Culture

The Royal Navy's Napoleonic campaigns are a popular subject of historical novels. Some of the best-known include Patrick O'Brian's Aubrey-Maturin series, C.S. Forester's Horatio Hornblower chronicles, Showell Styles' The Midshipman Quinn stories, Dudley Pope's Lord Ramage novels and Douglas Reeman's Richard Bolitho novels. Alexander Kent is a pen name of Douglas Reeman who, under his birth name, has written many novels featuring the Royal Navy in the two World Wars. Other well-known novels include Alistair MacLean's HMS *Ulysses*, Nicholas Monsarrat's *The Cruel Sea*, and C.S. Forester's *The Ship*, all set during World War II.

The Navy can also be seen in numerous films. The fictional spy James Bond is 'officially' a commander in the Royal Navy. The Royal Navy is featured in *The Spy Who Loved Me*, where a missile submarine is stolen, and in *Tomorrow Never Dies* when a media baron sinks a Royal Navy warship in an attempt to trigger a war between the UK and People's Republic of China. *Master and Commander: The Far Side of the World* was based on Patrick O'Brian's Aubrey-Maturin series. The *Pirates of the Caribbean* series of films also includes the Navy as the force pursuing the eponymous pirates. Noël Coward directed and starred in his own film *In*

Which We Serve, which tells the story of the crew of the fictional HMS *Torrin* during the Second World War. It was intended as a propaganda film and was released in 1942. Coward starred as the ship's captain, with supporting roles from John Mills and Richard Attenborough. Other examples of full length feature films focusing specifically on the Royal Navy, have been: *Seagulls over Sorrento; Yangtse Incident,* the story of HMS *Amethyst*'s escape down the Yangtze river; *We Dive at Dawn; The Battle of River Plate; Sink the Bismarck!.*

CS Forester's Hornblower novels have been adapted for television, as have Bernard Cornwell's *Sharpe* series, which, although primarily involving the Peninsular War of the time, includes several novels involving Richard Sharpe at sea with the Navy. The Royal Navy was the subject of an acclaimed 1970s BBC television drama series, *Warship,* and of a five-part documentary, *Shipmates,* that followed the workings of the Royal Navy day to day.

Television documentaries about the Royal Navy include *Sailor,* about life on the aircraft carrier HMS *Ark Royal;* and *Submarine,* about the submarine captains' training course 'The Perisher'. A book based on the series, and also called *Submarine,* was produced by Jonathan Crane.

The popular BBC radio comedy series *The Navy Lark* featured a fictitious warship ("HMS *Troutbridge*") and ran from 1959 to 1977

ECHO CLASS SUBMARINE

The Echo class submarines were nuclear cruise missile submarines of the Soviet Navy built during the 1960s. Their Soviet designation was Project 659 class for the first five vessels, and Project 675 for the following twenty-nine. Their NATO reporting names were *Echo I* and *Echo II.*

Echo I Class

The Soviet Echo I class (Project 659 class) were completed at Komsomolsk in the Soviet far east in 1960 to 1962. The Echo I class were classed as SSGNs armed with six launchers for the P-5 Pyatyorka (SS-N-3C, "Shaddock-B") cruise missile. The Echo I class had to operate in a strategic rather than attack role because of the lack of fire control and guidance radars. As the Soviet SSBN force built up, the need for these boats diminished so they were converted to the Project 659T SSN's between 1969 and 1974. The conversion involved the removal of the cruise missiles, the plating over and the streamlining of the hull to reduce underwater noise of the launchers and the modification of the sonar systems to the standard of the November-class SSNs.

All the Echo Is were deployed in the Pacific Fleet although *K-122* was damaged by a fire in compartment VII during a patrol mission near Okinawa in August 1980 and had to be towed back to Vladivostok for emergency dry docking (the submarine was removed from active service in October 1985). The last two boats were deleted in the early 1990s.

Echo II Class

The Echo II class (Project 675 class) were built at Severodvinsk (18 vessels) and Komsomolsk (11 vessels) between 1962 and 1967 as anti-carrier missile submarines. The Echo II class carried eight P-6 (SS-N-3a "Shaddock-A") anti-ship cruise missiles mounted in pairs above the pressure hull.

To fire the missiles, the ship had to surface and the missile was elevated to about 25 to 30 degrees. The Echo II class also had fire control and guidance radar. The Echo II class could fire all eight missiles in 30 minutes, but would have to wait on the surface until the missile mid-course correction and final target selection had been sent unless guidance had been handed over to a third party. From the mid-1970s, fourteen of the 29 Echo II class were converted during overhauls to carry the P-500 Bazalt (SS-N-12 "Sandbox") anti-ship cruise missile. The conversions could be distinguished by the fitting bulges to each side of the sail.

The Echo II class were divided evenly between the Pacific and Northern Fleets. The boats were obsolete by the mid-1980s, and were deleted in 1989 and 1994.

10

Sonar

Sonar (originally an acronym for sound navigation and ranging) is a technique that uses sound propagation (usually underwater, as in Submarine navigation) to navigate, communicate with or detect other vessels. There are two kinds of sonar: active and passive. Sonar may be used as a means of acoustic location and of measurement of the echo characteristics of "targets" in the water. Acoustic location in air was used before the introduction of radar. Sonar may also be used in air for robot navigation, and SODAR (an upward looking in-air sonar) is used for atmospheric investigations. The term *sonar* is also used for the equipment used to generate and receive the sound. The frequencies used in sonar systems vary from very low (infrasonic) to extemely high (ultrasonic). The study of underwater sound is known as underwater acoustics or sometimes hydroacoustics.

History

Although some animals (dolphins and bats) have used sound for communication and object detection for millions of years, use by humans in the water is initially recorded by Leonardo Da Vinci in 1490: a tube inserted into the water was said to be used to detect vessels by placing an ear to the tube. In the 19th century an underwater bell was used as an ancillary to lighthouses to provide warning of hazards.

The use of sound to 'echo locate' underwater in the same way as bats use sound for aerial navigation seems to have been prompted by the *Titanic* disaster of 1912. The world's first patent for an underwater echo ranging device was filed at the British

Patent Office by English meteorologist Lewis Richardson a month after the sinking of the Titanic, and a German physicist Alexander Behm obtained a patent for an echo sounder in 1913. Canadian Reginald Fessenden, while working for the Submarine Signal Company in Boston, built an experimental system beginning in 1912, a system later tested in Boston Harbor, and finally in 1914 from the U.S. Revenue (now Coast Guard) Cutter Miami on the Grand Banks off Newfoundland Canada. In that test, Fessenden demonstrated depth sounding, underwater communications (Morse Code) and echo ranging (detecting an iceberg at two miles (3 km) range). The so-called Fessenden oscillator, at ca. 500 Hz frequency, was unable to determine the bearing of the berg due to the 3 meter wavelength and the small dimension of the transducer's radiating face (less than 1 meter in diameter). The ten Montreal-built British H class submarines launched in 1915 were equipped with a Fessenden oscillator

During World War I the need to detect submarines prompted more research into the use of sound. The British made early use of underwater hydrophones, while the French physicist Paul Langevin, working with a Russian immigrant electrical engineer, Constantin Chilowski, worked on the development of active sound devices for detecting submarines in 1915 using quartz. Although piezoelectric and magnetostrictive transducers later superseded the electrostatic transducers they used, this work influenced future designs. Lightweight sound-sensitive plastic film and fibre optics have been used for hydrophones (acousto-electric transducers for in-water use), while Terfenol-D and PMN (lead magnesium niobate) have been developed for projectors.

ASDIC

In 1916, under the British Board of Invention and Research, Canadian physicist Robert William Boyle took on the active sound detection project with A B Wood, producing a prototype for testing in mid 1917. This work, for the Anti-Submarine Division, was undertaken in utmost secrecy, and used quartz piezoelectric crystals to produce the world's first practical underwater active sound detection apparatus. To maintain secrecy no mention of sound experimentation or quartz was made-the word used to describe the early work ('supersonics') was changed to 'ASD'ics, and the quartz material to 'ASD'ivite: hence the British acronym *ASDIC*. In 1939, in response to a question from the Oxford English Dictionary, the Admiralty made up the story that it stood for 'Allied Submarine Detection Investigation Committee', and this is still widely believed, though no committee bearing this name has been found in the Admiralty archives

By 1918, both the US and Britain had built active systems, though the British were well in advance of the US. They tested their ASDIC on HMS *Antrim* in 1920, and started production in 1922. The 6th Destroyer Flotilla had ASDIC-equipped vessels in 1923. An anti-submarine school, HMS *Osprey*, and a training flotilla of four vessels were established on Portland in 1924. The US Sonar QB set arrived in 1931.

By the outbreak of World War II, the Royal Navy had five sets for different surface ship classes, and others for submarines, incorporated into a complete anti-submarine attack system. The effectiveness of early ASDIC was hamstrung by the use of the depth charge as an anti-submarine weapon. This required an attacking vessel to pass over a submerged contact before dropping charges over the stern, resulting in a loss of ASDIC contact in the moments leading up to attack. The hunter was effectively firing blind, during which time a submarine commander could take evasive action. This situation was remedied by using several ships cooperating and by the adoption of "ahead throwing weapons", such as Hedgehog and later Squid, which projected warheads at a target ahead of the attacker and thus still in ASDIC contact. Developments during the war resulted in British ASDIC sets which used several different shapes of beam, continuously covering blind spots. Later, acoustic torpedoes were used.

At the start of World War II, British ASDIC technology was transferred for free to the United States. Research on ASDIC and underwater sound was expanded in the UK and in the US. Many new types of military sound detection were developed. These included sonobuoys, first developed by the British in 1944 under the codename *High Tea*, dipping/dunking sonar and mine detection sonar. This work formed the basis for post war developments related to countering the nuclear submarine. Work on sonar had also been carried out in the Axis countries, notably in Germany, which included countermeasures. At the end of World War II this German work was assimilated by Britain and the US. Sonars have continued to be developed by many countries, including Russia, for both military and civil uses. In recent years the major military development has been the increasing interest in low frequency active systems.

SONAR

In World War II, the Americans used the term *SONAR* for their systems, coined as the equivalent of RADAR. RADAR was considered very glamorous and effective, and they wanted to cash in on the name. Standardisation of signals for all NATO countries led to the dropping of *ASDIC* in favour of *SONAR*.

PERFORMANCE FACTORS

The detection, classification and localisation performance of a sonar depends on the environment and the receiving equipment, as well as the transmitting equipment in an active sonar or the target radiated noise in a passive sonar.

Sound Propagation

Sonar operation is affected by variations in sound speed, particularly in the vertical plane. Sound travels more slowly in fresh water than in sea water, though the difference is small. The speed is determined by the water's bulk modulus and mass density. The bulk modulus is affected by temperature, dissolved impurities (usually salinity), and pressure. The density effect is small. The speed of sound (in feet per second) is approximately:

4388 + (11.25 × temperature (in °F)) + (0.0182 × depth (in feet)) + salinity (in parts-per-thousand).

This empirically derived approximation equation is reasonably accurate for normal temperatures, concentrations of salinity and the range of most ocean depths. Ocean temperature varies with depth, but at between 30 and 100 meters there is often a marked change, called the thermocline, dividing the warmer surface water from the cold, still waters that make up the rest of the ocean. This can frustrate sonar, because a sound originating on one side of the thermocline tends to be bent, or refracted, through the thermocline. The thermocline may be present in shallower coastal waters. However, wave action will often mix the water column and eliminate the thermocline. Water pressure also affects sound propagation: higher pressure increases the sound speed, which causes the sound waves to refract away from the area of higher sound speed. The mathematical model of refraction is called Snell's law.

If the sound source is deep and the conditions are right, propagation may occur in the 'deep sound channel'. This provides extremely low propagation loss to a receiver in the channel. This is because of sound trapping in the channel with no losses at the boundaries. Similar propagation can occur in the 'surface duct' under suitable conditions. However in this case there are reflection losses at the surface. In shallow water propagation is generally by repeated reflection at the surface and bottom, where considerable losses can occur.

Sound propagation is also affected by absorption in the water itself as well as at the surface and bottom. This absorption is frequency dependent, with several different mechanisms in sea water. Thus sonars required to operate over long ranges tend to utilise low frequencies to minimise absorption effects.

The sea contains many sources of noise that interfere with the desired target echo or signature. The main noise sources are waves and shipping. The motion of the receiver through the water can also cause low frequency noise, which is speed dependent.

Reverberation

When active sonar is used, scattering occurs from small objects in the sea as well as from the bottom and surface. This can be a major source of interference but does not occur with passive sonar.

This scattering effect is different from that in room reverberation which is a reflection phenomenon. An analogy for reverberation is the scattering of a car's headlights in fog or mist. A high-intensity pencil beam will penetrate the fog; main headlights are less directional and result in "white-out" where the returned reverberation dominates. Similarly, to overcome reverberation, an active sonar needs to transmit in a narrow beam.

Target Characteristics

The target of a sonar, such as a submarine, has two main characteristics that influence the performance of the sonar. For active sonar it is its sound reflection characteristics, known as its target strength. For passive sonar the target's radiated noise characteristics are critical. The radiated spectrum in general will consist of an unresolved continuum of noise with spectral lines in it, the lines being used for classification. Echoes are also obtained from other objects in the sea such as whales, wakes, schools of fish and rocks.

Countermeasures

Active (powered) countermeasures may be launched by a submarine under attack to raise the noise level and/or provide a large false target.

Passive (i.e., non-powered) countermeasures include:

- Mounting noise-generating devices on isolating devices.
- Sound-absorbent coatings on the hulls of submarines, for example anechoic tiles.

ACTIVE SONAR

Active sonar uses a sound transmitter and a receiver. When the two are in the same place it is monostatic operation. When the transmitter and receiver are separated it is bistatic operation. When more transmitters (or more receivers) are used, again spatially separated, it is multistatic operation. Most sonars are used monostatically with the same array often being used for transmission and reception. Active sonobuoy fields may be operated multistatically.

Active sonar creates a pulse of sound, often called a "ping", and then listens for reflections (echo) of the pulse. This pulse of sound is generally created electronically using a Sonar Projector consisting of a signal generator, power amplifier and electro-acoustic transducer/array. A beamformer is usually employed to concentrate the acoustic power into a beam, which may be swept to cover the required search angles. Generally, the electro-acoustic transducers are of the Tonpilz type and their design may be optimised to achieve maximum efficiency over the widest bandwidth, in order to optimise performance of the overall system. Occasionally, the acoustic pulse may be created by other means, e.g. (1) chemically using explosives, or (2) airguns or (3) plasma sound sources.

To measure the distance to an object, the time from transmission of a pulse to reception is measured and converted into a range by knowing the speed of sound. To measure the bearing, several hydrophones are used, and the set measures the relative arrival time to each, or with an array of hydrophones, by measuring the relative amplitude in beams formed through a process called beamforming. Use of an array reduces the spatial response so that to provide wide cover multibeam systems are used. The target signal (if present) together with noise is then passed through various forms of signal processing, which for simple sonars may be just energy measurement. It is then presented to some form of decision device that calls the output either the required signal or noise. This decision device may be an operator with headphones or a display, or in more sophisticated sonars this function may be carried out by software. Further processes may be carried out to classify the target and localise it, as well as measuring its velocity.

The pulse may be at constant frequency or a chirp of changing frequency (to allow pulse compression on reception). Simple sonars generally use the former with a filter wide enough to cover possible Doppler changes due to target movement, while more complex ones generally include the latter technique. Today, pulse compression is usually achieved using digital correlation techniques. Military sonars often have multiple beams to provide all-round cover while simple ones only cover a narrow arc. Originally the latter was often scanned around mechanically but this was a slow process.

Particularly when single frequency transmissions are used, the Doppler effect may be used to measure the radial speed of a target. The difference in frequency between the transmitted and received signal is measured and converted into a velocity. Since Doppler shifts can be introduced by either receiver or target motion, allowance has to be made for the radial speed of the searching platform.

One useful small sonar looks roughly like a waterproof flashlight. One points the head into the water, presses a button, and reads a distance. Another variant is a "fishfinder" that shows a small display with shoals of fish. Some civilian sonars approach active military sonars in capability, with quite exotic three-dimensional displays of the area near the boat. However, these sonars are not designed for stealth.

When active sonar is used to measure the distance from the transducer to the bottom, it is known as echo sounding. Similar methods may be used looking upward for wave measurement.

Active sonar is also used to measure distance through water between two sonar transducers or a combination of a hydrophone (underwater acoustic microphone) and projector (underwater acoustic speaker). A transducer is a device that can transmit and receive acoustic signals ("pings"). When a hydrophone/transducer receives a specific interrogation signal it responds by transmitting a specific reply signal. To measure distance, one transducer/projector transmits an interrogation signal and measures the time between this transmission and the receipt of the other transducer/hydrophone reply. The time difference, scaled by the speed of sound through water and divided by two, is the distance between the two platforms. This technique, when used with multiple transducers/hydrophones/projectors, can calculate the relative positions of static and moving objects in water.

In wartime, emission of an active pulse is so compromising for a submarine's stealth that it is considered a very severe breach of tactics.

A very directional, yet low-efficiency type of sonar (used by fisheries, military, and for port security) makes use of a complex nonlinear feature of the water known as non-linear sonar, the virtual transducer being known as a *parametric array*.

Project ARTEMIS

Project ARTEMIS was a one of a kind low frequency sonar for surveillance that was deployed off of Bermuda for several years in the early 1960s. The active portion was deployed from a World War II tanker, and the receive array was a built into a fixed position on an offshore bank.

Transponder

This is an active sonar device that receives a stimulus and immediately (or with a delay) retransmits the received signal or a predetermined one.

Performance Prediction

A sonar target is small relative to the sphere, centred around the emitter, on which it is located. Therefore, the power of the reflected signal is very low, several orders of magnitude less than the original signal. Even if the reflected signal was of the same power, the following example (using hypothetical values) shows the problem: Suppose a sonar system is capable of emitting a 10,000 W/m² signal at 1 m, and detecting a 0.001 W/m² signal. At 100 m the signal will be 1 W/m² (due to the inverse-square law). If the entire signal is reflected from a 10 m² target, it will be at 0.001 W/m² when it reaches the emitter, i.e. just detectable. However, the original signal will remain above 0.001 W/m² until 300 m. Any 10 m² target between 100 and 300 m using a similar or better system would be able to detect the pulse but would not be detected by the emitter. The detectors must be very sensitive to pick up the echoes. Since the original signal is much more powerful, it can be detected many times further than twice the range of the sonar (as in the example).

In active sonar there are two performance limitations, due to noise and reverberation. In general one or other of these will dominate so that the two effects can be initially considered separately. In noise limited conditions at initial detection:

SL " 2TL + TS " (NL " DI) = DT

where SL is the source level, TL is the transmission loss (or propagation loss), TS is the target strength, NL is the noise level, DI is the directivity index of the array (an approximation to the array gain) and DT is the detection threshold.

In reverberation limited conditions at initial detection (neglecting array gain):

SL " 2TL + TS = RL + DT

where RL is the reverberation level and the other factors are as before.

MARINE MAMMALS

Active sonar may harm marine animals, although the precise mechanisms for this are not well understood. Some marine animals, such as whales and dolphins, use echolocation systems, sometimes called *biosonar* to locate predators and prey. It is conjectured that active sonar transmitters could confuse these animals and interfere with basic biological functions such as feeding and mating.

Hand-held sonar for use by a diver

- The LIMIS (= Limpet Mine Imaging Sonar) is a hand-held or ROV-mounted imaging sonar for use by a diver. Its name is because it was designed for patrol divers (combat frogmen or Clearance Divers) to look for limpet mines in low visibility water. Links:
  - 1. Abstract of article by the International Society for Optical Engineering
  - 2. Used to find debris from the Space Shuttle Columbia crash
  - 3.Used in fish passage research at hydropower facilities
- The LUIS (= Lensing Underwater Imaging System) is another imaging sonar for use by a diver. Links:
  - 4.Used for counting salmon in a river
- There is or was a small flashlight-shaped handheld sonar for divers, that merely displays range.
- For the INSS = Integrated Navigation Sonar System see:
  - an image.
  - short description
  - description

PASSIVE SONAR

Passive sonar listens without transmitting. It is often employed in military settings, although it is also used in science applications, e.g. detecting fish for presence/absence studies in various aquatic environments-see also passive acoustics and passive radar. In the very broadest usage, this term can encompass virtually any analytical technique involving remotely generated sound, though it is usually restricted to techniques applied in an aquatic environment.

Identifying Sound Sources

Passive sonar has a wide variety of techniques for identifying the source of a detected sound. For example, U.S. vessels usually operate 60 Hz alternating current power systems. If transformers or generators are mounted without proper vibration insulation from the hull or become flooded, the 60 Hz sound from the windings can be emitted from the submarine or ship. This can help to identify its nationality, as most European submarines have 50 Hz power systems. Intermittent sound sources (such as a wrench being dropped) may also be detectable to passive sonar. Until fairly recently, an experienced trained operator identified signals, but now computers may do this.

Passive sonar systems may have large sonic databases, but the sonar operator usually finally classifies the signals manually. A computer system frequently uses these databases to identify classes of ships, actions (i.e. the speed of a ship, or the type of weapon released), and even particular ships. Publications for classification of sounds are provided by and continually updated by the US Office of Naval Intelligence.

Noise Limitations

Passive sonar on vehicles is usually severely limited because of noise generated by the vehicle. For this reason, many submarines operate nuclear reactors that can be cooled without pumps, using silent convection, or fuel cells or batteries, which can also run silently. Vehicles' propellers are also designed and precisely machined to emit minimal noise. High-speed propellers often create tiny bubbles in the water, and this cavitation has a distinct sound.

The sonar hydrophones may be towed behind the ship or submarine in order to reduce the effect of noise generated by the watercraft itself. Towed units also combat the thermocline, as the unit may be towed above or below the thermocline.

The display of most passive sonars used to be a two-dimensional waterfall display. The horizontal direction of the display is bearing. The vertical is frequency, or sometimes time. Another display technique is to color-code frequency-time information for bearing. More recent displays are generated by the computers, and mimic radar-type plan position indicator displays.

Performance Prediction

Unlike active sonar, only one way propagation is involved. Because of the different signal processing used, the minimum detectable signal to noise ratio will be different. The equation for determining the performance of a passive sonar is:

SL " TL = NL " DI + DT

where SL is the source level, TL is the transmission loss, NL is the noise level, DI is the directivity index of the array (an approximation to the array gain) and DT is the detection threshold. The figure of merit of a passive sonar is:

FOM = SL + DI " (NL + DT).

WARFARE

Modern naval warfare makes extensive use of sonar. The two types described before are both used, from various platforms, i.e. water-borne vessels, aircraft and fixed installations. The usefulness of active versus passive sonar depends on the radiated noise characteristics of the target, generally a submarine. Although in WW II active sonar was mainly used, except by submarines, with the advent of modern signal processing passive sonar was preferred for initial detection. As the submarines have become quieter, active operation is now more used. In 1987, a division of the Japanese company Toshiba reportedly sold the machinery to the Soviet Union that allowed it to mill the submarine propeller blades so that they became radically quieter, creating a huge security issue with their newer generation of submarines.

Active sonar is extremely useful sometimes, since it gives the exact bearing to a target (and sometimes the range). Active sonar works the same way as radar: a signal is emitted. The sound wave then travels in many directions from the emitting object. When it hits an object, the sound wave is then reflected in many other directions. Some of the energy will travel back to the emitting source. The echo will enable the sonar system or technician to calculate, with many factors such as the frequency, the energy of the received signal, the depth, the water temperature, etc., the position of the reflecting object. Active sonar is used when the platform commander determines that it is more important to determine the position of a possible threat submarine than it is to conceal his own position. With surface ships it might be assumed that the threat is already tracking the ship with satellite data. Any vessel around the emitting sonar will detect the emission. Having heard the signal, it is easy to identify the type of sonar (usually with its frequency) and its position (with the sound wave's energy). Moreover, active sonar, similar to radar, allows the user to detect objects at a certain range but also enables other platforms to detect the active sonar at a far greater range.

Since active sonar does not allow exact classification and is very noisy, this type of detection is used by fast platforms (planes, helicopters) and by noisy platforms (most surface ships) but very rarely by submarines. When active sonar is used by surface ships or submarines, it is typically activated very briefly at intermittent periods, to reduce the risk of detection by an enemy's passive sonar. As such, active sonar is normally considered a backup to passive sonar. In aircraft, active sonar is used in the form of disposable sonobuoys that are dropped in the aircraft's patrol area or in the vicinity of possible enemy sonar contacts.

Passive sonar has several advantages. Most importantly, it is silent. If the target radiated noise level is high enough, it can have a greater range than active sonar, and allows an identification of the target. Since any motorized object makes some noise, it may be detected eventually. It simply depends on the amount of noise emitted and the amount of noise in the area, as well as the technology used. To simplify, passive sonar "sees" around the ship using it. On a submarine, the nose mounted passive sonar detects in directions of about 270°, centred on the ship's alignment, the hull-mounted array of about 160° on each side, and the towed array of a full 360°. The invisible areas are due to the ship's own interference. Once a signal is detected in a certain direction (which means that something makes sound in that direction, this is called broadband detection) it is possible to zoom in and analyze the signal received (narrowband analysis). This is generally done using a Fourier transform to show the different frequencies making up the sound. Since every engine makes a specific noise, it is straightforward to identify the object. The classified databases of unique noises are part of what is known as *acoustic intelligence* or ACINT. Another use of the passive sonar is to determine the target's trajectory. This process is called Target Motion Analysis (TMA), and the resultant "solution" is the target's range, course, and speed. TMA is done by marking from which direction the sound comes at different times, and comparing the motion with that of the operator's own ship. Changes in relative motion are analyzed using standard geometrical techniques along with some assumptions about limiting cases.

Passive sonar is stealthy and very useful. However, it requires high-tech components (band-pass filters, receivers), and it is costly. It is generally deployed on expensive ships in the form of arrays to enhance the detection. Surface ships use it to good effect; it is even better used by submarines, and it is also used by airplanes and helicopters, mostly to a "surprise effect", since submarines can hide under thermal layers. If a submarine's commander believes he is alone, he may bring his boat closer to the surface and be easier to detect, or go deeper and faster, and thus make more sound. Examples of sonar applications in military use are given below. Many of the civil uses given in the following section may also be applicable to naval use.

ANTI-SUBMARINE WARFARE

Until recently, ship sonars were usually with hull mounted arrays, either amidships or at the bow. It was soon found after their initial use that a means of reducing flow noise was required. The first were made of canvas on a framework, then steel ones were used. Now domes are usually made of reinforced plastic or pressurised rubber. Such sonars are primarily active in operation. An example of a conventional hull mounted sonar is the SQS-56.

Because of the problems of ship noise, towed sonars are also used. These also have the advantage of being able to be placed deeper in the water. However, there are limitations on their use in shallow water. These are called towed arrays (linear) or variable depth sonars (VDS) with 2/3D arrays. A problem is that the winches required to deploy/recover these are large and expensive. VDS sets are primarily active in operation while towed arrays are passive. An example of a modern active/passive ship towed sonar is Sonar 2087 made by Thales Underwater Systems.

Torpedoes

Modern torpedoes are generally fitted with an active/passive sonar. This may be used to home directly on the target, but wake following torpedoes are also used. An early example of an acoustic homer was the Mark 37 torpedo. Torpedo countermeasures can be towed or free. An early example was the German Sieglinde device while the Pillenwerfer was a chemical device. A widely used US device was the towed Nixie while MOSS submarine simulator was a free device. A modern alternative to the Nixie system is the UK Royal Navy S2170 Surface Ship Torpedo Defence system.

Mines

Mines may be fitted with a sonar to detect, localize and recognize the required target. Further information is given in acoustic mine and an example is the CAPTOR mine.

Mine Countermeasures

Mine Countermeasure (MCM) Sonar, sometimes called "Mine and Obstacle Avoidance Sonar (MOAS)", is a specialised type of sonar used for detecting small objects. Most MCM sonars are hull mounted but a few types are VDS design. An example of a hull mounted MCM sonar is the Type 2193 while the SQQ-32 Mine-hunting sonar and Type 2093 systems are VDS designs.

Submarine Navigation

Submarines rely on sonar to a greater extent than surface ships as they cannot use radar at depth. The sonar arrays may be hull mounted or towed. Information fitted on typical fits is given in Oyashio class submarine and Swiftsure class submarine.

Aircraft

Helicopters can be used for antisubmarine warfare by deploying fields of active/passive sonobuoys or can operate dipping sonar, such as the AQS-13. Fixed wing aircraft can also deploy sonobuoys and have greater endurance and capacity to deploy them. Processing from the sonobuoys or dipping sonar can be on the aircraft or on ship. Helicopters have also been used for mine countermeasure missions using towed sonars such as the AQS-20A

UNDERWATER COMMUNICATIONS

Dedicated sonars can be fitted to ships and submarines for underwater communication.

Ocean Surveillance

For many years, the United States operated a large set of passive sonar arrays at various points in the world's oceans, collectively called Sound Surveillance System (SOSUS) and later Integrated Undersea Surveillance System (IUSS).

A similar system is believed to have been operated by the Soviet Union. As permanently mounted arrays in the deep ocean were utilised, they were in very quiet conditions so long ranges could be achieved.

Signal processing was carried out using powerful computers ashore. With the ending of the Cold War a SOSUS array has been turned over to scientific use. In the United States Navy, a special badge known as the Integrated Undersea Surveillance System Badge is awarded to those who have been trained and qualified in its operation.

Underwater Security

Sonar can be used to detect frogmen and other scuba divers. This can be applicable around ships or at entrances to ports. Active sonar can also be used as a deterrent and/or disablement mechanism. One such device is the Cerberus system.

Hand-held Sonar

Limpet Mine Imaging Sonar (LIMIS) is a hand-held or ROV-mounted imaging sonar designed for patrol divers (combat frogmen or clearance divers) to look for limpet mines in low visibility water. The LUIS is another imaging sonar for use by a diver. Integrated Navigation Sonar System (INSS) is a small flashlight-shaped handheld sonar for divers that displays range.

Intercept Sonar

This is a sonar designed to detect and locate the transmissions from hostile active sonars. An example of this is the Type 2082 fitted on the British Vanguard class submarines.

CIVILIAN APPLICATIONS

FISHERIES

Fishing is an important industry that is seeing growing demand, but world catch tonnage is falling as a result of serious resource problems. The industry faces a future of continuing worldwide consolidation until a point of sustainability can be reached. However, the consolidation of the fishing fleets are driving increased demands for sophisticated fish finding electronics such as sensors, sounders and sonars. Historically, fishermen have used many different techniques to find and harvest fish. However, acoustic technology has been one of the most important driving forces behind the development of the modern commercial fisheries.

Sound waves travel differently through fish than through water because a fish's air-filled swim bladder has a different density than seawater. This density difference allows the detection of schools of fish by using reflected sound. Acoustic technology is especially well suited for underwater applications since sound travels farther and faster underwater than in air. Today, commercial fishing vessels rely almost completely on acoustic sonar and sounders to detect fish. Fishermen also use active sonar and echo sounder technology to determine water depth, bottom contour, and bottom composition.

Companies such as Raymarine UK, Marport Canada, Wesmar, Furuno, Krupp, and Simrad make a variety of sonar and acoustic instruments for the deep sea commercial fishing industry. For example, net sensors take various underwater measurements and transmit the information back to a receiver onboard a vessel. Each sensor is equipped with one or more acoustic transducers depending on its specific function. Data is transmitted from the sensors using wireless acoustic telemetry and is received by a hull mounted hydrophone. The analog signals are decoded and converted by a digital acoustic receiver into data which is transmitted to a bridge computer for graphical display on a high resolution monitor.

ECHO SOUNDING

An echo-sounder sends an acoustic pulse directly downwards to the seabed and records the returned echo. The sound pulse is generated by a transducer that emits an acoustic pulse and then "listens" for the return signal. The time for the signal to return is recorded and converted to a depth measurement by calculating the speed of sound in water. As the speed of sound in water is around 1,500 metres per second, the time interval, measured in milliseconds, between the pulse being transmitted and the echo being received, allows bottom depth and targets to be measured.

The value of underwater acoustics to the fishing industry has led to the development of other acoustic instruments that operate in a similar fashion to echo-sounders but, because their function is slightly different from the initial model of the echo-sounder, have been given different terms.

Net Location

The net sounder is an echo sounder with a transducer mounted on the headline of the net rather than on the bottom of the vessel. Nevertheless, to accommodate the distance from the transducer to the display unit, which is much greater than in a normal echo-sounder, several refinements have to be made. Two main types are available. The first is the cable type in which the signals are sent along a cable. In this case there has to be the provision of a cable drum on which to haul, shoot and stow the cable during the different phases of the operation. The second type is the cable less net-sounder – such as Marport's Trawl Explorer-in which the signals are sent acoustically between the net and hull mounted receiver/hydrophone on the vessel. In this case no cable drum is required but sophisticated electronics are needed at the transducer and receiver.

The display on a net sounder shows the distance of the net from the bottom (or the surface), rather than the depth of water as with the echo-sounder's hull-mounted transducer. Fixed to the headline of the net, the footrope can usually be seen which gives an indication of the net performance. Any fish passing into the net can also be seen, allowing fine adjustments to be made to catch the most fish possible. In other fisheries, where the amount of fish in the net is important, catch sensor transducers are mounted at various positions on the cod-end of the net. As the cod-end fills up these catch sensor transducers are triggered one by one and this information is transmitted acoustically to display monitors on the bridge of the vessel. The skipper can then decide when to haul the net. Modern versions of the net sounder, using multiple element transducers, function more like a sonar than an echo sounder and show slices of the area in front of the net and not merely the vertical view that the initial net sounders used.

The sonar is an echo-sounder with a directional capability that can show fish or other objects around the vessel.good

Ship Velocity Measurement

Sonars have been developed for measuring a ship's velocity either relative to the water or to the bottom.

ROV and UUV

Small sonars have been fitted to Remotely Operated Vehicles (ROV) and Unmanned Underwater Vehicles (UUV) to allow their operation in murky conditions. These sonars are used for looking ahead of the vehicle. The Long-Term Mine Reconnaissance System is an UUV for MCM purposes.

Vehicle Location

Sonars which act as beacons are fitted to aircraft to allow their location in the event of a crash in the sea. Short and Long Baseline sonars may be used for caring out the location, such as LBL.

SCIENTIFIC APPLICATIONS

Biomass Estimation

Detection of fish, and other marine and aquatic life, and estimation their individual sizes or total biomass using active sonar techniques. As the sound pulse travels through water it encounters objects that are of different density or acoustic characteristics than the surrounding medium, such as fish, that reflect sound back toward the sound source. These echoes provide information on fish size, location, abundance and behavior. Data is usually processed and analysed using a variety of software such as Echoview.

Wave Measurement

An upward looking echo sounder mounted on the bottom or on a platform may be used to make measurements of wave height and period. From this statistics of the surface conditions at a location can be derived.

Water Velocity Measurement

Special short range sonars have been developed to allow measurements of water velocity.

Bottom Topography Measurement

Side-scan sonars can be used to derive maps of the topography of an area by moving the sonar across it just above the bottom. Low frequency sonars such as GLORIA have been used for continental shelf wide surveys while high frequency sonars are used for more detailed surveys of smaller areas.

Sub-bottom Profiling

Powerful low frequency echo-sounders have been developed for providing profiles of the upper layers of the ocean bottom.

Synthetic Aperture Sonar

Various synthetic aperture sonars have been built in the laboratory and some have entered use in mine-hunting and search systems. An explanation of their operation is given in synthetic aperture sonar.

Parametric Sonar

Parametric sources use the non-linearity of water to generate the difference frequency between two high frequencies. A virtual end-fire array is formed. Such a projector has advantages of broad bandwidth, narrow beamwidth, and when fully developed and carefully measured it has no obvious sidelobes: see Parametric array. Its major disadvantage is very low efficiency of only a few percent.. P.J. Westervelt's seminal 1963 JASA paper summarizes the trends involved.

Bibliography

Bellamy, C.: *Knights in White Armour: The New Art of War and Peace*, London, Random House, 1997.

Chandra, R.: *Judicial System in India Navy*, Lucknow, Print House (India), 1992.

Davies .A.: *Telecommunications and Politics. The Secentralised Alternative*, London, Pinter, 1994.

Friedman, G.: *The Future of War: Power, Technology and Indian Army*, N.Y., Random House, 1996.

Heimanson, Rudolph: *Dictionary of Political Science and Law of Sea War*, N.Y.: Oceana Publications, 1967.

Huntington, S.P.: *The Soldier and the Indian Army*, N.Y., Vintage Books, 1964.

Jones, W.H.: *The Government and Politics of Indian Army*, London, Hutchinson, 1971.

Kelly, John B.: *India and the Pakistan War*, Oxford, Clarendon Press, 1968.

Mary, W.: *Asian Power and Politics: the Cultural Dimensions of Authority*, Cambridge, Belknap Press, 1985.

Nair, A. M.: *Role of Indian Navy*, Bombay, Orient Longman, 1983.

Posen, B.R.: *The Sources of Indian Military*, Cornell Univ. Press.

Rosen, P.: *Societies and Military Power: India and its Armies*, Ithaca, Cornell University Press, 1996.

Simon, D. : *Modernization in Indian Milatery Defence*, New York, Knopf, 1950.

Index

□□□